Socially
Engaging the Po
in Iberoamerica

MW01254246

A Collaborative Research Project of the
SOCIAL ENTERPRISE KNOWLEDGE NETWORK

Editorial Committee
Patricia Márquez
Ezequiel Reficco
Gabriel Berger

Published by Harvard University
David Rockefeller Center for Latin American Studies and Inter-American Development Bank
Distributed by Harvard University Press
Cambridge, Massachusetts
London, England
2010

Library of Congress Cataloging-in-Publication Data

Socially inclusive business : engaging the poor through market initiatives in
    Iberoamerica / a collaborative research project of the Social Enterprise
    Knowledge Network.

        p. ; cm.

    Includes bibliographical references.
    ISBN: 978-0-674-05336-6

1. Social entrepreneurship—Latin America. 2. Social entrepreneurship—
Spain. 3. Poor—Latin America. 4. Poor—Spain. 5. Economic development—
Latin America. 6. Economic development—Spain. I. SEKN.

HD60.5.L29 S63 2010
658.0017/561

Contents

List of Figures

List of Tables

Prologue

It has been nearly a decade since the pioneering research of C. K. Prahalad, Stuart Hart, and Allen Hammond[1] inserted onto the agendas of business researchers and practitioners the possibility of creating innovative business models that would simultaneously be profitable and socially beneficial to the overlooked resource represented by the world's billions of low-income people. As with all breakthrough ideas, managers increasingly began pursuing the potential opportunities and researchers began studying the phenomenon and testing the hypotheses. Steadily the momentum has grown and a significant field of inquiry and practice has emerged. The importance of this movement resides in the appealing potential impact of using the powerful forces of market mechanisms to attain social betterment. The vision of a triple win for business, the poor, and society is very enticing.

Over the years researchers have made significant advances in understanding the phenomenon; however, the field is still young and there remain significant knowledge gaps. So what is the value-added of this book? It represents an important contribution to narrowing those gaps by deepening and broadening our comprehension in a variety of ways. This contribution emanates first from the Social Enterprise Knowledge Network's distinctive research capabilities. As a research network consisting of ten leading schools of management education in Latin America, the United States, and Spain, SEKN is uniquely positioned to carry out comparative research on a hemispheric and transatlantic scale and scope utilizing a common research framework and standardized methodology. Accordingly, this book's research is based on thirty-three experiences of socially inclusive businesses in eleven countries. The research is derived from field-based, clinical studies that enable one to understand deeply operational realities, which makes the research particularly enriching in terms of managerial insights as well as empirical testing of prevailing hypotheses.

The Network's capacity to produce high value-adding research that advances the collective knowledge frontier for researchers and practitioners has been demonstrated by its previous books and accompanying articles, which also provide a highly relevant knowledge base for this current book's research on socially inclusive businesses. The first SEKN book, *Social Partnering in Latin America: Lessons from Collaborations between the Private Sector and Civil Society Organizations,* was a pioneering documentation of critical factors in cross-sector collaborations in the hemisphere. Creating such alliances is one of the important elements in developing successful socially inclusive businesses. The second SEKN book, *Effective Management of Social Enterprises: Lessons from Businesses and Civil Society Organizations in Iberoamerica*, identified and compared key success determinants in businesses and civil society organizations deemed leaders in producing social and economic value. A significant finding from that research was a deep understanding of areas of convergence between the businesses and CSOs. Convergence between strategies that simultaneously produce social and economic value is at the heart of the socially inclusive businesses studied in this current book. A common dimension of exploration in these first two books that is continued in this current research is the identification of barriers to effectiveness and approaches to overcoming those hurdles. Thus, this book analyzes the business models of socially inclusive businesses in terms of the resources, capabilities, and strategies that enable the LIS (low-income sectors) to be effectively integrated into the market system and specific value chains.

This book's research design in terms of the organizations included in the sample was explicitly structured so as to explore understudied aspects in the existing Base of the Pyramid (BOP) literature. Most of the existing studies have usefully emphasized the role of LIS as consumers who represent a significant and underserved economic market segment. The sample in this book also looks at LIS as consumers, but broadens the inquiry to examine their economic agent roles as producers, suppliers, and distributors. Furthermore, while existing studies have tended to look at LIS as dependent entities that are integrated into the market initiatives by the proactive efforts of companies, this sample also incorporates examples of LIS-led initiatives and their important role as entrepreneurs.

The sample was also designed to explore more broadly different types of organization. The origins of the BOP research gave special emphasis to multinational companies and their significant potential to incorporate the low income sector into their systems. While this research continues that focus on MNCs as well as large local companies, it also encompasses small enterprises and startups. Furthermore, the sample includes social enterprises (cooperatives and civil society organizations), which have been understudied as BOP protagonists.

A final dimension that permits new insights is the type of business studied. The sample examines agribusinesses, public utilities, and recycling enterprises. This diversity allows us to explore how barriers and success determinants vary or conform across distinct types of businesses. Other categories of businesses and products that have been more frequently examined in the literature and understood in practice were explicitly excluded from the sample. Last, the study expands the unit of analysis in the organizational framework from individual enterprises to the dynamics of the larger ecosystems within which socially inclusive businesses can be impeded or nurtured.

Of fundamental importance to researchers and practitioners in this field is value creation. This study makes a significant contribution to advancing our understanding of economic and social value creation in socially inclusive businesses. Along both dimensions, the research enriches our perspective by the framing of how to determine value, and by the empirical assessments. Value determination is methodologically complicated and solid data are scarce, so advancements are incremental, but each step forward moves us toward a fuller comprehension.

Overall, the findings that you will encounter in this book contribute to advancing our knowledge in four ways. First, some extend our understanding of socially inclusive businesses by introducing new dimensions previously overlooked or underexamined. Second, some contradict the conventional wisdom and prevailing hypotheses, which importantly leads us to rethink and reexamine the phenomenon more deeply and carefully. Third, other findings provide new empirical data that confirm existing findings, thereby solidifying parts of the knowledge foundation. Last, even where the findings are insufficient to provide firm conclusions, the book formulates new hypotheses that are helpful in guiding future paths of inquiry.

The book judiciously helps us to be realistic. While there may be fortunes to be made at the BOP and there may be significant social betterment to be produced, there is no quick and easy road to attaining these goals. However, the examples and findings in this study are uplifting in that they reveal very useful paths of progress that are within our capabilities. The imperative of continuing this very important and arduous journey of creating socially inclusive market capitalism is clear, and *Socially Inclusive Business in Iberoamerica* will greatly help us reach our hoped for destination.

James E. Austin
Eliot I. Snider and Family Professor of Business Administration, Emeritus
Harvard Business School

Note
1. Prahalad, C. K., and Allen Hammond. "Serving the World's Poor, Profitably." *Harvard Business Review* (2002); Prahalad, C. K., and Stuart Hart. "The Fortune at the Bottom of the Pyramid." *Strategy + Business* 1, no. 26 (2002).

Preface

This book marks the completion of a long and fruitful journey; a process of intellectual discovery and wonder that we undertook collectively starting in 2005. For readers unfamiliar with SEKN, it may be appropriate to explain what this network is, and what it stands for. The work of the Social Enterprise Knowledge Network is guided by its collective mission: "to advance the frontiers of knowledge and practice in social enterprise through collaborative research, shared learning, participant-centered teaching, and the strengthening of management education institutions' capabilities to serve their communities." SEKN was launched in 2001 under the vision and leadership of James Austin (Harvard Business School), and with the generous funding of the Avina Foundation. As of late 2009, the Social Enterprise Knowledge Network was comprised of:

- Argentina: Universidad de San Andrés (UdeSA)
- Brazil: Universidade de São Paulo (USP)
- Central America: Instituto Centroamericano de Administración de Empresas (INCAE)
- Chile: Pontificia Universidad Católica de Chile (PUCCh)
- Colombia: Universidad de los Andes (Uniandes)
- Mexico: Escuela de Graduados en Administración y Dirección de Empresas (EGADE)
- Perú: Universidad del Pacífico (UP)
- Spain: Escuela Superior de Administración y Dirección de Empresas (ESADE)
- United States: Harvard Business School (HBS)
- Venezuela: Instituto de Estudios Superiores de Administración (IESA)

At the dawn of this decade, the idea that markets could be leveraged to improve the living conditions of the poor began to expand among practitioners and academics. It was a novel proposition when applied to poverty alleviation, deserving careful scrutiny. Given our mission, SEKN could not remain indifferent. Composed of leading institutions in management education in Latin America and Spain, SEKN had the capabilities and the responsibility for steering its academic resources to advance the emerging field of inclusive business. With that goal in mind, in 2005 we undertook an ambitious research effort, which would span three years and encompass 33 Iberoamerican experiences of inclusive business.

In those years, the concept of inclusive business was permeated by a legitimate debate between those who genuinely saw value in bringing the market closer to the poor, and those who thought that *selling to the poor* was the problem, not the solution. How would we deal with this dilemma? Where would we stand? As has always been the case in all SEKN research undertakings, we sought to stay away from dogma and build our knowledge from the ground up, based on in-depth analysis of empirical data. We sought to generate knowledge that was relevant to Iberoamerica's business community and civil society, while at the same time contributing to the ongoing debate on the promise and pitfalls of inclusive business worldwide. The result of this effort, presented in the ensuing chapters, has the value added of encapsulating the views of research teams from the region's most prestigious business schools, operating in an array of very different national settings. By looking horizontally at dozens of cases in the countries, SEKN has the rare privilege of reaching conclusions that go beyond the specificities of a single country and the thinking of a few individuals.

A research project this ambitious would have been impossible to complete without the active collaboration of many institutions. First among them is Avina, our long-standing partner, which has been by our side ever since our network was created back in 2001. We are also grateful to Harvard University's David Rockefeller Center for Latin American Studies, which since 2001 has been an outstanding outlet for collective research, as part of a special book series published by the Harvard University Press. A similar word of gratitude goes to the Inter-American Development Bank, whose resources have been critical in projecting the knowledge created affordably and effectively throughout Latin America, our primary region of attention. In this book, we also welcome Cemex and Femsa as SEKN's corporate donors, whose support has proven invaluable to sustain SEKN'S collective work. Anyone who has worked in strategic partnerships knows that it is impossible to make any real progress without the support of the organization's top authorities. Thus, the researchers who worked on this project would like to acknowledge the unwavering support each of us received from our institutions: Department chairs, Deans and even university Chancellors. These acknowledgments would not be complete without recognizing the assistance received from the organizations featured in our sample (see Annex at the end of the book for a complete list). By opening up to our scrutiny, these organizations have contributed to our collective understanding of inclusive business—and, we hope, learned something in the process. Last but not least, we also thank the anonymous reviewers whose constructive inputs helped to sharpen our analysis. Needless to say, any shortcoming of the final product remains our exclusive responsibility.

We have collectively learned important lessons concerning this novel approach. Despite the undeniable progress made in understanding the role that markets can play in building a more sustainable and socially inclusive world, the road ahead is still long; challenges abound in Latin America and other continents riddled with poverty. With this book, we have come together from different parts of the world to offer a humble yet substantial contribution that advances our understanding of inclusive business, challenges prevailing common wisdom in the corporate and non-profit worlds, and points to productive avenues for further work by fellow researchers from other universities and networks. Large as it is, our network is tiny when compared to the magnitude of the problem of global poverty. We hope this book becomes an invitation for a long-term intellectual discussion with new friends, who may share our passion for societal betterment. At the same time, and foremost, we hope this book becomes a call for action, a catalyst for greater experimentation among both companies and non-profits that may dare enter this field.

Patricia Márquez, Ezequiel Reficco, and Gabriel Berger
San Diego, Bogotá, and Buenos Aires,
December 2009

1

Introduction: A Fresh Look at Markets and the Poor

Patricia Márquez, Ezequiel Reficco, and Gabriel Berger

Marcela made a living gathering wild fruit and mushrooms in Chile's Bio-Bio area, the country's second poorest region. The job itself was disparaged, left to women and children. Marcela's meager earnings from selling highly perishable produce to middlemen barely provided subsistence. Her shack lacked running water and electricity. In 2000, the non-profit Taller de Acción Social (TAC) began training and organizing local collectors; eventually, fruit gatherers began dealing directly with the produce companies, and the way their occupation was perceived by the rest of the community changed for the better. Four years later, 70 families had joined in an organization, with gatherers drawn from eight local communities. Soon enough they learned that dehydrated produce sold for higher prices and began to process fruits and mushrooms that way. Today they only sell dehydrated produce.

In 1998, Jose left his shanty just outside Morelia, the state capital of Michoacan, in Mexico, to join relatives in California. There he got a job demolishing cars, while saving all he could in hopes of building a new house for his family in Morelia. Six years later Jose heard of Construmex, a program launched by Cemex to sell cement and home improvement goods to the poor in association with local distributors offering credit terms in towns across Mexico. A Construmex architect designed the blueprint for the house and, after two years, Jose's family had a three-bedroom home with two bathrooms, living room, and kitchen.

What both Marcela and Jose sought—higher income and dignity and a home to return to, respectively—was made possible by business-generating market initiatives that turned the poor into consumers, producers, and business partners. The idea that market mechanisms can mobilize social change by engaging the poor in win-win scenarios is gaining increased world attention. Companies, civil society organizations (CSOs), and development agencies are all beginning to glean the potential to be gained from energizing the human capabilities that lie among the billions of the world's poorest people.

Behind this newly found interest in markets lies the realization that any effective response to global poverty will have to meet three fundamental characteristics.[1] First, it will need to have **scale**. The sheer magnitude of the problems calls for solutions that can be scaled up or replicated to meet demand. Well-intended efforts of philanthropic agencies are unlikely to pass this test. Second, it will need to have **permanence**. Given the intractability of the problem, any serious effort will have to span generations, for governments come and go, and multilateral agencies change their priorities according to the agenda of the moment. Third, any solution to poverty would need to have **efficiency and efficacy**. Resources are scarce, and have to be stretched if we are to make the most out of them. Governments do have scale, but efficiency and efficacy is hardly their strongest suit. On the other hand, even the private sector's detractors concede its ability to deliver value to the point in which marginal benefits equal marginal costs. Managers may change, and companies may go bankrupt, but there are very good chances that resources will flow to serve any need that can be served profitably through a tested business model.

Yet for the private sector to become part of the solution to poverty will not happen spontaneously, or overnight. Historically, both private and public companies have failed to serve the poor in Iberoamerica. Even public utilities, chartered to serve all homes in entire cities, are known to have overlooked low-income consumers. Yolanda, in 1974, erected her shack on the edge of the El Junquito road, 9 kilometers outside Caracas, Venezuela. Along with other Kilometer 9 squatters, she tapped the nearest lamp post for free electricity—for the power company's policy required land titles to provide service to dwellings. Despite a precarious hillside location, over the years Yolanda added room after room to her shack in order to provide shelter for her children and grandchildren. In time, power service was so weak that Yolanda couldn't turn on her TV set while ironing clothes. By 2005, the power company, concerned over mounting power losses from illegal connections, offered Kilometer 9 community dwellers reliable service if the head of household showed an identity card and agreed to become a paying customer. But why did it take the company 30 years to do so?

The answer to this question lies in a host of geographical, socio-cultural, political, and economic issues that distance companies from people living in poverty, who in effect become invisible to the rest of society. Yolanda's shack was hardly isolated geographically, located as it was on the edge of a public road in plain view of passing traffic. Her case was hardly unique either; on the contrary, it was quite representative of the challenges that large swaths of Latin America's population face on a daily basis. To be sure, low-income sectors (LIS) have long participated in trade, but they often do so in a technological and organizational context of limited opportunity and multiple hurdles—even exploitation. Indeed, the poor must often pay higher prices than those with higher income for similar goods and services: the so-called poverty penalty.[2] Supermarkets offering the lowest prices, for example, are seldom conveniently located near poor communities; and poor consumers are rarely able to buy supplies for more than a day or two.

The results of traditional efforts to alleviate poverty have been rather disappointing, despite the massive resources invested in the last 50 years,[3] and this makes the investigation of novel or complementary approaches all the more urgent. In this book, the Social Enterprise Knowledge Network (SEKN) takes stock and assesses the progress made so far in fostering market initiatives with LIS in Iberoamerica. We look at how different kinds of organizations have engaged LIS communities from across the region in market-based initiatives, and analyze the outcomes of these processes. A task force drawing on 9 teams of researchers from various business schools and universities examined in depth a total of 33 experiences, to learn what is needed for building new business value chains that help move people out of poverty.

The first section of this chapter defines its object and the main research questions that guided our collective efforts. In the second section we place this study in the context of the existing relevant literature. We then shed some light on the population segments that have benefited from the initiatives analyzed: the poor and the socially excluded. The following section describes the sample and the roles performed by LIS in the various cases. Finally, we give an overview of the book's content, with a succinct summary of each chapter.

The "Business" of this Book

A fitting point to start is with the precise meaning of the book's title. In our study of "socially inclusive **business**," we looked into business models that proved effective in connecting low-income sectors with mainstream markets and had the potential and the aspiration to improve the living conditions of the poor. This feature is what justifies the use of the term "inclusive" (which we will generally use henceforth)—as opposed to simply selling to the poor—in that it allows poor communities to take one step closer to mainstream markets and broader, meaningful citizenship.

Our collective research was guided by a common protocol of questions (see Annex, at the end of the book) seeking quantitative and qualitative information on three issue areas. First and foremost, we examined the organization that developed the venture, paying close attention to its business model. What kind of resources and capabilities need to be in place to make the connection with LIS? What kinds of barriers hindered that connection, and how were they overcome? Second, we analyzed the organization's milieu, and particularly the array of collaborative arrangements that sustained its business model. Given the magnitude of the challenges, solutions often require the engagement of various organizations, working together in pursuit of a common goal. What kinds of linkages between private, public, and non-profit sectors are built around these initiatives? Finally, we sought to assess the economic and social value created by the venture.

Business models are useful in providing blueprints that can be adapted and adopted. A business model defines how a new solution will create value for the client, and how the organization will capture some of the value in the form of profit. The analysis of the selected organizations' business models shed light on the way in which they (1) articulate a value proposition; (2) identify their market segment; (3) define the value chain required by the offering and the complementary assets required to support the organization's position within it; (4) specify the revenue-generating mechanisms, the cost structure, and profit potential; (5) position the organization within its setting (ecosystem), linking suppliers and customers, identifying potential complementors and competitors, and (6) establish a competitive strategy to gain and hold advantage over rivals.[4] In the initiatives examined, the business models were not always completely developed or even entirely clear to company managers, and our analysis aimed at making them explicit.

As we saw, these models were quite diverse; what they all had in common was that their ultimate driving force was the pull from demand, as opposed to other poverty alleviation approaches, based on the push that may emanate from grants or social investments, in top-down philanthropic or development programs.[5] Some push from mission-driven support organizations may be present, but these initiatives primarily aim at creating value for the end user of the value chain. The commercial dimension is what keeps them going. As defined here, market initiatives do not rule out the presence of targeted philanthropic or public interventions. As a matter of fact, these were a pervasive presence across the sample. However, they were either temporary or established by the regulatory framework and leveraged by entrepreneurs to externalize some of the costs implicit in building a new market. In all cases, the driving force behind the initiative's growth has been the connection of supply and demand.

The initiatives analyzed in this book found business opportunities in low-income sectors. All initiatives were part of the organization's core business—

although many of the sample cases were pilots, representing a mere fraction of the organizations' overall revenue. The cases were filtered through a double lens: *prima facie* they had to create economic and social value. The extent to which they succeeded is analyzed throughout the book, and particularly in chapters 9 and 10.

The word "business" in our title was not used to denote simply private companies. Our sample of market initiatives spanned 20 companies and 13 social enterprises that included cooperatives and civil society organizations (CSOs). Companies varied in size from multinational corporations (MNCs) to medium- and small-scale enterprises (SMEs); similarly, participating cooperatives and CSOs also varied in size.[6] A conscious decision was made to structure our inquiry upon the focal points of different organizational forms, for various reasons. While most the research focused on the BOP (Bottom or Base of the Pyramid) and inclusive business implicitly or explicitly emphasizes the potential of MNC in the fight against poverty, this approach would be somewhat out of line in a region where 90 percent of all productive organizations are micro-enterprises or small and medium enterprises (SME). Cooperatives have a rich tradition in the region, and many inclusive ventures made use of this tradition to build innovative business models, integrating the poor into vibrant value chains. Finally, most of Latin America's CSOs have stopped looking at the market as the root of the problem and started to embrace it as part of the solution in the fight against poverty alleviation. Public-sector enterprises, however, were deliberately left out of the sample. Undoubtedly, useful lessons could be drawn from public-sector market initiatives, but these are often subsidized on a continuous basis, which was inconsistent with the criteria that led our case sample selection.

The case set we selected does not pretend to be representative of the totality of inclusive businesses currently under development in Iberoamerica. Our selection meant to reflect variety in terms of organizational form, types of industries, and geographical scope. We also sought to make sure that the cases were balanced in the ways in which low-income citizens were engaged, such as consumers, distributors, or suppliers. Additional criteria included:

- The initiative must actively seek business opportunity with LIS;
- The initiative must prove significant for the organization, preferably as part of its core business (although the LIS initiative could represent a mere fraction of that business);
- The initiative had to generate economic value (EV) and social value (SV). The resources generated by the venture had to cover all factors of production as well as depreciation, administrative costs, and other

types of costs. For CSOs, EV was defined as *financial sustainability*; i.e., an organization's capacity to operate indefinitely. For private companies, EV required *profitability*; the initiative should be capable of creating value after repaying all factors of production—not simply their *cost*, but also their *opportunity cost* (the most valuable forgone alternative). As working definition for SV, we adopted the one forged in SEKN's previous book: "the pursuit of societal betterment through the removal of barriers that hinder social inclusion, the assistance to those temporarily weakened or lacking a voice, and the mitigation of undesirable side-effects of economic activity."[7]

In principle, cases in our sample had to be free of subsidies, with two exceptions: (a) subsidies could be acceptable in startup ventures, as a temporary resource with an expectation that in some foreseeable future the initiative could be either profitable or sustainable; (b) subsidies were also deemed acceptable when they were horizontal, that is, granted to an entire industry or sector by regulation, rather than channeled towards a specific initiative on an ad-hoc basis. Our primary unit of analysis was single organizations, or even subunits (those in charge of managing initiatives targeted to the poor). At the same time, we paid close attention to the interactions between the organization and its milieu. This was particularly important, as many of these initiatives were managed not by individual organizations, but by means of cooperative arrangements between various organizations. Thus, this is an embedded multi-case study: our primary emphasis was placed on the organizations that functioned as the "center of gravity" of the initiatives, determined its overall direction and articulated participant energies, but when needed the analysis was carried further out to encompass key partners.

Inclusive Business and the BOP Approach

In recent years, the pioneering work of C. K. Prahalad, Stuart Hart, and Allen Hammond on the concept of "serving the poor profitably,"[8] coupled with the widely shared view that development organizations failed to mobilize major social transformation, have triggered the emergence of a field of intellectual enquiry and practice known as the BOP.[9] This study seeks to make a contribution to that emerging literature. The initiatives analyzed here share some of the principles that, according to Ted London, define the BOP approach. The rest of this section draws heavily on his work, particularly on "The Base-of-the-Pyramid Perspective: A New Approach to Poverty Alleviation."

Connecting the local with the non-local. The possibility of inserting LIS in the global economy—"democratizing the economy," as Prahalad puts it—may provide a passkey to social transformation. All too often the poor are captives of unscrupulous middlemen, who benefit from LIS disconnection from mainstream markets. Usually the poor are underpaid as workers and overpay as consumers, as they do not have the benefit of multiple and competing bidders. Inclusive businesses connect supply (producers) with demand (consumers), and the local dimension with the global, thereby unleashing positive self-reinforcing processes of economic wealth creation and social empowerment.

Patient innovation. Most BOP scholars have signaled the need to tackle these ventures with a long-term view. Rather than considering the poor as the periphery of mainstream markets—the "next 20 percent"—that can be served through "business as usual," they should be considered as uncharted territory, an entirely different market. Those profound differences call for ad-hoc business models.[10] Much as what happens in the development of any new market of product line, the productive potential of the poor can only be unleashed through "patient capital": focused on the long run, willing to accept below-market returns at the beginning, and combined with assistance.[11]

The leverage of local assets. The BOP places a premium on the pragmatic leverage of the existing infrastructure. Albeit not ideal, its assets provide a useful starting point to start building a new institutional environment from the bottom up. Earlier BOP studies have shown that "in accessing low income sectors, the leverage of existing social organizations, networks and practices proved to be highly effective."[12] As Ted London points out, this approach marks a departure from traditional development models that focus more on building enabling environments from the top down, on a macro level.[13]

At the same time, however, our approach to inclusive business departs somewhat from mainstream, U.S.-inspired, studies of BOP. The differences are not fundamental, but they are nonetheless relevant to understand the precise purpose of this study.

Ventures' protagonists. The movement to utilize the market in the fight against poverty began as a call to action to multinational corporations:[14] for example, as one influential article suggested in its title, to employ "The Corporate Key: Using Big Business to Fight Global Poverty."[15] Prahalad's seminal work was based on the premise that multinationals corporations (MNCs) were best positioned to tackle the daunting task of truly alleviating global poverty, as they commanded the financial clout, global distribution channels, and brainpower needed to address the challenge. In fact, even those early works counted among their cases ventures led by SMEs or CSOs,[16] but they were not acknowledged in the conceptual frameworks developed inductively from the experiences. Later formulations were broader,[17] but as of this writing BOP publications still place most emphasis on MNCs. While CSOs are considered important, they tend to be seen as "unconventional partners,"[18] not protagonists. The difference divides practitioners working in the field. For example, some support organizations, such as SNV,[19] concentrate on large companies in their BOP work, while others, such as Avina, include initiatives led by CSOs in their understanding of socially inclusive markets. In this regards, our approach is closer to that of social enterprise, open to the leadership of various organizational forms, than to the mainstream BOP literature.

The principle of external participation. Another constant in the BOP literature is the "principle of external participation," according to which BOP initiatives must be launched by "an exogenous . . . venture or entrepreneur," a "non-native" agent operating outside the informal economy where the poor live.[20] The external agent is at the center of the wealth-generating activity. It does not merely "assist" the poor, financially or technically: it is directly involved in the wealth-generating activities.

On this point too, this study purposely took a broader approach. As the rest of the book will show, external actors did play a key role in many of the initiatives studied. At the same time, many of those initiatives were self-centered efforts by the poor to strengthen and scale up their business models, through a combination of learning by doing with trial and error, and external advice and support. Whereas the traditional BOP model relies on exogenous actors who intervene through radically new business models,[21] in the social entrepreneurship model the native players are central. External organizations, such as MNCs, contribute by helping to remove bottlenecks (for example, providing distribution channels, technology, financial or technological assistance) and bring the initiative up to scale.[22] Thus, the approach followed to select the cases included in this study falls between the BOP and the "social entrepreneurship" models.[23]

Co-creation of ad-hoc models v. incremental adaptation. As a corollary of the principle of "external intervention" BOP scholars often posit that to be successful, solutions must be "co-created" by the exogenous actor and the poor. The model proposed is the combination of "knowledge developed at the top of the pyramid with the wisdom and expertise found at the bottom."[24] As London explains, this feature differentiates BOP strategies from traditional corporate strategies, which import existing business models into the BOP.

Here too, this study has taken a somehow different line. While the co-creation of value is desirable, and often achieved, it has not been considered a defining trait of socially inclusive market initiatives in this study. As indicated earlier, some of the ventures analyzed here were conceived and executed by the poor, denying the symbolic marriage between bottom and top of the pyramid at the strategic level. It should be noted that co-creation does not allude to technical or financial assistance, but rather to "pilot-testing, evaluating, and formalizing the enterprise in a collaborative and equitable manner."[25]

Co-creation appears in our sample, but we have also included ventures in which companies intervened unilaterally in low-income sectors through incremental adaptations of existing business models, which would not be considered legitimate BOP ventures in the terms outlined above. The rationale behind this decision by the authors is clear: to work with familiar business models that prospective readers could relate to and be inspired by. As has been noted, incremental change though the assembly of existing building blocks (in collaborative arrangements in which various organizations bring together their expertise) is more feasible than the creation of radically new business models.[26]

Self-financed growth and sustainable social value creation. The initial wave of writings on BOP was presented as an enormous untapped business opportunity: as a "fortune" to be made at the bottom of the pyramid.[27] Perhaps because the message was tuned to the ears of mainstream business people—as opposed to the mission-driven crowd of CSR (corporate social responsibility) officers, social entrepreneurs, or development professionals—the business case was heavily stressed. Later formulations of the BOP approach presented a more balanced picture, stressing the need to put in place "mutually beneficial economic and social incentives."[28] To some BOP analysts, it is essential that growth be fueled by self-generated profits for the venture to be scalable. In this view, economic and social returns go hand in hand, and mirror each other: "the greater the ability of the venture to meet the needs of the poor, the greater the returns to the partners involved."[29]

This of course, is the ideal of inclusive business: radically innovative solutions, delivered at a fraction of the cost of old solutions, and to great benefit to previously ignored customers or producers. In this study we have taken a more down to earth approach. We purposefully left aside initiatives that generated high economic returns, but questionable social benefits—such as selling carbonated drinks to the poor. At the same time, we willingly included in our sample self-sustaining ventures with limited profits, provided that they were economically sustainable and generated substantial social and environmental benefits.

Figure 1.1
Profits and Social Impact in Socially Inclusive Business

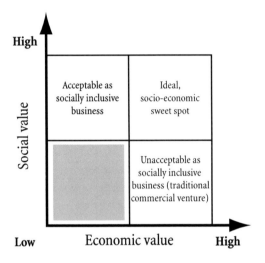

Who is to be "Included" in Inclusive Businesses?

After defining "business" in the context of this study, it is worth reflecting on the target of these efforts. Whom do we have in mind when we talk about the "poor" or LIS? Marketing studies that rely on socio-economic classification usually place this population sector in categories D and E—with high-income segments in A and B, and the mid-income group in C. However, it is difficult to pinpoint with precision the boundaries between these segments at the global level. In his seminal work, C. K. Prahalad defined the LIS category as those with an annual income of less than US$1,500 in purchasing power parity (PPP).[30] According to Hammond et al., the world's "base-of-the-pyramid" is comprised of the four billion people whose annual income is below US$3,000 in PPP.[31]

In Latin America, the task of defining with precision a region-wide poverty line is also problematic because of the heterogeneity of LIS income. As of 2006, it ranged from a monthly income of US$45 to $161 in urban areas, and US$32 to $101 in rural areas at current exchange rates. For people in extreme poverty, the range was US$21 to $81 in urban zones, and US$18 to $58 in rural zones.[32] The ventures in our case sample engage groups of both urban and rural poor, which feature marked differences. The urban poor generally lived in informal settlements—*barrios, favelas,* or *villas miserias*—and some live on the streets. Their main problems are crowdedness, everyday violence, insufficient basic services, and poor urban infrastructure. On the other hand, their spatial proximity facilitates social ties, an asset that was leveraged by many inclusive ventures. These urban dwellers also live close to some new technologies, such as mobile phones and the Internet, that permit increasing connection to national and global happenings. These features were capitalized in many inclusive business models.

Rural LIS challenges, on the other hand, include lack of access to basic services, insufficient infrastructure and cash scarcity, sometimes exacerbated by geographical dispersion and distance from urban centers. The rural poor tend to have less education and less access to information, basic services, and resources than their urban counterparts. They own fewer assets and generate low productivity.[33] For instance, in Brazil, 90.2 percent of the urban population has access to piped water, as compared with only 16.6 percent in rural areas.[34] In Costa Rica, 44.3 percent of the city dwellers have access to waste disposal systems, while only 5.4 percent of rural populations have such access.[35]

In contrast to Latin America, Spain has no absolute poverty as measured in absolute levels of per capita income, at purchasing power parity. However, 14 percent of the population lives in relative poverty, as defined by the OECD: those below a threshold set at half of the median income.[36] In Catalonia, Spain, there are around 1.2 million people in risk of falling below the poverty line,[37] such as former prison inmates, physically or mentally handicapped individuals, or women who are victims of domestic violence. Our case sample includes three ventures that dealt with relative poverty (see Table 1.1).

Table 1.1
Social Exclusion in Spain

Organization	Targeted group
Andrómines	Gypsies, immigrants, women heads-of-household
Fageda	Handicapped
Fundación Futur	Ex prison inmates, immigrants, women heads-of-household, indigents

The definition of beneficiaries of inclusive business is further complicated by the fact that income deprivation is only one aspect of poverty. As

Amartya Sen has observed, poverty is complex and multi-dimensional, with such additional facets as inequality, informality, and exclusion.

Latin America suffers from huge inequality in the distribution of income. Although the overall number of poor Latin-Americans has diminished in the last 15 years, socio-economic inequality continues to be extremely high,[38] as measured by the Gini coefficient[39] which ranged from .44 for Venezuela to .6 for Brazil,[40] making Latin America the most unequal region of the world. It is clear to all that low economic growth generates poverty; the real problem is that the reverse is also true: poverty and low economic growth reinforce each other in a vicious cycle.

Figure 1.2
Evolution of poverty and extreme poverty in Latin America

2.a. Volume of people (millions)   2.b. Percentage of population

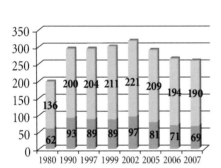 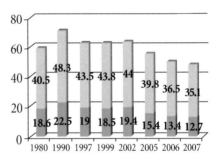

Source: "Panorama social 2007 de América Latina," Comisión Económica para América Latina, 2007.

According to Latinobarómetro, over 70 percent of people in Latin America perceive income distribution as either "unfair"[41] or "very unfair." If perceptions of inequality and exclusion are not addressed, they can easily translate into social unrest and rising crime. Over time, this trend may worsen, leading to disenfranchisement and ultimately to political polarization. The longer such conditions persist, the greater the prospects of socio-economic conflict. Economic growth generally contributes to poverty reduction, but significant increases recorded in Latin America's economic growth during the 1990s accomplished little in this regard, and may in fact have widened income inequality.

Latin America also features high levels of informality: more than half of its labor force earns a living in the informal economy, with LIS likely to make up the largest share.[42] It is true that studies of successful informal economy business units, suggest significant opportunity for linking embryonic entrepreneurs with the formal economy,[43] as some of the recent research on entrepreneurship suggests.[44] This finding was confirmed by our research: several of the market initiatives examined in this study interacted with the informal economy. Workers active in the informal economy, however, often become more vulnerable to exploitation and poor working conditions, as the law and institutions scarcely protect them. In Spain, informality can be useful to understand poverty, as both tend to go hand in hand. Strong redistribution policies and public subsidies keep those "inside the system" out of absolute poverty, but those benefits do not reach people who remain in the shadows, such as illegal immigrants.

The LIS also suffer "social exclusion," a concept coined in the 1970s[45] to describe the crisis of the European welfare state.[46] In the context of Latin America, it can be defined as a "process whereby individuals and groups are denied access to opportunities."[47] Various barriers and restrictions prevent low-income citizens from becoming fully autonomous agents: chronic unemployment, insufficient access to basic services such as health or education, or race or gender-based discrimination.

Consider Venezuela's health services industry. On the one hand, the private sector delivers a quality service, but only 15 percent of Venezuela's population can afford it. On the other hand, public hospitals are chronically under-funded, lacking even the most basis supplies such as cotton, gypsum, or medicines. "Mandatory" social security insurance–co-funded by companies and workers—reaches only 14 percent of the population, in a country where informality is rampant. Net result: market research showed that 88 percent of respondents considered that they did not have any place to go to in case of a medical emergency. Can we really talk of an untapped "niche" or even a "segment" when we are addressing a basic, unmet need of 85 percent of a country's population? Such potentially explosive context surely shapes the perception of opportunities and risks of the private sector in the region. This reality was very much present in our minds as we designed and carried out this research project, and helps to understand why the poor were only recently "discovered" by companies.

LIS as Broad Economic Agents

Prahalad's pioneering research on the BOP urges businesses to view the poor not as victims or a burden on society, but as resilient and creative entrepreneurs and value-conscious consumers.[48] Experiences documented in Latin America substantiate this view.[49] In 33 market initiatives, LIS groups in Latin America and Spain played various roles.

The Poor as Consumers

Prahalad focused on LIS as potential consumers under-served by large companies, pointing out the revolutionary impact that broadening consumer choice could bring about for the poor in terms of economic growth and individual self-esteem. Obviously, the idea of "selling to the poor" as such was not exactly new. The radically new concept behind the inclusive business approach is that the private sector was now given a role hitherto assigned to governments, charities, or multilateral agencies. The prospect of making profits was for the first time linked with improvements in the living conditions of the poor. Later formulations then expanded the concept to encompass market initiatives led by other type of organizations.

Why would the market succeed where other efforts to reduce poverty had failed? The key to success lies in entrepreneurial and organizational capacity to shape models that can overcome long-standing economic, geographic, cultural, and social barriers faced by the poor, which limit access and affordability. In the course of our research we examined 15 organizations serving LIS as consumers with a wide array of products and services (Table 1.2). In four experiences (Activo Humano, Cruzsalud, Comunanza and Supermercados Pali) LIS were at the center of the organization's mission, while in the

Table 1.2
The Poor as Consumers in Case Sample

	Organization	Product/Service	Country
LIS as main focus	Activo Humano	Work placement	Chile
	Cruzsalud	Health services	Venezuela
	Fundacion Comunanza	Micro-finance	Venezuela
	Supermercados Pali	Perishable and non-perishable goods	Central America
LIS as peripheral focus	AES-Electricidad de Caracas	Electricity	Venezuela
	Aguaytía	Gas	Peru
	Amanco	Irrigation systems	Mexico
	Cemex-Construmex	Cement and home improvement products	Mexico
	Codensa	Electricity and appliances	Colombia
	Colcerámica	Tiles	Colombia
	Edenor	Electricity	Argentina
	Ejercito de Salvacion	Clothing and furniture	Argentina
	Empresario Azteca	Credit	Mexico
	Gas Natural Ban	Gas	Argentina
	INACAP	Education	Chile

remaining 11, LIS were targeted as an additional market segment that supplemented the core business. In both types of situations we sought to uncover the driving forces that led to undertaking the activity, such as pursuing new business opportunity, reacting to threats in the environment, or following up philanthropic endeavors.[50] For each activity we asked: how did the forces leading to the initiative shape the business models deployed and the outcomes attained? What particular factors appear to have influenced the capacity of the initiative to generate economic and social value?

Finally, it should be noted that most of the initiatives included in the sample case did not target the poorest among the region's poor—at least not as potential consumers. The initiatives studied tended to target the "middle of the road" among the poor: the populations served looked like the middle of the bell curve of the income pyramid. Figure 1.3 below illustrates this point with three rather different cases: the Aztec Entrepreneur program (Programa Empresario Azteca), an initiative that sought to finance and sell machinery to the poor in Mexico; the National Institute for Professional Training (Instituto Nacional de Capacitación Profesional, or INACAP), a non-profit organization which provides top quality professional training to disadvantaged youth in Chile at a profit; and Codensa, a Colombian public utility company that sought to increase customer loyalty through the financing and selling of electronic products.

Figure 1.3
Segmenting the Low-income Sector Consumers

1.3.a. *Programa Empresario Azteca:* Selling tools to the poor in Mexico

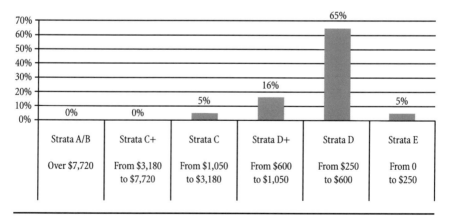

Socio-economic status of EA customers. Adapted by authors from data by EA and the Asociación Mexicana de Agencias de Investigación de Mercados y Opinión Pública (AMAI).

1.3.b. INACAP: Giving top-quality professional training to the poor in Chile, profitably

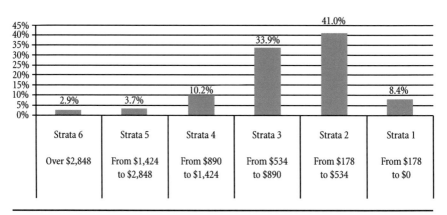

Socio-economic status of INACAP students, by 2006. Adapted by authors from data from the Sistema nacional de medición de resultados de aprendizaje (SIMCE), Chilean Ministry of Education.

1.3.c. Codensa: Democratizing credit in Colombia through a public utility company

Socio-economic status of Codensa customers, by 2006. Adapted by authors from company data.

The Poor as Producers and Suppliers

After the initial wave of BOP scholarship, which saw the poor primarily as an untapped consumer market, later formulations pointed out that significant progress in poverty reduction could not be achieved without increasing their income—improving their "balance of payments" vis-à-vis the rest of society, with more money flowing in and less coming out.[51] To raise income, it is necessary to "turn LIS into partners."[52] Thus, we examine not only how to "serve" the needs of the poor, but also how to work with them, in different capacities, in the construction of socially inclusive market initiatives.

In another 15 cases we analyzed, LIS participated as producers. This group falls into two categories (reflected in two columns in Table 1.3): self-organized efforts of the poor to bring goods to market or to supply other organizations, and LIS producers who joined an initiative led by a larger organization, participating in its value chain as suppliers. In the first category we have recyclers, wild fruit gatherers, sisal growers, seamstresses, and miners. In all cases we analyzed the challenges LIS groups faced in their quest to undertake initiatives in local and global markets.

Table 1.3
The Poor as Producers in Case Sample

LIS Organization	Country	Organization launching initiative	Country
APAEB	Brazil	Agropalma	Brazil
ASMARE	Brazil	Cativen	Venezuela
Centro Interregional de Artesanos del Peru (CIAP)	Peru	Costa Rica Entomological Supplies (CRES)	Costa Rica
Coopa-Roca	Brazil	Explorandes	Peru
Cooperativa de Recicladores Porvenir	Colombia	Hortifruti-Tierra Fertil	Central America
Coordinadora Regional de Recolectores y Recolectoras de las Región del Bio Bio	Chile	Irupana	Bolivia
Corporación Oro Verde	Colombia	Palmas del Espino	Peru
El Ceibo Recuperadores Urbanos	Argentina		

Organization of the Book

This book is organized in three modules. The first centers on actors: LIS groups participating in market initiatives, and organizations to which they are linked. A second part examines sectors where initiatives were developed, and the final section reviews the extent to which value creation was achieved.

Actors

Four chapters describe the actors involved in market-based initiatives with LIS as well as the collaborative arrangements among them. Chapter 2 focuses on the experience of thirteen large companies, critically assessing the comparative advantages held by large private firms in developing market initiatives with LIS as consumers and suppliers. A key query in this chapter is the centrality of LIS in the organization's purpose, a feature that appears to influence the venture's effectiveness.

Chapter 3 offers an in-depth look at LIS ventures led by SMEs. Issues discussed include how mission centrality focused on LIS markets, flexibility of management policy and practice, ongoing attention to opportunity for innovation and containment of operating costs, together with proximity to LIS, can lead to success in developing inclusive business ventures. These issues, considered crucial for inserting LIS in value chains, are examined against the backdrop of limitations that often plague SMEs and chip away profit margins. These may include diseconomies of scale, limited geographic reach, limited product portfolio, and (in emerging economies) access to external sources of financing.

Chapter 4 puts forward the concept of "social enterprise," a non-traditional category that encompasses both CSOs and cooperatives. This chapter seeks to uncover similarities among cooperatives and nonprofit organizations as they operate in socially inclusive market initiatives. Study of thirteen experiences yields insights into the potential for innovation through market mechanisms that feature the venture's beneficiaries in prominent roles. Also examined are the business models employed in building market initiatives with LIS, highlighting the role of creative leadership.

The final chapter in this module reviews the different organizational ecosystems where the various ventures were undertaken. Attention focuses on exploring the particular features of each, assessing those that appear to have been crucial in breaking down barriers that hindered fruitful value exchanges with the poor. A particular feature of socially inclusive ventures is that they are often built upon communities of interest, of different groups that interact in pursuit of a common goal. The chapter examines various types of players that perform a number of roles. The nature of their relationships can vary greatly: from semi-hierarchical to horizontal and cooperative linkages; and from loose, contract-based ties to structured joint-ventures.

Sectors

The guideline for our case selection was to shape a set that would be heterogeneous in terms of organizational form, industries, and geographical scope. Yet once the data gathering was completed, it became evident that three sectors stood out: agribusiness, recycling, and public utilities. This made sense: LIS have traditionally played a major role as producers and suppliers in the first two. The third one, however, exemplified an emerging field of concern in inclusive business, with the potential of having enormous impact on the living conditions of the poor. The initiatives encompassed in this last group reacted creatively to contextual challenges, and broadened their reach to include LIS in their respective value chains.

In chapter 6 five experiences in public utilities are examined: three in electric power supply, and two in natural gas. The electric services were delivered in large metropolitan areas in Argentina, Colombia, and Venezuela; the natural gas ventures took place in Argentina and Peru. Each experience provides the opportunity for discussing how tradition-bound companies crafted innovative business models to serve LIS consumers. One overcame a long-standing practice whereby poor consumers tapped power lines to obtain free electricity; another succeeded in halting pressures on state regulatory agencies to hold utility prices artificially low for political gain. These companies learned to develop attractive value propositions for poor consumers—by highlighting the tradeoff between delivering improved service to the poor and generating profit.

Chapter 7 focuses on LIS as recyclers. For decades, the Latin American urban poor made a living through the recycling of solid waste in metropolitan areas. The importance of this activity has recently increased, as the global economic crisis expelled individuals from the formal economy, and as the sustainability agenda created demand for recycled goods. The authors examine the experience of entrepreneurial organizations led by LIS groups, focusing on the leadership and innovation that enabled them to transform the recycling practices in their respective communities.

Chapter 8 examines the challenges firms face when they seek to bring rural communities, where insufficient infrastructure and poverty are a common denominator, into value chains linked to mass markets or high-end consumers. The discussion shows how the companies involved learned to overcome such challenges, weighing the benefits of long-term versus short-term gains.

Value Creation

Can profit be made by serving the poor? This overriding question remains an issue of current debate: Prahalad[53] holds there is a fortune to be made by eradicating poverty; whereas Karnani[54] and others deem this a mirage, for in their opinion business engagement with the poor, even in the best of circumstances, is costly and difficult. Both views may be right: our sample harbors both solid success stories and others that failed to fulfill their alleged "great potential."

The final section of this book examines economic and social value created by the array of initiatives included in the study. Building on previous SEKN work, new approaches deemed valid for gauging social impact on individual's lives, communities, and society as a whole are explored. To measure economic value in market initiatives with LIS, the authors take into account margins, earnings, and sustainability. Results attained by organizations where engagement with LIS lies at the core of the venture, are compared to those where the initiative is limited to a particular project. Similarly, results obtained by different kinds of organizations are assessed. Also examined are tensions emerging from efforts to create economic and social value in market-based initiatives with LIS.

How successful were these initiatives in creating material wealth for participants? Chapter 9 deals with this question and examines economic success in doing business with LIS. The analysis highlights the differences in economic value creation between organizations whose business engagement with LIS lies at the core of their mission, vis-à-vis social projects undertaken within, for example, the realm of corporate social responsibility. SEKN authors review a wide set of conditions that must be met in order to generate profits. These include cost controls, facilitating credit and payment terms for poor consumers, and developing appropriate yardsticks and indicators for measuring market success.

Chapter 10 deals with the other half of the value creation process. How was social value generated for LIS participating as consumers, suppliers, or partners in each of the ventures examined? In what ways did these initiatives favorably impact individuals, communities, or society as a whole? This chapter seeks to determine how the experiences analyzed lowered the market barriers hitherto encountered by LIS, thus opening access to goods and services, promoting human rights and dignity, and expanding individual and family income. The authors investigate whether significant differences emerged from one experience to another, depending on the kind of organization or sector, and bring up issues related to scalability and opportunity for experience replication.

The overall purpose of all the chapters in this book is to expand the ongoing debate on business at the socio-economic base-of-the-pyramid in Iberoamerica. Beyond generating knowledge, SEKN has sought to contribute to practice by dissecting specific challenges faced by the organizations in the sample and the paths taken to overcome them. This book is an invitation to imagine new possibilities in business for greater economic prosperity and positive social transformation. With that in mind, we offer lessons on how market initiatives engaging the poor can be a powerful force to foster more equal and fair societies in the region.

Notes

1. James E. Austin and Michael Chu, "Business and Low-Income Sectors: Finding a New Weapon to Attack Poverty," *ReVista Harvard Review of Latin America* (2006): 3.

2. C. K. Prahalad, *The Fortune at the Bottom of the Pyramid: Eradicating Poverty through Profits* (Upper Saddle River, NJ: Wharton School Publishing, 2005), 11; Allen L. Hammond et al., *The Next 4 Billion: Market Size and Business Strategy at the Base of the Pyramid* (Washington, DC: World Resources Institute and International Finance Corporation, 2007).

3. Craig Burnside and David Dollar, "Aid, Policies and Growth," *American Economic Review* 90 (2000); William Russell Easterly, *The Elusive Quest for Growth: Economists' Adventures and Misadventures in the Tropics* (Cambridge, MA: MIT Press, 2001).

4. Henry Chesbrough, "Business Model Innovation: It's Not Just about Technology Anymore," *Strategy & Leadership* 35, no. 6 (2007): 13.

5. Ted London, "The Base-of-the-Pyramid Perspective: A New Approach to Poverty Alleviation" (Working Paper, William Davidson Institute/Stephen M. Ross School of Business, 2008), 12.

6. Latin American countries use different criteria to classify companies as SME or large. In deciding how to classify each case, this study followed the criteria prevailing in the company's country of origin. These criteria vary significantly from nation to nation. For instance, in Argentina the criteria used is annual sales, but this differs among manufacture, commerce and service. In Chile there are two criteria: employment and sales. In Colombia SME status is determined by number of employees and total assets (www.fundes.org).

7. SEKN, ed. *Effective Management of Social Enterprises Lessons from Businesses and Civil Society Organizations in Iberoamerica* (Cambridge, MA: Harvard University Press with David Rockefeller Center for Latin American Studies, 2006), 226.

8. C. K. Prahalad and Stuart Hart, "The Fortune at the Bottom of the Pyramid," *Strategy + Business* 1, no. 26 (2002); C. K. Prahalad and Allen Hammond, "Serving the World's Poor, Profitably," *Harvard Business Review* (2002).

9. Prahalad and Hart, "The Fortune at the Bottom of the Pyramid"; Prahalad and Hammond, "Serving the World's Poor, Profitably"; Stuart L. Hart and Clayton M. Christensen, "The Great Leap: Driving Innovation from the Base of the Pyramid," *MIT Sloan Management Review* 44, no. 1 (2002); Prahalad, *The Fortune at the Bottom of the Pyramid: Eradicating Poverty through Profits* (Upper Saddle River, NJ: Wharton School Publishing, 2005).

10. James Austin et al., "Building New Business Value Chains with Low Income Sectors in Latin America," in *Business Solutions for the Global Poor: Creating Social and Economic Value*, ed. Kasturi Rangan, et al. (San Francisco, CA: Jossey-Bass, 2007).

11. Ted London, "The Base-of-the-Pyramid Perspective: A New Approach to Poverty Alleviation" (Working Paper, William Davidson Institute/Stephen M. Ross School of Business, 2008); Jacqueline Novogratz, "Meeting Urgent Needs

with Patient Capital," *Innovations: Technology | Governance | Globalization* 2, no. 1/2 (2007).

12. James Austin et al., "Building New Business Value Chains with Low Income Sectors in Latin America," in *Business Solutions for the Global Poor: Creating Social and Economic Value*, ed. Kasturi Rangan, et al. (San Francisco, CA: Jossey-Bass, 2007).

13. Ted London, "The Base-of-the-Pyramid Perspective: A New Approach to Poverty Alleviation" (Working Paper, William Davidson Institute/Stephen M. Ross School of Business, 2008), 24.

14. C. K. Prahalad and Stuart Hart, "The Fortune at the Bottom of the Pyramid," *Strategy + Business* 1, no. 26 (2002).

15. George C. Lodge, "The Corporate Key: Using Big Business to Fight Global Poverty," *Foreign Affairs* 81, no. 4 (2002).

16. Aneel Karnani points out that many of the cases used by Prahalad in "Fortune at the Bottom of the Pyramid" are not MNCs: Casas Bahía is a large Brazilian Company; Voxiva is an SME, and Aravind is a CSO. Aneel G. Karnani, "Fortune at the Bottom of the Pyramid: A Mirage" (Working Paper No. 1035, University of Michigan, Stephen M. Ross School of Business, 2006).

17. "While a number of authors have highlighted the important role that non-native multinational corporations (MNCs) can play in serving the base of the pyramid . . . BOP ventures are not the sole purview of these large companies. In fact, a variety of different external organizations and individuals can launch BOP ventures. As discussed in the BOP literature, these ventures also emerge from the host-country private sector as well as nonprofit organizations and other socially-oriented enterprises." Ted London, "The Base-of-the-Pyramid Perspective: A New Approach to Poverty Alleviation" (Working Paper, William Davidson Institute/Stephen M. Ross School of Business, 2008), 14. See also, David Wheeler et al., "Creating Sustainable Local Enterprise Networks," *MIT Sloan Review* 47, no. 1 (2005).

18. Allen L. Hammond et al., *The Next 4 Billion: Market Size and Business Strategy at the Base of the Pyramid* (Washington, DC: World Resources Institute and International Finance Corporation, 2007).

19. *Stichting Nederlandse Vrijwilligers*, the Netherlands' Development Organization.

20. Ted London, "The Base-of-the-Pyramid Perspective: A New Approach to Poverty Alleviation" (Working Paper, William Davidson Institute/Stephen M. Ross School of Business, 2008), 14.

21. "The aspiring poor present a prodigious opportunity for the world's wealthiest companies. But it requires a radical new approach to business strategy." C. K. Prahalad and Stuart Hart, "The Fortune at the Bottom of the Pyramid," *Strategy + Business* 1, no. 26 (2002). In this view, radical innovation should not be restricted to products, but encompass also processes. C. K. Prahalad, *The Fortune at the Bottom of the Pyramid: Eradicating Poverty through Profits* (Upper Saddle River, NJ: Wharton School Publishing, 2005).

22. Christian Seelos and Johanna Mair, "Profitable Business Models and Market Creation in the Context of Deep Poverty: A Strategic View," *The Academy of Management Perspectives* 21, no. 4 (2007): 60.
23. Christian Seelos and Johanna Mair, "Social Entrepreneurship: Creating New Business Models to Serve the Poor," *Business Horizons* 48, no. 3 (2005).
24. Ted London, "The Base-of-the-Pyramid Perspective: A New Approach to Poverty Alleviation" (Working Paper, William Davidson Institute/Stephen M. Ross School of Business, 2008), 16.
25. Erik Simanis et al., "Strategic Initiatives at the Base of the Pyramid: A Protocol for Mutual Value Creation." Base of the Pyramid Protocol Workshop Group Wingspread Conference Center, Racine, WI, 2005.
26. Christian Seelos and Johanna Mair, "Profitable Business Models and Market Creation in the Context of Deep Poverty: A Strategic View," *The Academy of Management Perspectives* 21, no. 4 (2007): 61.
27. C. K. Prahalad and Stuart Hart, "The Fortune at the Bottom of the Pyramid," *Strategy + Business* 1, no. 26 (2002); C. K. Prahalad, *The Fortune at the Bottom of the Pyramid: Eradicating Poverty through Profits* (Upper Saddle River, NJ: Wharton School Publishing, 2005).
28. Ted London and Stuart L Hart, "Reinventing Strategies for Emerging Markets: Beyond the Transnational Model," *Journal of International Business Studies* 35 (2004): 362.
29. Ted London, "The Base-of-the-Pyramid Perspective: A New Approach to Poverty Alleviation" (Working Paper, William Davidson Institute/Stephen M. Ross School of Business, 2008), 22.
30. C. K. Prahalad, *The Fortune at the Bottom of the Pyramid: Eradicating Poverty through Profits* (Upper Saddle River, NJ: Wharton School Publishing, 2005), 4.
31. Allen L. Hammond et al., *The Next 4 Billion: Market Size and Business Strategy at the Base of the Pyramid* (Washington, DC: World Resources Institute and International Finance Corporation, 2007), 3.
32. CEPAL, "Panorama social de América Latina 2007." (Comisión Económica para América Latina y el Caribe, 2007), http://www.eclac.org/publicaciones/xml/5/30305/PSE2007_Cap1_Pobreza.pdf.
33. Ramón López and Alberto Valdés, *Rural Poverty in Latin America* (New York: St. Martin's Press, 2000).
34. Comisión Económica para América Latina, "Anuario estadístico de América Latina y el Caribe." Naciones Unidas, División de Estadísticas y Proyecciones Económicas. Santiago: 2007.
35. Ibid.
36. Michael Förster and Marco Mira d'Ercole, "Income Distribution and Poverty in OECD Countries in the Second Half of the 1990s" (OECD Social, Employment and Migration Working Papers. Paris: 2005).
37. "La pobresa a Catalunya. Informe 2003," Fundació UN SOL MÓN de l'Obra Social de Caixa Catalunya, http://obrasocial.caixacatalunya.es/CDA/ObraSocial

/OS_Plantilla3/0,3417,1x3y355,00.html. The autonomic parliament approved the creation of social enterprises for labor inclusion (*empresas de inserción*) to develop market activities for the integration of people under great risk of social exclusion.

38. "Panorama social 2007 de América Latina," Comisión Económica para América Latina y el Caribe, http://www.eclac.org/publicaciones/xml/5/30305/PSE2007 _Sintesis_Lanzamiento.pdf.

39. The Gini coefficient is the indicator utilized to measure inequality of income distribution, where 0 corresponds to perfect equality of income, and 1 to perfect inequality (with one person capturing 100% of available income, and everyone else 0%).

40. "Indicadores de concentración del ingreso, total nacional, 1990–2006 (cuadro 14)," Comisión Económica para América Latina y el Caribe, http://www.eclac .org/publicaciones/xml/5/30305/PSE2007_AnexoEstadistico.xls.

41. World Economic Forum, "Latin America@Risk. A Global Risk Network Briefing," www.weforum.org/pdf/grn/LatinAmericaRisk.pdf.

42. Leonardo Gasparini and Leopoldo Tornarolli, "Labor Informality in Latin America and the Caribbean: Patterns and Trends from Household Survey Microdata." Documento de Trabajo Nro. 0, Centro de Estudios Distributivos, Laborales y Sociales, Universidad Nacional de La Plata. La Plata, Prov. Buenos Aires: 2007.

43. The informal economy embraces ordinary trade together with illicit activities, although in the informal economy literature illegal activities are not considered. Patricia Marquez and Henry Gomez, *Microempresas: alianzas para el éxito* (Caracas: Ediciones IESA, 2001).

44. Self-funding by entrepreneurs and funding from informal investors constitute the lifeblood of an entrepreneurial society. Aside from providing 65.8 percent of the start-up capital for their own companies they are four times as likely as non-entrepreneurs to be informal investors in another entrepreneur's business. Informal investors supply more than the external capital needs of entrepreneurs. Zoltan J. Acs et al., "Global Entrepreneurship Monitor. 2004 Executive Report" (Babson Park, MA: Babson College, 2005).

45. René Lenoir, *Les exclus* (Paris: Seuil, 1974).

46. Gabrielle Quinti, "Exclusión social: el debate teórico y los modelos de medición y evaluación," in *De Igual a Igual: El desafío del Estado ante los nuevos problemas sociales*, ed. Jorge Carpio and Irene Novacovsky (Buenos Aires: Fondo de Cultura Económica de Argentina y Secretaría de Desarrollo Social de la Nación, 1999), 289–304.

47. Gustavo Márquez et al., *Outsiders? The Changing Patterns of Exclusion in Latin America and the Caribbean* (Washington, DC and Cambridge, MA: Inter-American Development Bank and David Rockefeller Center for Latin American Studies, Harvard University, 2007).

48. C. K. Prahalad, *The Fortune at the Bottom of the Pyramid: Eradicating Poverty through Profits* (Upper Saddle River, NJ: Wharton School Publishing, 2005), 1.

49. María Eugenia Boza, "El consumidor venezolano: nuevas categorías y herramientas para entenderlo," *Debates IESA* 2004; John Ireland, "Mercadeo en Venezuela hoy: en busca de las mayorías," *Debates IESA* 8, no. 3 (2003); Marquez and Gomez, *Microempresas: Alianzas Para El Éxito*, Hernando De Soto, *The Other Path: The Invisible Revolution in the Third World*, 1st ed. (New York: Perennial Library, 1990).

50. James Austin et al., "Building New Business Value Chains with Low Income Sectors in Latin America," in *Business Solutions for the Global Poor: Creating Social and Economic Value*, ed. Kasturi Rangan et al. (San Francisco, CA: Jossey-Bass, 2007).

51. "Increasing income generated in the low-income community requires interventions or changes that alter one or more of these balances—that increase consumption that is locally-produced, that increase investment activities using local materials, that provide government services using inputs from the local community, or that expand exports." Herman B. Leonard, "When Is Doing Business with the Poor Good—for the Poor? A Household and National Income Accounting Approach," in *Business Solutions for the Global Poor: Creating Social and Economic Value*, ed. Kasturi Rangan et al. (San Francisco, CA: Jossey-Bass, 2007).

52. Kapil Marwaha et al., "IBENEX: Business Effectiveness—the Next Level: Being Served by the Poor, as Partners" (paper presented at the Harvard Business School Conference on Global Poverty, Boston, MA, December 1–3, 2005).

53. C. K. Prahalad, *The Fortune at the Bottom of the Pyramid: Eradicating Poverty through Profits* (Upper Saddle River, NJ: Wharton School Publishing, 2005).

54. Aneel Karnani, "The Mirage of Marketing at the Bottom of the Pyramid," *California Management Review* 49, no. 4 (Summer 2007).

2

Market Initiatives of Large Companies Serving Low-Income Sectors

Josefina Bruni Celli, Rosa Amelia González, and Gerardo Lozano

To the question whether it is possible to create an "inclusive capitalism," one that will contribute to diminishing global poverty, C. K. Prahalad[1] answers yes, *to the extent that large domestic and global firms become more involved in making it happen.* In his view, when compared to government, multilaterals or CSOs, large companies have greatest potential in bringing solutions to "those at the bottom of the economic pyramid around the world," given the large resources they command and mobilize, their capacity to apply learning and transfer knowledge globally, their nodal position in economic networks,[2] and the large scale and scope of their operations.

Though to date the involvement of large-scale private sector in dealing with the problems of 80 percent of humanity remains marginal, since 1999, Prahalad and other scholars have argued that companies can create profitable markets at the bottom of the pyramid (BOP), and that engaging in BOP market creation provides a competitive edge.[3] According to this view, the reason why large companies have not seized the opportunity is that management is making the wrong assumptions about the poor and therefore has not invested in building necessary capabilities or in making the required innovations in products, supply chains, and delivery systems.[4] In order to secure the necessary combination of low cost, good quality, sustainability, and profitability at the BOP, strategies comprising "an entirely new perspective" are proposed.[5]

This literature seeks to convince management of large corporations that developing BOP markets is possible, and to offer general guidelines as to "how to make it happen."[6] Thus, as Prahalad tells his readers, "judicious use of capital is a critical element of success in BOP markets," "innovations must become value oriented from the consumer's perspective," "firms must focus on all elements of cost," and companies must "learn to live with a wide variety of relationships."[7] However, there is little systematic comparative analysis of how BOP business ventures by large companies have evolved, in terms of profitability and scale.[8] This chapter contributes systematic evidence from 12 Latin American market initiatives by large private companies, acting with a profit motive, targeted at the low-income sector (hereafter, LIS). We address three questions. The first is how the managers of this set of business ventures have gone about developing a working business model with LIS, what challenges they have faced, and how they have dealt with them. The second is the extent to which recommendations put out by the BOP literature have worked for these companies. In this empirical verification special emphasis is placed on the role of innovation and ecosystems in the building of the business model. The final question considers the scale reached by ventures and their determinants.

All sampled initiatives are fairly recent[9] and connect a low-income segment to markets it did not have access to previously. Cases include both low-income producers and low-income consumers. The former either did not previously produce goods sold to the company, or sold them under inferior terms of trade. The latter either had limited access to products or services, or obtained them in conditions of inferior quality. All ventures are attempts at developing a relationship featuring direct market transactions between the companies and LIS.

The selected sample has two characteristics that affect the extent to which our results can be generalized, but which also inform about LIS market ventures in areas that have been under-explored. First, with few exceptions,[10] LIS customers involved were not rural people living in extreme or absolute poverty, as defined in this book's introductory chapter, but rather a better-off set of dwellers of urban slums and popular housing: a group living in "moderate poverty" that represents most of Latin America's LIS, whose income distribution in the BOP market segment ($500 to $3000 a year range) has been found to be "top heavy."[11] It is also important to recall that the cultural heritage—beginning with the Spanish language and the Catholic religion—of LIS in Latin America makes them less distant from Western culture than LIS in Asia or Africa.

Second, none of the selected ventures featured the kind of mass consumer products that can be packaged in small or single servings. We chose not to focus on these because, like Prahalad's single most cited company, Unilever, many mass-marketing companies have been successfully delivering goods such as candy, cigarettes, and soft drinks to Latin American LIS for many decades. Instead, we chose to analyze ventures featuring goods to which Latin American LIS have traditionally had less access, such as durables (equipments, appliances, homes, and home improvements) and public utilities (electricity, water, and gas). These are often called merit goods: products and services that, by social consensus, are basic needs of consumers. Our focus on durables and public utilities brings in new issues into building business relationships with low-income sectors. For example, in contrast to mass-market consumer goods, durables are indivisible and cannot be re-packaged in smaller or single-serving formats. Thus, while creating new product concepts and effective forward distribution channels may be the key for the mass-market goods, in the area of durables, the central challenge lies in establishing effective billing and collection mechanisms. This is also a central issue for public utility companies.

In the first section of this chapter we analyze how companies built a business model to engage LIS, giving special attention to venture drivers, attributes of designed business models, and key issues addressed in successive adjustments during implementation of the models. The second section looks into the features of innovation and ecosystems in analyzed ventures in the light of the BOP literature. The third section addresses the challenges faced by sampled companies when seeking to scale up their LIS ventures. The chapter ends with a summary of findings, a discussion of their implications for managers, and recommendations for advancing further down the road of inclusive capitalism.

Building the Business Model

Before engaging in a venture, companies must first see a business opportunity. They then go about designing a model that shows how the different pieces of their business concept fit together.[12] Finally, they implement and test their initial plan and assumptions and make the necessary adjustments. We describe the experience of sampled companies in all these phases of the business model-building process. Challenges specific to LIS markets are analyzed.

Venture Drivers

All 12 sampled ventures were profit-driven (see Table 2.1 below). Perceived opportunities for achieving high sales volumes were the business drivers (see chapter 9) behind six of the nine "LIS-as-customer" ventures. In the remaining "LIS-as-customer" ventures—pursued by electric energy companies—drivers were instead defensive: to secure consumer loyalty (Codensa) or to avoid "non-technical losses" (i.e., illegal connections) in urban slums (Edenor, AES-EDC). In turn, among all LIS supplier ventures, the core business driver was increased value chain efficiency. In particular, management of the two palm oil companies (Palmas del Espino and Agropalma) ventured to develop LIS suppliers because company lands surrounding their palm-oil

Table 2.1. Large Company Business Ventures with LIS

Company	LIS customer venture	Business driver of venture	Starting year
AES-EDC (electric energy)	Electric service provision in urban LIS	Loss reduction	2003
Agropalma (palm oil)	Procurement of palm for palm oil plant from small farmers	Using idle capacity (increased efficiency)	2001
Aguaytia (gas)	Provision of liquid gas in cylinders in the region neighboring the refinery (Peruvian Amazon)	Penetrating volume market; savings in transportation	2002
Amanco (irrigation systems)	Provision of irrigation systems to small farmers	Penetrating volume market	2004
Cativen (retail)	Procurement of vegetables for supermarkets from farmers	Capturing intermediation margin; increasing small supply chain efficiency	2001
Cemex (cement) "Construmex"	Provision of construction materials and homes to LIS	Penetrating volume market	2004
Codensa (electric energy)	Provision of electric household appliances to urban LIS (Codensa Hogar)	Securing customer loyalty	2001
Colcerámica (ceramic tiles)	"Su casa como nueva paso a paso" Provision of ceramic tiles to urban LIS	Penetrating volume market	2004
Edenor (electric energy)	Electric service provision in urban LIS	Loss reduction	2001
Gas Natural BAN (direct gas)	Direct gas provision in urban LIS	Penetrating volume market	2003
Grupo Salinas (banking and retail)	"Empresario Azteca" Provision of tools and equipment to micro-entrepreneurs	Penetrating volume market	2004
Palma del Espino (palm oil)	Procurement of palm for palm oil plant from small farmers	Using idle capacity (increased efficiency)	2003

processing plants did not yield enough to cover capacity. Developing peasant productivity in the area was more efficient than bringing in palm products from elsewhere, which was very expensive in these remote locations. Similarly, Cativen, a large retailer catering fresh produce through hundreds of stores in Venezuela, set out to buy directly from small farmers to increase quality control in the supply chain, reduce produce attrition, and capture intermediation margins.

The availability of relevant technology, the possibility of taking advantage of existing complementary company assets, and lack of better options were conditions that spurred some, but not all, of the initiatives (see chapter 9). The utility company Edenor saw in pre-paid meters an opportunity to bring electric energy to LIS without risk of nonpayment, and at the same time to adapt to their cash flow, which is ill-suited to afford bi-monthly invoicing. In order to sell durables to LIS, Codensa and Banco Azteca leveraged existing company or corporate platforms—a billing system, and a credit-scoring institution (Círculo de Crédito), respectively—both of which had already been used to penetrate the LIS market. Cativen, subsidiary of the giant retail multinational Groupe Casino, used the latter's logistics technology to set up the mechanism whereby it would purchase directly from LIS. And as we saw, Aguaytia, Agropalma, and Palma del Espino chose to create a LIS market because the gains derived from physical proximity to company plants were balanced against the costs of transporting out of or into the area. In all three cases, the company had spare resources (liquid gas in the case of Aguaytía, and spare processing plant capacity in the other two) that could not be put to use without incurring high transportation costs or substantial capital investment, unless the company worked with LIS located in the adjacent territory.

Designed Business Models

All companies in the sample took the time to design business models tailored to either serve the unmet needs of low-income consumers or to make use of LIS capacities as suppliers. These designs were substantially different from business models used by companies to serve their traditional markets, and in many cases expressly followed recommendations in the BOP literature.

Table 2.2 shows major innovations in five categories which have been identified by Osterwalder et al. as building blocks of business models:[13] value proposition, distribution channel, relationship with customers, partner network, and revenue model.

The manner in which the firm relates to its customers or suppliers is novel in all cases. New ways of enrolling customers and suppliers, of rating

Table 2.2: Major Novelties Featured in Original Business Model

Company	Value proposition	Distribution channel	Relationship with customers	Partner network	Revenue model
AES-EDC (electric energy)	None: traditional electric energy	None: traditional distribution network	New: illegally connected individuals become clients through collective meters.	New: close collaboration with community leaders	New: community leaders collect individual payments
Agropalma (palm oil)	New: otherwise unavailable palm supply and social license	New: company purchases directly from farmers cooperatives	New: company involvement in the organization and development of small farmers	New: collaboration with governmental agencies financing crop development	Implementation pending
Aguaytia (gas)	New product: liquid gas in cylinders	New: company sets up its own truck fleet	New: company "sows" free gas motors and stoves among future customers	None: no partnering involved	None: simple cash and carry
Amanco (irrigation systems)	New product: small tailor-made irrigation systems	None: traditional delivery remains in place	New: company promotes collective effort to build distribution network	New: close collaboration with CSOs, and national government	None: company traditionally sells on credit
Cativen (retail)	New: timely supply of fresh vegetables at stable prices	New: company purchases directly from farmers cooperatives	New: company involvement in the organization and development of small farmers	New: collaboration with government agencies and universities during setup	New: the company makes regular scheduled payments to farmers through bank accounts
Cemex (cement)	New products: houses and construction materials other than cement	New: company sets up a network of sales offices	New: unprecedented direct relationship with individual consumer instead of traditional b to b relations	New: partnerships with International remittances company, construction companies, and local distributors of construction materials	New: sale on credit to final consumer instead of traditional sale on credit b to b

Table 2.2: Major Novelties Featured in Original Business Model (continued)

Company	Value proposition	Distribution channel	Relationship with customers	Partner network	Revenue model
Codensa (electric energy)	New product: household appliances	New: company leverages on distribution channel of existing retail chain	New: applies credit scoring tailored for LIS customers	New partner serving distribution: large national hypermarket chain	New: unprecedented sale on credit
Colcerámica (ceramic tiles)	None: traditional ceramics	None: traditional delivery channel through local hardware stores remains in place	New: unprecedented sale relationship with individual consumer through local promoters	New: close collaboration with CSO, community organizations, and local hardware stores	New: layaway sale to LIS; community organizations collect payments
Edenor (electric energy)	None: traditional electric energy	New: distribution of pre-paid energy cards through dispensing machines	New: relates with customers through dispensing machines and pre-paid meters.	None: no partnering involved	New: pre-payment instead of post-payment of electric service
Gas Natural BAN (direct gas)	None: traditional gas service	None: traditional distribution network	New: company promotes collective effort to build distribution network	New: close collaboration with CSOs, local governments and multilateral agencies	None: traditional post-payment remains
Grupo Salinas (banking and retail)	New product: tools and equipment for micro-entrepreneurs	None: traditional retail chain	New: company uses credit scoring tailored for LIS customers	None: traditional close collaboration between companies of the Salinas Group	None: company retail chain traditionally sells on credit
Palmas del Espino (palm oil)	New: otherwise unavailable palm supply and social license	New: company purchases directly from farmers cooperatives	New: company involvement in the organization and development of small farmers	New: collaboration with governmental agencies financing crop development	Implementation pending

them, and of interacting with them in sales or purchasing transactions were developed. Major departures from traditional business models also occurred in the revenue model, which featured unprecedented credit or pre-paid mechanisms. Finally, most business models also involved a new product or service. In those cases where companies did not venture into new products or services, nontraditional elements were added to the distribution channel, the partner network, or the revenue model components of their business model.

Successive Adjustments in Implementation: LIS Markets' Specificities

In the ventures we observed, timetables for reaching profitability had to be rescheduled various times. During those delays, many successive adjustments were made to the original business model. The process of adjustment in these companies was continuous and incremental, akin to evolutionary changes associated with persistent troubleshooting to correct faulty assumptions underlying the initial business model design. This is no different from what usually occurs during the early implementation of any business model. Nevertheless, many of these adjustments were unique to LIS markets: how to build mutual reliance in a context of information asymmetries, how to correctly address LIS's perceived value of goods and services, and how to draw the fine line between informality and illegality.

Building Mutual Reliance and Two-Way Trust

After reading Prahalad's *The Fortune at the Bottom of the Pyramid*, Carlos Espinal, Colcerámica's Mass Market General Manager, set out to develop a BOP business model with the assistance of an Ashoka fellow. The model was founded on two central innovations: first, an expansion of the original product (ceramics) package to include nearby delivery and a payment plan; second, structuring of a local ecosystem (see chapter 5).

Closely in line with Prahalad's recommendations, for three months, the company and the partnering CSO did in-depth field research in Usme, a low-income neighborhood; and, after three additional months, they identified what they thought would be the relevant ecosystem for the initiative. During this process, the company decided that a layaway payment mechanism was the most appropriate for selling ceramics to LIS. But for the building of a working business model, this initial formulation had to be adjusted in ways that involved building greater mutual reliance and mutual trust between the company and LIS customers.

When the company initially presented to the community its business model, it proposed the creation of cooperatives that would serve as formal interlocutors between the company and the buyers. The community's reaction was that the company was not relying sufficiently on the existing local organizations, and that cooperatives were not necessary. The company reformulated its business model to include "existing community networks" to manage a sales force made up of female members of that community.

Not many months had passed when the LIS customers and the community sales force became suspicious that the tiles being sold were factory rejects, for as one community leader said: "how could an international organization come here just like that . . .it had to be seconds." Visits to the factory were organized to show them that this wasn't the case.

The company also discovered that its sales were lagging because LIS were not very willing to enter its layaway plan, a payment policy that had been established to reduce risk of buyer default. In order to increase sales, in 2006 management decided it was time to trust the customers: products began to be delivered to buyers after 50 percent had been paid. Demand increased, and there were no defaults. Chapter 5 elaborates on the importance of developing embedded relationships and gaining "business intimacy" along with "business friendships" with those targeted by the venture.

Adjusting the Product Concept to a Demanding Customer Segment
The literature on disruptive innovation has emphasized "more modest packages" or simplified, less expensive versions of products consumed at the higher end of the market.[14] This may be true for many consumer goods, but findings in this study show that for comparatively expensive durables that require credit loans or payments by installments, LIS tend to be an exacting market segment, because the purchase represents an important feat involving a large commitment and the costly surrender of other consumption. In various cases, companies had to adjust their initial product concepts accordingly.

Managers of Grupo Salinas had identified a business opportunity with LIS when bank analysts realized that many LIS loan applications at the group's bank (Banco Azteca) were not for acquisitions of home appliances at the group's chain of retail stores (Elektra), but rather to buy equipment for developing productive activities in stores that did not belong to Grupo Salinas. These buyers were self-employed small entrepreneurs. It was thus decided in 2004 that Elektra would now offer equipment for this segment. Managers assumed they could leverage the existing retail chain infrastructure and the previous experience of their Elektra sales force in serving this segment, but it soon became clear that these did not suffice to serve what turned out to be sophisticated, knowledgeable, and demanding buyers.

Self-employed small entrepreneurs expected and demanded quality service and prompt delivery of their purchased equipment. For them this was a very important and expensive purchase, a significant family event. Likewise, they were well versed in the technical features of the specialized equipment they wished to buy. In contrast, the Elektra sales force was trained to manage a technically simpler set of products, such as home appliances, furniture, and clothing. Moreover, as Elektra stores were not prepared to manage small inventories of specialized equipment, purchases were not in stock at the time of purchase and orders took as long as a month to be delivered, when small entrepreneurs demanded the equipment for immediate use. As of 2007, Grupo Salinas was working on putting together an integrated information system of its suppliers in order to make faster deliveries to small entrepreneurs.

Prahalad had observed that LIS are "value buyers," expecting "great quality at prices they can afford."[15] We found that improving the product-price ratio is not sufficient for the exacting LIS customer. Delivery, sales service, and post-sale service also have to be closely addressed. This implies that "more modest packages" can be very complex.

Tracing the Boundary between Informality and Illegality

Recent literature has insisted that in order to work better at the BOP, and as part of acquiring "native capabilities," companies must not insist on creating Western-style legal business environments,[16] but rather rely on existing informal community-level economic organizations to do business with the poor.[17] The problem is that in many situations, at least in Latin America, the informal and the illegal are closely related, as informal economic activities take place outside the formal institutional boundaries or laws and regulations.[18] Thus, companies will often find that as they advance in the implementation of a model of exchange with LIS, they must carefully note the thin line between informality and illegality and make corresponding adjustments. For example, when Construmex identified a business opportunity in remittances sent to their families by Mexican workers in the United States, management expanded its central product (construction materials) to include construction advice and payment facilities in the United States as well as construction advice and local delivery in Mexico. Initially Cemex planned to serve all of the Mexican immigrant market, including undocumented residents. The trend towards criminalization of illegal immigration in various U.S. states forced Cemex to re-think the market segment it was willing to serve, for ethical and legal reasons.

In Venezuela, Cativen was faced with the fact that tax authorities do not recognize for tax deduction purposes any purchase not backed by authorized receipts. Thus in order to develop a business relationship with small LIS farmers, Cativen found it necessary to help them comply with all the formalities required by law. LIS farmers did not feel comfortable going to government offices and banks, nor did they know how to go about the process of formalizing. Company employees (members of the purchasing team) thus attended weekly meetings with farmer groups to provide advice and drafts of bylaws. In addition, they accompanied farmers to government offices to register and obtain tax ID numbers, took them to government-authorized presses to purchase legally recognized receipts, and helped them open bank accounts.

In Peru, the poor farmers that Palmas del Espino was hoping would become suppliers of palm were illegal squatters of 1,200 hectares of company lands as well as illegal coca leaf farmers. Originally the company opposed the presence of these squatters and fought against a government program that sought to give them legal ownership of the land, but this only pushed squatters into illegal coca farming and joining rebel groups. In 2001–2002 the company negotiated a deal to provide squatters with land titles in exchange for return of half the land, but this did not solve the problem of illegal coca farming. Organizing farmers into a formal association of palm producers and complying with all the requirements for obtaining a company-guaranteed bank loan for plantation development was a way of bringing this group into a situation of legality.

How Innovation and Ecosystems Actually Worked

How to create a business model that is appropriate for exchanging with LIS consumers or producers is at the heart of the BOP literature. In this regard, the literature has identified two key requisites for success: innovation and market-based ecosystems. In this section, we look at sampled cases to verify the role those factors played in their business model-building process.

With regard to innovation, Prahalad puts product, service, and process innovation at the center of company efforts to create or develop BOP markets.[19] Milstein, Hart and London speak of the importance of revolutionary routines, that is, "problem solving approaches that enable transformative change," which is deemed necessary for entering BOP markets.[20] The advantages of "co-creation" between company and low-income consumers, as a means for developing new, locally relevant products, have also been emphasized.[21] Our empirical findings show that innovation was important in all ventures. Nonetheless, we found that in the process of building the business model, making small successive adjustments opportunely was as important as innovation—something that has been barely highlighted in the literature, with few exceptions.[22]

The researchers have also emphasized the importance of social embeddedness,[23] or market-based ecosystems,[24] for creating BOP markets. We found, however, that this was not an important element in the business model of many of the large companies in the sample. Moreover, despite suggestions that companies can gain an advantage by utilizing existing social infrastructure to venture into low-income markets,[25] we found that to operate in low-income markets, companies had to strengthen community organizations.

The Role of Innovations in Creating the Business Model

As in any new market venture, without exceptions, innovations were a central feature of all 12 ventures. These fell into four categories: technological, product, institutional, and relational.

All these innovations share one key feature of the "disruptive innovations"[26] referred to in the BOP literature: they seek to overcome "non-consumption." By tearing down barriers of access to mainstream markets, these initiatives create social value—as chapter 10 will discuss in greater detail. Nevertheless, they lack some of the attributes that the BOP researchers have assigned to "disruptive innovations." First, most of these innovations don't provide a simpler or more modest version or a higher-end product (a "more modest package of functionality").[27] Instead, in these cases—possibly due to the types of products involved (durables and public utilities)—the disruption consists of facilitating payment or the enforcement of payment. Condensa and Grupo Salinas created or activated scoring mechanisms (institutional innovations) that permitted non-consumers to acquire durables through installments. Edenor and AES-EDC made it possible for non-legal consumers to have access to electric service through pre-paid meters and cards (technological innovation). Cemex and Colcerámica expanded the reach of their products (construction materials and ceramics) by including in the offered package both advice and credit plans (product innovation).

Second, though some analysts suggest that companies must be very creative and innovative because LIS markets are so different from what is know in terms of "needs, suppliers, customers, technologies, product requirements, service demands, distribution channels, marketing approaches, manufacturing realities, sourcing, and production methods,"[28] innovations

Table 2.3: Innovations in Large Company Business Ventures with LIS

Company	Innovation	Status of business model
AES-EDC (electric energy)	Technology: application of pre-paid card digital technology to purchase electricity Relational: managers entered community spaces, social workers hired to engage LIS	Billing and collection unsolved. Also affected by government regulation of LIS electricity rates.
Agropalma (palm oil)	Relational: managers entered community spaces relying partly on community leaders	Not yet operational
Aguaytía (gas)	Product: original product (LPG cylinder) expanded to include means of consumption (stove, adapted motor) Technology: conversion of gasoline motors to use with LPG (liquefied petroleum gas) cylinders	Developed
Amanco (irrigation systems)	Product: irrigation system adapted for small acreage Relational: company initially entered community spaces through alliance with CSO	Profitable scaling model unsolved
Cativen (retail)	Relational: purchasing agents entered community spaces relying partly on community leaders, existing community organizations, and local public agencies	Profitable scaling model unsolved
Cemex (cement)	Product: original product (construction materials) expanded to include home design, international money transfers, and delivery in Mexico Technology: application of internet tools in marketing and sales of houses in Mexico	Profitable model unsolved
Codensa (electric energy)	Institutional: created organizational unit generating information and scores based on LIS specific standards	Developed
Colcerámica (ceramic tiles)	Product: original product (ceramics) expanded to include home design, and payment plan Relational: managers entered community spaces in alliance with CSO, community organizations and local salespeople	Delivery problem unsolved. Affects scaling.

Table 2.3: Innovations in Large Company Business Ventures with LIS (continued)

Company	Innovation	Status of business model
Edenor (electric energy)	Technology: application of pre-paid meter digital technology to purchase of electricity	Developed but offset by government regulation of LIS electricity rates
Gas Natural BAN (direct gas)	Relational: company initially entered community spaces through alliance with CSO, and then management carried on alone	Scaling model unsolved
Grupo Salinas (banking and retail) Empresario Azteca (tools and equipment to microenterprises)	Institutional: created program called Empresario Azteca coordinating three other group institutions (Elektra, Banco Azteca and Círculo del Crédito) for the purpose of serving the new market	Delivery problem unsolved. Affects scaling.
Palmas del Espino (palm oil)	Relational: managers entered community spaces relying partly on community leaders and existing community organization	Not yet operational

in the sample are not fundamentally new. Rather, they are adaptations or expansions of existing state-of-the-art products and technologies. For example, Edenor and AES-EDC adapted pre-paid technology to the sale of electricity; Cemex introduced the use of the Internet to sell houses; Aguaytia converted motorcycle and boat motors from gasoline to LPG (liquefied petroleum gas). Similarly, product innovations featured the incremental expansion of product boundaries (Aguaytia, Colcerámica and Cemex) or product adaptations (Amanco). Institutional innovations included adopting LIS credit-scoring systems from the world of microfinance (Codensa) or incrementally adding new schemes to boost intra-group synergies (Grupo Salinas).

The most radical type of innovation observed in the sample was the relational one, a kind not usually found in traditional new market ventures— a new pattern of personal relationships seen in some of these ventures, called "business friendships" (see chapter 5). These innovations comprised ways of bringing together LIS and the company wishing to include them as costumers or suppliers and included active participation of company personnel in LIS communal spaces. Such relational innovations have been revealed in BOP research and amply documented by it.[29] But our findings diverge with the BOP literature in one important respect: we found that the ventures featuring relational innovations were precisely the ones that had not yet managed to assemble a working business model (see last column of Table 2.6). The section in this chapter addressing challenges to scaling will look further into this.

The Role of Local Ecosystems in Building the Business Model

Authors have proposed that having a "capability of social embeddedness"— i.e., the "ability to create a web of trusted connections with a diversity of organizations and institutions, generate bottom up development, and understand, leverage, and build on the existing social infrastructure"[30]— is key for a successful BOP market entry.[31] They have also emphasized that the development of ecosystems (see chapter 5) with "non-traditional" partners, such as non-profits, community groups, and local governments, is a more successful strategy than reliance on traditional partners such as national governments and large local companies, because the former are better sources of expertise and local legitimacy.[32]

Social embeddedness patterns in the 12 companies do not quite fit findings or recommendations in the literature. Note in Table 2.4 that two companies (Aguaytia and Edenor) did not rely on connections with any organizations or institutions to engage with LIS. This does not seem to affect performance, for Aguaytia is one of the few companies whose venture is already profitable and growing in scale (see Table 2.6). Second, only three companies worked with traditional partners (Cemex, Codensa and Grupo Salinas). Again, this does not seem to affect performance given that the case of Codensa is the only other venture in the sample which is clearly profitable and growing in scale (see Table 2.6). Third, most of the seven companies that did rely on connections with non-traditional actors also made alliances with traditional actors. Fourth, few companies (only 3) relied on CSOs to enter LIS markets, a surprising result given the emphasis placed in the literature on CSOs as bridging organizations offering expert knowledge of the field.[33]

Table 2.4: Company Reliance on Non-Traditional and Traditional Actors

Company	Non-traditional actors	Traditional actors
AES-EDC	Local leaders, local policy arenas, community groups	None
Agropalma	Local leaders	National government
Aguaytia	None	None
Amanco	CSO, local leaders	National government, large multinational company
Cativen	Community groups, local leaders, local public agencies	None
Cemex	None	Companies in Mexico (distributors, construction companies) and international remittance companies
Codensa	None	Large national hypermarket chain
Colcerámica	CSO, community groups, local leaders	Local distributor companies
Edenor	None	None
Gas Natural BAN	CSO, local leaders, local governments, community groups	Multilateral agencies
Grupo Salinas	None	Cluster of companies in the group
Palmas del Espino	Community groups, local leaders	National government

In observed results, relations with non-traditional actors comprise local or community-level ecosystems, not wider regional or national ones like those cited by Seelos and Mair,[34] who examined an alliance between Grameen Bank, a large non-profit in Bangladesh, and Telenor, a Norwegian telecommunications company. Thus, growth of sampled ventures involving non-traditional actors required the multiplication of partnerships at the local level.

All partnerships formed with non-traditional actors had another important related feature: they responded to a need for local collective action. One of the rationales for collective action was the low purchasing power or low production capacity of individual LIS; from the point of view of the company, this meant engaging in a large number of small exchanges. Given the right technology[35] such multiple interactions could be managed at a low cost, as was the case of Edenor's pre-paid electricity venture. But if the technology is not available, a multiplicity of small exchanges significantly raises transaction costs for companies, unless LIS act collectively. This is why farmers had to organize in cooperatives or associations for selling to Cativen, Agropalma, and Palmas del Espino. This is also why in the case of Colcerámica, local community organizations aggregated small purchases before sending a large order to the factory. Similarly, LIS customers of AES-EDC had to group around collective meters.

Collective action was also necessary in a situation where participation requires building a large piece of common infrastructure, such as a grid, in a community where individual members do not have the purchasing power to pay for it in advance, or have little or no independent access to the credit market. The case of Gas Ban illustrates this type of situation. Usually, the company will invest in building the grid in a middle-class area, knowing that residents can afford and are willing to buy and pay the connection fee. In LIS neighborhoods, however, it is the residents who must take the initiative or organize to obtain non-refundable funding from government or a multilateral agency to partially cover the cost of building the grid, and also to obtain a collective bank loan for completing installation costs. Gas Ban's business venture with LIS consisted partly in adapting company policies and practices to the needs and expectations of the communities served, as well as acting as guarantor of LIS communities seeking loans.

Analysts have argued that one of the advantages of connecting with non-traditional actors is that they already exist; that they are a part of an existing social infrastructure or social capital that the company can leverage on.[36] Results in this study show, instead, that many non-traditional actors in local ecosystems had limited capacity to operate autonomously when the companies approached the community, and required significant tutoring. Often companies suffered from lack of CSOs that fit company requirements: some were not prepared to manage large projects and the core competencies of others were not sufficiently related to what was required for building the value chain. Moreover, CSOs that looked like good candidates had other priorities and were often busy with other projects. With regards to community groups, we found that companies had to invest important resources in either creating or strengthening them.

The case of Amanco exemplifies the problem of CSO supply. Amanco approached the Mexican LIS market segment with the help of Ashoka, a non-profit organization that supports social entrepreneurship, which identified local CSOs with relevant know-how and experience to serve as bridges between the company and small farmers. According to management, during the two pilot experiences these CSOs played a key role in approaching small farmers and in designing a business model. But management also reported that the capacities and resources of these organizations turned out to be insufficient for the purpose of taking on large infrastructure projects at a rapid pace. Amanco managers felt pressed to accomplish the mandate of 10 percent sales to LIS by 2008, but by 2007 they had not found a local CSO that would help achieve this goal.

The case of Gas Ban shows that to solve the problem of insufficient supply of local CSOs, companies may need to invest in creating equivalent organizations. In its first attempt at entering the Argentine LIS market, Gas Ban made an alliance with Fundación Pro Vivienda Social (FPVS). This organization had ample experience in improving LIS housing and had recently won the World Bank Development Market Place contest. FPVS devised the financial strategy which overcame the obstacle that hitherto had prevented disadvantaged neighbors from joining the grid. The proposed solution was a fiduciary fund, a tool that many found innovative and well suited to the initiative, for various reasons (see chapter 5). Moreover, that CSO also developed much of the marketing strategy for bringing direct gas to LIS. FPVS promoters would meet with the neighbors and assist them in creating associations in each block, which would then elect a "golden neighbor." "Golden neighbors" who managed to convince 75 percent of those living in the same block to join the grid and collect all required documentation would gain various benefits in return. FPVS facilitated and oversaw this, as well as other phases of the process, such as billing and collecting the loan obtained from a private bank to partially cover grid construction.

Though from the point of view of management working with FPVS was the ideal situation, the alliance with FPVS took place in only one neighborhood, Cuartel V (in Moreno city, on the outskirts of Buenos Aires) simply because this CSO did not have the operational capacity to spread its effort out any further (Cuartel V was a large community of 40,000 households). While Cuartel V was still negotiating with FPVS, the company sought to develop LIS markets in three smaller neighborhoods. As they could not find a financially savvy CSO that could replicate FPVS's role, they partnered with a grass-root organization and the local government. The partnership worked well, but the characteristics of these new partners, who lacked FPVS's operational capacity, forced to company to internalize many of the functions that FPVS had carried out in the original pilot program. The company was successful in entering these markets, but the strategy turned out to be very demanding for the company's operating units. At the time when the SEKN team was doing field work, the company was considering embarking on a joint venture with FPVS, in effect creating a "social development company," a hybrid which would combine features of a social organization and a private business. Gas Ban planned to replicate through this "social development company" the role played by FPVS, in other neighborhoods.

Table 2.5 shows the extent to which companies managed to rely on existing social infrastructure at the community level, and the extent to which they had to create or strengthen the groups that would make up the local ecosystem.

Table 2.5: Reliance and Investment in Communal Infrastructure

Company	Area	Reliance and investment in communal infrastructure	Details
AES-EDC	Urban	Company relied on existing communal social infrastructure.	Initial entry relied on community leaders, "electric tables" (government organized local policy arenas) and condominium boards. Community leaders actively participated in billing and collections.
Agropalma	Rural	Company invested in creation of community groups.	Initial entry relied on community leaders. The venture organized suppliers directly for the purpose of engaging in exchange.
Amanco	Rural	Company invested in creation of community groups.	Initial entry relied on community leaders. The venture organized customers directly for the purpose of engaging in exchange.
Cativen	Rural	Company invested in creation of community groups.	Initial entry relied on community leaders and community organizations. The venture organized suppliers directly for the purpose of engaging in exchange.
Colcerámica	Urban	Company relied solely on existing communal social infrastructure.	The company relied on community organizations to manage sales force, billing, and collections.
Gas Natural BAN	Urban	Company worked with existing community groups or with the municipality.	Initial entry relied on community leaders. The venture organized customers directly for the purpose of engaging in exchange.
Palmas del Espino	Rural	Company invested in creation of community groups.	Initial entry relied on community leaders and an existing but inactive peasants' association. The latter had to be re-recreated by the venture.

Cases in table 2.5 suggest that companies relied primarily on community leaders and some local government agencies to obtain information during initial entry, less on existing community or "self-help" groups.[37] In fact, companies seemed to face a sparse social fabric, especially in rural areas, and consequently had to invest resources in creating or strengthening community groups. The contrast between the more dense social fabric of urban areas and the less dense one of rural areas is illustrated by the experiences of Colcerámica and Amanco. Following the recommendations received, both companies sought to rely on local social infrastructure to build a market relation with LIS. Colcerámica discovered that existing community organizations were ready to support sales and distribution. Amanco, however, had to invest in organizing geographically disperse peasants in Mexico.

The experiences of Palmas del Espino, Agropalma, and Cativen also illustrate the efforts companies have made to remedy the weak social fabric in rural areas. All three companies sought to leverage existing social infrastructure. Venezuela's Cativen took advantage of irrigation committees, rural communal banks, and three peasant cooperatives that had been fostered with care by Catholic priests since the 1960s. But in order to develop a business relationship with a sufficiently large pool of small farmers, Cativen found it necessary to organize and incorporate ten additional producers' associations. Peru's Palmas del Espino sought out an existing peasant organization called Asociación de Productores Agropecuarios José Carlos Mariátegui that had been created in 1990, only to discover that it was no longer active. The company promoted its reactivation to set up a "head with which to interact and negotiate"[38] a regular supply of palm trees from 760 hectares of LIS-owned lands. For similar reasons, Brazil's Agropalma promoted the creation of a brand new peasant association: Associação de Desenvolvimento Comunitário Arauaí. Company technicians go to monthly meetings at the association's headquarters to analyze difficulties, possibilities for improvement, and action plans, which have already led to the construction of local roads, school, and public transportation. Company managers deem the creation of this association as a very important company achievement with great social impact in providing social capital and giving peasants access to true citizenship. Company willingness to invest in organizing rural communities is consistent with previous SEKN research findings whereby "organizing the poor in cooperatives is a widespread resource . . . whose importance cannot be underestimated. The feasibility of doing so (or not) in some cases was considered a make-or-break factor by the private sector when it came to venturing into this (LIS) market."[39]

Companies are faced with a further challenge after investing in organizing and strengthening LIS communities: continued participation in a collective process is not easy to sustain. "Superimposing an economic logic on a social organization or a community of new customers, may create problems. It may be akin to partnering with your block neighbors: some of them may be hard-working partners, and others may be chronic under-achievers, but insofar as they live in the block they have a legitimate right to be heard. You cannot simply fire them and move on."[40] The case of Cativen illustrates the precariousness of collective action: of the ten small farmers' associations that Cativen helped form, five had disbanded within a few months. Governance was not easy to establish in these collective entities, and conflicts developed among members of the associations around issues of equity, burden of duty, and management of common assets. When such conflicts went unresolved, the associations dissolved.

In sum, we have found that for all the advantages that previous studies have attributed to the idea of social embeddedness, the concept may be relevant or useful only under some conditions. Many of the large companies we analyzed relied on traditional partners more than on non-traditional ones. Moreover, and contrary to what has been suggested in the literature, in our sample the capacity to develop embedded relationships does not correlate in a positive way with performance. We also found that alliances and networks of relations with non-traditional partners were confined to very local ecosystems, usually emerging out of the need to secure collective action among low-income consumers or suppliers. Even though analysts have argued that an advantage of relying on non-traditional actors lies in that they compose the existing social infrastructure, we found that companies most often were agents of social fabric building. The writers are not unaware of the need of companies to invest in social capacity building,[41] but they have mostly emphasized investment in "educational awareness and skill building" of existing organizations. The type of investment in local capacity building here observed was in the creation of the non-traditional organizations and institutions required to secure collective action. In addition, we found that the organizations that resulted from these investments were in many cases fragile, implying that constructing social infrastructure is no simple task.

Scaling: An Unfulfilled Promise

The reason why Prahalad considered that large companies could make an important impact on global poverty alleviation was because of their capacity to operate at a large scale at the BOP. The emphasis on this is such in the BOP literature that upon establishing the distinguishing features of BOP ventures, Ted London[42] indicated that being "scalable" was a defining trait.

Table 2.6 (below) summarizes the major features of analyzed ventures as of 2007, with a focus on scale of operations. Independently of economic drivers and other encouraging factors, between 3 and 6 years after launching, all but two (Aguaytia and Codensa) of these LIS ventures were still operating at a very small scale. The patterns of results on Table 2.6 suggest that scaling and profitability are related, for the only two cases which are profitable are also the ones that have achieved the greatest—though still moderate—scale (again Aguaytia and Codensa). It is not possible to tease out the direction of causality for all sampled ventures, but evidence in these cases suggests that starting conditions which were strongly favorable to profitability were in place before scaling took place. Codensa leveraged, with a small investment, on its billing platform and the distribution networks of established hypermarket chains to set up a service whereby its LIS electric energy clientele could buy home appliances on installments on credit. Aguaytia, which created a market for liquid gas cylinders in the remote region surrounding its gas processing plant, faced a very low opportunity cost in engaging in this ambitious project, because the cost of transporting liquid gas by road for home consumption to large cities would have been too high.

Lack of scale of sampled ventures does not seem to be related to poor management practice, as the case of Amanco illustrates. In 2004 this company partnered with Ashoka to develop a pilot program to provide irrigation systems to small farmers. Ashoka's concept of "hybrid value chains" was used to develop the business model. The company leveraged the expertise of local CSOs that had experience working with small farmers to understand their irrigation needs and practices. The product was modified to fit small farmer needs; that is, an irrigation system designed for large areas was modified for a 40–hectare plot, the minimum optimal scale for economic sustainability. Service to small farmers went beyond the provision of irrigation systems. It also included system design, technical assistance, topographical surveys, provision of financing opportunities, applications for subsidies, and assistance in marketing of agricultural products. The company had full support of the holding company, Grupo Nueva, which in 2006 mandated that by 2008, 10 percent of the group's sales were to cater to BOP (15 percent by 2010). To incubate the BOP initiative, Amanco created a new unit within the Commercial Department called "New Businesses" that would insulate the initiative from the company's commercial and logistics

Table 2.6: Level of Scaling and Economic Sustainability of LIS Ventures

Company	LIS customer venture	Starting year	Level of scaling in 2007	Economic sustainability in 2007
AES-EDC (electric energy)	Electric service provision in urban LIS	2003	Pilot, small scale.	Operations are not self-sustaining.
Agropalma (palm oil)	Procurement of palm for palm oil plant from small farmers	2001	Small scale. Not yet operating.	Investment phase still running.
Aguaytia (gas)	Provision of liquid gas in cylinders in the region neighboring the refinery (Peruvian Amazon)	2002	Moderate scale.	Profitable. Low opportunity cost.
Amanco (irrigation systems)	Provision of irrigation systems to small farmers	2004	Two pilots implemented. Very small scale. Very slow expansion.	Investment requires social funding. Not profitable if all capital is private. High opportunity cost associated with working with LIS.
Cativen (retail)	Procurement of vegetables for supermarkets from small farmers	2001	Small scale, no expansion.	Positive net gain but there is an opportunity cost associated with working with LIS.
Cemex (cement)	"Construmex" Provision of construction materials and homes to LIS	2004	Small scale, little expansion.	Negative net income. High opportunity cost associated with working with LIS.
Codensa (electric energy)	Provision of electric household appliances to urban LIS (Codensa Hogar)	2001	Has been scaled moderately.	Positive net income. Secures market share of core business.
Colcerámica (ceramic tiles)	"Su casa como nueva paso a paso" Provision of ceramic tiles to urban LIS	2004	Small scale, some expansion.	Negative net income.

Table 2.6: Level of Scaling and Economic Sustainability of LIS Ventures (continued)

Company	LIS customer venture	Starting year	Level of scaling in 2007	Economic sustainability in 2007
Edenor (electric energy)	Electric service provision in urban LIS	2001	Pilot, small scale.	Operations are self-sustaining. Positive net income. Recovery of investment depends on government regulation of rates.
Gas Natural BAN (direct gas)	Direct gas provision in urban LIS	2003	Small scale. Slow expansion.	Operations are self-sustaining. Positive net income. Investment requires social funding. Not profitable if all capital is private.
Grupo Salinas (banking and retail)	"Empresario Azteca." Provision of tools and equipment to micro-entrepreneurs	2004	Small scale, little expansion.	Incipient profitability.
Palmas del Espino (palm oil)	Procurement of palm for palm oil plant from small farmers	2003	Small scale. Not yet operating.	Investment phase still running.

units. The result of this effort was that by 2007, only two pilot experiences, covering 620 famers, had been partially implemented.

This story is just one example of how the companies in the sample followed good practices suggested by the BOP literature: strive for innovation,[43] attain social embeddedness,[44] be patient.[45] With respect to innovation, products, delivery systems, and payment systems were continually readapted. With regards to social embeddedness, many companies built ecosystems, entering the communities, identifying and negotiating with their leaders, partnering with local actors. As to patience, none of the managers interviewed seemed discouraged or ready to give up. During the interviews, managers of all ventures recounted, with much enthusiasm, the effort, creativity, and perseverance of their companies in developing their LIS ventures. Most projected a bright future in terms of scale and profitability, and willingness to continue betting on their ventures even though timetables had been rescheduled.

Noting that "billions of poor people are still waiting" for large firms to act, in a recent article Seelos and Mair asked a provocative question: "If the BOP proposition is right, why then is the profit opportunity not picked up by companies on a large scale?"[46] In this section we examine some of the key challenges to scaling faced by companies in the sample.

One finding is that capabilities attained by companies to work with LIS in one community or site are not easily transferred to the next. A second major finding is that efforts made by companies (Amanco, Colcerámica, Gas Ban, Cativen, AES-EDC) to develop complex local ecosystems served the purpose of learning to work with LIS at a small scale, but—contrary to suggestions in the literature[47]—they may constitute an impediment to scaling. Finally, in many of the sampled cases, management has not yet identified a profitable business model or prototype, despite much experimentation; and the decision to bring the venture to scale is being postponed because of this.

Capabilities Attained in One Community or Site are Not Easily Transferred to the Next

Ted London pointed out that "organizations should not assume that a business model successfully implemented in one BOP community automatically transfers to another."[48] Similarly, London and Hart affirmed that "social embeddedness" capabilities cannot be transferred from one community and investment and applied to the next.[49] According to collected evidence, these assertions proved true in all those large firm ventures in which the marketing and delivery (or sourcing when LIS were suppliers) efforts required reliance on communal social infrastructure (Gas Ban,

Amanco, Colcerámica, Cativen). Unfortunately, the need to innovate at every attempt increases the complexity and reduces the speed of scaling LIS market ventures.

The case of Gas Ban illustrates how community-specific attributes have an enormous effect on how the business model is set up in each neighborhood, and how this constraint undermines scaling. After investing much time and effort in developing a working business model in Cuartel V, management realized that the most it could transfer to other neighborhoods was a protocol for approaching neighbors and other possible stakeholders. The protocol did, to some extent, speed up project startup and implementation in new sites, but as the neighbors in each place were organized differently, each undertaking was unique and consequently time-consuming. In Cuartel V, a partner CSO (FPVS) facilitated the process, but such a partner could not be found in other neighborhoods. In Cuartel V the municipal government was not involved in the venture, but in other neighborhoods (Los Troncos, Las Tunas, Los Tábanos) it was a key ally, not only because it funded the installation of the gas grid, but also because it served as interlocutor between the company and the LIS. In each neighborhood the strategy for financing construction of the grid varied, depending on particular combinations of funding by local governments, multilateral agencies, government lending agencies, and neighbors. Even though the company showed flexibility in attending the specificities of each neighborhood, the Commercial Director of Gas Ban wished for a more generally applicable business model: "We did benefit from our previous experiences with LIS in terms of our capacities. The challenge is that now each project requires higher modeling efforts, each project with LIS requires more craftsmanship."[50] Company management simply views this tailor-made approach to growth as an impediment to scaling. As discussed in chapter 5, this does not seem to be an accidental or idiosyncratic problem, but rather a shortcoming that is built into this modus operandi.

The necessity of adjusting capabilities from one community to the next would not be much of a problem if the task at hand at every new site was simple and not so time-consuming. But in each community companies must construct complex ecosystems, and this takes many hours and resources. The case of Amanco exemplifies the time and effort required to create an ecosystem and getting it to work in a single site. In order to ensure access of small producers to an irrigation system, the company sought to involve many actors in the project: the federal government of Mexico through the National Water Commission (Conagua), various agricultural councils, AMUCCS (Asociación Mexicana de Uniones de Crédito del Sector Social, a CSO with

15 years' experience in the creation and operation of rural financial institutions in Mexico), various private foundations, and government financial institutions. After contacting, interacting and negotiating with this varied set of actors, certain agreements were reached. Conagua would provide non-reimbursable funding for 50 percent of the required investment. The agricultural councils would put 20 percent of the investment. AMUCCS would create a revolving fund with resources provided by the Wal-Mart Foundation, the Bimbo Foundation, Fundemex, and Firco (a government funding institution). Despite these agreements, in 2007 the credit system that was to finance an important proportion of the investment was not yet operating, in part because AMUCSS's experience was with small rural loans, not with the large ones required to build irrigation systems.

BOP analysts call for company hyper-flexibility to attend to the specific conditions and needs of each new local market.[51] The case of Gas Ban exemplifies flexibility, learning capacity, and willingness to co-create with every LIS community the model that best fits its case. Nevertheless, evidence indicates that management, both in this one and in other sampled companies, finds this work exhausting. Gas Ban's most recent idea (in 2007) of creating a subsidiary "social development company" specializing in crafting and monitoring tailor-made projects in each neighborhood is one way in which management plans to deal with this challenge without wearing out the company's commercial department.

Complex Local Ecosystems Are Hard to Scale

Evidence shows that having to tailor every venture to the community level is not the only impediment to scaling. Often times, local business models[52] that work well in the pilot phase cannot be scaled. The case of Colcerámica offers a good example. When this organization ran its pilot program in the community of Usme, it engaged various social actors of the local ecosystem. This served the company's learning process well, but to make scaling feasible, the company had to simplify its local business model.

In Usme, Colcerámica set up a business model that included four community organizations, nine promoters, a local distributor, and Colcerámica. The promoters would communicate directly with potential clients and negotiate sales; they would then turn in customer orders to the community organizations. The community organizations (CO), in turn, were in charge of relaying orders to Colcerámica's factory, and also managed the promoters (selection, supervision, and payment using company-defined standards), displayed products, and collected client payments. After receiving the orders, Colcerámica's factory would send a delivery to the independent local distributor closest to the neighborhood (the factory cannot attend to small orders directly and the company's trucks are tool large to circulate through the narrow and precarious streets of LIS neighborhoods); upon receiving the factory's order, the distributor turn the ceramic tiles over to the customer.

Over time, the company realized the above scheme had too many actors and left too many variables outside the control of the company. In particular, the COs, which were neighborhood associations (Juntas de Acción Comunal) and mothers' associations, had been assigned duties that exceeded their institutional capabilities. Furthermore, as these organizations were informal, the company and the COs engaged in cash transactions, and this procedure generated problems of transparency and accountability. In order to simplify structures and processes, Colcerámica decided to rely less on the non-traditional partnerships and created Ibérica Service Centers, local showrooms, and coordination units attended by a company employee. Each Ibérica Service Center (ISC) took over the tasks of various COs in the previous model. The ISC's employee would coordinate 15 promoters in each neighborhood, provide information to local customers, and display the ceramic tiles.

Profitable Prototypes Are Elusive

In most of our cases managers postponed scaling because they have not yet come up with a prototype that promises acceptable returns when brought to scale. Data showed three principal reasons for postponement. First, some companies have not managed to identify economically satisfactory solutions to the logistics of distribution. For example, Colcerámica knows that to assure the profitability of its local business model, the company must capture the margin of independent distributors by taking over their role. Nevertheless, doubts as to what course of action to take, and the potentially fatal consequences of making the wrong decision given tight margins, have inhibited investment. Action in this case will be contingent on the opportunity cost of capital available for financing the investment. Second, the opportunity cost of scaling ventures, given other portfolio options available to companies, also seem to be inhibiting action in this direction. Finally, external factors, such as government regulation in rates that can be charged to LIS using public utilities, has also inhibited investment in scaling, especially when rates have been set below the marginal cost of service provision. Chapter 9 offers detailed analysis of challenges to profitability of ventures with LIS.

Summary and Discussion

By looking at a set of ongoing market ventures with LIS, we sought to gain a better understanding as to how large companies can build viable large-scale inclusive businesses. The business-model building process showed us that all companies ventured into the LIS market with a clear profit motive, and that the business models tailored by management for that purpose were quite distinct from those applied in traditional company markets. We also found that companies made numerous adjustments during early implementation, many of which concerned issues that were unique to LIS markets: the challenge of building mutual reliance in a context of information asymmetries, addressing the exacting demands of LIS customers, and tending the fine line between informality and illegality.

Innovation was found to be important in all business model-building, and all models addressed the problem of non-consumption. However, product and technological innovations were not fundamentally new but rather adaptations or expansions of existing ones. The only radical innovations observed were of a "relational" sort, that is, new patterns of relationships between company actors and LIS.

As to the advantages that previous studies have attributed to the idea of social embeddedness, we found that most analyzed companies relied on traditional partners rather than on non-traditional ones. Moreover, and contrary to what has been suggested in the literature, the capacity to develop embedded relationships does not correlate in a positive way with venture performance. Despite claims that relying on non-traditional actors allows companies to make use of an existing social infrastructure, we found that companies themselves were often agents of social fabric building. The type of investment here observed was in the creation of the non-traditional organizations and institutions required to secure collective action. In addition, we found that the organizations that resulted from these investments were in many cases fragile.

In all our cases, management made earnest and continuing efforts to strengthen these ventures, but even after several years of launching, most ventures were still operating at a very small scale. One reason for this is that capabilities attained by companies to work with LIS in one community or site are not easily transferred to the next. A second problem is that efforts made by companies in developing complex local ecosystems served the purpose of learning to work LIS at a small scale, but they may constitute an impediment to scaling. Finally, in many of the sampled cases management has not yet identified a working and profitable prototype or business model, despite much experimentation; and the decision to bring the venture to scale is therefore postponed.

The slow pace at which analyzed ventures have developed, their low impact on the company's overall bottom's line, and the fact that management has not yet figured out ways to bring them to scale brings to the forefront the risk of ventures turning into permanent demonstration or pilot programs. Many of the recommendations put forward in the literature (to innovate, to utilize existing social infrastructure, to build local ecosystems) seem to work for pilot programs but do not offer an answer to the question of scaling, because propagating[53] unique and complex business networks is a resource-intensive and time-consuming endeavor. Ultimately, evidence suggests it is not the complex model that easily gains scale in LIS markets, but rather those featuring simple individual exchange, facilitated by state-of-the-art technological platforms.

It is clear that companies must have patience, because learning during implementation inevitably involves much trial and error. Given this, the principle of "changing the metrics"[54] that has been put out in the literature seems like a reasonable recommendation. But it must be pointed out that a permanent expectation of lower returns from ventures with LIS only works for small-scale pilots tantamount to R&D; for large companies are not willing to accept such changed metrics in a large-scale operation unless opportunity costs are completely reframed. One way of reframing opportunity costs is by changing the rules of the game in stock markets in such a way that the set of systemic incentives guiding management decisions are modified. This route, which has to some extent been followed for the purpose of "greening" management decisions, would require a more political approach[55] to attending the problem of world poverty on the part of top management of large firms. Another way that management could reframe opportunity costs is by placing LIS ventures in associated social enterprises. The problem with this course of action is that if fundraising efforts are insufficient, such buffered ventures would not go beyond being small-scale showcases.

Attempts at leveraging on existing social infrastructure often failed because local CSOs and community groups lacked capabilities for value chain creation. Companies in the sample invested individually in the development of some of these organizations, but such efforts take time and resources. Pooling of resources or collective efforts by companies at the local and national levels to strengthen required social fabric is a course of action to consider, given associated savings from synergies, access to scaled social assets, and reduced individual effort.

Contrary to the emphasis of some analysts on partnerships with non-traditional local actors,[56] partnerships and alliances among large companies to create complementary assets along the value chain may play a key role in assuring scaling. The case of Grupo Salinas, in which the Empresario Azteca initiative is, after several adjustments, successfully leveraging the complementary assets of various companies in the group, also points to the advantages of collective approaches among large companies. The same can be said of Codensa, where a growing LIS venture makes use not only of the company's technological platform, but also the network of a large retail company. Joint efforts among companies can generate institutional spin-offs, such as specialized services that facilitate LIS ventures (as for example Círculo de Crédito in Grupo Salinas, a LIS scoring agency that now serves many companies in Mexico).

Finally, bringing in the issue of inclusive business into the policy agenda in each country could also facilitate scaling and increase profitability, because it would raise the number of joint efforts and the amount of public resources invested in this kind of venture. Governments are often reluctant to invest public resources in ventures that generate private profit, but extreme transparency and a broad-based social coalition that supports and legitimizes the idea that large companies can improve the lives of the poor through inclusive business, could attenuate this problem.

The creation of viable large-scale LIS markets continues to be a major challenge for large firms. Progress in this area may require more than the perseverance and action of individual firms. At the level of top management, it will require political agency among collections of companies to form governing institutions that would modify the structure of incentives for management decisions. At the level of upper-middle and middle management, it will require coordinated efforts to create complementary assets along the value chain, and pools of resources for strengthening social infrastructure in LIS communities.

Notes

1. C. K. Prahalad, "The Innovation Sandbox," *Strategy + Business* (2005).
2. C. K. Prahalad and Stuart Hart, "The Fortune at the Bottom of the Pyramid," *Strategy + Business* 1, no. 26 (2002).
3. C. K. Prahalad and Stuart Hart, "Strategies for the Bottom of the Pyramid: Creating Sustainable Development" (unpublished paper, 1999); C. K. Prahalad and Allen Hammond, "Serving the World's Poor, Profitably," *Harvard Business Review* (2002); Prahalad and Hart, "The Fortune at the Bottom of the Pyramid,"; C. K. Prahalad, "Why Selling to the Poor Makes for Good Business," *Fortune*, Nov 15, 2004; Stuart L. Hart, *Capitalism at the Crossroads: The Unlimited*

Business Opportunities in Serving the World's Most Difficult Problems (Upper Saddle River, NJ: Wharton School Publishing, 2005); Stuart L. Hart, *Capitalism at the Crossroads: Aligning Business, Earth and Humanity* (Upper Saddle River, NJ: Wharton School Publishing, 2007).

4. C. K. Prahalad, "Why Selling to the Poor Makes for Good Business," *Fortune*, Nov 15, 2004.

5. C. K. Prahalad and Stuart Hart, "The Fortune at the Bottom of the Pyramid," *Strategy + Business* 1, no. 26 (2002).

6. Two additional experiences in our collective sample were led by large corporations, namely, Pali and Hortifruti. However, chapter authors decided to leave those out of the subset used for this piece, as data collected for those experiences was insufficient to judge performance.

7. C. K. Prahalad, *The Fortune at the Bottom of the Pyramid: Eradicating Poverty through Profits* (Upper Saddle River, NJ: Wharton School Publishing, 2005), 55–62.

8. Two important pieces are, to date, some of the few major contributions to systematic empirical research: Ted London and Stuart L. Hart, "Reinventing Strategies for Emerging Markets: Beyond the Transnational Model," *Journal of International Business Studies* 35 (2004); Ted London, "Beyond 'Stepping Stone' Growth: Exploring New Market Entry at the Base of the Pyramid" (Working Paper, William Davidson Institute/Stephen M. Ross School of Business, 2006)..
The former piece compares strategies used by MNCs pursuing BoP opportunities in a set of successful and unsuccessful ventures, and found that successful ventures "developed a deep understanding of the local environment, and focused on generating bottom-up business creation based on identifying, leveraging, and building the existing social infrastructure," a capability that they called "social embeddedness." The latter publication, on the other hand, compared a set of ventures that had been effectively launched in BOP markets with ventures that had been abandoned, been put on hold, or veered toward the middle-income market. The author found that those ventures, which had been effectively launched, featured particular patterns in components (structure, problem-solving routines, prioritization routines and source of context-specific resources) affecting "capability development." In particular, successful ventures had been incubated in "white spaces" serving as firewalls against existing prioritization routines, which threaten innovation. They also feature diverse problem-solving settings, leveraging on non-traditional partners and investing in building new context-specific assets.

9. When SEKN researchers did their field work in 2006–2007, the nine market initiatives involving LIS customers were taken on between 2001 and 2004; the three initiatives involving LIS suppliers were founded between 2001 and 2003.

10. Amanco and Aguaytia.

11. Allen L. Hammond et al., *The Next 4 Billion: Market Size and Business Strategy at the Base of the Pyramid* (Washington, DC: World Resources Institute and International Finance Corporation, 2007), 19.

12. Alexander Osterwalder, Yves Pigneur, and Christopher Tucci, "Clarifying Business Models: Origins, Present, and Future of the Concept," *Communications of the Association of Information Systems* 16 (2005).

13. Alexander Osterwalder, Yves Pigneur, and Christopher Tucci, "Clarifying Business Models: Origins, Present, and Future of the Concept," *Communications of the Association of Information Systems* 16 (2005).

14. Stuart Hart and Clayton Christensen, "The Great Leap: Driving Innovation from the Base of the Pyramid," *MIT Sloan Management Review* 44, no. 1 (2002).

15. C. K. Prahalad, *The Fortune at the Bottom of the Pyramid: Eradicating Poverty through Profits* (Upper Saddle River, NJ: Wharton School Publishing, 2005), 14.

16. Stuart Hart and Ted London, "Developing Native Capability: What Multinational Corporations Can Learn from the Base of the Pyramid," *Stanford Social Innovation Review* (2005); Ted London, "The Base-of-the-Pyramid Perspective: A New Approach to Poverty Alleviation" (Working Paper, William Davidson Institute/Stephen M. Ross School of Business, 2008).

17. Patricia Márquez and Henry Gomez, *Microempresas: alianzas para el éxito* (Caracas: Ediciones IESA, 2001).

18. Manuel Castells and Alejandro Portes, "World Underneath: The Origins, Dynamics, and Effects of the Informal Economy," in The Informal Economy: Studies in Advanced and Less Developed Countries, ed. Alejandro Portes, Manuel Castells, and Lauren A. Benton (Baltimore: Johns Hopkins University Press, 1989).

19. C. K. Prahalad, *The Fortune at the Bottom of the Pyramid: Eradicating Poverty through Profits* (Upper Saddle River, NJ: Wharton School Publishing, 2005).

20. M. B. Milstein, Ted London, and Stuart Hart, "Revolutionary Routines: Capturing the Opportunity for Creating a More Inclusive Capitalism," in *Handbook of Cooperative Collaboration: New Designs and Dynamics*, ed. S. K Piderit, R. E. Fry, and D. L. Cooperrider (Stanford, CA: Stanford University Press, 2007).

21. Ted London, "The Base-of-the-Pyramid Perspective: A New Approach to Poverty Alleviation" (Working Paper, William Davidson Institute/Stephen M. Ross School of Business, 2008).

22. Christian Seelos and Johanna Mair, "Profitable Business Models and Market Creation in the Context of Deep Poverty: A Strategic View," *The Academy of Management Perspectives* 21, no. 4 (2007).

23. Ted London and Stuart L. Hart, "Reinventing Strategies for Emerging Markets: Beyond the Transnational Model," *Journal of International Business Studies* 35 (2004); Ezequiel Reficco and Patricia Márquez, "Socially Inclusive Networks for Building BOP Markets" (Working Paper, School of Business Administration, University of San Diego, October 2007).

24. C. K. Prahalad, *The Fortune at the Bottom of the Pyramid: Eradicating Poverty through Profits* (Upper Saddle River, NJ: Wharton School Publishing, 2005).

25. Ted London and Stuart L Hart, "Reinventing Strategies for Emerging Markets: Beyond the Transnational Model," *Journal of International Business Studies* 35 (2004).

26. Clayton Christensen, Thomas Craig, and Stuart Hart, "The Great Disruption," *Foreign Affairs* 80, no. 2 (2001); Stuart Hart and Clayton Christensen, "The Great Leap: Driving Innovation from the Base of the Pyramid," *MIT Sloan Management Review* 44, no. 1 (2002).

27. Clayton Christensen, Thomas Craig, and Stuart Hart, "The Great Disruption," *Foreign Affairs* 80, no. 2 (2001): 56.

28. Ibid., 90; C. K. Prahalad, *The Fortune at the Bottom of the Pyramid: Eradicating Poverty through Profits* (Upper Saddle River, NJ: Wharton School Publishing, 2005).

29. C. K. Prahalad, *The Fortune at the Bottom of the Pyramid: Eradicating Poverty through Profits;* London and Hart, "Reinventing Strategies for Emerging Markets: Beyond the Transnational Model"; Erik Simanis and Stuart Hart, "The Base of the Pyramid Protocol: Toward Next Generation Bop Strategy"(2008), http://www.wdi.umich.edu/files/BoPProtocol2ndEdition2008.pdf.

30. Ted London and Stuart L. Hart, "Reinventing Strategies for Emerging Markets: Beyond the Transnational Model," *Journal of International Business Studies* 35 (2004): 164.

31. James Austin et al., "Building New Business Value Chains with Low Income Sectors in Latin America," in *Business Solutions for the Global Poor: Creating Social and Economic Value*, ed. Kasturi Rangan et al. (San Francisco, CA: Jossey-Bass, 2007).

32. Ted London and Stuart L. Hart, "Reinventing Strategies for Emerging Markets: Beyond the Transnational Model," *Journal of International Business Studies* 35 (2004); Christian Seelos and Johanna Mair, "Profitable Business Models and Market Creation in the Context of Deep Poverty: A Strategic View," *The Academy of Management Perspectives* 21, no. 4 (2007).

33. Christian Seelos and Johanna Mair, "Profitable Business Models and Market Creation in the Context of Deep Poverty: A Strategic View"; Ezequiel Reficco, "Towards Social Inclusion: Do Strategic Networks Work?" *ReVista Harvard Review of Latin America* VI, no. 1 (Fall 2006); James E. Austin, *The Collaboration Challenge: How Nonprofits and Businesses Succeed through Strategic Alliances*, 1st ed. (San Francisco, CA: Jossey-Bass Publishers, 2000); Ted London and Stuart L. Hart, "Reinventing Strategies for Emerging Markets: Beyond the Transnational Model," *Journal of International Business Studies* 35 (2004).

34. Christian Seelos and Johanna Mair, "Profitable Business Models and Market Creation in the Context of Deep Poverty: A Strategic View," *The Academy of Management Perspectives* 21, no. 4 (2007).

35. The ventures of Edenor and Codensa leveraged on existing individual LIS customers; furthermore, their technology-based billing and payment systems lowered transaction costs to the point where no community organizing was necessary. Technology is not the only relevant factor. Situations where buying involves a single visit to a point of sale also facilitates firm-to-individual exchange. For example, in the cases of Construmex (Cemex) and Empresario Azteca, where the individual low-income consumer approached the point of

sale to make one large purchase on credit, no local ecosystem was necessary. But in the case of Colcerámica, where the low-income consumer made a number of several small purchases of ceramic tiles, the company found that building the local ecosystem was required.

36. Ted London and Stuart L Hart, "Reinventing Strategies for Emerging Markets: Beyond the Transnational Model," *Journal of International Business Studies* 35 (2004).

37. Ted London, "The Base-of-the-Pyramid Perspective: A New Approach to Poverty Alleviation" (Working Paper, William Davidson Institute/Stephen M. Ross School of Business, 2008).

38. Interview with Ángel Irazola Arribas, former CEO (2001–2006) of Palmas del Espino, January 30, 2006.

39. James Austin et al., "Building New Business Value Chains with Low Income Sectors in Latin America," in *Business Solutions for the Global Poor: Creating Social and Economic Value*, ed. Kasturi Rangan, et al. (San Francisco, CA: Jossey-Bass, 2007).

40. Ezequiel Reficco and Patricia Marquez, "Socially Inclusive Networks for Building BOP Markets" (Working Paper, School of Business Administration, University of San Diego, October 2007).

41. Ted London, "The Base-of-the-Pyramid Perspective: A New Approach to Poverty Alleviation" (Working Paper, William Davidson Institute/Stephen M. Ross School of Business, 2008).

42. Ibid.

43. C. K. Prahalad, *The Fortune at the Bottom of the Pyramid: Eradicating Poverty through Profits* (Upper Saddle River, NJ: Wharton School Publishing, 2005).

44. Ted London and Stuart L. Hart, "Reinventing Strategies for Emerging Markets: Beyond the Transnational Model," *Journal of International Business Studies* 35 (2004).

45. Ted London, "The Base-of-the-Pyramid Perspective: A New Approach to Poverty Alleviation" (Working Paper, William Davidson Institute/Stephen M. Ross School of Business, 2008).

46. Christian Seelos and Johanna Mair, "Profitable Business Models and Market Creation in the Context of Deep Poverty: A Strategic View," *The Academy of Management Perspectives* 21, no. 4 (2007): 49.

47. Ted London and Stuart L. Hart, "Reinventing Strategies for Emerging Markets: Beyond the Transnational Model," *Journal of International Business Studies* 35 (2004); Ted London, "The Base-of-the-Pyramid Perspective: A New Approach to Poverty Alleviation" (Working Paper, William Davidson Institute/Stephen M. Ross School of Business, 2008); Eric Simanis and Stuart L. Hart, "The Base of the Pyramid Protocol: Toward Next Generation BOP Strategy." http://www.wdi.umich.edu/files/BoPProtocol2ndEdition2008.pdf.

48. Ted London, "The Base-of-the-Pyramid Perspective: A New Approach to Poverty Alleviation" (Working Paper, William Davidson Institute/Stephen M. Ross School of Business, 2008).

49. Ted London and Stuart L. Hart, "Reinventing Strategies for Emerging Markets: Beyond the Transnational Model," *Journal of International Business Studies* 35 (2004).
50. Interview with Horacio Cristiani, Director of Gas Natural BAN.
51. M. B. Milstein, Ted London, and Stuart L. Hart, "Revolutionary Routines: Capturing the Opportunity for Creating a More Inclusive Capitalism," in *Handbook of Cooperative Colaboration: New Designs and Dynamics*, ed. S. K Piderit, R .E. Fry, and D. L. Cooperrider (Stanford, CA: Stanford University Press, 2007).
52. We define "local business model" as one that is designed to attend a limited territory, usually a neighborhood or community.
53. Erik Simanis and Stuart Hart, "The Base of the Pyramid Protocol: Toward Next Generation BOP Strategy," (2008), http://www.wdi.umich.edu/files/BoPProtocol2ndEdition2008.pdf.
54. Ted London, "The Base-of-the-Pyramid Perspective: A New Approach to Poverty Alleviation" (Working Paper, William Davidson Institute/Stephen M. Ross School of Business, 2008).
55. A.G. Scherer and G. Palazzo, "Toward a Political Conception of Corporate Responsibility: Business and Society Seen from a Habermasian Perspective," *Academy of Management Review* 32, no. 4 (2007).
56. Ted London and Stuart L Hart, "Reinventing Strategies for Emerging Markets: Beyond the Transnational Model," *Journal of International Business Studies* 35 (2004).

3

How Small Firms and Startups Shape Inclusive Businesses

Henry Gómez Samper, Mladen Koljatic, and Mónica Silva

In this chapter our analysis focuses on six comparatively small firms, four of them startups, which developed inclusive businesses: Mariposas de Costa Rica (CRES), a firm that purchased butterfly pupae from subsistence growers and exported them to butterfly exhibitors abroad; Irupana, an assembling, processing, and trading company that dealt in organic foodstuffs grown by Bolivian farmers; Titikayak Consortium, a partnership organized by a leading Peruvian travel agency (Explorandes) together with a micro-enterprise (Llachón Turismo Rural, or LlachónTurs) to promote kayaking at Lake Titicaca; Activo Humano, a Chilean labor placement agency for unskilled workers; and two Venezuelan organizations—Cruzsalud, which offered pre-paid healthcare services in poor Caracas neighborhoods, and Comunanza, established to offer financial services to subsistence entrepreneurs.[1] These six firms, defined as small to medium-sized according to criteria employed by Ayyagari et al., are discussed together, apart from those examined in chapter 2.[2]

Table 3.1 shows, for all six organizations, years in business, number of employees, and roles played by low-income sectors (LIS) engaged. Except for CRES and Irupana, all companies had only operated for three to four years by the time this study was completed.

Leaders of all six companies engaging the poor as consumers or suppliers showed a remarkable commitment to make their business succeed and improve LIS living conditions in their respective countries. Cruzsalud's founder Jean Paul Rivas, who was determined to offer the first pre-paid health care plans to consumers in poor Caracas neighborhoods, stated his aim eloquently:

> We want to improve the living conditions and well-being of the poor . . . Nation building requires doing the kind of things we do at Cruzsalud. For a few bolivars, we provide health care for children, for

Table 3.1. Data on the Six Companies Analyzed

Organization	Country	Years	Headcount	Industry	LIS Role	Type of organization
Mariposas de C. R. (CRES)	Costa Rica	24	19	Agribusiness	Suppliers	Company
Irupana	Bolivia	21	150	Agribusiness	Suppliers	Company
Explorandes/ Llachón Turs	Peru	4	40[1]	Adventure tourism	Suppliers	Alliance
Activo Humano	Chile	3	11	Employment services	Consumers	Company
Cruzsalud	Venezuela	3	74	Pre-paid medical services	Consumers	Company
Comunanza	Venezuela	3	16	Financial services	Consumers	Foundation

1. Llachón Turs operates as a grassroots organization, with no employees. It works with 16 associations that provide several services, building a network of 80 families who live in the Llachón area. Explorandes employs 40 people and hires others to escort tourist groups as guides, carriers, cowboys, etc.

example, giving them medicine and making this a sustainable business. That is my personal view on how a country is developed.

Other leaders voiced similar sentiments: Javier Hurtado, founder of Irupana, aimed to improve the living conditions of Bolivian quinoa growers by offering fair prices. He echoes Rivas by declaring, "to build a nation, we need to produce, create wealth, and do so in an ethical manner." Joris Brinckerhoff, at CRES, pursued the same goal for Costa Rican butterfly pupa suppliers. Activo Humano's leader conceived his company to serve as "headhunter for the poor." Alfredo Ferreyros, of Explorandes, recalled that before sealing its kayak partnership with Llachón Turs, the company board had committed itself to offer new travel products featuring high social value, while its partner micro-entrepreneur, Valentín Quispe, had long encouraged Llachón dwellers to welcome tourists to their lakeside community. Lastly, Albi Rodríguez founded Comunanza to offer a wide range of financial products to subsistence entrepreneurs. Over and above generating economic return, all company leaders aimed for social purpose.

We will describe management features shared by all six firms, the challenges each faced, ways in which they innovated, extent to which they were profitable, and lessons drawn from their initiatives in engaging LIS. We first discuss the significance of small companies in Latin America's organizational landscape, and suggest comparative advantages such firms may hold for developing inclusive businesses.

The Virtues of Small Organizations

Whether small companies hold an advantage in the marketplace is subject to debate, especially in the light of challenges posed by the global economy.[3] Would modest size favor them in launching ventures with LIS? We will probe these questions by examining the six firms in depth. Except for certain public agencies in some countries, few organizations based in Latin America may be deemed large. Worldwide, an estimated 90 percent of firms are small or medium-sized;[4] whereas in Latin America, over 90 percent of all productive units are micro-enterprises.[5]

In exploring the potential comparative advantages of small companies for developing inclusive businesses, Márquez and Reficco[6] cite the following: focused mission, proximity, flexibility, and capacity for innovation. As it happens, all six firms examined here confirm these four virtues. We discuss their relevance before turning to each experience.[7]

Focused Mission

Small firms squarely focused on the LIS market may enjoy certain advantages when compared with larger companies. An owner of a small business in a LIS community likely knows the customers personally and can cater more readily to their individual needs and wants; in contrast, the large firm seeking to serve a mix of upper- and middle-income consumers must rely on indirect profiles drawn from market research. This could explain how, for instance, a small shopkeeper, unable to offer low prices or a wide assortment of goods, manages to compete with supermarkets and keep LIS customer loyalty, despite their limited purchasing power.[8] The smaller the business, the more likely it can focus its mission on delivering a given good or service in a particular way to a targeted customer.

Microfinance businesses provide a noteworthy example of focused mission for companies targeting LIS markets. Long before the term "base of the pyramid" was coined, poverty mitigation efforts in several Asian, African, and Latin American countries featured small loans made to people who failed to qualify for ordinary bank credit.[9] These pioneering organizations were chartered as banks, cooperatives, public or private foundations or other CSOs to operate in LIS markets, adapting loan conditions to the needs of poor consumers. Not until the 21st century did the sheer size of the LIS market prompt certain large international banks to begin offering microfinance services.

Why did large banks take so long to tap microfinance markets? For one, traditional collateral as a loan guarantee was inapplicable, for the poor lack adequate property. Assessing credit worthiness among low-income citizens applying for micro-credit is time consuming and entails intense interaction with customers.[10] Perhaps this explains why new, smaller organizations, driven by goals different from traditional banking and committed to their mission, were the ones to serve LIS, utilizing new organizational and operational procedures, sometimes designed by trial-and-error.[11] In time, management practices evolved to serve micro-enterprises, benefiting from new technology applications developed by large financial institutions.

Mission focus is not only about targeting constituents; a firm may feature a particular goal as part of its mission, such as manufacturing leading-edge products. Neither are small companies the only firms that feature focused missions. Yet there is no comparison between the singular efforts made by these six firms to fulfill their goal of improving the lives of LIS by running a successful business operation while adjusting management practices time and again, and run-of-the-mill business plans designed to serve a given market segment profitably. CRES built its business by developing LIS pupae suppliers. Irupana turned LIS growers of organically farmed cereals, who had depended on state or other aid, into micro entrepreneurs. Titikayak mobilized families in a LIS community to pioneer kayaking as a tourist business. Activo Humano singled out unskilled job seekers from a poor population sector of the capital city (Santiago, Chile). Cruzsalud marketed its healthcare service to a particular low-income sector and redesigned its business practices as it acquired information on target consumer needs, wants, buying habits, and attitudes. And Comunanza offered a technologically innovative service designed to suit subsistence entrepreneurs operating from a fixed location (as distinct, e.g., from peddlers).

Proximity to LIS

Studies of small companies targeting LIS show they are often located closer to their customers than larger companies, as illustrated by atomized business units operating in poor communities. Proximity provides small entrepreneurs a clearer view of customer needs, a kind of social and cultural intimacy with LIS not easily attainable by professional management teams attached to large firms.[12] Small companies are thus better able to integrate with surrounding LIS populations and overcome the barriers that hinder developing business ventures with LIS.[13] Moreover, social integration builds trust, a strategic factor for business startups as they search out networks that help ensure future success.[14]

In several Latin American countries leading companies are increasingly locating operations in or near poor communities, including banks, franchise businesses, and, in Venezuela, chain stores with limited product assortment.[15]

Presence of such companies in poor communities provides LIS with access to new shopping options and better prices for regularly purchased products. Yet a question remains as to whether business proximity alone enables companies to gain improved understanding of LIS consumer patterns and gauge potential market demand.

All six firms based their operations in or near targeted LIS communities. CRES's founder ran his own butterfly farm and regularly visited pupa growers. Irupana operated quinoa stores in outlying rural areas of Bolivia. Titikayak Consortium was based in the lakeside community that delivered boating and lodging services for tourists. The jobless clientele of Activo Humano, the "headhunter of the poor," was based in the company's own neighborhood. Cruzsalud's health care center was located on a street through which most of its targeted customers passed daily. Comunanza loans could be applied for at the place of business of subsistence micro-enterprises.

Flexibility and Capacity to Innovate
It stands to reason that small organizations are more flexible than are larger counterparts. Large companies serving traditional middle-income consumers cannot readily adjust their business model to serve LIS markets— e.g., by adjusting collection mechanisms to serve consumers who seek to purchase an ongoing service but cannot commit to fixed payments for lack of steady income. Moving away from their managerial policies and practices can pose serious challenges to large companies. For instance, Gómez, Márquez and Penfold[16] reviewed the tortuous experience of a large power company when it sought to transform its organization to serve LIS consumers (see chapter 6).

Small companies often operate in limited markets—usually a single city or part of it. A small company that targets LIS—assuming it previously served an ordinary middle-income market—will likely encounter lower opportunity cost than a large company, whose benchmark may be national or global. When building business ties with LIS, small firms focus their operations without having to pay attention to several businesses, product categories, or market segments. Proximity to LIS may enable small firms to establish trust-based relationships with prospective customers, suppliers, or partners by drawing on shared social and cultural bonds. Their modest size may hold the key of their ability to move from one market segment to another.

Each of the six firms illustrates management flexibility and capacity for innovation. CRES organized workshops to establish a code of ethical practices as it battled with growers to maintain quality standards. Irupana adapted modern thrashing and drying methods to assist quinoa growers in expanding output. Titikayak Consortium organized dozens of village families into 16 associations to ensure that food and lodging services for visiting tourists would be distributed fairly. Activo Humano devised job candidate screening tools suited for unskilled workers. Cruzsalud undertook its own door-to-door consumer survey, led by its president, to shape promotion practices better suited to LIS than those drawn from professional market research. Comunanza outsourced micro-enterprise loan disbursement and payment operations to leading financial institutions capable of providing online services. Significantly, strategies and management practices were reshaped as each company overcame problems in dealing with LIS.

Shared Management Features

Despite significant differences in business models, all six companies display management similarities. These include: (1) a strong commitment by the founding leader to engage LIS in pursuing business goals; (2) innovative and resilient management; and (3) management complexity, requiring leadership skills and extensive support networks to shape and learn management practices even as the business was being grown.

Commitment to Serving LIS

As noted earlier, founders of all six firms pursued social goals with a commitment akin to passion. Many times over, Cruzsalud searched out ways to deliver its low-priced product to targeted LIS segments instead of taking the easy way out by servicing companies in need of low-cost healthcare plans for employees; and to gauge a subsistence entrepreneur's credit worthiness, Comunanza staff visited the prospect's neighbors to obtain character references. In all six experiences, relationships were forged by leader–entrepreneurs with LIS target groups for the express purpose of improving their livelihood; yet none of the leader–founders was driven by charity motives. Profits were sought to ensure venture continuity and, in the case of Comunanza, to attract new investors and expand sales volume.

New Market Development

Any business that combines employment opportunity with expanded output of goods and services is both socially and economically beneficial, but ventures that are bold enough to build new markets for formerly undetected needs and wants make a greater contribution. Such ventures test the viability of innovative business models that, if successful, are soon replicated. All six firms engaged LIS by serving new markets, the most exotic being

Titikayak Consortium. By bringing kayak boating and tourists to Lake Titicaca—the world's largest lake, located at 3,810 meters (12,500 feet) above sea level—the venture acquainted customers with the subsistence farmers in the village of Llachón, even getting tourists to share their humble homes. At first, Llachón dwellers were wary that incoming tourists might not respect local traditions; hence considerable effort had to be made to overcome community concern. Explorandes' link with Llachón Turs features a twofold relationship with LIS: a partnership between a medium-sized company and a micro-enterprise, and supply of local services by community members.

The other firms also developed new markets. CRES was the first company to organize pupae growers of more than 50 butterfly species bred in Costa Rica's impressive biodiversity, and ship them to exhibitors in America and Europe. Irupana promoted organic products long before market demand for them expanded. Activo Humano launched the first privately operated labor placement service for unskilled workers in Chile. And Cruzsalud offered a pre-paid healthcare service previously unavailable in poor neighborhoods. The two older firms, Irupana and CRES, sparked competition from market followers; whether the remaining four startups will do likewise remains to be seen. CRES's lead in developing the butterfly pupae market was soon followed by other suppliers, who took advantage of low entry barriers and lowered prices and forced CRES to strengthen promotional efforts for its high-quality product.

Other similarities in management practices are evident. Comunanza, Cruzsalud, and Activo Humano all recruited LIS prospects from nearby poor communities, thus illustrating the practice of geographical proximity. For the latter two firms, this practice proved crucial to legitimize their operation in the eyes of LIS. To assist state-certified tourist guides required by law, Explorandes recruited and trained Llachón youths, who could readily relate to community members charged with lodging tourists as well as learn needed kayak skills—i.e., navigation and rescue methods to battle Lake Titicaca's treacherous waves.

Another management practice shared by all six companies was early attention to developing external support networks. Building these networks entailed painstaking efforts and proved crucial for business growth.

CRES was launched in 1984, two years after a visiting scientist told Joris Brinckerhoff about an overseas market opportunity for butterflies. Brinckerhoff started out by breeding butterfly pupae at his farm, but output was soon short of market demand. He sought to offer his growing network of suppliers a fair price, given the meticulous inspection process required to collect eggs and pupae: leaves of plants where pupae are bred must be cleaned daily. Brinckerhoff also visited Costa Rica's rural areas to locate micro-climates with unique butterfly species, enlisted support from community leaders, and met with small farmers—some of whom were occasional day workers at banana plantations. In time, he managed to turn 100 growers into butterfly pupa suppliers by hosting quarterly meetings and workshops to explain business challenges and offer technical assistance. He then organized the first butterfly fair, attended by buyers from North America and Europe, which in following years became an annual event. Moreover, he enlisted support from the National Biodiversity Institute (Instituto Nacional de Biodiversidad, INBIO) to promote butterfly breeding and develop educational materials to foster biodiversity-related micro-enterprises.CRES still produces butterfly pupae for research and quality control purposes, but 90 percent of exports are sourced from its supplier network.

Irupana started out in 1987. Its founder, Javier Hurtado, drew on his prior experience in international aid programs, which facilitated a ready network of quinoa crop assemblers, farm associations, agricultural state agencies, CSOs, and foreign aid agencies. Hurtado built on his contacts to establish a storage network that appears to have been his core activity for some years. When business declined, Hurtado tapped into his political capital and, in 2001, secured a municipal contract to provide breakfast for 160,000 schoolchildren, an operation that lasted for three years. Irupana then ventured into exports by partnering with the CSO Bolivian Rural Development Association (Asociación Boliviana para el Desarrollo Rural— Prorural) to provide financing for suppliers. In 2005, Irupana external support was further buttressed when ties were forged with the Inter American Foundation and the World Bank's International Finance Corporation.

Titikayak Consortium, established in 2003, drew on networks built by Alfredo Ferreyros, of Explorandes, and partner Valentín Quispe, of Llachón Turs. Explorandes pioneered adventure tourism in Peru by introducing trekking, hiking, and kayak operations. A vast external promotion network of airlines and international travel wholesalers, plus direct contact with customers via its website, enabled Explorandes to run dozens of travel programs. Moreover, Ferreyros chaired the Machu Pichu Institute, a historical preservation agency, and was an active member of the National Tourism Chamber and other industry associations. He also promoted his business by attending international trade shows and fairs.

Quispe, in turn, organized the Llachón Tourism Promotion Association (Asociación Pro-Turística de Llachón-Aprotur) to overcome the local people's resistance to visiting tourists years before the Consortium was launched. Together with Llachón Turs, Aprotur provided kayak storage and

maintenance services, promoted home improvement to accommodate visiting tourists (e.g., by installing showers and toilets), and outsourced food
and lodging services to 80 families organized in 16 associations that aim to
ensure fair rotation practices. Interestingly enough, the Consortium agreement allowed Quispe's company to independently serve customers from 20
other travel agencies.

Activo Humano started out in 2005 by approaching large and small companies in need of unskilled workers, such as trucking assistants and han-
dlers who for the most part had been unemployed and drawn from LIS. Job
seekers were screened by means of personnel tests and LIS neighborhood
recruiting, as well as checking out character references. To overcome oppo-
sition from a state agency responsible for helping place the unemployed,
the firm's founder sought support from La Pintana's mayor, who was concerned about high unemployment in his constituency, and from local cler-
gymen and community leaders. A major move to draw external support
took place when Activo Humano merged with a seasoned British placement
company targeting similar job seekers.

Cruzsalud had organized support networks even before it started in
2005. These included information technology assistance to operate elaborate cost controls; to assess, record, and monitor customer health conditions; to organize a call center manned by physicians and paramedics; and
to set up a soon discarded mobile telephone fee payment service. Much
more demanding was building a suitable network of health care providers,
including physicians on hand 24 hours, medical specialists for patient refer-
rals, nurses, clinical test labs, and cooperating pharmacies to promote the
sale of health care plans in LIS neighborhoods.

Additionally, Cruzsalud required support from key actors in its immediate environment, including police, public health officials, community
leaders, and parish priests, to ensure the safety of physicians, nurses, and
ambulances venturing into dangerous neighborhoods. The firm's community network subsequently enabled Cruzsalud to open two primary health
care centers by partnering with local cooperatives.

Comunanza started out in 2005 by drawing on its founding partners'
close ties with financial institutions, including state agencies charged with
regulating micro-finance. Loan officers were recruited from Petare, a LIS
area from which prospects were drawn. The firm also obtained information technology and commercial support by outsourcing most operating
tasks. For example, Banco Mercantil opened online accounts for customers
who were granted loans, where payments could be deposited; and Seguros
Carabobo provided life insurance policies to cover loans, funeral service

charges for deceased borrowers, and a family livelihood stipend while a micro-enterprise was organized. These services were offered at market prices. An agreement with Petare's parish priest allowed Comunanza to meet with customers on church premises in exchange for a quarterly donation. The company's ambitious plans for future growth entailed investment promotion efforts targeted at individuals, companies, and international institutions.

Complex Business Ventures That Learn on the Go

Dependence on such diverse external support networks rendered the management of all six firms a complex operation. These networks spanned institutional, political and community linkages, and equally important, operating, financial, and commercial ties. Such management complexity underscores the comparative advantages held by small companies—focused mission, market proximity, and operating flexibility. When initial plans failed to work out, each firm was flexible enough to reshape management practices. Indeed, most of the six companies had to learn new management practices for dealing with LIS consumers or suppliers. Consider CRES's experience first.

CRES significantly contributed to improving living conditions of butterfly pupae suppliers—subsistence growers and squatters (i.e., families who build shacks and raise crops on unoccupied land, a common practice in much of Latin America). According to data provided by field support staff at Costa Rica's Environment and Energy Ministry and other sources, benefits accruing to CRES suppliers are substantial: previous pupae breeder income was around the minimum monthly wage of US$235; but on becoming CRES suppliers, income was multiplied by factor of two, in the low-season, or four, in the high-season.

Nonetheless, when CRES started out, Brinckerhoff had a huge training challenge ahead of him: he had to acquaint growers with market building, and service requirements, and to promote customer loyalty by imposing rigorous quality standards and timely delivery. Untimely pupae sales to third parties made by some suppliers, either to seize opportunity or unload overproduction, led CRES to draw up a code of ethics to which all suppliers subscribed, providing incentives to ensure product quality. Suppliers who failed to abide by the rules and standards were barred. It was not easy for CRES to turn subsistence growers into micro-entrepreneurs keen to improve productivity and respond to changes in market demand for different butterfly species.

In the face of growing competition from other exporters in Costa Rica and neighboring countries, Brinckerhoff tried to boost customer loyalty by shipping 30 percent more than what was ordered to cover potential transport loss, thus cutting profit margin. Additionally, building on Costa Rica's growing fame as an ecological travel destination, Brinckerhoff's wife opened a butterfly lodge and gift shop—The Butterfly Farm—to mitigate export seasonality.

Irupana built early relationships with growers by making mutual oral commitments—with both parties agreeing to perform their respective duties. But suppliers often failed to deliver on time because of weather or harvest mishaps, making it necessary to write up contracts. To render them enforceable, Irupana searched for a source of financial support acceptable to all parties.

When Irupana linked with international agencies to export quinoa and amaranth, growers were rewarded to expand output and produce a cleaner product. But traditional manual methods for harvesting, drying, and thrashing grain proved inadequate. Harvesting was improved by providing growers with sickles; and tents were supplied to prevent contamination by birds when the crop was drying. Thrashing proved more challenging: growers had improvised a quick method by placing grain on open roads for passing trucks or tractors to crush it, but this contaminated the product. Irupana then ingeniously adapted rice thrashers to quinoa specifications and supplied them to farmers. Even as these measures were taken, other problems emerged. Metal silos were provided to store grain but growers were unable to accurately measure what they contained; storage rooms were then built next to the homes of growers, who proceeded to move in their families! To hasten a solution, Irupana built community storage warehouses.

Titikayak Consortium operated at Llachón, where only 12 percent of the population had completed primary school and many villagers did not speak Spanish. Community members had good reason not to trust tourists: years earlier a foreign promoter tried to seize their land to build a hotel, and reckless tourism had led to environmental and cultural damage on Lake Titicaca islands. To overcome village hostility to visiting tourists, Valentín Quispe of Llachón Turs organized Aprotur, made up of 16 neighborhood associations, which then agreed to welcome tourists. Negotiations were already under way when Alfredo Ferreyros, of Explorandes, visited the community in 2002 to explore the consortium project. But many villagers remained wary: when Explorandes recruited Llachón youths as kayak lifeguards, their families feared the strange boats. Villagers also complained that guides used fiberglass boats to follow the kayaks and insisted that their own craft be used. Explorandes agreed, and the conflict was solved. Quispe handled food and other complaints by tourists. Had Explorandes not partnered with a community leader, consortium governance would have likely failed.

At the start, only 56 families collaborated with the kayak venture, but by 2006 as many as 80 families engaged. Villager income from the venture complements what they earn from subsistence farming.

Activo Humano was set up by its founder to help curb high unemployment rates among unskilled laborers and overcome the state agency's widely recognized incapacity to assist the jobless; the agency simply referred them to companies posting job vacancies, providing little or no information on candidate background. The founder undertook to assemble the job seeker's character references for prospective employers. But even so, candidates for job openings failed to elicit employer trust. Means had to be developed to assess candidate qualifications, and performance standards designed for management control. After three years, Activo Humano's job placement indicators were positive: over 90 percent held their jobs three months after hiring, the number of client companies had grown, and companies reported they cut turnover after retaining Activo Humano services. Operations expanded by advertising for job candidates, which required greater attention to evaluation and selection.

Cruzsalud focused on the poorest LIS consumer segment, known as social stratum E. This group depended almost entirely on deficient public health services: hospitals usually required patients to bring their own surgical supplies and medications, as well as plaster, bandages, and screws for bone fractures. Hence Cruzsalud pre-paid healthcare plans included surgical supplies. For as little as US$5 per month, subscribing families could access a physician 24 hours a day by mobile phone, and if needed obtain a physician house call and ambulance service—significant benefits given the dangers present in Caracas' poor communities, especially at night.

Soon after signing up, however, many plan subscribers failed to pay their membership fees on time. Fee levels drew on initial market research findings showing what consumers could afford to pay. Founder Rivas and his management team then visited neighborhoods where early subscribers and potential prospects lived, searching out reasons for nonpayment. They learned that LIS commonly lack a steady income, setting money aside only for food expenditures. Hence Cruzsalud payments were viewed as a contingent expense and competed with other key outlays, such as mobile phone cards. Once the marketing strategy was revamped, a step that proved effective was to offer consumers a free health check-up by Cruzsalud doctors and nurses before they subscribed, thus showing consumers that service quality was well worth its price.

Other management practices were also shaped on the go. At first, Cruzsalud mistakenly relied on a sales representative pyramid, as used worldwide by companies such as Avon and Amway in serving LIS consumers. More effective was using the company's own nurses and cleaning staff as sales promoters, as many of them lived in LIS communities from which customers were drawn. This strategy proved particularly effective when Cruzsalud opened a healthcare center on a street where hundreds of LIS consumers from nearby communities walked every day. In short, Cruzsalud learned how to shape its sales, pricing, and promotion management practices as it learned how to deal with LIS consumers.

Comunanza charged interest rates up to five times higher than those of state-owned banks specializing in micro-finance, yet customers were happy to pay them. Comunanza visited prospects at their place of business and processed loan applications in only five days, whereas its competitors, including a leading private institution that pioneered micro-finance in Venezuela, required that people go to them, so most micro-entrepreneurs had to close their business to get to a bank, wait in line, and apply for a loan.

Months passed before Comunanza could fine-tune its business plan, adapting micro-finance management practices used elsewhere in Latin America to Venezuelan LIS needs. An information technology platform was designed in close collaboration with financial institutions to which operations were outsourced. To attract investor capital and protect against country risk, Comunanza built a complex organizational structure. The operating arm was set up as a foundation, using loan portfolio as collateral to borrow funds from a Venezuelan holding company that obtained credit from a financial institution abroad owned by shareholders. Despite precautions to reduce shareholder risk resulting from potential regulatory changes in Venezuela, Comunanza is aware that its chief risk stems from serving subsistence micro-enterprises, which could default on loan payments at any time. To enhance debt commitment by its customers, the firm has planned to partner with parallel services such as pre-paid health care plans and educational loans.

These stories illustrate the management complexity of all six companies, despite being small and, in most instances, led by experienced managers. The steps they took to forge suitable management practices evidence the lack of available knowledge and experience when dealing with LIS populations. Note some of the management innovations these firms introduced in addressing their respective challenges.

Innovative Companies

The six firms show both entrepreneurial and organizational innovation, assessed in terms of functional, structural, and behavioral criteria.[17] This characterization, together with the strong commitment made by these firms to successfully engage LIS, may explain why they overcame challenges that might have led to business failure.[18]

CRES's founder was the first to glean a business opportunity in the world market for Costa Rican butterflies. Brinckerhoff's company's record is innovative from a functional standpoint:[19] it built an ambitious local and international network to render the business operational; it turned dozens of subsistence suppliers into micro-entrepreneurs; it undertook bold measures to withstand competition; and it overcame fluctuations in market demand for different butterfly species. Despite such innovation, CRES cannot escape the small size of the world butterfly market and its low business entry barriers.

Irupana's founder launched the company with a clear social goal: to reduce poverty within a wide network of rural suppliers. Such commitment may be viewed as innovative in terms of entrepreneurial behavior.[20] Also innovative is Hurtado's early grasp of the market for organic produce. Other innovative capabilities surfaced as output levels expanded, e.g., adapting rice thrashers to quinoa. Still another move with broad social impact, which took place in 2006, was turning most company retail stores into franchises. This measure marked a shift in Irupana's course, and followed the firm's growing ties with the Inter American Foundation and the International Finance Corporation.

Titikayak Consortium brought kayaking to Lake Titicaca, and drew on a social network of unschooled, subsistence Bolivian villagers to host international tourists. The venture is innovative from a structural standpoint.[21] The governing arrangement between Explorandes and Llachón Turs is also innovative in forging a partnership between a travel agency and a micro-entrepreneur; an unusual feature is that Explorandes contributes only 30 percent of Llachón Turs' sales, but receives preferential treatment from its partner in exchange for strategic guidance to handle 70 percent of sales from other travel agencies.

Activo Humano's leader foresaw a market opportunity in one of Chile's pressing social problems, unemployment among LIS. Labor placement services for unskilled workers were organized at low cost by developing a network of freelance recruiters, generating political and community support, and designing methods suited to screen unskilled candidates for jobs. By merging with a foreign company, the founder gained capital plus experienced management, yet continued as the firm's head.

Cruzsalud displayed innovation by offering healthcare services never before available to LIS: access to a physician by means of a 24-hour call center, together with emergency house calls and ambulance service if needed. Its business model called for a high volume, low-profit operation that relied on world-class information technology to help anticipate the health problems of consumers served. Moreover, management practices were improved as experience with LIS customers was gained.

Comunanza introduced a number of functional innovations in processing loans to subsistence micro-enterprises in Venezuela. An advanced information technology platform outsourced disbursement, payment, and other operational needs to leading financial institutions, so that loan applications could be made at the borrower's place of business and approved within five days. Also, a novel legal and organizational structure was designed to reduce shareholder risk and attract new investors.

In sum, all six companies displayed innovation capability by virtue of their unusual business models, and by shaping new management practices as each learned to engage LIS as consumers or suppliers.

Financial Returns

Financial results for the small firms' business with LIS were mixed. Two companies reported profit in the first year of operations, an unusual feat; but these firms and two others were startups, too early to gauge profitability. Not all six companies provided sufficient information to adequately assess financial performance.

CRES has operated for 24 years. From 2001 to 2005, net earnings dropped from US$35,000 to US$15,000, recovering in 2006. Investment figures are more revealing: in 2004–05, return on assets (ROA) fell from—3.27 percent to—3.83 percent, while return on equity (ROE) decreased from—4.43 percent to—5.68 percent. Nonetheless, CRES continues to pay its LIS suppliers higher prices than its competitors.

Irupana posted financial losses after 2004, and failed to draw profits from export shipments since 2002. But exports grew rapidly, from US$21,000 in 2003 to US$658,880 in 2006. The firm projected a profit for 2008, and ROE of 11.24 percent by 2011.

Consorcio Titikayak sales tripled in 2004–06, from US$3,700 to US$16,800. Explorandes (annual sales, US$4 million), which claims 60 percent of net income, assessed Titikayak earnings as excellent. The operation draws investment from all participants: Explorandes staked US$20,000 in kayak equipment and promotion; Llachón Turs spent US$7,000 to build a storage warehouse and docking facilities; and to accommodate tourists, Llachón villagers spent about US$900 to improve their dwellings.

Activo Humano's financial results do not appear promising. In 2007, the company reported losses in excess of earlier projections. The company expected to break even by late 2008 and post earnings from 2009.

Cruzsalud's shareholders and board members, after one year of operations, considered its 2006 earnings unsatisfactory: ROA 0.64 percent, and ROE 1.51 percent. Lessons learned in engaging LIS have led to changes in business practices and increased the growth rate of new subscribers; 2007 earnings were 13 times higher than those of the previous year, with projected annual profit growth of 1.9 percent.

Comunanza made 2,960 loans to 720 customers over 27 months (to March 2007). In 2006–07, ROA rose from 3.0 percent to 4.3 percent, while ROE declined from 67.0 percent to 38.5 percent. The latter figure compares favorably with an estimated opportunity cost of 29.5 percent (average return, Caracas Stock Exchange).

Altogether, financial performance for the six small companies has been fair, with only two firms showing moderate to robust results. Four were startups. Of these, three (Titikayak, Cruzsalud, and Comunanza) appeared to make progress toward becoming going concerns, but it is too early to assess financial performance. Financial challenges besetting these firms, however, can hardly be attributed to engaging LIS.

Insights on Small Companies Doing Business with LIS

Do small companies hold comparative advantages in doing business with LIS? Does the experience of the six firms support or disprove this view? We address these questions by assessing the six firms in light of the following: focused mission, proximity to LIS, operating flexibility, capacity for innovation, operating a complex business, need to learn by doing, and evidence of becoming socially embedded with LIS. On the basis of the challenges faced by the six firms, we note the limitations of small companies when doing business with LIS.

Focused mission. All six enterprises grounded their business plans on involving LIS as consumers, suppliers, or partners. Explorandes partnered with Llachón Turs expressly for the purpose of enlisting subsistence Llachón village dwellers to operate kayak services and provide tourists with food and lodging; CRES and Irupana engaged LIS as suppliers, while Activo Humano, Cruzsalud, and Comunanza focused exclusively on LIS consumers. It appears comparatively easier for small companies to serve LIS as consumers rather than as suppliers—a finding consistent with results drawn from all business ventures with LIS, presented in chapter 9.

Proximity. Our sample of small firms operated in areas near to the particular LIS they engaged in business; their leaders displayed a special sensitivity to the needs of poor communities and conceived their business ventures by building on their familiarity with LIS. CRES engaged butterfly pupae suppliers from Costa Rica's rural areas for 90 percent of its volume. Irupana started out buying organic coffee near its namesake town, where it opened the first of several storage units in LIS villages. Consorcio Titikayak operated its kayaking service in a lakeside village where subsistence farmers provided lodging and food services to kayak customers. For its unskilled labor placement service, Activo Humano hired recruiters who resided in the same areas as the unemployed workers it served. Cruzsalud headquarters and its primary health care center were located on the outskirts of a poor area, home to 30 percent of the capital city's population. Lastly, Comunanza recruited loan officers from the same area from which it drew micro-enterprise customers and prospects, who were attended at their respective place of business. Day-to-day interaction with LIS was a common feature of all firms.

Flexible operations. All six enterprises proved flexible in adjusting management practices to dealing with LIS. CRES organized workshops to explain to its suppliers the quality and customer service standards required for serving world markets; Irupana partnered with several institutions in order to broaden financial and marketing support to suppliers; Explorandes departed from its standard practice of dealing directly with travel service suppliers as it entrusted its micro-enterprise partner with handling all Consorcio Titikayak issues emerging in Llachón; Activo Humano's leader merged his firm with a larger, more experienced organization with headquarters outside the country, yet maintained his leadership; Cruzsalud learned, by trial-and-error, the marketing and fee collection practices needed to serve LIS consumers profitably; and Comunanza partners allocated months on end to hone the legal, organizational, technological, and administrative mechanisms required to offer speedy customer service and reduce shareholder risk.

Capacity to innovate. As noted in chapter 9, startups often originate in innovations that intend to exploit market opportunities; and four of the six firms are startups. Evidence of flexibility in operations reveals a capacity for innovation in dealing with LIS consumers and suppliers that is all the more significant given comparatively little experience in developing businesses with such groups. When innovation capacity is coupled with other attributes, such as focused mission, proximity to targeted LIS, and flexibility in management practices, smaller ventures such as those studied appear to generate synergies seldom matched by larger companies in dealing with LIS.

Complexity. A company that is small in size is not necessarily easier to run than a large firm. All six firms operated complex businesses. Engagement with LIS added even greater complexity as the firms had to set up intricate networks to render the business viable, learn to deal with cultural differences, and shape new management practices.

Learning by doing. Every organization learns from experience. But in dealing with comparatively uncharted business relations with LIS, our six companies had more to learn. Inevitably, such learning brought delays that affected investment payback. Accordingly, companies that engage LIS must make allowance for learning time to develop appropriate management practices.

Partnering with micro-enterprises. In Latin America, unregistered micro-business units vastly outnumber those legally chartered, and an overwhelming share belong to LIS.[22] Such ventures should find it easier to do business with other LIS than companies run by managers drawn from higher social strata. Our sample of small firms featured only one partnership with a micro-enterprise (Explorandes and Llachón Turs), and appears to show that without the latter partner, Explorandes could not have engaged LIS suppliers successfully; over and above the venture's profitability, Explorandes came across as a socially responsible company that respects both nature and indigenous cultures. Accordingly, linking large companies with micro-enterprises in Latin America might well serve to promote business development.

Capacity for social embedding. The focused mission of a small firm centering its business model on LIS presents a markedly different operating context than that of a large firm serving many markets. In each of the six cases examined, targeting LIS as consumers or suppliers shaped the very identity of the organization and, for the most part, the business motives of the founding leaders. As noted in chapter 5, such a degree of social commitment in business development generates significant advantage when dealing with LIS.

Yet despite all the competences evidenced by the cases examined, such virtues may not suffice to overcome challenges faced by small firms. Although some of the six firms appeared headed towards success, not all had securely established prospects for sustainability. Likewise, small firms lack features likely to favor larger companies, such as financial muscle to overcome market volatility, exert control over the value chain, and remain a "patient investor." All such limitations affected the sample firms, while market-related issues challenged CRES and Irupana. Nonetheless, our in-depth review suggests a combination of competences that larger companies would find difficult to match; furthermore, all six firms benefited their targeted LIS.

Key attributes shared by our sample firms, notwithstanding their widely different business models, suggest a promising area for further exploration of competences held by small firms in dealing with LIS, and by ventures that draw support from both large and small firms along lines suggested by Bruni Celli, González and Gómez Samper.[23] An ongoing challenge is to build a greater body of evidence to determine whether small firms feature inherent advantages for mounting inclusive businesses. Additionally, as noted by Chu (2005), further research is required to learn whether success in doing business with LIS goes beyond income improvement; for the ultimate goal of market-based initiatives with LIS is to advance social inclusion. As stated by the founders of Irupana and Cruzsalud, the idea is that such business ventures should become cornerstones for nation building.

Notes

1. Comunanza was legally incorporated as an NGO to offset current micro-credit regulations in Venezuela. It is included in this chapter because it operates with a business company rationale.

2. According to one definition, micro-enterprises employ as many as 10 persons, featuring total assets of up to $10,000 and annual sales of up to US$100,000; whereas small companies employ up to 50, with total assets and sales of up to US$3 million. Medium-sized companies employ up to 300 persons, with total assets and sales of up to US$15 million. Meghana Ayyagari, Asli Demirguc-Kunt, and Thorsten Beck, *Small and Medium Enterprises across the Globe: A New Database* (SSRN, 2003).

3. Asli Demirguc-Kunt, Thorsten Beck, and Ross Levine, *Small and Medium Enterprises, Growth, and Poverty: Cross-Country Evidence* (SSRN, 2003).

4. Michael Klein, in *Creating Opportunities for Small Business* (Washington, DC: International Finance Corporation, World Bank Group, 2007), 3.

5. Emilio Zevallos, "Micro, pequeñas y medianas empresas en América Latina," *Revista de la CEPAL* 29 (2003).

6. Patricia Márquez and Ezequiel Reficco, "SMEs and Low-income Sectors," in *Small Firms, Global Markets: Competitive Challenges in the New Economy*, ed. Jerry Haar and Jörg Meyer-Stamer (London and New York: Palgrave Macmillan, 2008).

7. Other criteria used to analyze SME success in inclusive businesses include regulatory framework, access to funding, information technology, and human resources. Emilio Zevallos, "Micro, pequeñas y medianas empresas en América Latina," *Revista de la CEPAL* 29 (2003).

8. Guillermo D'Andrea and Gustavo Herrero, "Understanding Consumers and Retailers at the Base of the Pyramid in Latin America" (Paper presented at the Harvard Business School Conference on Global Poverty, Boston, MA, Dec. 2005).

9. Marc J. Epstein and Christopher A. Crane, "Alleviating Global Poverty through Microfinance: Factors and Measures of Financial, Economic, and Social Performance." (Paper presented at the Harvard Business School Conference on Global Poverty, Boston, MA, Dec. 2005).

10. Michael Chu, "Commercial Returns and Social Value: The Case of Microfinance." (Paper presented at the research symposium at Harvard Business School "The Business of Reaching the Global Poor," Boston, MA, Dec. 2005).

11. Tom Easton, "The Hidden Wealth of the Poor," *The Economist*, Nov. 5, 2005.

12. Ted London and Stuart L Hart, "Reinventing Strategies for Emerging Markets: Beyond the Transnational Model," *Journal of International Business Studies* 35 (2004).

13. James Austin et al., "Building New Business Value Chains with Low-Income Sectors in Latin America," in *Business Solutions for the Global Poor: Creating Social and Economic Value*, ed. Kasturi Rangan, et al. (San Francisco, CA: Jossey-Bass, 2007).

14. Carlos Jarillo, "On Strategic Networks," *Strategic Management Journal* 9 (1) (1988).

15. Raquel Puente, "Mercadeo para las mayorías," in *Compromiso Social: gerencia para el siglo XXI*, ed. Antonio Francés (Caracas: Ediciones IESA, 2008).

16. Henry Gómez, Patricia Márquez, and Michael Penfold, "Cómo AES-EDC generó relaciones rentables en los barrios pobres de Caracas," *Harvard Business Review América Latina* (Dec. 2006).

17. Jan Fagerberg, David C. Mowery, and Richard R. Nelson, *The Oxford Handbook on Innovation* (Oxford, UK: Oxford University Press, 2004).

18. In developing countries, 50% to 75% of startups cease to exist during their first three years, while only 10% to 20% remain in business after five years. "La pequeña y mediana empresa. Algunos aspectos." LC/R. 1330, CEPAL. 1993.

19. Michael E. Porter, *The Competitive Advantage of Nations* (New York, NY: The Free Press, 1990).

20. Peter F. Drucker, *Innovation and Entrepreneurship: Practice and Principles*, 1st ed. (New York: Harper & Row, 1985).

21. Henry Mintzberg and James Brian Quinn, *The Strategy Process: Concepts, Contexts, Cases*, 2nd ed. (Englewood Cliffs, NJ: Prentice Hall, 1991).

22. Patricia Márquez and Henry Gómez Samper, *Alianzas con microempresas* (Caracas: Ediciones IESA, 2001).

23. Josefina Bruni Celli, Rosa Amelia González and Henry Gómez Samper, "Las empresas grandes y las Pymes como emprendedoras sociales," *Harvard Business Review América Latina* (May 2009).

4

Social Enterprises and Inclusive Businesses

Gabriel Berger and Leopoldo Blugerman

In Iberoamerica, poverty and exclusion are issues of long-standing relevance in public and social agendas. While private companies have only recently started to consider the best ways to use their capabilities to develop productive and market-based initiatives to serve the needs of the poor, civil society organizations (CSOs) and cooperatives traditionally involved in fighting indigence and exclusion have worked with low-income sectors (LIS) to engage in market-based activities for quite some time already.

It may be argued that civil society organizations' and cooperatives' greater "proximity" to low-income sectors, as well as the inclusiveness embedded in their missions, values, and operations, facilitate their development of market-based initiatives that promote social inclusion. Based on this premise, this chapter explores lessons that can be learned from social enterprises in Iberoamerica pursuing business strategies that promote social inclusion.

In these pages we make a comparative analysis of 13 business ventures by, for, or involving poor sectors, carried out by nonprofit organizations—associations and foundations as well as cooperatives. Cases studied include cooperatives and CSOs—most of them established organizations with a proved track record—that undertook diverse market-based initiatives. Five of the 13 ventures started in the 1980s or earlier; seven ventures began in the early and mid 1990s; while only one of them was created in this decade (2004).

Initiatives involving LIS as producers. This first group includes five cases that feature low-income producers. The Association for the Hemp Region's Sustainable and Solidarity-Based Development (Associação de Desenvolvimento Sustentável e Solidário da Região Sisaleira, hence APAEB) was created by hemp fiber producers to carry out trade and to seek higher income through industrialization. Rocinha's Handicraft Work and Sewing Cooperative (Cooperativa de Trabalho Artesanal e de Costura da Rocinha, hence Coopa-Roca) managed and coordinated the work of women who produced handicraft fabrics and design goods at the Rocinha *favela* (slum) in Rio de Janeiro. Bio Bio Wild Fruit Pickers (Coordinadora Regional de Recolectoras y Recolectores del Bio Bio) is an association of collectors from communities in Southern Chile, who joined together to harvest and market wild fruits, medicinal herbs, and vegetables that they dehydrated in wholly owned plants to secure better trading conditions. The Green Gold Corporation (Corporación Oro Verde) sought to organize African-Colombian producer families at the Colombian Chocó region to set up the business of extracting, processing, and marketing of certified gold. Finally, Peru's Cross-Regional Handicraft Center (Centro Interregional de Artesanos del Perú, hence CIAP) was created and managed by handicraft workers from several Peruvian areas to streamline their production to fair-trade international markets as well as to undertake other business ventures.

Initiatives involving LIS as urban recyclers. This second group includes producers and workers who formed solid-waste collecting cooperatives to build recycling chains in urban areas. *El Ceibo* Cooperative, in Buenos Aires, forged ties with residents and apartment building porters, training them to separate waste categories in order to collect inorganic waste to be processed and sold to recyclers. Belo Horizonte's Association of Paper, Cardboard and Recyclable Material Collectors (Associação dos Catadores de Papel, Papelão e Material Reaproveitável, hence Asmare) collected waste from the streets or from several companies or public agencies, processing and adding industrial value to the material in order to sell it to recyclers. Last, Bogotá's Porvenir Recyclers' Cooperative members collected and processed solid urban waste later sold to recyclers or paper industry companies in the Colombian capital.[1]

Initiatives for LIS job opportunities. A third group includes three Spanish ventures set up to provide job opportunities for people excluded from regular labor markets. La Fageda offered jobs to mentally challenged individuals at La Garrotxa—a town near Barcelona—in its dairy product manufacturing and marketing operations as well as other productive ventures. Futur Foundation placed immigrants and former convicts in catering and food services to schools, using organic products and fair trade practices. Catalonia's Andrómines Social Association offered job opportunities in furniture, computer, and clothing collection and sale.

Initiatives for sales to LIS. The fourth group includes two cases of goods or service sales to low-income sectors: Escudo Rojo, a store that sold donated clothing, furniture, and equipment in Buenos Aires in partnership with a local Salvation Army chapter: and Chile's National Institute for Professional

Training (Instituto Nacional de Capacitación Profesional, hence INACAP), an institution offering private higher education services to low-income individuals across Chile.

In this chapter, an initial conceptual section discusses the type of organizations used as a basis for our analysis, different interpretations about how to define these actors, and keys for the social sector to develop market-based strategies. The second section presents research findings, showing patterns identified in the 13 organizations featured in this study. The last section offers conclusions and management lessons drawn for the development of inclusive businesses led by nonprofits and cooperatives.

Social Enterprises and Market Strategies

We have chosen to characterize CSOs and cooperatives together as *social enterprises*. As it is unusual to view them within the same organizational category, a brief description of this type of organizations is in order to justify this characterization.

Non-profits are organizations that pursue benefits or improvements for their beneficiaries, members, or communities through several social intervention strategies. They do not distribute the proceeds from their operations. While their governance bodies may or may not include beneficiaries, their primary task is to accomplish their mission as well as to protect their organizations' assets and resources. According to Salamon and Anheier,[2] non-profits are organized and institutionalized; do not distribute profits; are private, self-governed, volunteer; and have no electoral purposes. These organizations often have small scale, ample flexibility, and a capability to mobilize community efforts.[3]

Cooperatives are institutions with strategies that tend to focus on solving problems shared by their members—income creation, trade, purchases, or utility supply. Cooperative members are partners and owners of the organization—they are involved in key decisions and appoint governance body members. In addition, proceeds from cooperative operations belong to the entire group and are distributed equitably among members. These organizations are guided by the so-called cooperative principles, including democratic control, limited compensation for capital contributions, earnings distribution based on contributions to operations, collaboration among cooperatives, and a concern for the community.

However, these conceptual differences between non-profits and cooperatives do not always translate so neatly into practice, as shown by several cases studied in this research, which have adopted a hybrid format. Thus, the legal format adopted by these organizations does not necessarily match their operations. Indeed, some organizations displayed ambiguous formats despite their legal status, and, as a result, some cooperatives acted like non-profits and vice versa.

For instance, La Fageda was legally incorporated as a cooperative, but it actually operated as a CSO. On the one hand, it promoted income generation through compensations to its beneficiaries—all formal partners in this venture. The cooperative's producer partners were mentally challenged individuals who enjoyed economic benefits and job opportunities but could hardly be expected to make decisions on the organization's business strategies. In turn, legally incorporated as a non-profit, Bio Bio Pickers acted as a cooperative of eight fruit and mushroom collectors' committees that later processed all products and compensated pickers for their contribution to sales.

This hybridization may be attributed to constraints imposed by the legal frameworks in some countries on non-profit and cooperative statuses, rather than to explicit model choices made by organizations. In addition, some non-profits and cooperatives do in fact share commonalities that enable them to be characterized as part of the same organizational category. Thus, we shall adopt a working definition of social enterprises as mission-driven private organizations, which rely primarily on market-based strategies to raise the necessary funds to create social value for their members, specific groups, or communities—whether these organizations are legally incorporated as non-profits or cooperatives.

These organizations fit the category of "social enterprise," a term that has commanded increasing attention among both American and European scholars,[4] though from different perspectives.[5] Social enterprises' search for revenues through market-based initiatives, with strategies commonly associated with business companies, has received significant attention in the scholarly literature. Although non-profits have traditionally relied on public (subsidies) or private (donations from individuals, foundations, etc.) funding from domestic and international donors, offering services and products in the marketplace enables organizations to diversify their revenue sources, thereby enhancing their autonomy, sustainability, and scale. As non-profits start to develop market-based and productive activities and strategies that involve payments as a result of product exchanges or service delivery, and as these transactions create revenues that support their social mission, these organizations become social enterprises.[6]

Earlier studies have provided a basis to identify critical dimensions for the success of market-based ventures developed by social enterprises. These dimensions will be of use to analyze the initiatives explored in this chapter.[7]

First, in order to produce revenues through market-based initiatives, an organization needs to identify a demand. Often, social entrepreneurs who develop market-based initiatives fail to properly "read" the potential demand and its existing payment capability. This is frequently true for organizations that operate in low-income sectors, as it is not always easy to identify profitable activities associated with their missions. However, in some of the cases we examined (e.g., La Fageda and Futur), an inadequate early understanding of a business demand was later adjusted to cater to actual market needs.

A second key dimension comes into play after identifying a demand. To satisfy such a demand, initiatives must be developed with a multiple alignment—they need to make a natural fit with the organization's mission, resources, capabilities, and customer profile. The better the fit, the less likely will the venture run into mission drift—a important risk for these enterprises.[8] Note that in nearly all the cases analyzed in this chapter this natural alignment was present, as businesses activities were central to their organizations and missions.

According to earlier studies, the third critical dimension required for market-based initiatives to succeed hinges on the crafting of an attractive value proposition with a realistic price. A key requirement in this regard is conceiving a product or service that appeals to all key stakeholders involved in the venture. At the same time, in market-based initiatives, prices need to strike a delicate balancing act, with a revenue stream that contributes to organizational sustainability and autonomy, while at the same time ensuring inclusion and social impact.

Finally, social ventures need to find an adequate scale. Small-scale operations tend to fail to cover the fixed costs involved in efficient businesses. Based on traditional economic principles, these initiatives should embrace operating and business models that are scalable or can drive economies of scale (i.e., models in which unit costs decrease as production volumes increase). This has been a major hurdle faced by several cases in this research sample.

To launch market-based initiatives, organizations must meet several conditions. Gregory Dees[9] warns about the need for organizations to be financially healthy or to rely on significant external support in order to launch successful ventures,[10] for market-based initiatives require initial investments, working capital, and management capability development. As several cases will show, when organizations develop market-based initiatives to include vulnerable groups, external support becomes even more relevant. As Dennis Young adds:[11]

Where nonprofits utilize market enterprises as vehicles for producing social benefits such as employment for disadvantaged groups ... raising revenues through the charging of prices is ... justified, though not necessarily at a level that maximizes profit. Without charging for sales of their products, these ventures cannot simulate a market experience, hence they would not produce the intended social benefits. Yet, such ventures, because they generate social benefits, can be justified even if they do not generate profits. Unless they also entail some special competitive advantages ... , these ventures will probably need some external form of support, in the form of lower wage costs, special government contracts, or subsidies that underwrite market losses.[12]

Market-based initiatives seek to diversify ventures' funding portfolios with a view to securing their sustainability or broadening organizational autonomy. SEKN's previous research into effective management of social enterprises has revealed additional advantages drawn from market discipline and the "virtuous effects" it produces, such as stricter measurements and more rigorous accountability, enhanced donor autonomy, larger operating scale—and therefore greater social impact—as well as improved financials and greater organizational capability.[13] Yet, as several authors point out and as shown by the cases studied in this chapter, it is not easy or risk-free for social enterprises to turn into market players. The conditions and requirements for social enterprises to deploy sustainable business ventures are hard to meet. At the same time, social enterprises have limited capabilities and skills for formulating successful business models. Furthermore, by focusing on business opportunities to broaden their resources, social enterprises can risk drawing away from the needs of vulnerable groups that justify their existence.[14]

Social Enterprises' Inclusive Business Strategy Patterns

Our research revealed several patterns that shed new light on social enterprises' inclusive business strategies. This discussion covers a set of dimensions that clarify the origin and characteristics of the initiatives built by social enterprises.

Initial Context and Drivers of Market-Based Initiatives
The time frame for the origin of several social enterprises studied—i.e., the 1990s—is no minor detail, as economic turnaround, market deregulation, state withdrawal and shrinkage, and increasing globalization processes seem

to have created an environment conducive to the use of market mechanisms by CSOs and cooperatives.

Some cases illustrate the influence of countrywide crises, economic (domestic and regional) or political in nature, in the late 1980s and early 1990s (Chile's institutional crisis and Argentina's hyperinflation outbreak); others occurred later (Mexico's so-called "tequila" effect"[15]); and some happened nearer the turn of the century (Brazil's stagnant economy, Argentina's convertibility collapse and devaluation). Thus, it would have been unlikely for INACAP to forgo public funding to provide higher education services and rely instead on fees and donations if not forced by the fiscal and political crisis that besieged the Chilean economy in 1989. Neither would El Ceibo's "cardboard pickers" have come together in Argentina if it had not been for the severe economic downturn that steadily impoverished the country since the late 1990s, leading to social unrest in the final days of 2001. Other ventures, especially those concerning producers from low-income sectors in rural communities—namely APAEB, CIAP and Bio Bio Pickers—originated in settings that were not particularly crisis-ridden. Rather, these initiatives emerged as a result of long exclusion, exploitation, and patronizing of *Mineiro* hemp growers, Peruvian artisans, and Chilean wild fruit pickers.

In these settings, it is essential to recognize the role played by other social actors in the initiatives' inception. While nearly half of these ventures were initiated by the cooperatives or CSOs that worked with or served low-income sectors, the rest resulted from or were greatly promoted by organizational alliances. For example, the Oro Verde Corporation emerged from Amichoco Foundation's sustainable development promotion work with Las Mojarras Foundation—an organization doing community work at the Chocó region—as well as the Tadó and Condoto Community Councils—local administrations from African-Colombian communities. Also in Colombia, Porvenir was created with support from the Social Foundation and Bogotá's Recyclers Association, a second-tier organization of recyclers who worked at the nation's capital.[16] (This aspect is analyzed in greater detail in the section on collaboration.)

Four key drivers spurred the creation of these initiatives (see Table 4.1): higher income for producers; social and labor inclusion for workers; the supply of goods and services for the poor; and income generation for the organization.

The most frequent motive for the creation of these initiatives was to secure higher income for underprivileged individuals. Another key driver was to ensure social and labor inclusion for traditionally excluded segments.

Table 4.1: Drivers in Each Initiative

Drivers	Initiative
Boosting producers' income (initiatives developed by low-income sectors)	CIAP, APAEB, Coopa-Roca, Oro Verde, Bio Bio Pickers, El Ceibo, Porvenir, Asmare
Social and labor inclusion (initiatives developed with low-income sectors)	La Fageda, Futur, El Ceibo, Porvenir, Asmare, Andrómines
Providing access to services (initiatives developed for low-income sectors)	INACAP
Income generation for the organization (initiatives with the poor as clients)	Escudo Rojo

In 11 out of the 13 ventures examined, low-income sectors were engaged as producers or workers, while only two of these initiatives viewed the poor as customers or consumers.

When low-income sectors acted as producers, they came together to enhance their leverage and/or to move up in their industry's value chain in order to capture more of the value created, thereby increasing their income. In the ventures that sought to promote social inclusion through employment opportunities, social enterprises strove to create the appropriate organizational conditions required to overcome labor exclusion. Social enterprises involved in businesses engaging LIS seem to emerge—as suggested by these cases—primarily from efforts to remedy poverty and social exclusion, seeking solutions to the income creation problem that underlies these conditions

Building and Formulating a Business Model

To launch any market-based venture, it is necessary to design and build processes and relationships that combine productive factors into a business model for the creation of economic value, in order to ensure—at least, as far social enterprises are concerned—venture continuity and sustainability for the purpose of accomplishing the social mission that gave birth to it. These models cannot be static if they intend to be sustainable. Thus, it is important to understand how the 13 models studied were built and how they were reformulated.

The cases examined display three kinds of business models developed by social enterprises. The first model was based on membership aggregation and capturing greater value, either through greater bargaining power, improved efficiency, scale, an upgrade in the value chain, or product development.[17]

The second model, based on adapting the offer to the characteristics of the demand, was used by the two ventures which provided inexpensive goods or services to low-income sectors,[18] while the third model was based on identifying business opportunities in the market that could generate jobs for previously excluded groups.[19]

Examples of the first model had the hard task of engaging Peruvian artisans, Chocó miners, hemp growers in Northern Brazil, knitters at the Rocinha *favela*, or fruit pickers in Southern Chile to promote business schemes that sought to capture a greater share of value in each chain. Bringing producers together and coordinating their actions provided greater leverage to better prices. Previously, these producers, acting on their own or on behalf of their families, had no way to command better prices from intermediaries, who captured most of the value created by the primary producing groups. In general, these initiatives first set out to work with production units that preserved their initial, limited scale,[20] but, with the support from promoter CSOs, they coordinated their efforts—through governance mechanisms as well as operating schemes and processes—with other committees, families, and individuals to accomplish greater scale. Within the same type of business model, a variant was developed for urban solid waste collectors, based on increasing the efficiency of work. This scheme encompasses Argentine, Brazilian, and Colombian waste recoverers, who engaged scattered low-income individuals and families with no access to labor opportunities as a result of poverty-related social exclusion and lack of qualifications. These initiatives also sought to bypass or to the extent possible limit the role of intermediaries, who used to abuse individual or family waste collectors when selling inorganic waste to industry recyclers. Under the new initiative, the recyclers set out to expand the scale of their operations not only by gathering and organizing "cardboard pickers," but also by streamlining work processes, such as organizing, classifying, and storing the waste collected. This enabled them to secure the volume required to sell waste to recycling companies that turned it into industry raw materials, shunning intermediaries (not always successfully) or, at least, gaining more leverage in the often obscure recycling value chain.

Once producers were grouped and a larger scale was attained to secure better prices, some initiatives did manage to move forward in the value generation chain by doing away with intermediaries. The Bio Bio Pickers' case was a success in this process. By building fruit dehydrating plants themselves, the organization's committees were able to avoid wild fruit collection seasonality, incorporating an operation that was previously carried out by intermediaries and securing a kilo price five times higher than before.

Other ventures came to realize that they could bolster their revenues if they added more value to their primary products. Thus, in activities associated with LIS community traditions, such as CIAP's Peruvian handicrafts or gold mining at the Chocó region in Colombia, producers enriched raw materials, turning them into more value-added goods, or designed traditional products, such as the jewelry and wood handicrafts produced by the more active artisan committees at CIAP. Some of these ventures have even managed to add value by selling their products through international fair-trade networks, which promoted the adoption of quality assurance standards as well.[21] An aspect that should be noted in the development of this kind of business model was the creation of marketing agencies, legally independent from but controlled by parent social enterprises. This scheme provides a twofold benefit: a more business-like management and an often more transparent relationship with tax authorities. For example, Oro Verde created Biodiversa to streamline its trading operations, isolating them from the organization's community development and producer support activities. CIAP followed a similar path when it created Intercrafts Perú SAC, a company wholly owned by CIAP's partner artisans, with marketing and exports operations separated from production.

Waste collection organizations pursued a similar strategy by reformulating their business models to add more value to their products through processing of raw materials, plastic and cardboard cleaning and/or packing, and even moving forward into basic recycling industrialization processes. Thus, by joining seven other waste collector associations and cooperatives, Asmare raised funds to build a plastics recycling plant in order to both add value to products and to climb up in the recycling value chain ladder.[22]

For some ventures, efforts to boost revenues did not necessarily require organizing or aggregating producers to improve bargaining power, or adding value to raw materials or primary products. Neither did it mean moving forward along the value chain. Rather, it required a redefinition of their products. For instance, Coopa-Roca set out to increase its revenues by offering new, more value-added products to fashion and design industries.[23] Although it continued to employ traditional techniques at all times, the organization went from manufacturing carpets and bedspreads to producing pieces and accessories for the more dynamic fashion market, as the Brazilian fashion industry started to grow internationally in the mid 1990s. Indeed, Coopa-Roca began to manufacture bikinis with *fuxico,* a patchwork technique used in Brazil's northern region, significantly boosting its sales thereby.

A second business model was employed by initiatives providing goods (Escudo Rojo's second-hand store in Buenos Aires) or services (INACAP's higher education programs in Chile) to low-income sectors. This model is quite straightforward, for it adjusted its supply to its potential market. Escudo Rojo sold donated, second-hand clothes, appliances, and furniture at very low prices, creating a value proposition that appealed to the poor in terms of pricing, store location, store layout, service, etc. Donations to Escudo Rojo relied on the venture's ties to the Salvation Army. It should be noted that neither venture focused exclusively on serving underprivileged sectors, but they both zeroed in on market opportunities that included low-income sectors. Reformulations for this model were minor, including merely new product offerings and adjustments to operation, human resources, or marketing management practices.

Finally, some initiatives developed the third business model to remedy labor exclusion—either for mentally and emotionally challenged individuals or socially alienated people, like illegal immigrants, former convicts, the homeless. The business model pursued by these organizations was based on identifying market opportunities to generate profit. These groups were involved in the production of goods (La Fageda's yogurts) or services (Futur's catering services) that were outstanding and competitive for their markets by achieving differentiation.

All these business models had to be revised and reformulated in order to generate value. The organizations followed a distinctive business model reformulation path, with significant strategic shifts that forced them to forgo their initial operations in order to focus on other activities with greater growth and profitability prospects. It should be noted that these strategic turns continued to yield uncertain results. For instance, La Fageda ventured into gardening, later switched to productive, food-related activities, and, finally, it moved from milk production to yogurt manufacturing as a result of restraints imposed by the European Union to Spanish milk producers. Futur underwent a similar experience, migrating from the textile industry to the catering business. Possibly, these bold changes were supported by continued public support for efforts addressing the plight of excluded, discriminated groups.

In short, regardless of the business model pursued, several organizations in this sample managed to reformulate their business schemes and to follow growth strategies that consolidated their sustainability and enhanced their social impact (see Table 4.2). Their growth displayed several patterns.

Collaboration in Social Enterprises' Market-based Initiatives
Most social enterprises in this study were able to develop and sustain inclusive businesses by collaborating with other organizations. These partnerships

Table 4.2: Business Models and Reformulations

	Aggregation/bargaining power for LIS	Offering low prices to LIS (*for* and *to* LIS)	Identifying business opportunities (with LIS)
Initial Model	APAEB Collectors Coopa-Roca Oro Verde CIAP Asmare El Ceibo Porvenir	INACAP Escudo Rojo	Andrómines Futur La Fageda
Reformulation: Value chain step-up	APAEB (carpet factory), Bio Bio Pickers (dehydration and packing plants) Asmare (plastic recycling plant)		Andrómines (stores, exports)
Reformulation: Product/Service Redefinition	Bio Bio Pickers (other fruits, mushrooms, etc.) CIAP (design revamping for several textile, bijouterie, pottery, wood products) Coopa-Roca (new textile and design products)	INACAP (new program offerings) Escudo Rojo (new product categories)	Futur (organic products for catering services, etc.) La Fageda (new dairy products)
Reformulation: Diversification	CIAP (tourism and saving products, etc.) Porvenir (cleaning services— later discontinued) El Ceibo (consulting services, bar) Asmare (bar)		La Fageda (dairy products)
Reformulation: Strategic Turns			La Fageda (from religious artistry to dairy products) Futur (from textiles to food services)

took several forms, with three major types that unfolded successively or simultaneously: 1) a relationship with an *allied organization*—an institution that played a crucial role in venture development; 2) a relationship with a set of private, civil society, or public sector actors that were part of the ecosystem that enabled the existence of these ventures; or 3) ties with public sector actors. In any of these collaboration schemes, relationships were built on the basis of business arrangements (supplying goods to fair-trade networks, for instance), or through funding assistance, access to markets and networks, or training. In the case of public sector actors, in addition to these ties, other forms of advocacy were observed.

The inclusion strategies pursued by a significant number of cooperatives and CSOs studied in this chapter have featured an instrumental involvement of institutions other than the social enterprises launching these initiatives. These institutions—essential to the creation or sustainability of social enterprises' ventures—are the "allied organizations."

Alliance building is a dynamic process; to understand the type of relationship built, timing is a key factor to be taken into account. Allied organizations may thus be characterized (see Table 4.3) as *promoters,* with a primary role only during an initiative's inception; *protectors,* with an ongoing, crucial involvement throughout an initiative's lifecycle; and *partners,* with an essential strategic role in the successful development of an initiative, and a share of the benefits.

Table 4.3: Types of Allied Organizations

Promoter Organizations	Asmare-Pastoral da Rua (promoted collaboration, supported and strengthened waste collectors' activities in order to reinforce their dignity and citizenship); APAEB-Comunidades Eclesiais de Base or CEBs and Movimento de Organização Comunitária or MOC (CEB mobilized rural producers to support their self-organization, while MOC fostered economic project development and established funds to encourage and value local production); Porvenir-Fundación Social (provided funding for venture inception).
Protector Organizations	Bio Bio Pickers-Taller de Acción Cultural (at first, it supported collectors' organizing process; later, it strengthened production by training on fruit dehydration, management, accounting and marketing; it also helped pickers to contact local agribusinesses and forest companies in order to get more training and access to international markets); Oro Verde-Fundación Amichoco (currently performing a central role in Oro Verde's administrative, management and marketing processes).
Partner Organizations	CIAP–International Association for Alternative Trade or IFAT (international network for fair-trade promotion and practice that channeled 87% of CIAP's sales and provided training on accountability, reporting and evaluation); INACAP–Confederación de la Producción y el Comercio or CPC (Chilean business community association), Andrómines-Programa Roba Amiga (joint employment opportunity project by Fundació Un Sol Món, Aires and Cáritas Catalunya, using second-hand clothing collection, food services, recycling, and sales to offer labor inclusion to handicapped segments); Oro Verde-Association for Responsible Mining (ARM), international agency that promotes global transparency and legitimacy in mining and supported Oro Verde through training and standard setting.

Promoter organizations performed a crucial role in the formation of cohesive groups, as well as in their access to networks and resources. These organizations contributed resources, training, networking, raising awareness of operations' economic and social value, or boosting affiliates' self-esteem. Some of these promoters were ecclesiastical, like Asmare's promoter Pastoral da Rua,[24] others were grassroots organizations, or even second-level organizations, like MOC and ARB, promoters for APAEB and Porvenir, respectively. Promoter organizations ceased to have a dominant role when ventures started to show signs of autonomous, efficient behavior, but they did not withdraw entirely, remaining in contact—more or less formally—with the ventures' governance bodies (e.g., Pastoral at Asmare).

New ventures' relationships with protector organizations resembled those built with promoter organizations, but the protectors were also involved throughout venture evolution, as was TAC with Bio Bio Pickers in Chile or Fundación Amichocó at Oro Verde, supporting them by networking with other organizations or building trade. It was expected that social enterprises would gain greater autonomy and eventually carry out these tasks on their own, although the timing was not yet defined in the planning.[25] Both promoter and protector organizations match the development field's definition of "support organizations."

Partner organizations played a critical role in making the new ventures viable by providing continued access to markets, managing sales channels, or acting as regular customers. In some cases, these partners, such as IFAT for CIAP and Roba Amiga for Andrómines, included international networks or local civil society actors. In some cases, partner organizations supported the initiatives' improvement efforts. Such was the case of INACAP, with the CPC business association serving as "client," using the educational institution's capabilities to prepare the human resources it required. IFAT provided CIAP with access to fair-trade networks, but, at the same time, it drove the initiative to adopt performance measurement criteria and to focus on management skill development, encouraging CIAP to embrace an engaging, standardized, and transparent scheme.

Regardless of the relationship forged by some ventures with allied organizations, nearly all the social enterprises explored in this study were forced to network or to build collaboration ties with other agents—though to a lesser extent than with their allied organizations—in order to develop their initiatives. This type of collaboration materialized through networking, market access, trade agreements, funding, and training, although these relationships were not as intense as those established with partners. The actors involved included companies, other CSOs and public agencies, and, in some cases, these collaboration efforts were initially hindered by ideological prejudice or fear of curtailed autonomy.

Several examples illustrate these less profound, more ad-hoc, but still highly significant ties. For instance, Fundação Banco do Brasil provided funding for Asmare and seven other waste collector cooperatives from Belo Horizonte to build a US$2 million plastic recycling plant, enabling these initiatives to do away with market intermediaries, to move forward in their value chain, and to add more value to the enterprise. CLIBA (Compañía Latinoamericana de Ingeniería Básica Ambiental)[26] trained El Ceibo's waste collectors and furnished them with equipment, while Greenpeace offered them initial recycling and environmental care training. As a result, El Ceibo was able to innovate and enhance its waste collection process by forging ties with apartment building janitors and residents in its focal operating areas.

In addition to ties to allied organizations and private institutions, social enterprises often engage in relationships with public entities, as did organizations that worked in social and labor inclusion initiatives (La Fageda, Futur, or Andrómines in Spain) or in urban waste collection ventures (El Ceibo, Asmare). In these latter ventures, the support of the public sector seemed to be quite significant, either through subsidies or by providing usage rights over plots of land (in the cases of Asmare and El Ceibo).

In all Spanish labor-oriented initiatives in this study and the ventures created by Argentine and Brazilian waste collectors, state agencies provided subsidies that complemented existing funding or were used to purchase venture equipment. Relationships with state agencies seemed to last longer than those forged with private actors and international or domestic CSOs, probably as a result of a more favorable political determination to address exclusion (social and labor exclusion in Spain or environmental exclusion in the case of waste collectors). State agencies provided not only subsidies but also contracts for social enterprises' services, as illustrated by the case Andrómines—hired to collect, recycle, and dispose of urban waste by local administrations in Montcada and other neighboring Catalonian towns.

Likewise, social enterprises' relationship with local administrations often took a new turn, leading to a more active role in policy-making. For example, CIAP's artisans joined the executive committee of GRESP (Grupo Red de Economías Solidarias), an institution that promoted solidarity economics and included some 200 organizations. This committee discussed and lobbied for the approval of an Artisans' Act, which was later legislated.

Leadership and Governance in Social Enterprises' Inclusive Business

Two factors—leadership and organizational governance—help to explain how social enterprises manage to build market-based inclusive initiatives. Viewing leadership as the ability to perceive opportunities and drive the changes needed to yield results,[27] three characteristics associated with entre-preneurs can be clearly identified: an innovative approach to venture cre-ation or reformulation, a willingness to take risks in order to operate in competitive markets, and an ability to make any necessary internal adjust-ments to secure better results.

The innovative nature of leadership showed in the development of an attractive value proposition for some goods or services. These cases featured individuals who formulated an innovating strategy to accomplish their social missions. The Cock brothers did this at Amichocó, when, after studying abroad, they discovered that economic, social, and environmental improve-ments in responsible gold mining could be driven in Colombia: the operat-ing principle underlying Oro Verde. However, innovating leadership was found not only in production-related ventures, but also in service offerings. For example, El Ceibo's founder, Cristina Lescano, gave a twist to the tradi-tional notion of urban—often stealthy—inorganic waste recovery, building a network with "supplying" homes to collect waste in pre-set schedules. Thus, she reformulated the role of informal waste collectors, turning them into "urban waste recoverers" environmentally educated by Greenpeace.

Other leaders took risks in order to promote initiatives in competitive markets. For instance, psychiatrist Cristóbal Colón envisioned, through a productive labor program and close patient follow-up, a way to build a com-petitive venture with mentally challenged individuals at La Fageda, which became a successful yogurt manufacturer. Another example is provided by Teté, Coopa-Roca's founder, who promoted traditional handicraft tech-niques from Brazil's northeastern region, where most cooperative members came from, to create textile products of distinctive Brazilian design. Later, when Brazil's textile industry gained a greater share in international mar-kets, after their exposure in acclaimed fashion-week runway shows, Coopa-Roca's products were sought by renowned fashion and design brands around the world. Similarly, Almirall's entrepreneurial vision shifted Futur's business focus from the textile sector, where the organization was not per-forming as expected, to businesses with more potential in Catalonia, includ-ing the booming hospitality industry.

Several leaders showed their entrepreneurial ability to drive changes and improvements for ventures seeking to accomplish more ambitious results than their founders had envisaged. For instance, Colonel Páez, aided by Juan

Rodríguez, introduced significant changes to Escudo Rojo's operations and management, although the venture operated within a strong pyramidal structure. As a result, despite some resistance from long-time organization members, he managed to professionalize the institution's human resources and processes, turning Escudo Rojo into Argentina's second-hand goods leader. Its performance clearly proved the adequateness of these changes: Escudo Rojo's monthly sales rose from US$30,000 in 2003 to US$120,000 by mid 2007.

It should be noted that, in some ventures, entrepreneurial leadership was provided by other institutions—either promoter or protector organizations. These initiatives did not have an entrepreneur that put a defining mark in their inception or startup process. Rather, they have been developed, at least initially, with leadership provided by other organizations.[28] This scheme with outside leadership was also found in some initiatives at later stages.

The analysis of leadership in market-based inclusive initiatives developed by social enterprises should also inquire how concentrated and distributed leadership is in an organization. The ventures studied featured both strong leaderships—with one individual playing a highly influential role—and more distributed, horizontal leaderships, with individuals exerting less influence. Clearly, founders played a significant role in shaping the organizations' leadership model and style (Lescano at El Ceibo, Colón at La Fageda, Teté at Coopa-Roca). In other experiences, personal leadership was strengthened when an individual achieved success in changing the type of business (Almirall in Futur) and when internal consolidation occurred, as seen at Porvenir or Andrómines when this study was conducted.[29]

Organizations devoted to social and labor inclusion in Spain, as well as those selling goods or services to LIS in Latin America, like Escudo Rojo and INACAP, had strong personal leadership. Waste collection organizations—El Ceibo, Porvenir and Asmare—showed dissimilar leadership patterns, however. El Ceibo was created and led by one individual, with no significant support from, or involvement of, other organizations. Asmare presented a rather horizontal structure, with two organizations, MOC and CEB, playing a dominant leadership role in its inception. After a leadership change, Porvenir seemed headed for a centralized, more professional leadership scheme.

Regardless of the type of leadership embraced, the governance model that describes the organization members' involvement in major decision-making processes helps to understand the development of these ventures. Organizations whose business models included LIS as producers had to establish a more engaging governance scheme and a flatter decision-making structure.

Yet, despite formal governance schemes, governance models ultimately depended on leaders' or entrepreneurs' style. For instance, although El Ceibo's formal governance structure followed the usual participatory scheme of cooperatives, decisions in this organization tended to be entrusted to founder Lescano. While a wider governance scheme may respond to a business model that hinges on gathering LIS individuals, execution difficulties and strongly influential founders or support organizations may also affect governance; these variations may reflect the underprivileged sectors' inexperience in collective coordination, paternalistic traits, or the effect of promoter and protector CSOs' operating model, which led to their strong involvement in venture decisions—not only in the startup stages but also throughout venture development.

Conversely, concentrated decision-making power and vertical governance structures seemed to be naturally adopted by organizations embarking on sustainable, market-based initiatives including LIS as customers or primarily seeking their social and labor inclusion. For instance, INACAP was governed by its Board and Dean, with a highly pyramidal structure, while at Futur, the same scheme was marked by Almirall's strong leadership.

There is a close link between type of leadership and governance model. Indeed, CIAP's more distributed leadership matched the influence of each artisan committee on the organization's decision-making scheme. Also, a strong, innovating personal leadership at venture inception seems to accommodate a more vertical governance scheme. Thus, La Fageda established a pyramidal structure, while El Ceibo and Coopa-Roca formally instituted a horizontal structure, although actually Lescano and Teté made the important decisions. In short, leadership and governance seem to depend both on the business model adopted and the role played by LIS in value chains, as well as on organizational culture, environmental characteristics, and dynamics.

Social Enterprises' Funding Model and Economic Value

The ventures launched by CSOs and cooperatives in this study created funding models that turned to the market as their major source of sustainability and growth. Their performance as market-based initiatives, however, did not exclude the use and exploitation of other funding sources, as long as they contributed to their social missions.

Given the crucial role played by allied organizations to ensure ventures' inception, consolidation, growth, and sustainability, it comes as no surprise that, in most cases, there was extensive public, private, domestic, and/or international support (in the form of resources, supplies, etc.). Grants and assistance were key components of collaboration strategies and exerted significant influence on ventures' autonomy.

The funding scheme that included subsidies or external economic contributions—adopted by six of the 13 social enterprises studied—limited ventures' independence to some extent, primarily in economic terms. For instance, Futur received subsidies from the autonomous Catalan government equivalent to 29 percent of its sales. In some cases, like those of Argentine and Brazilian collectors, subsidies seemed to be embedded in their business models (funding and supply of facilities, equipment, or infrastructure). This support came not only out of a recognition of the excluded population working on waste collection in areas of great visibility (large cities), but also of new efforts by local administrations to promote cooperative activities in these sectors in order to mitigate the effects of economic crises on the poor or to respond to critical and urgent environmental issues. At the same time, both cooperatives of urban solid waste collectors relied on other resources (training, supplies, cash) provided by foreign agencies. These organizations intended for this aid to decrease in time, but neither Asmare nor El Ceibo included this intention explicitly or consistently in their strategies. In contrast, Oro Verde did move forward in this direction by formulating a business model that sought to do away with international subsidies, planning to cover all of Biodiversa's marketing costs autonomously by 2009.[30]

Ventures that managed to operate without economic contributions but relied on strong support or collaboration from individuals or domestic or international CSOs also experienced restrictions to their structural or governance independence. Such was the case of Andrómines' integration into the Roba Amiga Program. Andrómines benefited from a donation of 49 containers, a truck, and two stores as a result of Un Sol Mon Foundation's support to that program. This helped the Catalonian organization to collect in 2004 four times more clothing than in 2002, and, more important, to offer 20 times as many kilos of clothing, capturing a greater share of value. Andrómines also reorganized its structure and professionalized its culture as a result of its incorporation into the Ropa Amiga Program.[31] At the same time, the constraints imposed on Andrómines by this program seemed to be offset by tangible rewards in economic value creation.

In recent years, social enterprises receiving assistance showed good overall financial performance,[32] but their evaluation would be different if they ceased to receive that support—for example, from allied institutions that facilitated their access to trade networks. In some cases, venture short-term sustainability seemed secured, albeit with some dependence or vulnerability, as illustrated by CIAP. This organization channeled nearly 90 percent of its sales through IFAT, displaying its latent vulnerability to any changes in this network.

Greater independence may be found in ventures with no subsidies that managed to draw away from their allied organizations, such as Porvenir (that had overcome its separation from Fundación Social and was advancing towards leadership professionalization) and APAEB (with lower support from other actors at inception), and in initiatives featuring LIS as customers. Social enterprises of this type improved their economic performance as a result of long processes. INACAP was forced to learn to operate with no state assistance, while Escudo Rojo had to embark on management professionalization—an aspect of its development which had been neglected until the early 1990s—to pave the way for greater profitability. These social enterprises met an actual market demand, and therefore their more independent funding models spared them the need to seek other financial sources. In contrast, the funding models of most LIS organizations—nine out of eleven cases—did require other sources to complement operating revenues. Supporting themselves solely by market proceeds seemed more difficult for these organizations because they incurred greater costs to promote LIS productive or collaborative capabilities, to coordinate supply, to expand their scale in order to do away with intermediaries or to access international networks from excluded areas.

Multidimensional Social Value Creation

Because inclusive goals are embedded in their missions, values, and operations, CSOs and cooperatives are expected to create social value unequivocally. Market-based ventures with inclusive missions and goals, like the social enterprises studied, also create—not as an externality, but explicitly— social value in multiple dimensions: lowering barriers, helping underprivileged sectors, and/or mitigating side effects from business activities. At the same time, most of the cases studied created a so-called macro-social value: they expanded society's boundaries. In general terms, it should come as no surprise that the most prominent form of social value created is closely linked to mission-driven inclusiveness.[33]

The development of job-related skills and competencies as well as the enhancement of self-esteem for formerly excluded groups have been core components of the social value created by these ventures—not only those specifically focusing on labor inclusion, but also waste collection organizations and ventures engaging LIS as producers-workers in underprivileged communities—both urban (Coopa-Roca's artisans, who came from Brazil's northeastern region but resided at Rio de Janeiro's Rocinha slums) and rural (Bio Bio Pickers in southern Chile).

Access to goods and services provided by the removal or reduction of entry barriers or income limitations was another social value created in most cases. Barrier reduction was an explicit goal for organizations seeking to boost LIS producers' income as well as for initiatives offering job opportunities to excluded segments. However, this social value was also created by two cases that did not feature these drivers (Escudo Rojo and INACAP). Although barrier reduction was not Escudo Rojo's *raison d'être*, this venture enabled LIS to have disposable income for other purposes by offering clothing, home appliances, and furniture at lower prices, and even in some cases affording them a chance to serve as resellers at poor neighborhoods or slums.

Additionally, six initiatives succeeded in mitigating undesirable environmental side effects of business. For example, Oro Verde explicitly opposed large-scale extractive exploitation, which usually brings a harmful environmental impact as a result of cyanide utilization. While urban waste recovery cooperatives emphasized environmental care more (El Ceibo) or less explicitly (Porvenir) explicitly, they did contribute to its advancement.[34]

In addition to those mentioned, some of the ventures studied have created social value in associated fields. Producers' associations, usually located in underprivileged rural areas (CIAP, Oro Verde, APAEB, Bio Bio Pickers), not only enhanced LIS access to goods and services by increasing their income, but also infused other social values into communities, such as a sense of belonging, a reluctance to migrate to urban areas, revitalized local economy and culture, and social capital promotion as a result of collaborative efforts among workers. Solid waste collecting initiatives provided a sense of belonging while dignifying the group's work and enhancing its self-esteem. Thus, since most cases created social value in all three dimensions, it may be concluded that, by pursuing market-based strategies for low-income sectors, social enterprises seem to become multidimensional value-creating agents.

Finally, most experiences were found to create a macro-type social value: the recognition of some low-income and vulnerable groups as part of society. In general, before the initiatives were created, mentally handicapped Catalonians, Rocinha's knitting mothers, or cardboard collectors in Buenos Aires' Palermo neighborhood were usually ignored as actors or unintegrated into the social fabric. Furthermore, they were mostly considered as outsiders in local citizenship schemes—true pariahs, *lumpen*, forgotten segments, or troublesome groups. These initiatives changed that situation, enabling underprivileged sectors to acquire job skills, to increase their leverage, to gain access to goods and services, to enhance their self-confidence, to protect the environment, to avoid migration, and to revalue their community culture. Perhaps more important, these ventures have granted greater visibility to LIS, turning them into relevant social actors playing a role in collective issues and formal markets.

Conclusions and Managerial Lessons

Social enterprises that develop inclusive market initiatives have a significant capacity to fulfill their "social value proposition." Experiences encompassed in our research sample show how these organizations can simultaneously create several kinds of social value by eliminating access and economic barriers, strengthening excluded groups with weak collective identities, or mitigating negative market effects. Their capacity to do so affects not only low-income sectors' lives but also society at large, as it contributes to building social capital and inclusive societies. However, to deliver this social impact, these market-based initiatives need to face several management challenges described below.

1. Formulating Sustainable Business Models that Fit Social Missions

Good intentions and inclusive goals are not enough to build sustainable businesses. CSOs and cooperatives often have a hard time "reading" markets adequately and identifying business opportunities with sustainability potential. While this may happen to any type of organization, the difficulty is more severe for CSOs and cooperatives because of their emphasis on meeting social needs rather than on "doing business."

The key to success for socially inclusive, market-based initiatives has been their ability to make substantial adjustments to their behaviors and activities. Revisions of initial business models enabled organizations to move towards greater initiative sustainability, either through industry shifts, business diversification, or product line adjustments. In this reformulation and adaptation process, a clear alignment between organizational purpose and business models proved to be a primary driver for venture fulfillment, in the sense of creating more revenues and promoting social and labor inclusion or access to goods and services for LIS.

2. Seeking an Adequate Scale for Ventures

In business, "small is rarely beautiful." Finding a suitable scale is a major challenge for social enterprises. In general, this type of organizations finds it very hard to overcome some constraints (financing, business know-how, etc.), a situation which, in turn, leads to small-scale operations. These

restrictions make it difficult to build management teams or make infrastructure improvement investments, among others.

To some extent, business model adjustments may be attributed to a
search for greater volume and scope. Several sample organizations managed to increase their operating volume by means of alliances and collaborations with other organizations—working with other institutions is a way
to take a leap to larger scale. Another way to move on to a larger scale is to
pursue a strategy that only a few initiatives in this sample managed to adopt:
that of structure professionalization as well as commercial and management process revision to accomplish greater efficiency. In any case, developing a suitable business scale emerged as an ongoing challenge for sample
social enterprises.

3. Building Smart, Creative, and Pragmatic Alliances

Forging strategic collaboration ties with other organizations in various evolutionary stages turned out to be instrumental to ensuring venture emergence, consolidation, growth, and sustainability. This type of collaboration
was vital for social enterprises developing socially inclusive, market-based
initiatives.

There is always a risk that assistance received from the organizations we
have called "promoters" and "protectors" eventually comes to hinder creativity, autonomy, and independence. However, sample social enterprises
have smartly exploited these collaborations as leverage for greater sustainability.

At the same time, the initiatives examined displayed multiple engagements—of a more shallow and instrumental nature—with other social
actors, companies, or state agencies. The kind of value created by these relationships or network involvement was diverse, including business arrangements, technical assistance, training, contacts with relevant actors, or
financing. Managing these collaborative relationships, both with allied
organizations and with other value chain members, required flexibility and
pragmatism from the social enterprises.

4. Leading for Sustainability

It is not possible to reformulate business models, find a suitable scale, and
develop collaboration strategies without a sound leadership based on a clear
vision of the value of market-based approaches to organizational sustainability. Indeed, three key features of sample ventures' leadership help to
understand the success of these initiatives—willingness to innovate, to take
risks, and to make internal adjustments to boost economic performance. This

kind of leadership may be provided from inside the organizations—by founders or other members—or outside—by a partner organization. In any case, the role of leadership has proven to be crucial for sample initiatives.

Our research study also revealed the need for most social enterprises to further strengthen their organizational capabilities to develop market-based initiatives efficiently and profitably. To rise to this challenge, it is necessary to build consensus on the importance of understanding and introducing administrative and economic principles and criteria into social enterprises' management models. In addition, management and operating teams should strengthen and professionalize their practices through the acquisition of technical skills that are currently unusual for social enterprises.

A powerful image from a Greek myth may illuminate the challenges faced by social enterprises launching inclusive ventures. While at sea after leaving Circe, Ulysses asked to be tied to his ship's mast in order to avoid being lured into a certain death by mermaids' tempting songs. Social enterprises' leaders may find themselves in a similar position. On the one hand, they need to tie themselves to their masts to prevent excessive personalization, which curtails the development of management structures and jeopardizes venture continuity. On the other hand, they should avoid listening only to mission "songs," luring them away from business strategy formulation and the use of modern management tools to accomplish their social goals. Finally, this same self-discipline should be exercised when exposed to market "mermaids"—succumbing to their charm would imply (regardless of economic results) forgetting the inclusive purpose of these initiatives and foregoing the accomplishment of their social objectives.

Notes

1. For a more detailed analysis of these organizations, see chapter 7.
2. Lester M. Salamon and Helmut K. Anheier, *The Emerging Nonprofit Sector: An Overview* (Manchester, UK: Manchester University Press, 1996).
3. Lester M. Salamon, "The Rise of the Nonprofit Sector," *Foreign Affairs* 73, no. 4 (1994).
4. Lester M. Salamon and Dennis Young, "Commercialization, Social Ventures, and for-profit Competition," in *The State of Nonprofit America*, ed. Lester M. Salamon (Washington, D.C.: Brookings Institution Press, 2003); Ezequiel Reficco, Roberto Gutiérrez, and Diana Trujillo, "Empresas sociales: ¿una especie en busca de reconocimiento?" *Revista de Administração da Universidade de São Paulo* 41, no. 4 (Oct.–Dec. 2006).
5. In the United States, the term "social enterprise" has been primarily used to refer to social organizations applying business methods or building business ventures to support themselves entirely or partly, with management principles

and practices commonly associated with for-profit organizations. Yet, the legal definition of social enterprises is broad, ranging from for-profit organizations developing activities with explicit, positive social impact to organizations using business operations to accomplish a social mission. The organizational format used is irrelevant to define a social enterprise—what matters is its content and purpose: Dennis R. Young, "Social Enterprise in the United States: Alternate Identities and Forms" (paper presented at the conference L'Impresa Sociale In Prospettiva Comparata, Trento, Italia; Istituto Studi Sviluppo Aziende Non-profit, Universidad de Trento, December 13–15 2001); Janelle A. Kerlin, "Social Enterprise in the United States and Europe: Understanding and Learning from the Differences," *Voluntas* 17 (2006). This definition of social enterprise excludes institutions explicitly redistributing proceeds among organizational members. Although the American definition of social enterprises does not allow for private distribution of proceeds, its European counterpart does accept such distribution—albeit with moderation. Kerlin, "Social Enterprise in the United States and Europe: Understanding and Learning from the Differences," *Voluntas* 17 (2006). By allowing income redistribution among members, the European social enterprise also encompasses cooperatives and other organizations that address excluded groups' employment and inclusion issues. Dennis R. Young, "Social Enterprise in the United States: Alternate Identities and Forms" (paper presented at the conference L' Impresa Sociale In Prospettiva Comparata, Trento, Italia; Istituto Studi Sviluppo Aziende Nonprofit, Universidad de Trento, December 13–15 2001), 3. European academics view social enterprises as associated with social economics. The notion of social economics—popular, labor, or solidarity economics in Spanish-speaking nations; social or cooperative economics in French-speaking countries, and community economic development in English-speaking states—covers new productive (both formal and informal) forms based on cooperation and solidarity.

6. As noted by some authors, these market activities may even register losses, but they still diversify funding. Beth Battle Anderson, Gregory Dees, and Jed Emerson, "Developing Viable Earned Income Strategies," in *Strategic Tools for Social Entrepreneurs: Enhancing the Performance of Your Enterprising Nonprofit*, ed. J. Gregory Dees, Jed Emerson, and Peter Economy (New York, NY: Wiley, 2002), 192.

7. Ibid.; Leslie M. Fox and Bruce Schearer, eds., *Sostenibilidad de la sociedad civil. estrategias para la movilización de recursos* (Cali, Colombia: Civicus, 1998), especially pp. 21–43; Rolfe Larson, *Venture Forth! The Essential Guide to Starting a Moneymaking Business in Your Nonprofit Organization* (St. Paul, MN: Amherst H. Wilder Foundation, 2002), especially pp. 5–18; Sharon M. Oster, Cynthia W. Massarsky, and Samantha L. Beinhacker, eds., *Generating and Sustaining Nonprofit Earned Income: A Guide to Successful Enterprise Strategies* (San Francisco: Jossey-Bass, 2004).

8. In any case, it should be noted that if a market-based initiative has greater "multiple alignment," it may raise stronger moral objections. Beth Battle Anderson, Gregory Dees, and Jed Emerson, "Developing Viable Earned Income Strategies," in *Strategic Tools for Social Entrepreneurs: Enhancing the Performance of Your Enterprising Nonprofit*, ed. J. Gregory Dees, Jed Emerson, and Peter Economy (New York, NY: Wiley, 2002), 198. This was the case of the Brazilian handicrafts venture, showcased in this chapter.

9. Gregory Dees, "Putting Nonprofit Business Ventures in Perspective," in *Generating and Sustaining Nonprofit Earned Income: A Guide to Successful Enterprise Strategies*, ed. Sharon M. Oster, Cynthia W. Massarsky, and Samantha L. Beinhacker (San Francisco. CA: Jossey-Bass, 2004); Gregory Dees, "Why Social Entrepreneurship Is Important to You," in *Enterprising Nonprofits: A Toolkit for Social Entrepreneurs*, ed. J. Gregory Dees, Peter Economy, and Jed Emerson (New York, NY: Wiley, 2001).

10. Some authors argue that the fact that initiatives require external financial support to complement revenues obtained from the market is not intrinsically problematic. Foster and Bradach make this point quite eloquently when they state, "A mission-promoting activity that covers half its costs through earned income could have more impact per philanthropic dollar than a less mission-focused activity that covers three-quarters of its costs." William Foster and Jeffrey Bradach, "Should Nonprofits Seek Profits?" *Harvard Business Review* (February 2005): 9.

11. Dennis R. Young, "Nonprofit Finance Theory," National Center for Nonprofit Enterprise, http://www.nationalcne.org/index.cfm?fuseaction=feature.display&feature_id=27.

12. Ibid.

13. SEKN, ed., *Effective Management of Social Enterprises: Lessons from Businesses and Civil Society Organizations in Iberoamerica* (Cambridge, MA: Harvard University Press with David Rockefeller Center for Latin American Studies, 2006).

14. Dees, "Putting Nonprofit Business Ventures in Perspective"; Salamon and Anheier, *The Emerging Nonprofit Sector: An Overview*.

15. The impact of the Mexican economic crisis on the Southern Cone and Brazil came to be known popularly as the "Tequila Effect."

16. In addition, it should be noted that ASMARE relied on support from Belo Horizonte Archdiocese's Pastoral da Rua. Also, in APAEB's inception, a significant role was played by Comunidades Eclesiais de Base—which promoted critical awareness in local communities, debating social exclusion in the context of Bible discussion—and the Movimento de Organização Comunitária. Bio Bio Pickers was created by the Taller de Acción Cultural (TAC)—an organization that enabled communities to self-manage and overcome exclusion—and CIAP, supported by Servicio de Paz y Justicia (SERPAJ), an Evangelic institution devoted to non-violence advocacy.

17. APAEB, CIAP, Oro Verde, Bio Bio Pickers, Coopa-Roca, and the three waste collection organizations.
18. Escudo Rojo and INACAP.
19. La Fageda, Andrómines and Futur all seek inclusive employment.
20. For example, committees built by a dozen producers in Chile or artisan groups at CIAP.
21. Another business model reformulation option consisted of diversifying activities. For instance, CIAP did not reformulate its core business (handicraft sales); instead, it broadened and diversified its business portfolio, offering tourism and savings services to organizational members.
22. The fact that Asmare managed to do this only with a pool of collectors' associations indicates how hard it is for waste collectors to add value to their job and how effective their networking can be. This initiative was in the course of implementation by the time the fieldwork for this study was completed.
23. In 2003, the organization produced over 7,000 pieces and around 4,000 pieces in 2005. However, during the same period, Coopa-Roca's revenues rose by more than 60%, which proves the greater value added by each piece.
24. Salamon and Anheier highlight the significant role of the Catholic Church in Brazilian nonprofits: "[Support] . . . The remaining 25 percent comes from transfers from parent organizations like the Catholic Church." Lester M. Salamon and Helmut K. Anheier, *The Emerging Nonprofit Sector: An Overview* (Manchester, UK: Manchester University Press, 1996), 106.
25. Although the two organizations had not separated completely, their plans explicitly foresaw that Oro Verde would operate self-sufficiently in the near future.
26. Waste collection company in charge of one of the areas in Buenos Aires.
27. SEKN, ed. *Effective Management of Social Enterprises Lessons from Businesses and Civil Society Organizations in Iberoamerica* (Cambridge, MA: Harvard University Press with David Rockefeller Center for Latin American Studies, 2006).
28. For example, at APAEB, Asmare, or Bío Bío Pickers.
29. At organizations providing services to the poor, with a longer history and greater institutionalization (Escudo Rojo and INACAP), personal leadership was still present. Although these two cases present some differences in their governance bodies' specialization and formalization, their pyramidal leadership scheme was unquestioned and seemed to be part of their organizational models.
30. Biodiversa was an independent venture created by Amichocó to serve as Oro Verde's marketing affiliate.
31. The organizations that joined the Ropa Amiga Program had to meet some minimal criteria regarding institutional, legal (insurance, taxes), and social (teamwork and incorporation of new organizations) aspects as well as accreditations (ISO standards), hygiene, and safety plans, etc.

32. Regardless of currency exchange matters, as in the case of Brazil's APAEB and Coopa-Roca, which exported a share of their production with a local currency appreciating vis-à-vis the U.S. dollar.

33. The term key—somewhat ambiguous—is used to refer to the social dimension where initiatives create their greatest impact. By specific, we refer to the social value created purposefully for low-income sectors. For example, let us consider the case of La Fageda, whose key driver—traceable back to its social mission—was social and labor inclusion. While, once sustainably launched, this venture created revenues or helped to change collective views on job opportunities for the mentally handicapped, effectively overcoming social barriers, its key and most specific impact—comparing before and after social dimension statuses—was the enhanced job skills acquired by mentally handicapped individuals.

34. Other examples include Andrómines, which raised the amount of inorganic waste collection in Catalonia, and Futur, whose catering services based on organic products that comply with international environmental standards largely contribute to this social value dimension.

5

Engaging Organizational Ecosystems in Inclusive Businesses

Ezequiel Reficco and Alfred Vernis

> *"Progress toward sustainable development requires many more—and more complex—partnerships. Smart companies are recognizing that the most effective way to leverage change in our interdependent world is through common endeavor with others and by learning from the experience. We can manage cooperatively what we cannot manage individually. This is the essence of a very old, very powerful idea called community. The whole is more than the sum of its parts."*[1]

Carlos Espinal, marketing director at Colombia's Colcerámica company, never thought that he would have to become involved with so many people when he was assigned to launch a product line for low-income sectors. First, he contacted Haidy Duque, from Ashoka, to help him set up a project to sell floor tiles to low-income people. Carlos and Haidy soon understood that "social entrepreneurs who wished to work with the poor would have to build their own value chain, bringing together the knowledge from both the market and the community." They built their model and moved on to execute it at Usme, a low-income neighborhood in Bogotá. Their initial design was based on setting up women's cooperatives that would promote tile flooring in Bogotá's low-income neighborhoods.

At Usme, they met people like Ana Delia Ibarra, a 40-year-old mother who worked at home looking after neighborhood children. The ground floor at Ana's home—with no tiles—served as a day-care center, while its second floor was under construction. In early 2006, Bogotá's Health Department informed Ana that, for hygienic reasons, she had to build a tile floor at her home. Like the other 670 mothers at Usme's Day-Care Cooperative, Ana did not have the Col$207,000 (US$85) needed to upgrade her home. If Ana and her colleagues did not find a solution, their day-care centers would be shut down, not only rendering them jobless, but also preventing them from "looking after children who had no other care options."

When Haidy and Carlos met with Usme Cooperative's mothers, Haidy realized "it was the moment of truth: they wondered why we asked them to build new cooperatives when they already had one." Carlos explained that "after listening to the community leaders, I could not help but thinking 'who are the experts here?' We have failed to acknowledge the true value of the community's contribution." After the meeting, Carlos and Haidy outlined the model's components—product, funding, communications, community involvement, and design. They decided to use the community's existing networks and called the project, "Your Home, Built Anew, Step by Step."[2]

Colcerámica's example, with Carlos, Haidy, Ana and the other Usme mothers, clearly illustrates the notion of ecosystems that we will introduce in this chapter. If we analyze recent studies on socially inclusive, market-based initiatives, we find that collaborations and partnerships are recurring features. Most studies indicate how important it is, when working with low-income sectors, to "reach out of the organization,"[3] "to build long-term relationships,"[4] to work "with several actors,"[5] to "forge win-win collaborations,"[6] "to build unconventional partnerships,"[7] or "market-oriented ecosystems."[8]

The significance of cross-organization collaborations has been central for SEKN network's research agenda. Its first collective work cycle (2001–2003) focused on cross-sector partnerships.[9] The capacity to build successful partnerships also surfaced in SEKN's second research cycle (2003–2005) as a key success factor in management of social enterprises.[10]

In the context of inclusive businesses, collaboration schemes have often been placed under the "ecosystem" metaphor. This term, borrowed from biology, had been used by several research lines in management, with different scopes.[11] C. K. Prahalad was the first to use it in the context of inclusive business,[12] and since then it has become the terminology of choice in most studies published on the subject. However, as applied to inclusive business initiatives, the term has been more used than explained. Most BOP studies that used the term have taken its meaning for granted.

Thus, the goal of this chapter is twofold. On the one hand, it seeks to bring some clarity to this notion, showing how it differs from traditional terminology and pointing out its advantages, both analytical and pragmatic. On the other hand, the chapter seeks to showcase the dynamics at play in these collaborative arrangements.

What Is a Business Ecosystem?

An ecosystem is an economic community resting on a foundation of interacting organizations that revolve around the production of goods and services.[13] It is a concept that goes beyond traditional frameworks, such as the value chain, extended value chains, or value systems.[14] As Iansiti and Levien suggest, hundreds of organizations in many industries and sectors had to collaborate so that we could use the personal computer on which this text was written.[15] Many of these organizations fall outside the traditional value chain of suppliers and distributors that participate directly in the linear production process. The actions of each of these organizations, and particularly of those placed at the core of these systems, affect the strength of the entire community. In mainstream markets, companies such as Wal-Mart and Microsoft have realized this and pursued strategies that not only aggressively further their own interests but also promote the overall health of their ecosystems.[16]

Co-Dependency, Co-Evolution, and Co-Learning

The ecosystem notion strongly highlights the intimate connection between an organization and its environment—in the long run, if one fails to progress, the other's potential is curtailed. As in biological ecosystems, isolated organizations tend to be fragile and vulnerable. To stay alive and strong, companies need to open up to their environments, co-evolving with them.[17] James Moore, who applied this notion to large corporations (like Wal-Mart) as part of a research agenda unrelated to social inclusion, concluded, "An excellent restaurant in a decadent neighborhood is likely to fail."[18]

The ecosystem metaphor also conveys the notion of complementariness and interdependence among members. In ecosystems, several roles must be performed for the entire system to work. If those roles are not performed, members will be keen on developing them for their own good. Consider the Hortifruti experience; when this Costa Rican large-store supplier tried to increase its perishables' purchases to address a growing demand, Hortifruti encountered a problem: farmers lived in poor conditions, and their production was low-tech. As Jorge Cavallini, the company's Agribusiness Development Director, recalled, "we had to call the town's saloon to place our orders with a farmer who lived a mile away." Hortifruti came to the conclusion that it needed a different type of producers to boost its business. "We needed farmers who had a phone," explained Cavallini, "storage warehouses, and running water, both to irrigate their vegetables and to wash their harvests." This simple story illustrates the interdependence dynamics among ecosystem members. Much as it happens with fishing fleets, the group is as fast as its slowest member. If a community wants to move forward at a faster pace, its most privileged members will have to pay attention to the weakest ones.

Who Belongs To My Business Ecosystem? Who Is To Be Left Out?

It is quite simple to establish the components of an ecosystem: map the groups that are part of the economic community where an organization is embedded and reach out towards them. In Moore's words: "Understand the economic systems evolving around you, and find ways to contribute."[19] The guiding criterion should be **relevance**: as Iansiti and Levien point out, "Drawing the precise boundaries of an ecosystem is an impossible and, in any case, academic exercise. Rather, you should try to systematically identify the organizations with which your future is most closely intertwined and determine the dependencies that are most critical to your business."[20] The depiction that follows could be used as a framework for any economic venture, but it was devised specifically with inclusive business in mind.

At the core of any business community lies the organization's own **extended chain,** or value system,[21] which depends upon it for the delivery of its goods and services. This chain starts upstream, with the work of suppliers, and extends downstream, towards distributors, marketers, processors, or customers. The ecosystem includes **other actors,** outside the extended chain, that operate within ecosystem boundaries: competitors, producers of substitute and complementary goods, and interested observers, such as neighboring communities or other stakeholders.[22]

Figure 5.1
Organizational Ecosystems and Their Components

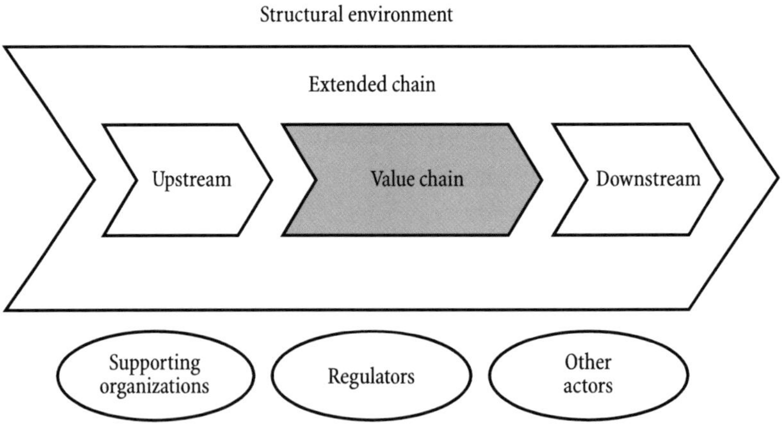

Ecosystems also encompass **support organizations** and **regulators.** The first group includes socially oriented organizations that provide "seed capital" (in its broadest meaning, financial, social, technological or other capital)

to nurture the ecosystem, enabling it to overcome its weaknesses and to prosper. Although these initiatives are not intrinsically charitable, philanthropy often plays a key role, especially in the early stages of inclusive businesses. Committing to an ecosystem generally means starting from scratch—for example, quantifying unmet demands or productive capabilities of sectors that are not included in population censuses; strengthening and institutionalizing fragile or informal organizations, or creating them where needed, or teaching accounting or tax regulations to illiterate individuals. Few private companies are willing to perform these tasks on their own. Instead of viewing these problems as insurmountable or as requiring indefinite funding, support organizations tend to regard them as bottlenecks that block ecosystems' productive potential. Thus, they seek to release that potential through ad-hoc philanthropic investments that lead to virtuous cycles of economic value creation and social empowerment. Once bottlenecks are overcome, support organizations often step aside and let market dynamics take over. As a rule of thumb, support organizations are not directly involved in value chains—rather, they help to render value chains feasible and, then, withdraw (although some NGOs join networks on an ongoing basis, for example providing LIS with steady funding). The chapter on social enterprises discusses support organizations in greater depth.

The regulator group includes state agencies, unions, consumer associations, or any other entity with the ability to set "the rules of the game." This group is particularly important for LIS initiatives, as very often they redefine the contours of established business models. The importance of regulation is obvious in public utility initiatives, where the role of state agencies is decisive,[23] but it is not limited to them. Given the asymmetries in power and influence among parties that characterizes these initiatives, it is often necessary to seek "buy-in" from those who issue "licenses to operate" with LIS.

Finally, biological ecosystems consist not only of interacting organisms but also include environmental conditions (such as water, air, etc.) that enable or hinder those interactions. As applied to the organizational realm, the notion of **structural context** encompasses the quality of regulations as well as the economic, cultural and various other conditions that surround and influence those interactions. Hence, when we analyze ecosystems involving LIS, we need to pay attention to the existence of these key supplies. In addition to efficient physical infrastructures and sustainable natural resources, we need, for example, easy access to affordable financing. In several of our cases, the existence of microfinance organizations in that country has been instrumental to consolidating initiatives with LIS. On a different note, the existence of a regulatory framework that facilitates employment for vulnerable groups in Spain has enabled the operations of that country's CSO. Due to space limitations, this chapter does not delve into the impact of regulatory frameworks, but it cannot fail to acknowledge its influence.

The Analogy with Biological Ecosystems

Traditionally, the interaction between the organization and its environment was seen in terms of industry or value chain analysis. Whatever lay outside those frameworks remained peripheral to most business radars, and tended to be handled by "specialists"—community relations or public affairs managers. Business ecosystems offer an alternative vision, where hitherto peripheral issues become central in business agendas.

From this perspective, the value chain is clearly too narrow to cover the universe of inclusive business initiatives. "This extended relational view of the firm goes beyond the traditional approach that involves value-chain partners and, on specific tasks, competitors . . . It encompasses not only relationships with firms, but also with other stakeholder groups (e.g., governments and civil society)."[24] As Miguel Rivera-Santos points out, value-chains are characterized by "linearity," a sequential process in which different players contribute to value creation in a chronological sequence, with each member receiving a product and enhancing it through the addition of value before handing it over to the next. This reflects both the homogeneous commercial nature of all players and the exclusively commercial nature of the interactions among them.[25] In inclusive business, by contrast, non-market actors usually play a key role, with interactions that are at once commercial and social. Something similar can be said of industry analysis, as business ecosystems often cut across established industries.

When it comes to collaborative arrangements, analysts have tended to study them under the rubric of networks, value systems, or strategic alliances. These terms reflect reality with greater transparency and rigor than a metaphor. At the end of the day, business "ecosystems" are organizational networks. But despite its merits, the network terminology offers little action-oriented guidance to practitioners. There are simply too many types of networks: from those run by news organizations (CNN) to those formed by affinity groups or computers. The term does not evoke any compelling reason to engage fellow community members, nor does it suggest any particular course of action.

Another contender to frame these collaborative relations would be the literature on stakeholder theory.[26] After all, the idea underlying the ecosystem notion—"enlightened self-interest" should lead any organization to map all relevant members of its community of interests and commit to them—does resonate strongly with this view. In recent decades, commitment to stakeholders has evolved from communication to dialogue and from dialogue to joint action. Large multinationals are increasingly engaging with their stakeholders on economic, social, and environmental issues. The notion of value creation for all stakeholders has been gathering momentum.[27] However, while stakeholders' theory and practice have tended to focus on openness and dialogue, the ecosystem view is geared towards action and helps identify the underlying dynamics of change and adaptation. Ecosystem members do not only engage each other in honest and transparent exchanges—they need each other for the whole community to survive and prosper.

The analogy between biological and business ecosystems, by contrast, offers strong and clear clues geared towards action. Biologist Stephen Jay Gould observed that natural ecosystems collapse when they fail to adapt to radical changes in their environmental conditions. Those who fail to adapt are marginalized by new combinations of species that take center stage.[28] As Iansiti and Levien note, there are strong parallels between business networks and biological ecosystems. Both are constituted by loosely interconnected participants that depend on one another for their effectiveness. In the long run, only if the ecosystem is healthy, will individual participants thrive. Increasingly, companies find themselves intertwined in mutually dependent relationships with various stakeholders, like species in a biological ecosystem. Moreover, despite clear power asymmetries between ecosystem members, the consequences of these relationships are often beyond the absolute control of any one of them. Finally, and most interesting, business and biological ecosystems are characterized by the presence of crucial hubs that assume the keystone function of regulating ecosystem health,[29] as we review in the next section.

Yet the analogy has its limits, as even its cited proponents acknowledge. While inputs to biological systems (sunlight, nutrients) are fairly predictable, inputs in business ecosystems (such as technology) are very dynamic. Most important, unlike biological communities that co-evolve blindly following a logic they do not understand, business communities are social systems, made of individuals who make conscious choices.

Why Commit To The Business Ecosystem?

We will now analyze some of the reasons driving organizations to commit to their ecosystems. These drivers do not necessarily apply to all kinds of ecosystems: the dynamics of an ecosystem led by a corporation may differ from that of an ecosystem led by a cooperative. However, these general traits seem to characterize most of the cases in our sample.

Incentives to Participants: Industry Platforms

Usually, business ecosystems revolve around the leadership of a key organization, called "pivotal,"[30] "keystone,"[31] "anchor,"[32] or "bridging"[33] organizations, which align the visions and investment decisions of the ecosystem members. While most studies point to the leadership role of large corporations, our sample does include business communities led by CSOs and cooperatives—see Exhibit 1 (at end of chapter) for a list of ventures led by private companies, CSOs, and cooperatives. "Participants in the shaper's broad ecosystem can use the strategy to create and capture enormous value as they learn from—and share risk with—one another."[34]

The cases in our sample show how pivotal organizations managed to align the behavior of different players with their own strategy through positive incentives. Previous research on mainstream business ecosystems agreed that this is done primarily through "platforms": assets that the leader offers to other ecosystem participants to make interaction fluid and effective.[35] In mainstream markets, these platforms often have a technological basis: think of Microsoft and its operating system. In the context of our sample of inclusive businesses, platforms consisted of clearly defined standards and practices that helped organize and support the activities of participants, enabling them "to do more with less."[36] Cativen, a Venezuelan retailer, set out to integrate farmers in its value chain so as to enhance the quality of its perishables, and to put an end to recurring oversupply and underproduction crises. Producers had earlier based their work on "gut feeling"—they planted their land without any knowledge of climate or soil advantages, of clients they would sell their crops to, or of pricing. To solve these problems, Cativen installed several multi-purpose "Logistic Platforms" near production areas. These functioned as storage, purchasing, and technical assistance centers, but also as social promotion hubs where producers coordinated their production processes and learned from each other's best practices.

Platforms were also used in some of the initiatives that targeted the poor as consumers. Let us go back to the experience of Colcerámica. Since 2000, this Colombian tile manufacturer had successfully targeted the low-middle classes with Ibérica, a value-for-money product line, with excellent cost/performance relation. By 2004, demand for these products was outstripping output capacity. However, company research showed that its sales were concentrated in the low-middle class; to bring in the bottom of the income pyramid would take additional thinking. The company approached a social

entrepreneur to design a collaborative scheme that could make use of existing social structures and leaders in the community. They designed a forum
called Community Organizational Nucleus (NOC), where the company, the
social entrepreneur, and grass-roots organizations consensually established
the value chain's modus operandi and how profits would be shared among
partners.

While this section described the incentives to external participants to
join the pivotal organization's platform, the following sections describe the
incentives and benefits accrued by the ecosystem's leader.

Redefining Relations with Stakeholders through Win-Win Arrangements

Creating the platform is only the first step; pivotal organizations then need
to make sure they generate win-win propositions, so that partners remain
on board and commit to venture success.[37] "The strength and sustainability of enterprises come from their ability to fit into the environmental,
social, and cultural context in which they function. By creating values for all
stakeholders, enterprises can involve them and gain deep support based on
their commitment."[38]

Appealing win-win propositions can reshape the relationships between
the company and some of its stakeholders. Consider the experience of Palmas del Espino, a Peruvian company that produces palm oil in that nation's
Amazon region. Its philanthropic programs[39] were not succeeding in building close ties to the surrounding communities. In the 1980s, a group of families gradually invaded a 1,200-hectare (2,965-acre) company property next
to its plant, later dubbed José Carlos Mariátegui village.[40] The company's
good intentions fell short of meeting the neighboring communities' needs
and expectations. Rather than periodic donations to schools and hospitals,
what these communities needed was a scheme that afforded them a decent
livelihood in a setting with rather limited economic opportunities.

In 2000, the company realized the value of building a long-lasting, cooperative relationship with the squatter community. Based on that belief, it
petitioned the government to formalize legal deeds to turn squatters into
rightful owners, in hopes of creating incentives for them to farm those lands
and escape poverty. However, the market did not respond as expected. The
distance to urban centers prevented demand from driving revenues. Palmas del Espino recognized that philanthropy alone would hardly have any
significant impact on farmers' living conditions. What farmers were looking for was not charity—they needed a viable business model. A local farmer
put it quite eloquently when he recalled his meeting with Dionisio Romero
Paoletti, Palmas del Espino's Board Chairman,[41]

> We said "Don Dionisio . . . we are poor, but we are your neighbors . . .
> We don't envy your estate, nor do we want to take away the wealth you
> have worked hard to amass. We just want to be as rich as you someday,
> as a result of our work." Dionisio liked those words . . . Since then, he
> opened a lot of doors for us.

Clearly, this expectation could not be met simply through the company's
"specialists" in social affairs, nor through philanthropy. The community
would have to be incorporated into its business core. To that end, the company reshaped its relationship with the farmers, turning them into suppliers for its own business. As Ángel Irazola, Palmas del Espino's general
manager, pointed out, "the people surrounding us should be our partners,
because, if they are our enemies, we are doomed."[42]

Turning subsistence farmers into partners meant implementing a collaboration scheme with other company stakeholders. First, Palmas del Espino
set out to "create an interlocutor," promoting the creation of a José Carlos
Mariátegui Producers' Association and its incorporation to regional and
national producers' organizations to access union representation.[43] According to Irazola, "with no formal institutions, there is nowhere to start from."
To fund new plantations, Palmas del Espino engaged Banco de Crédito del
Perú in an innovative system that enabled those farmers to be considered, for
the first time ever, as credit subjects.[44] Finally, the company hired Gestipalma,
a company built by retired Palmas del Espino former workers, to train new
vendors on oil palm planting, maintenance, and harvest.

Palmas del Espino's initiative thoroughly reformulated the relationship
between the company and its neighboring farmers through a model that
was later emulated by CSOs, development cooperation agencies, and banks
operating in the area. Society expects more and more from companies (to
produce with superior quality and lower prices and to do so in a sustainable,
socially inclusive fashion) and CSOs (as a watchdog safeguarding society
from potential excesses by corporations and governments, as well as to drive
transformation and sustainable impacts). As Palmas del Espino's experience suggests, working within one's ecosystem may create synergies while
addressing several organizational imperatives simultaneously.

Stabilizing the Environment, Enabling Investments

Platforms can serve to anchor expectations and clarify roles and commitments. As previous research on emergent industries has shown, this is particularly valuable in turbulent[45] or uncertain settings,[46] and inclusive
business certainly fits that mold. The general manager of such business

stated during an interview that he sometimes felt he was "betting the shareholders' money," given the uncertainty surrounding the implementation of an innovative inclusive business model. By reducing perceived risk, platforms enable investment and accelerate returns.[47]

Consider Bolivia's agricultural sector (see Figure 5.2). Traditionally, funding agencies (governments and development agencies) used to provide nonrefundable grants to implementing organizations that offered technical assistance, training, and infrastructure facilities (irrigation, silos, etc.) to producers. Neither storing and processing companies nor distributors and marketers were involved. The underlying assumption was that once farmers had a top quality product at a competitive price, the invisible hand of markets would absorb production, thus improving their living conditions. However, the expectation did not materialize. On the one hand, implementing organizations were out of touch with the quality standards demanded by the market. On the other hand, processors, distributors, and marketers had not made the necessary investments to handle farmers' expanded production. This lack of coordination was overcome through the collaboration scheme led by Irupana, a small company that stored, processed, and marketed organic products such as quinoa and amaranth. The company built a vendor network consisting of Bolivian farmers with the assistance of ProRural, a CSO that offered funding and training. With that scheme, Irupana was able to develop an institutional framework that allowed for the unfettered flow of information and resources, coordinating investment decisions and allowing partners to produce exactly what the market demanded.

At the same time, operating through this shared platform allowed Irupana to accelerate returns and capture economies of time. In the words of Javier Hurtado, Irupana's CEO, "The supplier development program has allowed us to reach in two years an exports volume that took other companies 10 to 15 years." Those who manage to position themselves at the center of an economic ecosystem, coordinating its members' actions, can capture significant economic benefits and shape their environment[48] (see chapter 3).

Reducing Transaction Costs

As previous research on mainstream business ecosystems has shown, pivotal organizations can increase the productivity of all participants by simplifying the complex task of connecting network participants to one another.[49] In the context of inclusive business, lowering transaction costs is critical: these initiatives operate with low margins per transaction, which means that they need scale to reach profitability. But managing relations with large

Figure 5.2
Irupana and Its Organizational Ecosystem

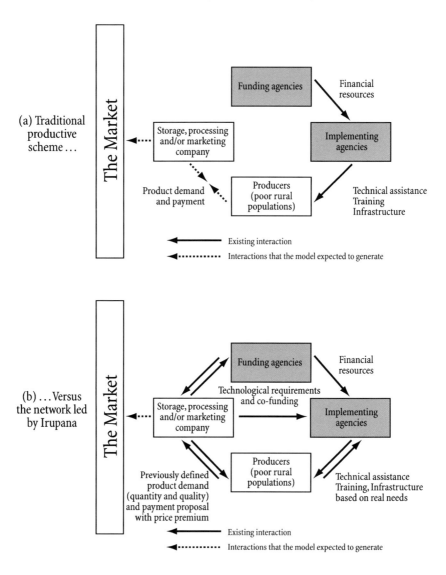

(a) Traditional productive scheme ...

(b) ... Versus the network led by Irupana

Source: Adapted from *Revista Pro Campo,* Issue 93, December 2004.

number of LIS customers or producers can be dauntingly complex. That is why many pivotal organizations set up cross-sector strategic alliances: it is easier and more effective to forge long-term agreements with a CSO or a cooperative than to negotiate with hundreds of independent producers. A suitable partner can simplify matters substantially for any company interested in engaging LIS.

In the cases analyzed, several companies collaborated actively to build an organizational interlocutor that could speak for their low-income partners. The feasibility of cooperation sometimes became a make-or-break factor when it came to decisions about whether or not to work with LIS. Let us explore the experiences of Orsa and Natura. Both Brazilian companies share a proven commitment to social development and environmental sustainability. The Orsa Group is a leading paper and paper byproduct manufacturer. One of its affiliates, Orsa Florestal, focused on socially and environmentally sustainable extraction operations in the Amazon region. Since 2003, Orsa Florestal had been working on the development of a sustainable agricultural and forest industry in the Almeirim district, with Vale do Jarí communities. By 2005, this initiative had yielded mixed results. The precedent of resounding failures by prominent local cooperatives, compounded by the local, individualistic culture, had hindered the company's efforts to organize communities in cooperatives. Farmers expected the company to purchase their products on an individual basis, which increased the initiative's governance costs to unacceptable levels. For Orsa Florestal, it was virtually impossible to align 500 individuals to the company's strategy or to streamline their work habits.

Natura's experience has moved in the opposite direction. The company created the Ekos product line, based on plants and oils traditionally used by indigenous communities in Brazil. Natura decided to launch a pilot program at the Iratapurú community on account of its environmental wealth and community members' willingness to build a cooperative. Early project stages were tough, with producers used to regarding each other as competitors. However, participating communities eventually came around the idea of working in cooperatives, and the venture took off.

Existing Social Infrastructure
Most companies have come to acknowledge that trust and legitimacy are extremely important in these initiatives. In their quest to generate trust, they seek to build on the social networks already in place. In turn, CSOs have realized that they can capitalize on their rich relationship portfolio and the trust built over years of commitment to LIS, as an asset that can be leveraged to obtain economic resources while pursuing their mission. Once a solid network has been built to help vulnerable individuals with a project, it makes sense to use it to launch a new project of a similar type, capturing

what economists call "economies of scale"—as production grows, unit cost tends to decrease. In addition, the same network may be also used to launch other complementary efforts—what economists call "economies of scope." Social capital seems to be crucial, as these trust and reciprocity networks enable groups of isolated individuals to become working communities, effectively reducing the cost of doing business with underprivileged sectors.

Gas Natural Ban, a natural gas supplier in Argentina, partnered with Fundación Pro-Vivienda Social (FPVS) to launch a pilot project for LIS. This foundation, devoted to housing solutions for the poor, had created Argentina's first micro-loan program for home improvement, building in the process a solid network of reliable customers at Cuartel V's low-income neighborhoods in the outskirts of Buenos Aires. The project—suitably entitled "strategic alliances and social capital"—received the World Bank's financial support and involved several grass-roots organizations, local administrations, and Argentina's national agency for social housing issues. Through this partnership, FPVS realized that the social network it had built could be further exploited as a vehicle for additional programs, and it quickly moved from running just one program to four.

Capacity to Shape the Environment

Commitment to the ecosystem members, as described in Figure 5.1, is an effective way to expand boundaries and possibilities. By working with other players in the business ecosystem, organizations can broaden their scope and pursue goals that would be simply unreachable on an individual basis. When this rationale is pushed to the limit, an organization may actually change the structural environment where ecosystem members operate. Previous research on mainstream business ecosystems shows that shared platforms can reshape the business environment where companies operate, sometimes creating whole new industries.[50] Our case sample does not include change on that order of magnitude, but it does show that engaging ecosystem participants through inclusive ventures can reshape "the rules of the game." This is the "structural change" (see Figure 5.1) described by Dees: a shift in environmental conditions that influences players' behavior.[51]

Oro Verde Corporation (COV) is a joint venture intended to improve living conditions for LIS at Colombia's Chocó region through socially and environmentally sustainable gold mining practices. This venture includes two CSOs (Fundación Amigos del Chocó and Fundación Las Mojarras) and several grass-roots organizations (Community Councils) that coordinate community interests. Its operating model was built on the basis of Productive Family Units (UFPs), a traditional organizational form at

Chocó communities. UFPs are economic and social units, each typically consisting of around seven family members.

A strategy based on partnerships with local units has enabled this organization to overcome resistance and entry barriers at some communities (such as Tadó and Condoto), as it provides an incentive for local people to join in. In addition, by networking, grass-roots organizations have managed to accomplish much more ambitious goals. COV's model seeks to create a livelihood means for poor populations and to build a business model that exploits the area's mining resources while mitigating the devastating effects of large-scale mining at Chocó's natural ecosystem. Thus, COV's value proposition includes intangible social and environmental components, much like Forest Stewardship Council's standards for "good wood" production.[52] The problem COV faced was that it offered a differentiated product—"responsible gold"—at a market dealing exclusively with commodities. On account of its intangible component, responsible gold is sold at a premium price 10 percent higher than its commodity counterparts. COV knew that there was a niche willing to pay a premium price, but in order to reach that demand, it had to create a standard that singled out responsible gold. By definition, this task cannot be performed in isolation.

Under the leadership of Fundación Amigos del Chocó (Amichocó), COV partnered with the Pacific Ocean Institute for Environmental Research (IIAP), an institution that reported to Colombia's Environmental Ministry. The IIAP agreed to participate in the technical development of responsible mining standards and, later, in certifying that mining families complied with those standards. However, COV's ecosystem is global rather than local—most of its sales are exports. Thus a local certification was not enough, as it would mean very little for European Union consumers. Led by Amichocó, COV focused on building a multi-stakeholder forum that could formulate legitimate, globally recognized standards for responsible mining practices. As a result of this effort, the Association for Responsible Mining (ARM) was created. As Lina Villa, COV's Executive Director, recalled, "we have networked to build a framework that will enable us to think about responsible mining, based on COV's model but acknowledging that mining operations are very different around the world."

Working with Low-Income Sectors in These Ecosystems

The initiatives studied display ties of diverse depth and density among extended value chain members. Considering this variability, cases may be plotted on a continuum of increased LIS engagement. On one extreme of this continuum, LIS were incorporated into an extended value chain unilaterally run by a pivotal organization; on the opposite extreme, LIS played a key role in defining the business model and running the enterprise.

Unilaterally Managed Value Chains

Some of the organizations in our sample managed to adjust their structures or processes to reach out to LIS with no outside assistance. This group of initiatives stands out because their value chains are vertically controlled by a single organization, even when they cooperated with support organizations or regulators to promote venture success.

Consider the case of Cemex. In the mid 1990s, this Mexican multinational corporation realized that part of its cement demand in Mexico was insensitive to the periodical financial crises that besieged that country. Research revealed that this resilient demand did not come from construction companies, but from end users with low-income and no access to the banking system. A deeper analysis found that this segment added up to approximately 45 million prospective consumers, with an aggregated purchasing power equivalent to 40 percent of Cemex's installed capacity at the time. This discovery led the company to launch Patrimonio Hoy, an initiative intended to allow LIS to build 10-square-meter rooms at two-thirds the historical cost in one-third of the time, through a combination of savings and micro-credit. The success of this program led the company to scan its economic and social environment for new ways to contribute to mitigating social problems profitably. This was the origin of Construmex, an initiative that channels money transfers from Mexicans residing in the United States towards the purchase of construction material and home building in Mexico.

Much as in Patrimonio Hoy, Cemex unilaterally controls the Construmex value chain. However, the success of this initiative to a large extent hinges on partnerships with other organizations. First, Cemex enjoys a strong business relationship with most Mexican construction companies—the next link in this ecosystem's expanded value chain—as Construmex intermediates between émigré customers and Mexican builders. Construmex also relies on a partnership with Conficasa, a Texas-based financial institution, for collections and customer loan account management. In addition, Cemex cooperates with support organizations, which consider the initiative to converge with their socially-oriented mission. For instance, the venture benefits from the Mexican Social Development Department's "three-for-one" program for émigrés whereby federal, state, and city administrations each match every Mexican peso contributed by émigré associations to community projects in their hometowns. Construmex also collaborates with émigré clubs in the cities where it owns points of sale by sponsoring sports and cultural events that raise funds for the "three-for-one" program. As sponsor, Construmex promotes its services among event participants. Finally, Construmex has entered into cooperation agreements with Mexican Consulates in U.S. cities with significant Mexican immigrant populations to promote its program among expatriates (see also chapter 2).

Value Chains Co-Managed Through Alliances

In other cases, cooperation dynamics yielded different results—in some, large parts of initiatives' value chains were handled by organizations and people over whom pivotal organizations had no direct control. These partnerships were managed by alliances, very often cross-sector, linking companies, CSOs, cooperatives, and social entrepreneurs, to achieve respective or common goals.[53] In these alliances, the members' fate is intertwined: they either succeed or fail collectively. There is no vertical authority—their cooperation aligns partner interests and creates incentives for joint work.

In general, collaboration tie density (quantity) and intensity (quality) are stronger in this group than in the previous one, probably on account of the strategic value these ties hold for pivotal organizations. As building these partnerships involves substantial resources (management time, money, and others), they are managed like a valuable asset. In fact, some organizations embrace the notion of "relational capital"[54]—i.e., the set of long-term, trust- and loyalty-based relationships that can yield competitive advantages. Once a solid network has been built to render a project viable, it makes sense to use that network to launch another project of a similar type, capturing economies of scale and scope. Social capital seems to be crucial, as these trust and reciprocity networks enable groups of isolated individuals to become working communities, effectively reducing the cost of doing business with underprivileged sectors.

In the vulnerable settings inhabited by LIS, where both the state and the market have had a weak presence at best, social capital may be one of the few cornerstones available to build new institutions. In 2002, Venezuela's Cativen supermarket chain developed an initiative to integrate farmers into its extended value chain, as direct vendors. Effective networking between the company and low-income farmers at Timotes was made possible by the existing social capital in the area, as the community had already worked in concert for other collective projects, successfully coming together and coordinating its efforts. For instance, since the 1970s, autonomous irrigation committees had effectively managed a crucial farming operation through cooperative decision-making. This relational fabric was used to build an effective company-community interface.

Another unique trait present in these partnerships is the active and central role played by unconventional actors. Ventures unilaterally managed by large companies also feature CSOs as customary participants (see Exhibit 1 at the end of the chapter), but they tend not to perform direct roles in the value chain—their business partners are other private companies. CSOs perform supporting roles that are socially meaningful, but economically secondary. By contrast, in initiatives with co-managed value chains, CSOs, grass-roots organizations or social entrepreneurs perform business-critical tasks. Consider the case of Amanco, a leading irrigation system manufacturer.

In 2006, Amanco decided to serve Mexico's small farmers, whose income potential was curtailed by their poor technology and low productivity.[55] To tap into this market, Amanco partnered with Ashoka and some of its entrepreneurs to build a cross-sector integrative alliance[56] in which this private company partnered with several social entrepreneurs, CSOs, and government agencies around a shared value chain. Amanco had to move beyond merely selling equipment. Instead, it crafted an enriched value proposition catered to the various specific needs of this target segment, including support services provided with partner CSOs, such as land surveys, design, quotations, permit application submission to the National Water Commission, contacts for loan and subsidy requests, technical advice for installation, and marketing support. The CSO Red de Agronegocios Austosustentables (RASA) distributed the irrigation systems and articulated the relation between Amanco and farmers. Loan design and application were handled by the Asociación Mexicana de Uniones de Crédito del Sector Social (AMUCSS), a federation of grass-roots organizations consisting of 32 farming credit unions. AMUCSS managed a revolving fund with several sources, including the Wal-Mart Foundation, Bimbo Foundation, Mexican Business Community Foundation, and the Shared Risk Trust Fund, a state agency. Finally, Wal-Mart provided advice to farmers on crop marketing, promotion, and sales, and offered a retail channel through which farmers could bring their expanded output to market on a large scale.

The feature that characterizes initiatives co-managed through alliances is their need for productive process coordination. "Functional fragmentation [in the value chain] requires securing technological compatibility and complementarity . . . in an effort to co-ordinate for quasi-reintegration and effective production on a now decentralized basis . . . Effective action is not feasible unless governed by a coordination mechanism that can deal with increased complexity."[57] In our sample, alliances could be grouped according the dynamics that prevailed in relations among partners: coordination, consensual cooperation, and co-governance.

a. Coordination

At some subcontractor networks, the pivotal organization outsourced portions of its value chains to producers' associations or cooperatives of low-income workers. In these cases, work plans need to be tightly coordinated to ensure synchronicity and quality standards, following guidelines set by the pivotal organization's business model to which low-income suppliers must simply adjust.

This dynamics is illustrated by the Cativen experience. As indicated earlier, this Venezuelan leader in large-store retailing set out to integrate farmers in its value chain through "Logistic Platforms" near production areas. The company made no spot purchases; instead, it negotiated long-term agreements that guaranteed purchase volumes in exchange for quality standard compliance. Both the company and the producers planned harvests and orchestrated their work based on weather conditions and demand fluctuations.

b. Consensual Cooperation

Some networks took their joint value-creation and decision-making a step further. They created special forums to build consensus, articulate partners' interests, and negotiate agreements. The case of Agropalma, Latin America's leading palm oil producer, illustrates this dynamics. In 2001, the company oversaw the creation of a sophisticated network, called Family Agribusiness Project, in northeastern Brazil. This network was meant to incorporate low-income farmers as suppliers, relying on the support provided by the state (Pará) and local (Moju) administrations, and a bank that funded the venture (Banco da Amazônia). This network operates by consensus. Strategic decisions are made at a multi-stakeholder forum, where all partners meet once a month. Tactical and operating decisions are made on a day-by-day basis bilaterally, by the company and farmers. Although the company is not on an equal standing with farmers, there is a commitment by all participant partners to find common ground and to build consensus.

c. Co-governance

Collaboration dynamics drove some alliances in our sample to grant partners a say on strategic decisions, such as the manner of running operations and the distribution of benefits among participants. As we have seen, Colombia's Colcerámica, a company that manufactured and sold ceramic tiles and bathroom fittings, created a product line specifically addressing the needs of the poor.[58] Its value proposition was excellent quality at low cost, by avoiding advertising and marketing expenses and restricting variety of products, which simplified logistics. But accessing this market successfully also required the development of an ad-hoc distribution and sales channel.

From the start, the company decided that it could not manage this initiative by itself, so it asked Haidy Duque, an Ashoka fellow, for help to design a collaboration scheme that could leverage existing social structures and leadership in the community. Community organizations were thus invited to join in as partners. These grass-roots organizations focused on delivery of social service delivery and strengthening the infrastructure, and they were recognized for their strong leadership and credibility as well as for their participative decision-making style.

Together, Colcerámica, the social entrepreneur, and community organizations designed a collaboration scheme based on a multi-stakeholder forum called Community Organizational Nucleus (NOC), which included all partners. This forum consensually established the value chain's modus operandi and how profits would be shared among partners. Initially, the NOC supervised sales and managed door-to-door sales revenues, while it served as a showroom for product display at accessible sites for the communities involved. Its work was supported by a 3 percent commission on profits. Eventually, the NOC was eliminated. At all times, sales were handled through "promoters"—female community members hired to go door to door to promote and conduct sales, to offer advice on purchases, to invoice and collect payments, and to provide post-market and guarantee services, with a compensation scheme based on sales commissions. These women became the initiative's face—they were trusted by their fellow community members and had unfettered access to their homes.

Coordination, Consensual Cooperation, or Co-Governance: Does It Matter?

At this point one may wonder what drives organizations to give away—partly, at least—control over business-critical processes. Ultimately, Colcerámica could have hired promoters on its own to market its products—it did not need to invest time and money in building consensus. The answer to this question is clearly complex, and this study can only hint at some clues to respond to it.

One possible explanation is the need to build commitment by letting low-income communities share venture ownership.[59] Only when communities feel they own the initiative, will the people involved fight tooth and nail for its success. Let us recall the experience cited at the beginning of this chapter. For Usme neighborhood mothers, like Ana Delia Ibarra, the success of this initiative was the only way they had to make a decent living and keep the community childcare center open, and they gave their all to make that happen.

A second clue that emerges from our sample cases is the opacity of LIS markets, understood as the lack of systematized information that may support decision-making. Anyone venturing into an unknown, slippery territory tries to find a local partner that can provide help and guidance. Even initiatives like Cemex's, which do not resort to alliances, hire local staff to serve LIS. Alliances take this logic further. Through horizontal, long-term relationships, companies venturing into these markets capture valuable business information that is rich, context-specific, and informal—called fine-grained data or tacit knowledge in management literature.

For instance, how can an individual's payment ability and willingness be measured if he has no credit record? Only his own community can determine that. This is not a trivial concern, for it may make the difference between getting rid of a chronic bad debtor and losing a loyal customer who is going through a rough patch. As Santiago Ataguile, from Gas Natural Ban's marketing department, put it,

> We handled the information from the meters out, while Comunidad Organizada and FPVS managed the information from the meters in. We knew how much people owed us, but we had no way of knowing why they owed us, and that was something we needed to know.

Two dynamics are useful for understanding why an organization is driven to build a network: externally, its new market's coordination and development level; internally, its corporate values and organizational identity.

Market "opacity" is related to its level of development. Some of the ventures in our sample were created in settings with established supply, production systems, and distribution channels. For example, initiatives like Construmex relied on a rich institutional fabric (see Exhibit 1 for a description of this initiative's ecosystem). There is no need to build sophisticated alliances in such a rich and well-structured environment. Conversely, it is hard to operate when such a fabric is not present. Consider the case of Cativen: it had no interest in entering the agricultural business. It was compelled to do so because of a weakness in its ecosystem: the low level of development of the Venezuelan agricultural sector. In the words of Jean Marie Hilaire, Cativen's CEO: "once a given country has developed enough, we go back to our business and focus on retail, letting producers mind the quality of produce. By the time we left the French agricultural cooperatives they knew about the agro-business industry much more than our people." Alliances may thus contribute to building an institutional framework that could not emerge spontaneously. Some speak of "the social construction of markets," understanding markets not as point of convergence between supply and demand, but rather as a setting where successive interactions between participating individuals, organizations, and companies spark wealth creation.[60]

Settings do not explain everything, however. Similar environments may create initiatives with varying degrees of engagement in decision-making processes. For instance, despite the fact that they operated in very similar markets, the ventures by Palmas del Espino (Peru) and Agropalma (Brazil) offered LIS very different participation schemes (see Exhibit 1 at end of chapter for a summary of their individual characteristics). Organizational values play a significant role here as well, as some organizations may view it as a value to engage with other ecosystem members.

Another element in this equation is communities. How important is for low-income communities to build coordination, consensual cooperation, or co-governance relationships? In the end, it may be argued that the only thing that matters is the value created by a venture, regardless of its management scheme. If LIS producers' income is raised, or better products are offered to LIS consumers at lower prices, then all other issues could be deemed secondary. Although this is true, management structure and processes are far from irrelevant.

When a low-income community is brought to the table, it is not only its income that improves. By participating in debates and exercising their ability to make significant decisions LIS develop key skills required to manage their own resources and future. Even if companies eventually leave, this knowledge remains—which does not happen when the poor are passive recipients of a model designed by others. For example, Colcerámica's initiative participants agree that, as a result of this experience, the community organizations involved have increased their management capability. By engaging in Ibérica Service Centers, Community Action Boards have realized several business projects that had been in their plans for some time. Those who have worked on poverty mitigation efforts have long learned that it is best to teach the hungry how to fish rather than giving them fish to eat. Just as important as learning how to fish is to decide what to fish, and to rally available physical and human resources to fish.[61]

Models enabling LIS co-management provide an added, intangible value to a venture's return. Indeed, some authors go as far as viewing this as a new paradigm that leaves traditional capitalist practices behind. Those traditional practices were based on "clinical interventions"—companies viewed LIS as distant outsiders and formulated "solutions" for "objective" needs, much like a physician who examines a patient and prescribes a treatment without asking for his/her opinion. In the new paradigm, ecosystem members co-create wealth and are committed to each other, contemplating their individual needs to build customized solutions.[62]

On the flip side, the value of co-governance forums is probably temporary for companies. If decision-making processes become more democratic only because companies need to rely on motivated partners when they venture into uncharted waters, the value of these engaging schemes will tend to depreciate once companies acquire the ability to operate by themselves in those markets. Colcerámica's experience seems to point in that direction. A year and a half after launching its pilot program at Usme, the company decided to replicate its program on a larger scale in other major Colombian cities (Cali and Medellín). Yet this new program did not focus on building trust, transparency, and consistency; rather, its goal was to capture economies of time and scale while enhancing efficiency by lowering costs. In other words, the company applied a purely economic management rationale that demanded greater standardization and, therefore, unilateral value chain control. At Usme, Colcerámica learned through trial and error, zeroing in on best practices and streamlining knowledge acquisition. Afterwards, the company set out to scale this knowledge in order to maximize its efficiency and profitability. Hence the collaborative arrangements built in Cali and Medellín did not feature a community organizational nucleus; horizontal components became weaker to favor a more vertical management approach. Usme's pilot program eventually got rid of its NOC as well.

"Business Friendships"

Pure market-based relationships are typically impersonal and focus on short-term value exchanges. Our case sample suggests that inclusive ventures require a different kind of relationship, one that is personalized and projects into the future. In practice, this translates into a willingness to accompany partners in bad times and even to invest in strengthening them. In this type of embedded relationships, an interpersonal commitment is built that goes beyond a purely market-based outlook. For instance, these relationships may involve remaining loyal to a partner despite the emergence of new competitors who may offer pricing advantages, or refraining from exploiting partners' temporary vulnerability, or not maximizing prices systematically. These behaviors should not be viewed as irrational or "suicidal"; indeed, they are often the most direct path to long-term business advantages. As it has been noticed,[63] the term "business friendship" refers to the need to build a close, personalized, and sustained relationship that goes well beyond a "one-shot" commercial value exchange, in order to operate in these markets. The idea of business friendship can be related to the concept of "business intimacy," advanced by Simanis and Hart, who consider it a prerequisite for the private sector to "co-create" value with non-traditional actors. This intimacy is built when companies and communities view each other interdependently, developing a mutual commitment to each other's long-term growth.[64]

This type of relationship seems to be customary in socially inclusive ecosystems. As Irupana's director put it, "this is how we view our low-income vendors—we are partners. Our relationship is both human and business-oriented ... we need to humanize our business interactions." Or, as a director from Construmex characterized it, "we try to befriend our customers."

It may be in order to wonder if there is some naïveté in referring to "friendship" or "intimacy" in business, with important economic interests at play. We are not suggesting that ecosystem members should be intimate or friendly in a literal sense. Rather, these terms are used as metaphors to refer to a relational dynamics with a long-term scope that goes beyond mere market transactions. The notion of "business friendship" has a dual nature: on the one hand, it emphasizes embeddedness and long-term commitment and stability; on the other hand, it features a materialistic, utilitarian component, as these relationships are ultimately developed in and for a business setting.

After all, business friendships are driven by management imperatives, not good intentions. Successful multinationals like Starbucks have turned the cultivation and development of this type of relationships into explicit policies, as they recognize its benefits.[65] Gas Natural Ban's experience provides additional evidence. As mentioned earlier, since 2003 Gas Ban has been developing a business model that incorporates LIS as customers. Whenever the company engages a poor community, its sales team is joined by the community relations staff, which immediately rolls out training programs focused on responsible and sustainable energy consumption. According to a member of the company's External Relations team,

> Our community involvement team supports the entire gas network expansion process, with CSR programs. We reach out to these communities holistically, from all our areas—it is not about getting there, building the network, and "so long." The company has a long-standing commitment to the communities where it operates.

This policy was instituted after learning from past experience. A few years earlier, the company had launched another program, Gas for Everyone, to incorporate LIS as customers with a purely commercial approach. Instead of forging relationships with communities, Gas Natural Ban followed the business-as-usual path: the initial contacts with poor consumers were handled through free-lance installers. In 1997–2001, nearly 100,000 new customers were incorporated; yet, in just a few months, a significant share of them ceased to pay for their service. After a while, the company discovered why—installers had not safeguarded either company or customers' interests; they had just sought to maximize short-term profits for themselves. Households that had done well with a single gas outlet had six or seven outlets installed. As a result, despite having access to a substantially cheaper energy source, users' invoices became impossibly high. Eventually, the company realized it was not just a matter of the quantity of its customer base, but also its quality. The company concluded that LIS were a viable market, but not a "quick buck": the business could only work by means of a stable, win-win relationship that provided benefits for both parties. Incorporating a customer that would stop paying six months later was a terrible outcome for the company and a source of frustration for consumers. Building a long-lasting relationship with users would mean, in this particular case, educating them on responsible natural gas consumption.

This experience also illustrates another characteristic of "business friendships": partners sometimes refrain from maximizing their profits; rather, they tend to satisfice—a neologism coined by combining "satisfy" and "suffice."[66] The idea is that foregoing a maximum, short-term profit may lead to securing steady, sustained long-term revenues. For Gas Natural Ban, selling a natural gas connection that consumers can afford and that satisfies their basic needs makes more business sense that selling six connections to each consumer, initiating a cycle that leads to default, disconnection, legal claims, and frustration for both parties.

Yet not everything is acceptable among "business friends." Just as personal friendships sometimes require boundaries, business friendships also practice tough love on occasion. As viewed by practitioners, commitment is no excuse for indulgence or inefficiency. Jonathan Nickel, Colcerámica's marketing manager, clearly stated, "despite this project's great emotional content, we are well aware of the fact that it is a business." Thus support is necessarily bound to effort: actors are convened because they have something valuable to contribute and are rewarded accordingly. Not all fall in line, however. According to Javier Hurtado, after working for so many years with development cooperation organizations, many farmers in Bolivia had gotten used to receiving charity-based donations, to "obtaining benefits without any effort."

To stress their expectations, pivotal organizations often establish incentives, with premium prices for partners abiding by quality and quantity standards, as well as sanctions for those who do not meet them. Costa Rica Entomological Supplies (CRES) works with a farmer network to produce silk cocoons for exports. Its production is subject to stringent quality standards, and producers who meet those standards are rewarded with a price that exceeds current market prices by 20 to 25 percent. When producers fail to meet those standards, they receive a warning; after three warnings, they are penalized. While there has been no need for sanctions, this rule has infused a culture of compliance in the network, as well as the belief that price premiums and improvements in their living conditions are contingent on the satisfaction of consumer needs.

What are the boundaries of the loyalty built on business friendships? Clearly, loyalty should be supported by a community with convergent economic interests. These collaboration schemes cannot be built away from or against the market. If that happens, loyalty is likely to crumble. In our sample, there were no cases of this sort, although CRES's experience may be used to test loyalty boundaries. The silk cocoon exports business has low entry barriers; and CRES partners' improved income attracted many other farmers to the business. Though inferior in quality, their additional supply drove local market prices down and threatened CRES's business model, based on improving farmers' income by means of superior quality and high retail prices. As prices go down, some farmers are said to be considering dropping out of the CRES network to deal directly with exporters, offering prices below those of CRES.

To Conclude

In these pages, we have discussed the relevance for any organization of the community of economic interests in which that entity operates. We have reviewed how understanding those communities, mapping their members, and evaluating the short and long-term forces that shape them can turn threats into opportunities. Specifically, we analyzed how commitment to market ecosystems can account for a path to social inclusion, when organizations—whether driven by profits or a social mission—set about remedying communities' bottlenecks. When this happens, passive observers—a source of potential conflict—become active producers—a source of wealth.

This final section intends to highlight some of the practical lessons drawn from one of our sample cases: the initiative led by Argentina's Gas Natural Ban and Fundación Pro Vivienda Social (FPVS).

1. Mapping and Understanding the Web of Relations in the Ecosystem
First, the preceding discussion showed how significant it is to have a clear understanding of the relationships with the different actors operating around a value chain. These relationships webs may be viewed as platforms to engage in ad-hoc or ongoing collaborations, which may expand the organization's capability set. Preceding cases illustrate how collaborations with support organizations, regulators and other ecosystem members can effectively expand organizations' possibilities. As shown by Figure 5.3 below, Gas Natural Ban realized the potential of a partnership with FPVS. This Foundation effectively organized a demand for gas in LIS. Through this partnership, both organizations found a way to overcome distribution and financial barriers to access that market. By means of a hybrid chain, communities themselves "took over" marketing and financing operations, enabling the natural gas network to expand to new districts that hitherto had remained off-limits.

Figure 5.3
Organizational Ecosystems around Gas Natural Venture in Cuartel V

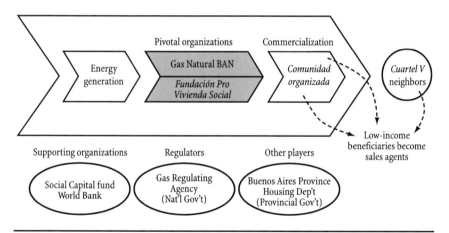

Source: Adapted from CSO documents.

2. Leverage the Existing Social Capital
Once the decision is made to explore ecosystem relationships associated with a value chain, experience suggests the advantages of **building on the existing social capital.** Knowing the structures, relationships, leaderships and non-written rules in place on site will enable organizations to save time and resources. In practical terms, a good place to start is the fabric of civil associations, cooperatives, grass-roots organizations and other actors with

long-standing presence on the ground. By approaching these organizations, it is possible to tap into a community's latent energy, and mobilize it with a view to ensuring venture success. Gas Natural Ban managed to secure an effective connection with LIS when FPVS, which had worked for some time at Moreno's Cuartel V district, offered a "social management model" that would provide the community poor with access to the natural gas network. According to Raúl Zavalía, FPVS executive director, "we turned the community's social capital into financial capital." To that end, FPVS supported a process that led to the creation of Comunidad Organizada (Organized Community), an umbrella including 45 grass-roots organizations at Cuartel V. As Fabián Chamadoira, the company's West Region Operations Manager, put it, "with no social fabric in place, failure is very likely."

3. Anchor Expectations, Reduce Uncertainty, and Enable Investments

Committing to other organizations in an ecosystem can stabilize uncertain environments, anchor expectations, and clarify commitments and roles, thus enabling investments. Many of the initiatives in our sample required the concerted efforts of several actors, which cooperatively built channels that enabled the flow of information, resources and products. At times, these organizational combinations gave way to new business models that would have been unfeasible with isolated efforts.

Several institutions were involved in the Solidarity Network Fiduciary fund:[67] the Social Capital Fund (FONCAP),[68] which contributed US$3 million to the fund; the World Bank, which donated US$750,000 as part of its Development Marketplace program; and neighbors—with their own contributions. The pooling of political will and resources produced a critical mass that infused the project with credibility. The fiduciary fund was used as a flexible, transparent financial tool that streamlined and captured investments from several sources—some of which could not have donated funds to a private company.

4. Securing Appropriation by the Community

A key lesson is how significant it is for beneficiary LIS communities to appropriate these projects, and become much more than mere "customers" or "consumers." For initiatives to enjoy long-term success, communities must perceive them as their own, particularly when markets are opaque, tacit data is crucial to the venture success, or the market features low-levels of development.

In the Gas Ban venture, building a fiduciary fund significantly influenced the community's "appropriation" process. When neighbors asked about natural gas network expansion costs, FPVS replied, "it's up to you." The cost for individual neighbors was the result of a division.[69] The total network expansion cost was the numerator, but the denominator, measuring the community's commitment to this project, was equally important (see Figure 5.4). The larger the denominator, the lower the cost for each neighbor. In addition, neighbors were not just making payments "to the company," but investing in themselves. The purpose of the fiduciary fund was to fund community projects. If the fund was oversold (as it eventually was), the surplus would not go to shareholders, but would be invested in community needs. Both arguments, added to monetary incentives for early subscribers, turned many community members into active promoters and sales people, by word of mouth, with a dynamics resembling "viral marketing" practices.

Figure 5.4
Community Involvement and Financial Burden

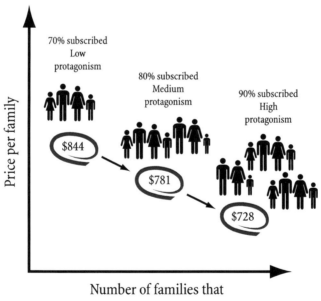

Number of families that
subscribe to adhesion contracts

5. Building Long-Term, Humanized Relationships
The dynamics of ecosystem interaction in initiatives targeted to the poor illustrate the constraints of traditional commercial approaches. Traditional commercial relations, based on depersonalized, one-time transactions, are

not suitable to work with low-income sectors. This conclusion bears significant implications for several corporate areas (marketing, finance, social responsibility, strategic planning, etc.). The notion of "business friendship" has a dual nature: on the one hand, it includes a personal component that emphasizes embeddedness, long-term commitment to individuals, and stability. On the other hand, it also features a materialistic, utilitarian component, as these relationships are ultimately about business and should be accountable for the resources they invest, even if the venture is not profit-seeking but mission-driven.

Gas Natural Ban devoted much attention to building long-lasting cooperation relationships that stressed continuity. This policy stemmed from pragmatic learning from previous experience, which revealed the limitations of purely commercial models in dealing with LIS. According to Raúl Zavalía, FPVS director, working together "implies an extraordinary effort for both parties. Neighbor interactions with utility companies and Gas Natural Ban's interactions with this type of customers required the development of several coordination mechanisms to promote and enable those interactions." These mechanisms are not developed overnight; they are built amidst deeply-rooted, embedded relationships based on mutual trust.

6. Legitimize Through Win-Win Results
Though this is probably self-evident, trust is bolstered by results. It is always helpful to have early victories to reverse a tradition of misunderstandings and distrust between LIS communities and companies.

The initiative led by Gas Natural Ban and FPVS shows significant results. From September 2003 until May 2006, 1,867 households accessed the natural gas network through this initiative. Family income allocations to energy purchase came down from US$35 a month (in natural gas substitutes such as bottled gas, wood, kerosene, electrical stoves, coal and other fuels) to US$7 monthly installments for natural gas network expansion works, plus a variable natural gas monthly expense (US$1 to $5).

Notes
1. Charles Holliday, Stephan Schmidheiney, and Philip Watts, *Walking theTtalk: The Business Case for Sustainable Development* (Sheffield: Greenleaf Publishing, 2002).
2. Diana Trujillo Cárdenas and Roberto Gutiérrez, "The Base of the Pyramid, Citizenship above Consumerism: Colombia's Colcerámica," *ReVista Harvard Review of Latin America* (Fall 2006).
3. Stuart Hart and Clayton Christensen, "The Great Leap: Driving Innovation from the Base of the Pyramid," *MIT Sloan Management Review* 44, no. 1 (2002).

4. Ibid.

5. C. K. Prahalad and Stuart Hart, "The Fortune at the Bottom of the Pyramid," *Strategy + Business* 1, no. 26 (2002).

6. John Weiser et al., *Untapped: Creating Value in Underserved Markets* (San Francisco, CA: Berrett-Koehler Publishers, Inc., 2006).

7. Allen L. Hammond et al., *The Next 4 Billion: Market Size and Business Strategy at the Base of the Pyramid* (Washington, DC: World Resources Institute and International Finance Corporation, 2007).

8. C. K. Prahalad, *The Fortune at the Bottom of the Pyramid: Eradicating Poverty through Profits* (Upper Saddle River, NJ: Wharton School Publishing, 2005), 65.

9. James Austin et al., *Social Partnering in Latin America: Lessons Drawn from Collaborations of Businesses and Civil Society Organizations* (Cambridge, MA: Harvard University, David Rockefeller Center for Latin American Studies, distributed by Harvard University Press, 2004).

10. SEKN, ed. *Effective Management of Social Enterprises Lessons from Businesses and Civil Society Organizations in Iberoamerica* (Cambridge, MA: Harvard University Press with David Rockefeller Center for Latin American Studies, 2006), 316.

11. "Organizational ecology" focuses on the environment where organizations compete, analyzing dynamics such as population evolution in these systems, as well as mortality and birth rates (company demise and inception pace). See Glenn R. Carroll, "Organizational Ecology," *Annual Review of Sociology* 10 (1984); Michael T. Hannan and John Freeman, *Organizational Ecology* (Cambridge, MA: Harvard University Press, 1989). In this chapter, this term is used with a different scope.

12. A "framework that allows private sector and social actors . . . to act together and create wealth in a symbiotic relationship". C. K. Prahalad, *The Fortune at the Bottom of the Pyramid: Eradicating Poverty through Profits* (Upper Saddle River, NJ: Wharton School Publishing, 2005), 65.

13. James F. Moore, *The Death of Competition: Leadership & Strategy in the Age of Business Ecosystems* (New York, NY: HarperBusiness, 1996), 26.

14. Michael E. Porter, *Competitive Advantage: Creating and Sustaining Superior Performance* (New York, NY: Free Press, 1985).

15. Marco Iansiti and Roy Levien, "Strategy as Ecology," *Harvard Business Review* (March 2004): 1.

16. Ibid.

17. Indeed, it may be argued that this idea is quite old—it was already developed in the Middle Ages, when cities flourished.

18. James F. Moore, *The Death of Competition: Leadership & Strategy in the Age of Business Ecosystems* (New York, NY: HarperBusiness, 1996), 3.

19. Ibid., 8.

20. Marco Iansiti and Roy Levien, "Strategy as Ecology," *Harvard Business Review* (March 2004): 2.

21. Michael E. Porter, *Competitive Advantage: Creating and Sustaining Superior Performance* (New York, NY: Free Press, 1985).

22. This category is not discussed extensively because it was not found to be particularly relevant in our sample. For a more detailed analysis, see Paul N. Bloom and Gregory Dees, "Cultivate Your Ecosystem," *Stanford Social Innovation Review* 6, no. 1 (Winter 2008).

23. Carlos Rufin, "The Role of Government: LIS Market Initiatives and the Public Sector," *ReVista Harvard Review of Latin America* (Fall 2006).

24. Antonio Tencati and Laszlo Zsolnai, "The Collaborative Enterprise," *Journal of Business Ethics* (2009): 374.

25. Carlos Rufin and Miguel Rivera-Santos, "Global Village vs. Small Town: Understanding Networks at the Base of the Pyramid" (unpublished paper, 2008), 15.

26. R. Edward Freeman, *Strategic Management: A Stakeholder Approach* (Boston: Pitman, 1984).

27. See, for example, ibid.

28. James F. Moore, "Predators and Prey: A New Ecology of Competition," *Harvard Business Review* (May 1993): 76.

29. "An example of a biological keystone is the sea otter, which helps regulate the coastal ecosystem of the Pacific Northwest by consuming large numbers of sea urchins. Left unchecked, sea urchins overgraze a variety of invertebrates and plants." Ibid., 5.

30. James Moore, *The Death of Competition: Leadership & Strategy in the Age of Business Ecosystems* (New York, NY: HarperBusiness, 1996), 26.

31. Marco Iansiti and Roy Levien, "Strategy as Ecology," *Harvard Business Review* (March 2004); *The Keystone Advantage* (Boston, MA: Harvard Business School Publishing, 2004).

32. SNV & World Business Council for Sustainable Development, "Inclusive Business: Profitable Business for Successful Development" (2008), http://wbcsd.typepad.com/wbcsdsnv/wbcsd_snv_alliance_brochure_march_08 _web.pdf.

33. Frances Westley and Harrie Vredenburg, "Strategic Bridging: The Collaboration between Environmentalists and Business in the Marketing of Green Products," *Journal of Applied Behavioral Sciences* 27, no. 1 (1991); Sanjay Sharma and Frances Westley, "Strategic Bridging: A Role for the Multinational Corporation in Third World Development," *Journal of Applied Behavioral Sciences* 30, no. 4 (1994); Ted London and Stuart L Hart, "Reinventing Strategies for Emerging Markets: Beyond the Transnational Model," *Journal of International Business Studies* 35 (2004); L. David Brown, "Bridging Organizations and Sustainable Development," *Human Relations* 44, no. 8 (1991).

34. John Hagel, John Seely Brown, and Lang Davison, "Shaping Strategy in a World of Constant Disruption," *Harvard Business Review* (October 2008): 3.

35. Annabelle Gawer and Michael A. Cusumano, "How Companies Become Platform Leaders," *MIT Sloan Management Review* 49, no. 2 (Winter 2008); John

Hagel, John Seely Brown, and Lang Davison, "Shaping Strategy in a World of Constant Disruption," *Harvard Business Review* (October 2008); Marco Iansiti and Roy Levien, "Strategy as Ecology," *Harvard Business Review* (March 2004).

36. John Hagel, John Seely Brown, and Lang Davison, "Shaping Strategy in a World of Constant Disruption," *Harvard Business Review* (October 2008): 7.

37. Marco Iansiti and Roy Levien, "Strategy as Ecology," *Harvard Business Review* (March 2004): 7.

38. Antonio Tencati and Laszlo Zsolnai, "The Collaborative Enterprise," *Journal of Business Ethics* (2009): 367.

39. Since its inception in 1979, Palmas del Espino embraced an active philanthropy, supporting schools, health centers and charities in its multiple operation areas.

40. José Carlos Mariátegui was a Peruvian reporter, politician, and thinker, considered to have been one of the most renowned theoreticians of Marxism in Latin America.

41. Farmer Honorio Espejo did not work for the José Mariátegui Producers' Association but for a small organization of small local producers that competed with Palmas.

42. Although it is not the purpose of this chapter, this example fittingly illustrates the problem faced by many companies when they confront these challenges with a corporate responsibility department that is not fully integrated to their business strategies. Palmas del Espino needed to integrate local producers to its value chain and could only do so with the contribution of company management and operation/production areas.

43. San Martín's Oil Palm Regional Federation (Federación Regional de Palma Aceitera, FREDEPALMA) and Peru's National Oil Palm Growers and Companies Confederation (Confederación Nacional de Palmicultores y Empresas de Palma Aceitera del Perú, CONAPAL).

44. The bank agreed to finance 500 hectares of palm plants, using the land as collateral. The loan (payable in 10 years at a 10% annual interest rate, with a five-year grace period) would be payable in monthly installments equivalent to half of the revenues from sales to the company. The company would serve as a collection agent for these payments, and, during the transition (while palm trees grew and became productive), it would pay farmers a salary equivalent with initial loan funds.

45. F. E. Emery and E. L. Trist, "The Causal Texture of Organizational Environments," *Human Relations* 18 (1965).

46. George B. Richardson, "The Organization of Industry," *Economic Journal* 82 (1972).

47. John Hagel, John Seely Brown, and Lang Davison, "Shaping Strategy in a World of Constant Disruption," *Harvard Business Review* (October 2008): 7.

48. "There can be a tremendous economic advantage in coordination when it comes to shaping the future—in terms of focusing investment, avoiding dead-ends, and finding a role in the center of a powerful community." James F. Moore,

The Death of Competition: Leadership & Strategy in the Age of Business Ecosystems (New York, NY: HarperBusiness, 1996), 61.

49. Marco Iansiti and Roy Levien, "Strategy as Ecology," *Harvard Business Review* (March 2004): 6.

50. John Hagel, John Seely Brown, and Lang Davison, "Shaping Strategy in a World of Constant Disruption," *Harvard Business Review* (October 2008): 2.

51. Paul N. Bloom and Gregory Dees, "Cultivate Your Ecosystem," *Stanford Social Innovation Review* 6, no. 1 (Winter 2008): 52.

52. The FSC is a global nonprofit that sets criteria for sustainable forest exploitation. It is governed by a multi-stakeholder scheme, with industry, civil society, and community representatives. FSC-sealed products are certified to have been produced in accordance to economic, social, and environmental sustainability practices. In the forest industry jargon, these products are known as "good wood"—they are physically identical to similar commodities but carry a significant, intangible value added. James E. Austin and Ezequiel A. Reficco, "Forest Stewardship Council," HBS Case No. 9-303-047 (Boston: Harvard Business School Publishing, 2002).

53. James Austin et al., *Social Partnering in Latin America: Lessons Drawn from Collaborations of Businesses and Civil Society Organizations* (Cambridge, MA: Harvard University, David Rockefeller Center for Latin American Studies, distributed by Harvard University Press, 2004), 9.

54. Ranjay Gulati, Sarah Huffman, and Gary Neilson, "The Barista Principle: Starbucks and the Rise of Relational Capital," *Strategy & Competition* Third Quarter (2002).

55. For instance, in lemon harvests, their yields ranged from 4 to 8 tons per hectare, while high-tech farms had an average yield of 30 to 40 tons per hectare.

56. For the concept of integrative alliances, see James Austin et al., *Social Partnering in Latin America: Lessons Drawn from Collaborations of Businesses and Civil Society Organizations* (Cambridge, MA: Harvard University, David Rockefeller Center for Latin American Studies, distributed by Harvard University Press, 2004).

57. "Functional fragmentation [in the value chain] requires securing technological compatibility and complementarity . . . in an effort to co-ordinate for quasi-reintegration and effective production on a now decentralized basis . . . Effective action is not feasible unless governed by a coordination mechanism that can deal with increased complexity." Wolfram Elsner, "The 'New' Economy: Complexity, Coordination and a Hybrid Governance Approach," *International Journal of Social Economics* 31, no. 11 (2004): 1031. The statement was made for markets that depend on net-based technologies, in which structural factors create incentives for collaboration. Interestingly, it seems to fit well the emerging field of market initiatives targeted at LIS.

58. Colombia's National Statistics Department divides the local population in six socio-economic strata—Colombians with the highest income are included in the sixth stratum.

59. A doctoral thesis, suggestively entitled "Because It Is Ours," presents a passionate defense of this argument in the context of Posada Amazonas, an ecological lodge in the Peruvian Amazon, where a company and an indigenous community built a joint venture as equal partners. Amanda Stronza, "Because It Is Ours: Community-Based Ecotourism in the Peruvian Amazon" (Ph.D. Dissertation, University of Florida, 2000).

60. Ezequiel Reficco and Patricia Marquez, "Socially Inclusive Networks for Building BOP Markets" (Working Paper, School of Business Administration, University of San Diego, October 2007).

61. Patricia Márquez and Ezequiel Reficco, "SMEs and Low-income Sectors," in *Small Firms, Global Markets: Competitive Challenges in the New Economy*, ed. Jerry Haar and Jörg Meyer-Stamer (London and New York: Palgrave Macmillan, 2008).

62. Erik Simanis and Stuart Hart. "Beyond Selling to the Poor: Building Business Intimacy through Embedded Innovation" (Working Paper, Cornell University. Ithaca, NY, 2008).

63. Ezequiel Reficco and Patricia Márquez, "Inclusive Networks for Building BOP Markets," *Business & Society* (forthcoming).

64. "Business intimacy . . . entails a deep interdependence wherein the company and community develop and nurture a shared commitment to each other's long term growth and development." Erik Simanis and Stuart Hart, "Beyond Selling to the Poor: Building Business Intimacy through Embedded Innovation" (Working Paper, Cornell University. Ithaca, NY, 2008).

65. Ranjay Gulati, Sarah Huffman, and Gary Neilson, "The Barista Principle: Starbucks and the Rise of Relational Capital," *Strategy & Competition* Third Quarter (2002).

66. Ezequiel Reficco and Patricia Marquez, "Socially Inclusive Networks for Building BOP Markets" (Working Paper, School of Business Administration, University of San Diego, October 2007).

67. A fiduciary fund is a legal instrument that enables a combination of several kinds of resources (money, machinery, buildings, land, tools, etc.) in a special fund or estate. These resources may only be used for a specific purpose.

68. State agency report to Argentina's Social Development Ministry.

69. As explained by FPVS: cost for each neighbor equals overall project cost (construction work plus administrative expenses plus financing cost) divided by percentage of subscribers.

Exhibit 1: Overview of the Ecosystems of the Initiatives Analyzed in Chapter

(a) Unilaterally managed value chains

	Initiative Leader	Business Partners	Support Organizations	Regulators
Private Companies	**Activo Humano** Private company specialized in labor intermediation, facilitates LIS access to employment.	Upstream: controlling group (Working Links) Downstream: franchisees, client companies	Local administrations, Labor Ministry's intermediation agencies, social organizations	
	Cemex Construmex Construmex channels money transfers from Mexican émigrés residing in the U.S. to Mexico for construction material and housing purchases. It also provides financial services to Mexicans employed in the U.S. who want to remodel or build a home in Mexico.	Construction companies, financial institution (Conficasa)	Émigré clubs, consulates, Social Development Department	
	Edenor Pilot program to provide pre-paid energy services to LIS, enabling fractioned payments in low installments, distributed overtime (as opposed to bi-monthly bill).	Downstream: LIS customers		
CSOs	**Asmare** Civil association that seeks to provide a livelihood for homeless citizens through urban waste recycling.	Upstream: large users (companies and government) Downstream: processing companies	Local administration (Social Assistance Department), CSO (Pastoral de Rúa)	Local administration (Urban Cleaning Supervisory Board)
	APAEB This cooperative intends to "promote sustainable and solidarity-based social and economic development, improving living conditions for hemp producing region's population" at Valent, Bahia, Brazil.	Exporters, distributors/marketers	Producers' associations, local CSOs, global CSOs	Unions
Cooperatives	**Bio Bio Pickers** This cooperative gathers wild fruit pickers from eight communities scattered in Southern Chile, who work together to market their fruits effectively and profitably.	Upstream: suppliers (forest companies) Downstream: distributors/buyers (agroindustry companies, fair-trade companies)		
	Porvenir It coordinates a group of urban waste recyclers to improve their living conditions.	Upstream: private suppliers, industrial suppliers. Downstream: processors (Cartón de Colombia)	Asociación de Recicladotes de Bogotá, Fundación Social	

Exhibit 1: Overview of the Ecosystems of the Initiatives Analyzed in Chapter (continued)

(b) Value chains co-managed through alliances

	Initiative Leader	Business Partners	Support Organizations	Regulators	Coordination, consensual cooperation or co-governance?
Private Companies	Agropalma This palm oil manufacturer has incorporated LIS as independent suppliers.	Upstream: financial institutions (Banco da Amazônia and Family Farming Strengthening Program), low income producers, affiliated with the Associaçao de Desenvolvimento Comunitário Arauaí	Technical assistance: Secretaria Executiva de Ciência, Tecnologia e Meio Ambiente (SECTAM), and Empresa de Assistência Técnica e Extensao Rural (EMATER). Land donations: Instituto de Terras de Pará	Instituto de Terras de Pará, which regulates land use. Also, the Pará State issues permits to release federal funding from PRONAF (Family Agriculture Strengthening Program).	Consensual cooperation. Strategic decisions are made consensually between the company, the local and state administrations, the bank and producers (affiliated with an association). Tactical, day-to-day decisions are made bilaterally, by company and producers: not equals, but committed to reaching consensus. Amanco
	This company markets irrigation systems for LIS through a cross-sector, integrative alliance.	Upstream: financing providers (AMUCSS). Downstream: marketers (Wal-Mart), distributors (RASA, Red de Agronegocios Autosustentables). Downstream: LIS farmers	Technical assistance: Ashoka Philanthropic financial support: Wal-Mart Foundation, Bimbo Foundation, Fundemex and Firco (government)		Coordination. No formal forum; ecosystem actors' interests and perspectives were articulated by social entrepreneurs, supported by Ashoka.
	Cativen Supermarket chain that has incorporated LIS as perishable produce providers.	Producers' cooperatives working on logistical platformss	ACET (Asociación Civil de Extensión Agrícola de Timotes), Riego Trujillano (parastatal organization) to identify producers, organizations and leaders; Universidad Central de Venezuela, to develop new internal farming competencies.		Coordination. The company and a large number of cooperatives coordinate quantity, quality and production standards based on demand fluctuations, seasonality as well as soil and weather conditions.

Exhibit 1: Overview of the Ecosystems of the Initiatives Analyzed in Chapter (continued)

(b) Value chains co-managed through alliances (continued)

	Initiative Leader	Business Partners	Support Organizations	Regulators	Coordination, consensual cooperation or co-governance?
Private Companies	Colcerámica Industrial group that manufactures and markets home improvement and construction products and intends to market a product line designed for LIS. LIS co-manage this market chain.	Downstream. (a) Community organizations: grassroots organizations that supervised promoters, managed sales revenues/ commissions, and displayed LIS product line. (b) Promoters: LIS citizens that sell products door to door, provide technical assistance, advice on payment plans, post-sales service.	(a) Through students, a group of universities researched the existence of a potential consumer market for Colcerámca products among LIS. (b) A social entrepreneur -Ashoka fellow- provided support and training for producers and advice to the company.		Co-governance. Integrative alliance with a value chain co-managed with non-traditional actors. Its Community Organizational Nucleus is a forum that makes strategic decisions, including distribution of profits among participants.
	CRES Costa Rica Entomological Supplies (CRES) is a company that purchases, breeds, packs and exports pupae to butterfly exhibitors in the U.S. and Europe. It has incorporated LIS farmers as vendors.	Upstream: LIS producers who supply pupae for the company.	The National Biodiversity Institute (InBio) provides scientific and technical support to pupae producers; Costa Rica's Environmental Ministry (MINAE) offers information on environmental requirements, and the International Trade Ministry (COMEX) provides information on exports.	MINAE, enforcement agency for the Wild Life Preservation Act (Nbr. 7317), regulates Costa Rica's pupae supply.	Coordination. The company and a large number of producers coordinate quantity, quality and production standards based on demand and regional climates.

Exhibit 1: Overview of the Ecosystems of the Initiatives Analyzed in Chapter (continued)

(b) Value chains co-managed through alliances (continued)

	Initiative Leader	Business Partners	Support Organizations	Regulators	Coordination, consensual cooperation or co-governance?
Private Companies	Gas Natural BAN This natural gas network provider led an initiative to expand its network to LIS neighborhoods in a partnership with CSOs and grassroots organizations.	Downstream. "Comunidad Organizada", which encompasses 45 grassroots organizations and whose Secretariat executes the decisions made by consensus at Assemblies; Fundación Pro Vivienda Social (FPVS) designed financing model (fiduciary trust) for the initiative, as well as unconventional promotion methods and commercialization channels.	Financing: Fondo de Capital Social (FONCAP), World Bank.		Co-governance. "Comunidad Organizada" is a forum that gives the community a voice on strategic decisions on the initiative, such as the need to expand the network, as well as the use to be given to surplus resources raised through the fiduciary fund. Decisions are made by consensus between C0, the company and FPVS.
	Hortifruti This agricultural product supplier for supermarkets developed a development program for small farmers, offering farming supplies, technical advice and ongoing follow-up.	Low income farmers who provide perishable produce to the company.	a) CSOs provide technical assistance, funding, training and overall education (in Nicaragua: Catholic Relief Services, Adventist Development & Relief Agency International; in Honduras: Fundación COVELO, Swiss Contact). b) Producers' associations (e.g., Corporación Nacional Arrocera). c) Public agencies, like the Agricultural Ministry's Farming Development Program, or the Food Research and Technology Center (CITA). d) Government or multi-lateral development agencies: USAID, Partnership for Food Industry Development, Economic Development Administration.		Coordination. The company and a large number of cooperatives coordinate quantity, quality and production standards based on demand fluctuations, seasonality as well as soil and weather conditions.

Exhibit 1: Overview of the Ecosystems of the Initiatives Analyzed in Chapter (continued)

(b) Value chains co-managed through alliances (continued)

	Initiative Leader	Business Partners	Support Organizations	Regulators	Coordination, consensual cooperation or co-governance?
Private Companies	Irupana Irupana Andean Organic Food is a private company that manufactures organic food products based on crops provided by indigenous farmers in the Andes, Amazon and Bolivian Chaco regions.	Upstream: financial institutions, farming communities that provide organic products. Downstream: stocking, transformation or commercialization companies.	CSO Asociación Boliviana para el Desarrollo Rural (Prorural) provides technical assistance, training, infrastructure, and funding; it also oversees agreements and mediates to solve conflicts.		Coordination. The company and a large number of producers coordinate quantity, quality and production standards based on demand and regional climates.
	Palmas del Espino This palm oil manufacturer has incorporated LIS as independent suppliers.	Upstream. Production: low income farmers (affiliated with José Carlos Mariátegui Farmers' Association) supply palm as raw material for oil production. Financing: Banco de Crédito del Perú. Training and technical support: GESTIPALMA, a private consulting firm built by former company employees.			Coordination. The company and associated producers coordinate quantity, quality and production standards based on manufacturing capacity and demand fluctuations.

Exhibit 1: Overview of the Ecosystems of the Initiatives Analyzed in Chapter (continued)

(b) Value chains co-managed through alliances (continued)

	Initiative Leader	Business Partners	Support Organizations	Regulators	Coordination, consensual cooperation or co-governance?
Civil Society Organizations	CIAP Peru's Cross-Regional Artisan Center (Central Interregional de Artesanos del Perú, CIAP) is a CSO that encompasses 20 artisan grassroots groups, selling their production with business criteria (scale, efficiency) in export markets.	Upstream: Handicraft producers' associations (associates), suppliers. Downstream: Commercialization agency focused on exports, Intercrafts (wholly owned private company). Financing: CIAP Savings and Loans Cooperative (wholly owned savings cooperative); PRO-Ecosol, solidarity economy shopping mall (wholly owned company). Fair-trade importers (SERVV International, Solidar Monde, CTM Altromercato, Commercio Alternativo and Cooperativa Equo Mercato).	a) International fair-trade networks (International Association for Alternative Trade or IFAT; Latin American Community Trade Network, Peru's Solidarity Economy Network Group, Peruvian Fair Trade and Ethical Consumption Network. IFAT is the most important: it contributes through networking capabilities and access to customers and peer organizations in other countries. b) Fair-trade stores in importing markets from developed countries that promote southern suppliers' development (CAFÉ, SERVV, Solidar Monde, etc.)		Co-governance. Grassroots organizations are represented at CIAP's governance bodies, and their interests and perspectives determine the group's (CIAP plus controlled private companies) business strategy.

Exhibit 1: Overview of the Ecosystems of the Initiatives Analyzed in Chapter (continued)

(b) Value chains co-managed through alliances (continued)

	Initiative Leader	Business Partners	Support Organizations	Regulators	Coordination, consensual cooperation or co-governance?
Civil Society Organizations	Corporación Oro Verde The Oro Verde Corporation (COV) is an integrative alliance intended to improve living conditions for African-Colombian populations through socially and environmentally sustainable mining operations.	Upstream. Producers: Productive Family Units (UFP), low-income social group (close relatives) that works in sustainable mining operations. Distributors: Community Councils aggregate and distribute production, coordinate sustainability certifications, and strengthen UFP work. Downstream. Gross metal processing companies (CUBIS y CIGSA).	Financing and promotion (Oxfam-Novib, Both Ends, CEPF, Ashoka, Fondo para la Acción Ambiental y la Niñez - FPAAN-, Conservación Internacional). Market research, business plans, mining, environmental impact, cultural identity (Instituto de Estudios Regionales, of the Universidad de Antioquia, Universidad Tecnológica del Chocó and Eafit). Community Development (Fundación Centro Internacional de Educación y Desarrollo Humano). Ad-hoc support from other organizations (Colombian Collegiate Design Institute and Professional Excellence Program, Alliance Française, Asociación Intercultural Antioquia Chocó, Antioquia Museum, American Colombian Center).	The Pacific Ocean Environmental Research Institute (Instituto de Investigaciones Ambientales del Pacífico, IIAP) issues certificates for minerals extracted with sustainable procedures. The Association for Responsible Mining (ARM) establishes global standards for responsible mining.	Co-governance. This joint venture is managed by two CSOs (Fundación Amigos del Chocó and Fundación Las Mojarras) and grassroots organizations (Community Councils) that articulate community interests. The poor perform a key role in the definition of overall strategy.

6

Utilities: Private Interests and Social Benefits

Verónica Durana, Natalia Franco, Roberto Gutiérrez, Iván Darío Lobo, and Diana Trujillo

> *Now, just a few pioneers have turned their eyes to low-income citizens; in ten years' time, this will be a standard for the entire electrical sector.*
> —Ivar Pettersson, COO, AES Brazil

Utilities typically satisfy basic needs, aspire to universal coverage, depend on dedicated physical networks for their distribution, and are profoundly conditioned by several kinds of public regulations and political pressures. As a result, serving low-income citizens becomes strategic and encompasses a range of challenges and opportunities. The following pages provide an analysis of companies that supply two residential utilities: electricity and natural gas. These companies have faced several operating challenges—from theft of a substantial portion of their output to new market development. We explore how the five companies in our sample rose to those challenges to effectively serve low-income sectors (LIS).

Among the five companies are some with long-term experiences and considerable scale, as well as others that have not successfully completed their pilot phase. Why have some of these enterprises had an impact on the lives of many thousands of people while others have influenced just a few? The answers to this question shed some light on the characteristics of both LIS consumers and utility service providers. This chapter presents these answers after describing the problems faced by these companies and analyzing how they addressed them.

Context and Challenges in the Value Chain of Utility Companies

Latin America registers increasing poverty in its cities. In 2007, nearly 32 percent of the urban population included families living in precarious housing conditions and without any basic utilities (electricity, water, sewage, among others). These citizens view utilities as a right and a need, and try to gain access to them either legally or illegally.[1] In these cases, providing utility services to market segments that are unattractive on account of their limited payment ability is not only a growth opportunity but also a strategic imperative.[2]

The five initiatives considered here have sought to turn some LIS into customers by building business models that suit their characteristics. We have classified these initiatives in two groups: three companies that provide energy services, and two natural gas companies. During the study period (1998–2006), these five companies were multinationals. Until the early 1990s, Edenor (Argentina), Gas Natural Ban (Argentina), and Codensa (Colombia) were state-owned companies, while Electricidad de Caracas had been a private company until its nationalization in 2007.[3] At the turn of the century, all five sample companies were owned by foreign multinationals. Then, in 2005, Edenor was transferred from the French multinational Electricité de France to an Argentine business group.

Challenges for Energy Distribution Companies

Around the world, 40 percent of urban poor populations have no access to modern electricity services, as stated by a recent USAID report.[4] That document starts with an overview of the predicament shared by energy distribution companies: "even within the poorest neighborhoods, electricity is almost universally available. A closer look reveals that this electricity is usually stolen (largely by third parties), which results in poor quality service provided at very high prices and extremely dangerous conditions."[5]

Any company that loses a substantial portion of its output is in trouble. Non-technical losses at AES-Electricidad de Caracas—including a significant share of illegal connections—rose until they reached 18 percent in 2004 (accounting for US$35 million losses). Confronted with this situation, some company officials recognized the importance of serving poor neighborhood dwellers. AES-EDC was the exclusive energy provider in metropolitan Caracas, a city with a population in excess of five million, half of whom resided in unplanned communities called *barrios* (neighborhoods).[6]

Another problem faced by electricity companies has been delinquent payments. Empresa Distribuidora Norte S.A. (Edenor), in charge of energy distribution in northern and greater Buenos Aires since 1992, has faced delinquent bills from low-income customers. In 2006, Edenor had 2.4 million customers in an area with an overall population of 6.8 million (20 percent of Argentina's total population)—600,000 of them were low-income customers, and nearly 200,000 had recurring payment arrears.

When theft and delinquent payments accumulate, electricity distributing companies face a crisis. Such was the case of Empresa de Energía Eléctrica de Bogotá in 1995, when it was declared nonviable by Colombia's Energy and Gas Regulation Commission. Two years later, Endesa, a Spanish group, acquired a controlling stake in the company, now called Codensa, which was awarded a license to provide energy to 8.1 million people in Bogotá and 96 townships in the region of Cundinamarca. Most of its customers, 88.8 percent, were private users (2.05 million households); 83.3 percent of them on socio-economic levels 1, 2, and 3.[7] Energy losses (US$82 million a year) amounted to 23.3 percent of the company's overall production, while late payments accounted for 115 percent of its monthly sales (US$42.9 million).

The three sample companies—and many other electricity distribution companies around the world—have made significant efforts to reduce nontechnical losses and defaults.[8] Before discussing how they chose to address these issues, it is important to take a look at the challenges faced by another type of utility companies.

Challenges for Natural Gas Distribution Companies

Because natural gas is a product with several substitutes, the challenge faced by these utilities was different from the one faced by energy distributors. Although natural gas features a lower unit cost as compared to other fuels, installation costs are high for LIS, forcing companies to develop innovative awareness, credit, and subsidy strategies to lower financial barriers hindering access and to ensure niche penetration.

Why does it make business sense to compete to serve LIS? When company operations are restricted to a specific geographical area, as is the case of licenses to operate in a given territory, serving LIS becomes a business expansion option. In late 1992, Gas Natural Ban—the Argentine affiliate of the Spanish energy multinational Gas Natural—was awarded a license to provide utility distribution services in Buenos Aires Province's northern area, the region with the largest population and industry concentration in the country. Out of the total 1.3 million customers served by the company in this area, 190,000 were in low-income sectors. The area managed by Gas Ban covered, on average, 79.5 percent of all households, but in low-income neighborhoods, only 55 percent of households were serviced. As an institutional brochure put it, "this counts for a great opportunity and challenge for both the company and the community." Some company officials were more emphatic in their statements about LIS: "these are the segments we need to approach. Penetration in these sectors stands at 20%, depending on the location. Clearly, this is where we need to grow, as opposed to other sectors that have 99% coverage."

For companies with license boundaries, the growth option involving LIS becomes most attractive. This appeal does not only stem from typical license restrictions; it may also result from high operating costs incurred to serve markets in other areas. Because of inadequate roads in the region exploited by Aguaytía Energy of Perú, transportation costs for liquefied petroleum gas (LPG or LP gas) from oilfields in the jungle area between Pucallpa and Iquitos to Lima amounted to US$12 per barrel. With one of the highest transportation costs in the world, the company set out to transform energy matrixes at communities surrounding oilfields, both for household and public transportation fuel applications, in order to expand its local customer base. While the overall investment for this oilfield exploitation project totaled US$300 million, accounting for a significant barrier to direct competitors, Aguaytía's products competed with other kinds of fuel, such as gasoline, diesel oil, kerosene, and wood, among other energy substitutes used by lower-income Peruvian communities.

Gas Ban and Aguaytía rose to local growth challenges in different ways. The analysis of the reasons for their different outcomes and the comparison of their approaches vis-à-vis those used by energy distribution companies yield interesting lessons.

Innovative Models That Allowed For the Inclusion of LIS

The sample utility companies embarked on multiple efforts to reduce their losses and to face the growth challenges described above. These efforts may be grouped according to their major goals: to improve services and associated consumer perceptions, and to provide convenience of payment.

Both electricity and natural gas distributors need to offer attractive services and products to LIS—the former, to change existing relations (based on illegal connections and delinquent payments) with these consumers, and the latter, to approach them. Offerings that are appealing to middle-income classes may not attract LIS. A US$10 electricity bill may go unnoticed in a middle-income family's budget, while it may leave a low-income family with no means to afford other basic expenses. The opportunity cost of scarce cash is quite high for a low-income family. If the value of a utility is perceived as high, consumers are more willing to pay for it, **even** if their income is low. Enriching value propositions becomes imperative for utility companies—if they don't succeed, they are threatened by illegal consumption or stagnated growth.

A Value Proposition That Appeals to LIS

In the specific case of electricity, value propositions must make it more attractive for LIS to become legal paying customers. Finding offerings that low-income consumers may view as valuable is not simple—more so when companies have remained detached from the reality of their lives. In contrast to strictly technical approaches used by former administrations, in 2003 AES-EDC started to explore ways to change its relationship with LIS. The company hired 30 social workers for three pilot projects. In the first project, special energy service meters were installed at 300 households in a downtown Caracas neighborhood (with 1,200 houses) in order to develop a pre-paid service system similar to schemes designed by mobile telephone services and widely used by LIS in Venezuela. This initial stage enabled the company to gain a better understanding of these target populations and their interest in having a better energy service and becoming regular customers. However, this initiative was thwarted because the regulating agency did not approve the use of a pre-paid system. Months later, two other projects were executed: one to drive payments for hundreds of invoices with years in arrears, all from a massive social housing development (154 buildings with an average of 400 apartments each), and another one, called "zero tangles," to remove highly dangerous illegal connection cables as well as to turn consumers into company customers.[9] These three efforts were intended to reduce energy losses, but they also served as a learning lab for AES-EDC on how to provide electricity services to LIS, transforming this challenge into a business opportunity.

Direct communications among companies and communities are crucial to build mutual knowledge and trust as well as negotiating schemes. AES-EDC agreed to provide better quality of service and more street lighting in exchange for users' debt recognition and acceptance to have meters installed. In addition to reducing company losses, this set of initiatives, called "Electrical Neighborhood," enabled AES-EDC to build a new kind of relationship with these communities, to recognize customer heterogeneity in this market segment, and to understand LIS consumption patterns. Eventually, the company enhanced its value proposition for LIS. In 2006, partnering with Banco Venezolano de Crédito, AES-EDC launched a cash card called "EDC Silver." With this card, users could deposit funds in their card accounts to purchase goods at neighborhood stores and pay their monthly energy service bills. For a monthly fee of 3,000 *bolívares* (around US$1.35 at the official exchange rate), two additional cards could be issued to relatives, with the possibility of wiring funds to any location across the nation. For individuals with no access to banking services, having a cash card brought significant benefits. Even after the company was nationalized, the bank continued this program with government support.

Convincing customers of the benefits of a legal, regular service was relatively easy. AES-EDC managed to turn 173,000 low-income citizens into customers over a four-year period. The hard part was retaining them as regular customers. That was the challenge faced by the company at the time of its nationalization in February 2007.

Another example of efforts to "legalize" thousands of consumers was provided by Codensa. The new management that took over in 1997, with Endesa as controlling shareholder, initiated the process. "At inception, Codensa's goal was to become financially viable," said David Felipe Acosta, its Marketing Manager. "We started focusing on communities rather than on technical issues, seeking their validation as citizens. Other experiences tackled technical problems, like building anti-theft networks . . . although losses were reduced, late payments increased. In some cases, like Lima, severe social problems resulted from confrontations with communities."

The company established a direct dialog with users through community programs. At the same time, Codensa increased street lighting services and improved technical systems to prevent electricity theft. To promote payments, it offered incentives (such as waiving interests on old debts and rewarding timely payments), and penalties (immediate service interruption in default cases). These activities involved countless efforts. Experiences by energy companies that have tried to "normalize" LIS services consistently point to difficulties such as finding people at home during the week, high dweller turnover, and hard-to-access, narrow streets with no clear and accurate names and numbers.

From 1997 to 2001, service quality improvements, timely payment promotion, and technical interventions successfully "normalized" the service provided by Codensa to nearly 300,000 customers, reducing energy losses to 11.3 percent and delinquent debt to 27 percent. The number of monthly service interruptions dropped from 86,500 to 47,500. Reducing energy losses by half and monthly late payments to less than a quarter brought yearly savings of nearly US$70 million for the company.

Codensa's process, which took longer than the one carried out by AES-EDC, shows other alternatives to maintain LIS legally connected. The company understood that without the ability to retain customers, service "normalization" for LIS might be just a "quick fix," a temporary relief from massive losses. In the same vein, the effort to keep low-income citizens as customers drove Gas Ban to reformulate its entire customer acquisition scheme for the natural gas network.

The need to expand its customer base and natural gas network led Gas Ban to create several programs to provide natural gas services to LIS. The company launched its "Gas for Everyone" program, with two campaigns carried out between 1997 and 2001. This experience marked its first approach to LIS. In this program, the company acted as a liaison among three actors: financial institutions, certified installers, and low-income customers. The latter used loans granted by financial institutions to cover natural gas service installation costs, which, on average, were four times as high as average LIS salaries. Installers contacted customers to build their connections to natural gas networks and to determine the technical requirements of each household. The company delegated customer demand management to installers.

Gas Ban's value proposition was fairly attractive—in the late 1990s, natural gas was seven times cheaper than propane tanks, and the loans took care of installation costs. Within this scheme, 100,000 new customers were incorporated. However, excessive consumption prevented families from paying their bills. Installers benefited by installing the largest possible number of outlets, while users failed to maintain a reasonable consumption level. Argentina's economic crisis compounded this situation, until only 90,000 customers remained. Ricardo Saponara, Gas Ban's Customer Service Manager, noted:

> With the *Gas for Everyone* program, we sought broad customer growth—penetrating the market as fast as possible or building new networks quickly. We focused on growing the number of customers, without enough attention to quality. Certified gas installers were the ones who chose which customers and neighborhoods to target for network expansion. We gave in to our sales force. If we had partitioned our demand, we would have done better.

After this experience, the company learned that "it is impossible to keep the traditional marketing rationale" with LIS. The program revealed that outsourcing its customer relationship management was not an effective approach to LIS. As Saponara put it, "we could no longer do things the way we used to, telling contractors, 'ok, see what you can do in that neighborhood, and, if it is a poor neighborhood, tough luck.' If we do not understand the reality we are working with, we haven't learned a thing."

Initiatives to Retain Customers

It is not enough to acquire new customers; it is crucial to retain them. While customer retention is always important—keeping a customer is usually less costly than gaining one—it is vital in inclusive business, which tends to require large volumes for profitability. In the words of Andrés Geringer, Gas Ban's Marketing and Trade Coordination Manager, "The margin provided by low-income customers is lower and more difficult to maintain; thus, it is necessary to be very smart about it."

Retaining customers has been challenging for residential utility companies. Natural gas and energy companies face somewhat different problems. When it comes to delinquent payments, for example, even though there may be illegal connections to natural gas networks, gas companies can easily interrupt their service and stop their losses. By contrast, it is harder to cut supply to electricity service customers, as energy does not have many obvious substitutes. Customer attrition, in the case of natural gas, and increased energy theft, for electric power, drove companies to reconsider their product marketing schemes.

The traditional marketing rationale, with massive marketing campaigns to stimulate a demand that is later served, does not work for LIS. "These customers don't come to our offices to request a gas connection; they demand a much larger effort from our marketing department," explained Horacio Cristiani, Commercial Director at Gas Ban. Most utility companies need to discover how to approach this population in order to attract and retain it as customers. Successful strategies to maintain LIS as customers at sample companies have involved careful selection processes, various payment facilities, and value proposition enhancement.

Selection Process

An effective strategy starts with a selection of prospective customers. This process goes beyond determining who will be served and who will not; it includes demand preparation and streamlining. After its "Gas for Everyone" program, Gas Ban began to explore more focused approaches to LIS. The first was an initiative developed by Fundación ProVivienda Social (FPVS), which mobilized community resources and organizations in order to engage Cuartel V neighbors, legitimize this initiative, and streamline demand. A fiduciary fund was created with contributions from several organizations as to fund infrastructure works required to provide service access. Both loan acquisition and payment demanded strong LIS community commitment—neighbors were in charge of streamlining demand, monitoring payment compliance, and reporting. On account of their knowledge of and proximity to LIS, organizations such as FPVS and other neighborhood associations were instrumental in helping Gas Ban to acquire and sustain customers.

At some of the neighborhoods where the gas network expanded to next, other civil society organizations (to streamline demand) and local administrations (to provide financing) were leading actors. From late 2003 until 2006, Gas Ban expanded its natural gas network to six low-income neighborhoods in the Greater Buenos Aires area, and nearly 3,000 new customers started to receive this utility service. Throughout these expansion projects, the company sought to promote, manage, collaborate, and work with low-income neighbors and community organizations. Here, from the beginning, Gas Ban maintained direct contact with neighbors, organizations, and local administrations, in contrast to its traditional business model. Tools and solutions were especially designed and adjusted to cater to each neighborhood's needs—rather than using massive campaigns. The notion of "fuel substitution" was reinforced to generate savings from the start, and payment follow-up and control were handled through monthly invoices.

The schemes relied on building trust and addressing community specificities, rather than applying preset, systematic operating approaches. At Gas Ban's initiatives, the support provided to LIS by social organizations (advice and online assistance) increased product satisfaction and encouraged agreement compliance. Gas Ban's Western Region Operations Manager, Fabián Chamadoira, elaborated, "The key to success is not the model itself; successful replication depends on location, scale and environmental conditions." Such specificities restrained service expansion to LIS. In 2007, Gas Ban's plans to reach 12,000 new customers with an average income of US$150 raised this question: how could installation costs of US$600 to US$700 be financed?

Payment Convenience

A basic way to retain customers is to make it easier for them to pay for their services. Payment issues relate not only to LIS scarce and unsteady cash flows, but also to payment conditions. Customers' willingness to pay decreases with inconvenient payment conditions, among other things. Another factor that eases payments is household consumption efficiency, which reduces expenses.

As most poor neighborhood or slum dwellers are part of informal economies, utility companies have been challenged to understand what conditions are more conducive to timely payments, given low-income population's income generation pace. Thus, a major business innovation lies in schemes to facilitate service billing and payment. These schemes start with clear, relevant information. The three sample energy companies—Edenor, Codensa, and AES-EDC—changed their invoices to make them more user-friendly, with clearer explanations of what is being billed and how much customers pay for kilowatt consumption.

Service-oriented companies have a vast infrastructure that transforms **payment logistics**. In 1998–2001, Codensa opened 13 customer service centers and looked for ways to make energy invoices easier to pay. Among other efforts, the company reduced billing periods to a month and expanded its collection network. Codensa has gradually added new options that are promptly announced on invoices—"You no longer need to find a place to pay; you just pick your location of choice. Now you have more than 3,700 ways to pay your bill." Choices include electronic payment, automatic-attendant systems (paying invoices over the phone has become a standard practice for most utilities in Bogotá), and various points of payment (Codensa bills can even be paid at supermarket cashiers).

Even the most extensive collection network is useless if customers do not have the means to pay. Hence some companies have tried to ensure that their customers use only as much gas or energy as they can afford. This is one of the reasons underlying the emergence of programs for **efficient and rational energy utilization**. It is crucial for utility companies that low-income consumers have the necessary information on efficient energy use and its benefits. Edenor officials preferred to approach LIS "not using traditional supply interruption methods, but training them on efficient energy utilization," as noted Alejandro di Natale, the company's Sustainable Development and Safety Manager. Gas Ban's management also realized how important it was to raise awareness among LIS on responsible consumption. As María Bettina Llapur, External Affairs Director, explained,

> We approach poor neighborhoods with our marketing area and explain to neighbors how much gas each appliance uses, how to read the bill properly, and to help them understand that they cannot install ten appliances and start squandering gas because it just doesn't make any business sense—two months later, those people stop being customers because they cannot afford their first bill. That is a business and social fiasco. It's better this way: we go talk to poor customers, and we explain to them how to use their gas more efficiently and how to really save . . . This means we provide something more than just a utility or a connection.

Peruvian Aguaytía has built its business around low cost. The cost of LP gas as transportation fuel was 50 percent lower than the cost of more contaminating fuels such as gasoline, and it increased daily earnings by 45 percent to 130 percent, depending on vehicle type and ownership. The company absorbed the cost of adapting small gasoline-powered engines and recovered its investment with local sales in periods ranging from two to three years, depending on the type of vehicle and its LP gas consumption. On another front, the families that cooked mostly with wood or kerosene received gas stoves for free or for a symbolic price, as well as a discount on their first LPG tank as part of Aguaytía's market expansion strategy. This initiative has already delivered nearly 50,000 stoves and converted 7 percent of local vehicles; the hope is to reach an overall 50 percent vehicle conversion rate.

In addition to promoting affordable consumption, some companies have explored other service payment systems—**pre-paid systems and fragmented purchases**. As an Edenor official explained, "payment issues at LIS segments were attributed not so much to customers' willingness to pay—for most were willing to pay—but to service payment terms. We needed to adjust our service to their capabilities." The company tried several options. In one of its programs, it allowed customers to purchase energy vouchers that they could later use to pay their bills. In a pilot project launched in 2002, Edenor installed 100 pre-paid meters in Escobar, in Buenos Aires Province's northern area. In view of its good results, in July 2003, the project was replicated in the Merlo area, where 4,200 low-income families switched from irregular energy supply to pre-paid meters.

By charging for actual energy consumption, this pre-paid system drove a consumption decrease of nearly 30 percent, while the share of customers who paid on time rose to 95 percent. This system, closely tailored to customer income, reduced the company's financial losses. Since its inception in mid 2002 and until 2006, 834,382 advance purchases were made for approximately US$800,000. Over 60 percent of these purchases were below a dollar and were sold at most 15 blocks away from customers' homes. "The purpose of this project is to incorporate people who are well below poverty and indigence lines. They have no saving capacity; therefore, they have no payment capacity, which creates a lot of costs for us. With this project, customers can make one-dollar purchases, instead of paying a 17-dollar (aprox. 50 Argentine pesos) bimonthly invoice," elaborated Jorge Rigamonti, Edenor's Regulatory Agency and Analysis Deputy Manager.

Small packaging has been a practice used by consumer companies for quite some time, and is not limited to them or to energy companies.

Aguaytía began to install service stations much like gas pumps, as LIS find it easier to purchase small LPG amounts than full tanks.

Multiple initiatives to facilitate payments reduce the likelihood of defaults by LIS, but do not eliminate them. **Flexible payment terms** constitute one last alternative when customers are experiencing payment difficulties. As part of its debt reduction program, Codensa designed easy finance plans and created payment schemes of up to 48 months with no interest—waiving all penalty interests for LIS customers—but established a service suspension policy for two-day defaults of these payments, while it improved its operating capacity for service interruptions and reconnections. Additionally, it built reward programs for timely payments with monthly raffles. According to company officials, the promotion of new payment habits has been instrumental for success.

LIS finances are especially vulnerable to economic crises. At such times, it is more important than ever to offer flexible payment terms. During Argentina's 2001–2002 economic crisis, Edenor took advantage of its controlling stockholder's (Electricité de France) sustainable development policy to build a payment scheme that enabled delinquent customers to pay their debt in weekly installments. The company's Sustainable Development and Safety Department was in charge of this development. At other companies, flexible payment terms were suggested by communities themselves. Female leaders, who served as "account executives" for AES-EDC, negotiated with their neighbors and even collected payments from users where housing conditions called for the installation of collective rather than individual meters. The company recruited a team of up to 50 female volunteer coordinators at the neighborhoods where new flexible payment procedures were tested.

In addition to these four types of payment convenience, companies like AES-EDC also found ways to exploit intangible assets (i.e., social fabric) to exercise social control for payment compliance. The combination of these measures has contributed to customer retention.

Value Proposition Enhancement

To turn consumers into legal customers, a company's value proposition must be *attractive;* to retain customers, it helps to *enrich* that value proposition. Codensa used two initiatives to attract and retain customers. The company had found that one of the causes underlying energy theft was that people could tell no difference between illegal connections and the company's regular services—there was no perception of value added in the legal connection. Tania García-Aranda, Household and Small Store Deputy Manager, knew that "when customers don't get any benefits, a product—no matter how inexpensive it might be—will always be viewed as expensive. Our assurance lies in communities wanting us, feeling that we validate them as citizens and deliver benefits that go beyond well-supplied energy."

At first, the company worked in four areas: network and service quality improvements, loss reduction, delinquent payment reduction, and social programs. As Codensa's Marketing Manager put it, its foremost goal was "operating excellence, and, only then, [did we focus on] consolidating our supply." Through "closer relationships with our customers and new product and service development," that consolidation was accomplished. The company did not only work on retaining its low-income customers, but it also worked to retain customers in general in case the energy distribution market were to become deregulated, and customers could then choose among several distributors. This posed a challenge for energy companies that were used to have relative monopolies. Companies would have to compete not only to capture new customers but also to retain/hold on to their existing ones as well.

Once it streamlined its operations, Codensa decided to enrich its value proposition for customers by means of a broad product and service portfolio. With this, it also raised entry barriers for potential competitors. In 2001, the Marketing Department led the creation of Codensa Home, a business line for consumer appliance financing, with credit installments payable along with energy bills. This initiative was based on three premises: (1) developing a business to enhance customer loyalty; (2) accomplishing self-sustainability; and (3) exploiting the company's competencies. Codensa Home's business model included partnerships with leading retailers and appliance manufacturers; outsourcing support services required to operate this business; developing finance systems; incorporating new product billing in energy service invoices; and building a marketing infrastructure to launch, maintain and deliver Codensa Home's products and services.

The company was in charge of managing the downstream value chain. Codensa contacted financial institutions so that, as business partners, they would grant consumer loans to LIS at competitive rates. This offering awoke little interest, given the formal banking institutions' poor information on low-income sectors and their "reluctance to grant loans to people with no banking record." Codensa's management then decided to use company surpluses to finance home appliance purchases. With the information from customers' payment records and the company's billing and credit systems, success was guaranteed. By 2007, Codensa Home had granted a little over US$600 million in loans for approximately 730,000 customers. The rate of 90-day late payment was only 1.88 percent (in October 2007), well below standard rates for credit cards and consumer loans. After Codensa Home's introduction, non-technical energy losses kept falling, and household energy consumption rose. Throughout, Codensa has achieved its goal of customer loyalty.

An enriched value proposition increases customers' willingness to pay. In 2006, AES-EDC built a team to create a value proposition specifically targeting low-income customer retention. The first step was to review studies and surveys to learn more about the average income and spending of nearly 380,000 prospects. The strategies formulated to reduce costs and to develop new services included a pilot test for a one-year payment in advance to get a free month, as well as a couple of additional initiatives to enhance customers' payment disposition—an "electrification kit," with safe wiring inspection and installation, and an appliance sale. EDC's nationalization in February 2007 somewhat hindered these initiatives.

The initiatives of these five utility companies increased LIS willingness to pay for their services. The relations between these companies and some LIS have changed, just like these citizens' perceptions about them. In addition to enriching their value propositions, companies contributed to streamlining demand and provided several choices for service payment. Yet some population segments still find it very hard to continue being customers.[10]

Variations in Scale and Corporate Goals

Among the initiatives deployed by sample utility companies, some are still experiments, while others have reached substantial scale. Edenor transformed its relationship with 4,300 customers, and Gas Ban acquired 3,000 new customers. While AES-EDC incorporated 173,000 customers to its system, Codensa provides an example of sustainability: in addition to incorporating 300,000 customers at an initial stage, it has used its capabilities to manage consumer transactions and to offer loans for appliance purchases to 730,000 customers. Gas Ban and Codensa have successfully retained customers after their connection to network services, even though Gas Ban's "handcrafted" efforts contrasted with Codensa's massive endeavors. These differences may be attributed to at least two reasons: the connection of these initiatives to other corporate objectives, and companies' perception of the obstacles they needed to overcome to accomplish venture growth.

There is a great difference between initiatives viewed by company executives as part of the business and those that are regarded as actions delivering social benefits. It is not enough for a company to develop an initiative. If figures or conditions are not sufficiently attractive, the initiative will be carried out on a small scale, emphasizing image and reputation over the potential to accomplish greater social impact.

Social Action

It is unlikely that an initiative viewed as a social intervention will reach a large scale. The reasons for limited growth may lie inside the company or its environment. Edenor's pre-paid system was still a pilot project while 200,000 household customers experienced payment difficulties. As opposed to similar experiences in other Latin American or African countries, Edenor's special pre-paid meters (six times as costly as standard meters) were not charged to customers, and all customers already had electricity before this system was developed.[11] This pre-paid system was only profitable in the long run, given the meter and marketing costs. Edenor's investment would be recovered in approximately 27 months, depending on fee and consumption levels. Despite a cost and profitability analysis, management viewed pre-paid meters as part of its sustainable development commitment. The regulatory setting did not promote growth either, for large-scale, pre-paid energy sales were still under consideration by Argentina's National Energy Regulatory Agency (ENRE) in 2007.

Business officials' perception of initiatives depends on venture profitability and development hurdles. High profitability prospects may offset difficulties, while low profitability highlights any existing hindrance. Gas Ban's potential market included 150,000 LIS customers and accounted for nearly 12 percent of its overall market. When asked about what was missing to approach that market, company executives replied that they needed to secure bank financing. For some officials, "it is so clear that this initiative is closely related to company profitability and values that this project is managed by its marketing department and not its foundation." Nonetheless, funding was not the only obstacle hindering LIS approaches—low consumption, high transaction costs, and the need for multi-stakeholder coordination were also significant concerns. It took Gas Ban 83 months to recover investments made to incorporate new customers. In the case of LIS customers, this recovery period rose to 107 months on account of greater marketing and financial costs as well as lower profitability due to less consumption.

Business Unit

Sample companies showed contrasts that clearly illustrate the difference between perceptions of their initiatives as social actions or business units. An initiative deemed as a business features particular traits. Building such initiatives requires vision and persistence—and both affect market opening and maturity. Without vision and persistence, initiatives fade. Aguaytía and Gas Ban were able to create a market, even though substitutes existed for the products they offered. However, growth perspectives for their LIS initiatives have differed greatly: while Aguaytía's goal was to expand its initiative massively and to sell its entire production at its Amazon rainforest site (by 2007, it was already selling half of its output there), LIS-oriented initiatives did not account for a significant component in Gas Ban's marketing strategy (its goal was to have a 10 percent growth fueled by LIS). Gas Ban's expectations associated with low-income niches did not seem to be very ambitious; its next major project zeroed in on incorporating 12,000 new customers to its current base of over 1.3 million. For Aguaytía, LIS had no financial entry barriers, and the company recovered its investment in three years; for Gas Ban, with no funding alternatives for its infrastructure network, LIS initiatives were not a core element in business growth strategies.

A business unit's acid test is profitability. In turn, high profitability is associated with added value as perceived by customers. For utilities, which may be viewed as commodities, service differentiation is crucial. By offering customers new products and services only accessible through Codensa, the Codensa Home business unit has largely contributed to the company's net profits through a combination of loan proceeds, increased energy consumption, and delinquent payment reduction. The latter resulted from customers' association of energy invoices with loan repayments. Although, by law, defaulting on loan payments does not lead to energy service suspension, very few citizens know this. Codensa's loan program alone accounted for, on average, 2 percent of the company's overall profits in 2005 and 2006 (a little over US$3 million a year); in coming years, these contribution is expected to rise to 8 percent.

Initiatives viewed as business ventures accomplished greater scale and impact than those regarded as social actions. In the case of social actions, a company may lower its growth expectations or accept the promise of future returns if an initiative provides other kinds of benefits. For instance, an initiative may be viewed as an investment on research and development in hopes of acquiring a significant knowledge on LIS that becomes a source of competitive advantage. In addition, the growth of an initiative with limited scope is also plagued by obstacles.

Barriers Faced By These Initiatives

Utility companies' initiatives with LIS face severe growth obstacles. If this were not the case, a larger number of companies would launch this type of initiatives. As mentioned in this chapter's epigraph, only a few companies are now on the path to innovation that others may follow later.

We have identified at least four types of hurdles for these initiatives, including the need to rely on financing for initial investments, to streamline demand, to introduce changes to offerings, and to elicit favorable regulations. In each one of these categories it is possible to find alternatives that lower barriers to action.

Financing

Utility unit prices for LIS are often higher than the prices available for other customers. What prevents LIS access to more inexpensive alternatives is their high connection costs, as a result, in general, of limited physical infrastructure networks. Without alternatives that are not dependent on physical networks, such as mobile telephone services, the lack of connections or adequate equipment "makes it expensive to be poor." New technologies are bringing electricity to remote areas through solar-energy, hybrid or combined micro-generators that were unimaginable until recently. However, the best outcomes are still associated with the expansion of dedicated distribution networks.[12]

Financial bottlenecks may be solved by utility companies themselves. Electricity distributors, such as Edenor, have used their resources to finance equipment that enables suitable consumption for LIS economic conditions. Other companies, such as Codensa, faced with banks' refusal to offer consumer loans, invested their own economic resources to build an initiative that rendered their value propositions more attractive for LIS. Natural gas companies, such as Aguaytía, have also provided financial assistance for LPG equipment purchases—the company increases its product sales, and consumers save money with a cheaper fuel.

In other cases, other parties have provided financial support. Gas Ban's network infrastructure has been funded with resources from FONCAP (Argentina's Social Capital Fund), local administrations, and funds secured by partner organizations. The company is still working to engage banks or multilateral agencies as financial supporters.

Streamlining Demand

A way to forge long-term relationships between companies and communities is to engage LIS in initiative startup and operation processes. For instance, a promising engagement process begins when local labor is hired to build the necessary infrastructure. This relationship consolidates over time when community members are involved in initiative operations. A couple of the five sample companies engaged LIS in roles other than end consumers. In addition to AES-EDC, Gas Ban expanded sections of its natural gas network with labor from served communities and hired local installers who provided legitimacy to the company, as in addition to their regular job they also worked to ensure the quality of service. The company also discovered the advantages of relying on communities to streamline demand—i.e., to enlist and manage new customers.

Given the scale of operations with LIS, companies can opt for building relationships with these populations through intermediaries. Yet only one of the five cases studied featured organizations that served as liaisons between companies and communities. The three sample energy companies have done away with intermediaries to approach communities, service their needs and work with them to their satisfaction. Direct communication benefits were mutual—on the one hand, direct communication increased the company's interest in and commitment to consumer well-being, and, on the other, it engaged LIS in electrical network expansion and care.

Gas Ban's case illustrates the advantages brought about by an organization that facilitates communications between companies and communities. The liaison caused the company to approach each community not only with its natural gas network expansion project but also with a set of social responsibility programs, including its School, First Export, Volunteer Work, Community Orchard programs and more. As of 2003, Gas Ban worked with Fundación pro Vivienda Social (FPVS) to supply natural gas to 2,000 people in Cuartel V, a district of Buenos Aires province. FPVS had designed an engagement scheme with neighbors and local organizations to build network infrastructure and to provide utility services. Its greatest contribution to Gas Ban has been its assistance in approaching communities from the inside, with a local partner.

By relying on several partners, learning from their experiences, and exploiting their capabilities, Gas Ban was able to reduce the design and startup complexity of every one of the six natural gas network expansion projects it launched until 2006. The company moved from approaching communities through independent installers (or "quack politicians" who distort information) to building relationships through liaison organizations and local administrations. The resulting advantages included easier physical access to LIS neighborhoods, knowledge about their conditions and needs, and enhanced project support. A more unusual result was communities' self-streamlined demand. In short, by strengthening or developing local partners, Gas Ban managed to build more efficient relationships with communities, local leaders, and civil society organizations present in its operation areas.

Supply Changes

For decades, cultural distance and distrust have prevailed between LIS and businesses. In the case of EDC, during a drastic layoff process upon the arrival of AES, company managers and workers met in exchanges that revealed valuable information on LIS customers. Company executives learned that "neglected" neighborhood families had little choice but to illegally connect their living quarters to electrical networks and that many dwellers would be willing to formalize their connections to receive quality service.

Awareness of LIS special features increased gradually. Many managers had been biased and ignorant, not only about LIS characteristics but also about ways to build initiatives that met their needs as customers.[13] Consequently, companies have had to learn about the demands and contingencies that emerge in initiative development, leaving behind technical, engineering, and hierarchical notions that turned stringent operating standards into a priority. The need to pay attention to specifics may be a deterrent for companies with highly standardized operations; however, the opportunity to find solutions for critical business issues and to learn in the process may be motivation enough. A subsequent step is to institutionalize the knowledge acquired in these experiences.

The development of innovative ventures has required the introduction of changes in companies. At least three factors have determined how fast these innovations have been implanted. First, regulatory agencies have sometimes hindered system development, as in the case of pre-paid systems. Second, citizens' mistrust has also fueled resistance to business propositions. For instance, AES-EDC's plans to improve energy services at a 154-building development drove 12 condominium boards to file complaints at the consumer protection agency. Third, the organizational culture prevailing at sample multinationals was quite removed from LIS and actually obstructed the construction of productive relationships and flexible offerings.[14] However, these conditions further illustrate that these are initiatives with a different pace, requiring new knowledge and skills.

Companies in this study were not used to deploying marketing efforts, and in order to sell their products to LIS, they had to change their service and marketing concepts. At every marketing stage, necessary adjustments were made to serve LIS. At first, companies embarked on systematic efforts to approach LIS and to get to know them better. During the selling stages, companies formulated several strategies to legalize connections and to facilitate infrastructure and consumption payments. As part of their post-market services, some initiatives pursued strategies to boost customer loyalty. Initiative outcomes prove the importance of these business innovations and point to the need of utility marketing, especially when these companies approach LIS. As initiatives drove a new knowledge of LIS, direct contact and communications changed both parties' perceptions, and mutual distrust subsided.

Venture initiatives transformed the sample companies' relations with several stakeholders. The most relevant changes in these cases affected companies' relationships with their own employees, LIS (mostly consumers but also suppliers, labor contractors, or product distributors), and other value chain actors and public officials.[15]

Regulations and Fees

Utility companies' environment includes regulatory agencies reporting to national, regional, and local legislatures and administrations. Companies are forced to forge close relations with state agencies setting the rules for competition. Within each country's regulatory framework, some national and local administrations have actively promoted utility coverage expansion.

Regulations encourage or prevent developments that could have an impact on LIS living conditions. Over this decade, Argentina's regulatory agency has set rather low prices for natural gas, while it does not control bottled gas prices. This differential has fueled a 7-to-1 ratio that favors natural gas consumption—this ratio would drop to 2-to-1 if natural gas prices were not state-controlled. Gas Ban's value proposition to LIS thus largely derives its attractiveness from the price difference set by the regulatory agency. Public intervention encourages demand, but, on the downside, it also constrains supply. The gap between the political and market prices of natural gas partly explains why Gas Ban did not pursue its initiative as a business unit and why the number of beneficiaries still lags behind the six-digit figures found in other cases explored.

Regulatory agencies are slow to adjust to innovations, hindering some private companies' new developments. The pre-paid system that held significant promise for AES-EDC's pilot projects was abandoned because it was not approved by Congress.[16] Conversely, the state has partially subsidized non-technical energy losses in Caracas. Although AES-EDC sometimes invested in infrastructure to reduce theft losses, network expansion investments were made by the state. Furthermore, the government promoted citizen mobilization to demand better water and energy services. After President Hugo Chávez himself asked for energy service improvements on his Sunday television show, officials inaugurated so-called Technical Energy Tables. In 2005, 24 "electrical tables" (policy meetings) were held in Caracas. In addition to AES-EDC, these tables were attended by

CADAFE, a state-owned energy company, representatives from each local administration, neighbor associations, and other stakeholders who were interested in improving local energy services, as well as the Fund for Development Investments (FIDES), which financed infrastructure works required to expand energy networks. Each table required the formulation of a project plan, including proper technical surveys and an estimated budget for required installations. At many neighborhoods, AES-EDC already had a project plan, and, in others, it agreed to prepare one in just a few days. Then the company presented its "Electrical Neighborhood" concept, with an emphasis on social rather than technical issues. "Electrical tables" served, amidst the tense local political atmosphere, as a means to connect the company to LIS markets and to strengthen its relationships with city administration (which had requested street lighting projects for areas with construction permits still pending) and other local administration agencies. These precedents were useful for the company when it negotiated its acquisition by the state in early 2007.

Grounds to Scale Initiatives

Sample initiatives contributed to both **economic and social value creation**. Companies and communities drew benefits from them. When customers recognized they were receiving a better service, they were more willing to pay for it. At the same time, innovations introduced to management systems enabled a suitable consumption level that matched customers' payment capacity. As a result, company losses dropped. Both natural gas companies in this sample built a market for their products. Although there are several substitutes for natural gas, it could compete with them on account of its low unit cost. However, many LIS did not count the product as an option because they had no payment capacity or financing available to cover its high installation costs. To overcome this barrier, Aguaytía included this cost in its natural gas prices, while Gas Ban has sought specific financial solutions for each of its projects.

Increased disposable income is one of the benefits afforded to LIS, especially for natural gas consumers. In addition to lower costs, LIS benefited from an increase in real estate property value as a result of legal utility connections—either for electricity or natural gas. Access to residential utilities makes houses more livable and valuable. As for vehicle use, gas-fueled engines suffer less wear and require less oil.

When a utility company serves LIS, benefits seem to outweigh new payment commitments for citizens as a result of installations and consumption. For beneficiaries, legal access to utilities holds an intrinsic value, for they can receive or demand better services, save on appliance repairs, and purchase cheaper fuels. Improvements occurred in service quality as well as in living conditions at both community level—through safety and cohesion—and at private homes. Gas Ban's president, Pedro Sáenz, noted,

> Fortunately, there are more companies that realize you can use your business to serve low-income people, providing a benefit to them and receiving a benefit as well. Some think it is immoral to sell stuff to low-income people, but I believe that if we provide them with a benefit, there is nothing immoral about it. We approach them in a straightforward, candid way, making a big effort to explain why they need to spend less, and I think that improves their living conditions.

In some cases, access to utilities can even **legitimize these individuals as citizens** to other organizations—in some countries, for example, a utility invoice is required to access financial or formal economy services. As argued by Rufin and Arboleda, "having a utility invoice is a legal proof of residence that entitles individuals to demand other public services, like education and, in some cases, land ownership."[17]

AES-EDC's experience illustrates the benefits of better service for LIS. Accidents diminished because connections were now in qualified hands, and the reduction of electrical network overload ensured a steadier, powerful energy service. The unstable, unsafe energy supply from illegal connections not only jeopardized LIS physical integrity but also their budget, as sudden voltage changes damaged home appliances. There were also aesthetic changes when "cable tangles" were replaced by legal, orderly connections, and neighborhood safety increased as a result of street lighting improvements (thus weekly average violent deaths at the 23 de Enero neighborhood dropped from 18 to 3).

Benefits from additional utility products have also been substantial. Loans offered by Codensa had fewer requirements than loans from traditional financial institutions. Such loans could triple customers' salaries, and credit bureau evaluations took no more than 48 hours. According to company analyses, 97 percent of Codensa Home's customers belonged to the three lowest socioeconomic strata. Their living conditions improved with greater access to consumer products and financial services. A loan customer commented:

> My husband and I wanted to buy a large TV set and were always saving. We just couldn't make it—something was wrong. I went to Codensa's office, filled out the forms, and, two days later, they called

me. They told me that my loan was approved and that I could go pick my TV set. Then, I realized I had more credit available. So, I decided to buy two sets. Now, I watch my soap operas; when my daughter comes home from school, she watches her cartoons, and we play her songs on the stereo so that she learns the numbers with them. I think it's just cool to pay my electricity and appliance bills at the same time, hassle-free.

Most low-income individuals have purchased washing machines, TV sets, and computers. Acquired goods may be classified into three categories: those with a positive impact on income (computers and washing machines), those with a direct impact on family well-being (refrigerators), and all other goods. It should be noted that in Bogotá only 40 percent of the population has **access to financial services.**[18] Among Codensa Home's loan beneficiaries, 66 percent had never been granted a formal loan or access to financial services; after successfully applying for a loan at Codensa, 45 percent of these individuals accessed other financial services.[19]

Finally, companies that wish to pursue further growth with initiatives involving LIS should examine the systems used by utility companies. The scope and impact of a program like Codensa Home illustrates how these companies can become **platforms** to reach out to large population groups. The Inter-American Development Bank's "Opportunities for Majorities" initiative on health issues currently studies the experiences of utility companies.[20] The example of mobile telephone services as a platform for financial services is telling. One of the lessons afforded by this experience is the industry transformation that was brought about by breaking away from physical infrastructure networks.

Lessons Drawn from Utility Services for Low-Income Citizens

By increasing their market share, companies can create more employment, earn more revenues, and pay more taxes. When their operations concentrate on a population that is not adequately served, like LIS, they transform these people's living conditions. When this segment is served in the right way, economic results are positive, and, at the same time, social value is created. The transforming power of the initiatives described in this chapter may be attributed to the importance of energy and natural gas in people's lives. It should be noted that most of the changes explored came as a result of improved LIS living conditions. By becoming "full-fledged" energy or natural gas network customers, the poor received other benefits, such as access to information, increased disposable income, and a proof of citizenship.

Throughout this chapter, we have discussed the features of several utility business ventures to serve low-income citizens. Sample companies have proved it is possible to provide quality services to both low- and high-income customers. The challenge for natural gas companies in this sample was to build a market, while energy distributing companies faced a different dilemma. As electricity has few substitutes, energy companies differ from other businesses in that they cannot easily draw away from consumers. Although a company may not want to provide its service to a specific segment, this segment will try to get the service in any possible way—even illegally. Therefore, for electricity distributors, it is important to clearly convey the advantages for "formal" customers and to offer a value proposition that attracts customers (larger service portfolio, timely payment rewards), especially for prospects with greater access restrictions. To reach LIS successfully, several activities are required in each marketing stage. In the absence of services that are tailored specifically to LIS features, relations with these population groups are troublesome and undermine utility companies' legitimacy.

An approach that does not take into account the high opportunity cost of people with scarce economic resources is sadly doomed. LIS willingness to pay and payment conveniences are key elements, and companies need to work on both.

A greater value proposition from companies enhances customers' disposition to pay. Company offerings may range from those directly associated with core services to those that lower access barriers to other goods and services. Gas Ban, for instance, has offered something that goes beyond material and economic benefits. "Through its External Relations department, the company provides all kinds of courses for neighbors, including lectures on efficient consumption to raise awareness. At the same time, its marketing department approaches them with connections, invoices and all the CSR programs for these neighborhoods that require more than just natural gas network expansion." Experiences prove Rufin and Arboleda[21] right: when customers' satisfaction increases, so does their payment disposition.

Another key element is to provide payment convenience, adjusting service models to LIS payment capacity. Companies can adapt their systems to low-income customers' irregular income flows by means of multiple alternatives, like shorter invoice periods, more extensive collection networks, consumer training in efficient and rational energy consumption, innovations in service purchases, or payment term flexibility.

An initiative that does not enhance willingness to pay and payment convenience will not successfully incorporate LIS as customers. To retain them as customers and scale initiatives, companies' value propositions will need to preserve their attractiveness for LIS, and companies will have to overcome both internal and external obstacles. Internally, companies will need to introduce changes into their cultures and operating systems. Financing and demand streamlining take place in an environment where regulatory frameworks can favor or hinder them. This complex path may lead to significant profits for companies and enhanced living conditions for consumers that will make the venture completely worthwhile. Some actors in our sample cases have realized this quite clearly. As Jaime Tupper, AES-EDC's Vice President, summarized it,

> First, the model always hinges on being very close to communities. It also involves having parallel projects: in addition to formal home electrification efforts, there should be formal street lighting projects. Third, people want to pay, and there is often an educational and a convenience problem to pay. Then the model should also include payment mechanisms that engage the community, and we need to adjust to neighborhood economics. Fourth, something we haven't explored enough, are service packages. We should offer value-added services to differentiate our offerings from commodities. This demands the development of additional value to improve customers' living conditions.

Notes

1. ONU-Hábitat, *El estado de las ciudades en el mundo 2006/2007* (New York, NY: Programa de las Naciones Unidas sobre Asentamientos Urbanos, 2007).
2. Carlos Rufin and Luis Fernando Arboleda, "Utilities and the Poor: A Story from Colombia" (paper presented at the Harvard Business School Conference on Global Poverty, Boston, MA, December 1–3, 2005).
3. This company's study covers a period starting in 2000, when it was acquired by the multinational AES, and concluding with its nationalization in 2007.
4. USAID, "Innovative Approaches to Slum Electrification" (Washington, DC: Bureau for Economic Growth, Agriculture and Trade, December 2004).
5. Ibid.
6. "Consejo Nacional de la Vivienda, Programa II: Habilitación Física de Zonas de Barrios," CONAVI, http://www.conavi.gov.ve.
7. To determine utility fees and some taxes, Colombia's population is officially classified in six socio-economic strata, with stratum 1 assigned to the poorest population segment. Strata 1, 2, and 3 receive subsidies for utilities, while strata 5 and 6 pay overprices.
8. USAID, "Innovative Approaches to Slum Electrification" (Washington, DC: Bureau for Economic Growth, Agriculture and Trade, December 2004).

9. "Cable tangles" are multiples wires hanging from a single light post to get energy. Poor service quality and accident hazards are part of this alternative's costs.

10. AES-EDC was particularly aware of LIS difficulties to remain customers. Efforts by technicians and social workers combined the described initiatives, which ranged from explaining household fees to inspecting home installations to check whether consumption was being affected, for example, by a refrigerator door that did not close properly. Neighborhood visits were announced in advance and provided information on fees, workshops on energy use optimization, customer service, new customer acquisition, and collections.

11. These are specificities of the system adopted in Argentina. In some countries, figures are astounding: in South Africa, there are six million pre-paid accounts because, since 1988, ESKOM, a state-owned company, developed a program called "Electricity for Everyone" for poor neighborhoods with no energy service; since the late 1970s, the United Kingdom's pre-paid system has recruited four million customers—most from low-income sectors (accounting for 16% of all registered electricity customers and 9% of all natural gas customers).

12. Allen L. Hammond et al., *The Next 4 Billion: Market Size and Business Strategy at the Base of the Pyramid* (Washington, DC: World Resources Institute and International Finance Corporation, 2007).

13. Aguaytía included its technical personnel in social awareness efforts to enhance employees' knowledge on cultural traits shared by low-income users.

14. Henry Gómez, Patricia Márquez, and Michael Penfold, "Cómo AES-EDC generó relaciones rentables en los barrios pobres de Caracas," *Harvard Business Review América Latina* (December 2006).

15. In a direct company intervention, Edenor engaged telecommunication companies to transfer data to collection companies and several pre-paid card POS. Codensa Home is another example of entire value chain coordination.

16. A similar delay affected Edenor's pre-paid system development.

17. Carlos Rufin and Luis Fernando Arboleda, "Utilities and the Poor: A Story from Colombia" (paper presented at the Harvard Business School Conference on Global Poverty, Boston, MA, December 1–3 2005), 4.

18. A. Manroth and T. Solo, "Access to Financial Services in Colombia: The "Unbanked" in Bogotá." *Policy Research Working Paper* No 3834. Washington, D.C.: World Bank, 2006.

19. M.A. Arbeláez, F. García and C. Sandoval, *El "Crédito Fácil para Todos" de CODENSA: un programa de impacto social para Bogotá.* (Bogotá: Fedesarrollo, 2007).

20. F. Díaz, "Platform Strategies for Scaling". Access on May 24, 2008 at http://www.nextbillion.net/blogs/2008/05/15/guest-post-platform-strategies-for-scaling.

21. Ibid.

7

Solid Waste Management: Integrating Low-Income Sectors in the Value Chain

Rosa Maria Fischer, Monica Bose, Paulo Rocha Borba, and Graziella Comini

> *"The 'mines' of the 21st Century will be old products at the end of their life cycle."*[1]

Latin America is witnessing a growing presence of social ventures formed by low-income individuals dedicated to the collection of solid waste discarded in the urban trash. These initiatives participate in political organization movements, which provide institutional support for social inclusion of these people. Such ventures seek to enter the production chain of waste management, which is becoming a driving sector in modern economy.

This chapter presents and analyzes this type of enterprise in three Latin American countries. It examines how such initiatives arise, develop and consolidate themselves in the adverse environments in which they operate.

The vast majority of these trash collectors are uneducated and extremely poor, often living in precarious circumstances or even in the streets. In several regions, they have formed groups to overcome the limitations and the risks of working individually with no support. Many of these groups then establish more structured organizations, such as associations and cooperatives, which become social ventures. They can be defined as collective-property initiatives (which adopt incipient management models with participative characteristics) aimed at individuals deprived of conditions for insertion in the formal labor market.

Within the specific legislation of each country, these enterprises exhibit characteristics of cooperative models of work organization and economic production.[2] In other words, they are collectively owned, democratically managed, and composed of individuals who coalesce to fulfill common economic, social and cultural needs.[3] Such organizational forms reflect the trend toward organizations more in tune with the paradigm of solidarity economy[4] than with the entrepreneurial architecture of market economy. Democracy, equality, and solidarity are values that serve as the basis for these initiatives, which have as their purpose not only the generation of wealth but also self-esteem and dignity.

The homeless people and the ones that work individually in the collection of solid waste residues from the urban garbage live in conditions of poverty, exclusion, and marginality, which limits their productivity and income as well as their economic and social mobility. Thus, any workable organizational arrangement for these collectors must offer conditions for sharing values, responsibilities, and opportunities, as well as an equitable distribution of rewards, thereby increasing their sociability and empowering them as citizens.

Given these conditions, a social venture may not only generate economic value from the more rational organization of resources and from the increase in productivity deriving from collective work; it may also create and consolidate the social capital of these low-income segments. Social capital can be defined as the value which results from horizontal collaboration networks, based on trust and on coexistence regulated by behavior rules and codes. Environments in which social capital is strengthened promote social cohesion. Literature on political science emphasizes that these social contexts are essential for the efficient operation of democratic institutions, as they assure and stimulate the participation of citizens in the construction of collective assets.[5]

The experiences of three social initiatives in the solid waste recycling sector: El Ceibo Recuperadores Urbanos (El Ceibo Urban Collectors, Argentina); Asmare—Associação dos Catadores de Papel, Papelão e Material Reciclável (Association of Paper, Cardboard, and Recyclable Material Collectors, Brazil); and Cooperativa de Recicladores Porvenir (Porvenir Recyclers' Cooperative, Colombia) have provided significant lessons on the development of social entrepreneurship. In general terms, we conclude that the institutionalization of solid waste collection, handling, and sale offers the prospect of transforming these people's economic and social conditions, both through the generation of income where it was nonexistent, and through the construction of more dignified living conditions and access to citizen rights. In addition, the more articulated and diversified these organizations' participation in the various stages of solid waste management, the more opportunities for social transformation will arise for the collectors, and the stronger the sustainability of the enterprises in which they participate. It is possible to infer that these enterprises make important contributions to local development, by increasing income generation and strengthening social relations for this sector of urban poverty.

Context and Challenges in the Value Chain of Solid Waste Management

Waste collection and recycling by low-income citizens[6] are no recent phenomena, but their magnitude and visibility have increased in recent years as a result of various converging factors. One is the problem of the worldwide quest for solutions to the management of waste generated from growing consumption. Another factor is the intensification of economic and social problems generated by recurrent economic crises in Latin America, which accentuate unemployment and poverty and push impoverished individuals to waste collection as a last, desperate resort, to avoid hunger.

From the second half of the twentieth century, accelerated population growth in Latin America and its concentration in urban areas, together with industrial development and changes in consumption patterns, have led to an increase in the quantity and variety of solid waste generated by the continent's inhabitants. In 2001, the urban population reached 406 million inhabitants, representing 78.3 percent of a total of 518 million inhabitants, with an urban production of solid waste estimated at 369 thousand tons per day. A population of 627 million inhabitants is projected for 2015, of which close to 501 million will be urban (80%). Maintaining the present rates of waste generation and production, the volume will surpass 446 thousand tons per day.[7]

Collection and final disposal of domestic waste are major problems in the region. The solutions are rendered unfeasible as a result of several concomitant factors: the governments' inertia in determining policies and specific practices; lack of information and interest of the public at large in committing to selective waste collection; and the conflicts of interest among the several firms and organizations that are part of the recycling production chain. Given this state of affairs, social enterprise initiatives emerge as innovative proposals that can reconcile the generation of economic value with a solution for the early stages of the waste recovery process and with the addition of social value for the low-income groups involved. In Latin America, 2.2 percent of the total solid waste is estimated as recovered, of which 1.9 percent is inorganic and 0.3 percent is organic.[8] That small percentage represents loss of usable natural resources and a waste of work and income generation opportunities.

Expanded collection by organized waste collectors in social enterprises could provide a livelihood for the population's poorest groups, who have posed a dramatic social problem for over 60 years in Latin American countries. Estimates indicate that more than 120 thousand families are currently dedicated to waste collection, under unhealthy, high-risk circumstances. In some countries, a few programs have been implemented during the last few decades to reduce the waste deposits and outdoor dumps where scavengers engage in informal and degrading waste collection. These initiatives tend to solve environmental problems but do not usually further social aspects.

Solid waste collection, whether carried out by organized or individual collectors, generates benefits for society and for the environment, but is neither recognized nor valued. This activity contributes considerably to the minimization of the negative environmental impacts caused by the physical waste, especially: a) reduction in soil contamination by chemical substances derived from the decomposition of waste; b) reduction of the pollutants released by the incineration of waste.

The solid waste collectors, as well as the cooperatives and associations through which they organize their activities, arise and multiply in social contexts in which the government has little presence; there is no assurance of fundamental rights. Poverty, exclusion, and inequality are high and unceasing, particularly in urban zones. The number of collectors usually increases during economic crises that cause greater unemployment and poverty. In Mexico, the 1994 devaluation of the peso and the consequent economic crisis led to an accelerated increase in the activity of informal collection. In Argentina, the economic crisis in the early 1990s caused a notorious growth in the number of people working in the streets of Buenos Aires, looking to survive.[9] This new category of workers provides fertile ground for the appearance of initiatives to fight poverty, even if they receive no support to become an institutional segment of the job market.

Collectors' organizations, usually in the form of cooperatives and associations, came into being during the last decades of the twentieth century, totaling, in 2005, more than 200 organizations of *catadores* (collectors), *segregadores* (sorters), *cartoneros* (cardboard collectors), *gancheros* (scrap metal collectors), *pepenadores* (scavengers) and *recicladores* (recyclers).[10] These organizational initiatives allow collectors to improve working conditions, eliminate their status as second-class citizens, coordinate their activities with municipal sanitation agencies, and negotiate, under better conditions, with the people and industries that comprise this chain of production.[11]

Preliminary data on garbage and solid waste produced in Argentina, Brazil, and Colombia signal the potential for economic, social, and environmental transformation of the market for solid waste recycling. Argentina generates 12,325,000 tons of waste per year, and only 2 percent of the solid waste produced is recycled.[12] Buenos Aires generates 4.5 tons of garbage per day, enabling work for close to 7,000 *cartoneros*.[13] Colombia produces 23,000 tons of garbage daily, of which 6,000 tons originate in Bogotá. In that country, 300,000 tons of paper and cardboard are recycled per year, and 50,000 collectors are active, of whom 18,000 operate in Bogotá, where the percentage of recovered waste reaches 10 percent.[14] In Brazil, 129,000 tons of garbage are produced per day, but only 2 percent of the 40 percent of solid waste found in urban garbage is recycled.[15] Estimates indicate that 400,000 people collect recyclable material to survive or to generate income, either regularly or occasionally; that 26,000 collectors live in waste dumps and in the streets; and that only 10,000 of them are organized into cooperatives and associations,[16] which number from 400[17] to 500[18] enterprises.

Innovative Models That Allowed For the Inclusion of LIS

The organization of the solid waste collectors allowed them to cross the economic and social barriers that kept them from achieving a dignified life. This benefit did not come about spontaneously. Social exclusion, destitution, and low self-esteem did not motivate the collectors to organize on their own. The interference of external players, with in-depth knowledge of these people's problems, was fundamental for the process of raising the collectors' awareness and of mobilizing them.

Once the enterprises brought the collectors together, their incorporation into the solid waste management chain only became possible thanks to links with players that enjoy political and economic influence. Building partnering networks with governmental institutions, CSOs, and private-sector firms has been decisive for the consolidation and the sustainability of these initiatives.

LIS Organizations

The organization of collectors in Belo Horizonte (in the Brazilian state of Minas Gerais), which culminated in the creation of Asmare, occurred in a context characterized by a strongly associative culture, and was framed by movements of resistance to the military regime, which gave rise to many initiatives aimed at increasing social justice. An important role was played by the Pastoral de Rua (Street Pastoral Mission[19]), linked to the archdiocese of that city, which continues to work to strengthen the involvement of homeless and former homeless people. The Mission stimulated the creation of Asmare jointly with other local social movements and with Cáritas, an entity related to the Catholic Church, which promotes development of areas with high levels of poverty. The Street Pastoral Mission started with a careful approach so as to gain the collectors' trust, asserting the value of their work and signaling the possibility of gaining self-esteem and dignity by organizing their work. As a result, ten collectors decided to organize a group to conduct collection together and thus overcome the limitations of individual activity. After holding a number of meetings, the group conceived Asmare, and structured it by involving other collectors, social actors, and partner organizations in the effort to create the enterprise.

Fundación Social, a Colombian welfare organization, played an important role in the process of collectors' organization in Colombia. Created by Jesuit priests with the mission of promoting human rights and basic development, this organization has substantial investment capability, as it owns important companies in the financial sector. Operating as an outside catalyst, it contacted groups of collectors and gave them support to organize the first cooperatives. With the support of Fundación Social and of government agencies, the number of collectors' cooperatives in the country grew steadily throughout the 1980s. Porvenir, for example, created in 1989, was among the enterprises that resulted from this involvement. In 1990, the Fundación Social sponsored the first national meeting of recyclers, which gave rise to the creation of the National Association of Recyclers (ANR). This group began to operate in 1991 and soon became an important partner of Porvenir's.[20]

In addition to these outside organizations, individual members of collectors' cooperatives have decisively influenced the formation of these associations. Among these groups of individual collectors, various entrepreneurs have the gift of vision and a keen sense of opportunity. These leaders can play a significant role as internal catalysts. Cristina Lescano was the main voice of the group of collectors that created the Argentine El Ceibo cooperative, with financial support from the Institute of Mobilization of Cooperative Funds, an entity focused on fomenting and strengthening cooperatives. Although Lescano had been middle-class with a good professional background, she was forced to live in abandoned houses occupied by the homeless, surviving from the sale of solid waste she collected in the streets of Buenos Aires, a city impoverished by economic crisis. At that time she participated in the creation of El Ceibo's "Trabajo Barrial" (District Labor), a group of women who lived in these houses and dedicated themselves to the improvement of reproductive health services. Later, the initiative began to take part in political actions focused on housing for the poor. At the same time, Lescano identified the opportunity to organize those who worked individually in the collection of solid waste from urban garbage. With the purpose of increasing the quantity of material in order to obtain better prices, Lescano encouraged these people to organize themselves and create the El Ceibo Urban Collectors' Cooperative.

Clearly, the support and participation of outside and internal actors was essential for the creation and strengthening of the initiatives studied. But the subsequent coalition of those enterprises with other partners and collaborators is also important for success. Such partnerships are needed to transform the situation of precariousness and exploitation to which solid waste collectors were subjected when they worked alone. However, the improvement of this category of workers has caused problems in their relationships with other players, a situation requiring that cooperatives constantly strengthen their capacity for social articulation and negotiation within their political network.

Private initiatives also discovered that solid waste management could be good business, and many companies entered this sector with the traditional purpose of profitability, without seeking any socio-environmental benefits. At this point, unfair competition gave rise to a conflict, given the huge discrepancy of bargaining power between the actors involved. Companies and local governments confronted the interests of the collectors, initially disregarding them and even boycotting them in public bidding procedures. In this context, the collectors benefited from political changes in the management of waste collection and disposal, leading Brazilian Asmare and Argentine El Ceibo to construct new ties with the government, creating partnerships necessary for the sustainability of the enterprises. In the Colombian case, however, the government continues to impose restrictions that devalue the potential of the collectors' cooperatives, which find their best strategy for sustainability in partnerships with private companies.

Incorporation into the Solid Waste Management Chain

Solid waste collectors build partnership networks with social organizations, private firms, and public bodies to gain space and legitimacy in the solid-residue management chain. This high degree of social connectedness has proven essential to consolidate gains and provide some social mobility, as well as sustainability to the collectors' associations and cooperatives. Successful initiatives seem to develop from a base built by the group's social capital and through structured forms of operation, which anticipate the very constitution of their associations and cooperatives as organizations with legal personality and administrative structure.

In Argentina, the first cooperatives of waste collectors were formed in 1999 and 2000. Among them is the El Ceibo (coral tree) cooperative, named after the national flower of Argentina. El Ceibo is comprised of families of *cartoneros*—the pioneers of recycling in Buenos Aires, for whom the collection of paper and cardboard has provided an escape from destitution. Today they have a key role in enforcing the ambitious "Zero Garbage Law," designed to prohibit landfilling of recyclable and compostable waste by 2020, which obliges the government and the three million inhabitants of the capital to reduce garbage generation and promote its selection, recovery, and recycling.[21]

In Brazil, the first cooperative of solid-residue collectors was constituted in the city of São Paulo in 1989: the Cooperative of Autonomous Collectors of Papers, Scrappers and Reusable Material (Coopamare). Though selective garbage collection processes have increased by 38 percent in Brazil in recent years, they are still conducted in only 6 percent of the country's cities and remain strongly concentrated in the south and southeast regions. Initiatives by the local public authorities account for 85 percent of the structured recycling programs and are limited to five states with cities involved in this type of collection (São Paulo, 114; Rio Grande do Sul, 40; Paraná, 39; Santa Catarina, 33 and Minas Gerais, 28). Out of these programs, 43.5 percent maintain a direct relationship with cooperatives—partnerships that have been growing because they offer better conditions of operation for the collectors, while reducing costs for local governments. In 1994, the average cost of selective collection was US$240 per garbage ton and, in 2006, US$151. Nevertheless, it is still five times more expensive than the conventional collection, with smaller volumes of collection and use of special waste collection vehicles that do not compact the rubbish.[22]

The Argentine and Brazilian cases illustrate the importance of official waste management programs to the development of collectors' organizations, whether these plans are designed to solve environmental issues, as in Argentina, or to improve socio-economic conditions, as in Brazil. To gain official recognition, it was crucial that collectors were strongly organized and had the support of social entities.[23]

In Colombia, the joint effort of groups of collectors, CSOs, and a few local and national governmental entities gave rise to a rapid proliferation of cooperatives between the late 1980s and the early 1990s. In twenty years, those initiators managed to found and foster 94 workers' cooperatives, in addition to regional and national networks of cooperatives, with the purpose of transforming the conditions of solid-residue management, creating a labor market for the collectors, and improving their quality of life. Though they do make a sufficient living, collectors have been historically exploited, and to this day face strong social discrimination, being often treated as social throwaways, much like the material they manipulate.[24]

Despite differences in the constitution of the recycling chains, El Ceibo, Porvenir, and Asmare have similar workflow models. Collection can be triggered either informally by the collectors, or formally by firms and cooperatives hired by the local government to render these services. Likewise, materials may be sold by garbage pickers directly to companies in charge of collection and destination, or a firm hired for this collection can be in charge of commercialization. In either case, collectors' organizations face severe competition when they fail to establish alliances with the public and private agents present in the supply chain.

Barriers Faced By These Initiatives

The populations of solid waste collectors studied in Argentina, Brazil, and Colombia have distinctive socio-economic features that explain why the collectors' incorporation into the production chain is precarious, a situation that the researched social enterprises plan to overcome. A recent survey[25] conducted in Minas Gerais, the Brazilian state in which the Asmare initiative was established, confirms that solid waste collectors suffer the lack of recognized formal jobs and carry the burden of accumulated successive losses extended throughout generations. Low schooling level, absence of professional qualifications, and use of child labor are predominant characteristics of this population. In addition to deriving income from garbage dumps, many families find in them basic goods for survival, such as food leftovers, clothing, footwear, and other materials. Deprived of information, of access to social rights, collectors submit to various forms of exploitation: at times they actually exchange the collected waste, the fruit of their labor, for food, alcoholic beverages, and drugs. Even the simple push cart where they carry the material is sometimes granted under conditions of extortion that reduce their earning possibilities.

Consumption of alcohol and other toxic substances is frequent, although organized collectors tend to drink less. Incidents of physical aggression and of sexual abuse are commonplace; they take place in the materials sheds, the waste dumps, and the city streets. Although there has been more information about the collectors' activities, giving rise to some appreciation of their role, they are invariably mistaken for beggars, delinquents, or demented people, and are considered incapable of coexisting socially.

The members of Asmare, Porvenir, and El Ceibo used to represent a socially excluded group whose main activity—collection of solid waste—was never recognized as work. These people have been living in extreme poverty for generations; to this population are added those who have suffered sudden loss of employment and economic power. All of them see solid waste collection as a means for survival. Although few are illiterate, the great majority have not completed primary or secondary school. The percentage of women is a little higher in Asmare (55%) and in Porvenir (60%), and is balanced in El Ceibo. While youths, adults, and elderly people work in the three initiatives studied, in Asmare, participants range from 35 to 40 years of age; in El Ceibo from 18 to 60, with a concentration of individuals aged 30 to 35; and in Porvenir the major concentration is of people aged 45 to 60, but individuals aged over 65 have also been noted.

Besides having to overcome poverty, informality, and precarious working conditions, solid waste collectors suffer prejudice and the violence of society and of the government itself. In the 1980s, with the intensification of economic and social crises, exclusion indicators rose and conflicts increased. In Belo Horizonte, the local government itself implemented so-called "Cleanup Operations," using violence against people who lived in the streets or obtained their sustenance from them. In the Colombian capital, Bogotá, this population was the target of "Social Cleanup" actions, in which armed gangs killed people from marginalized groups. In both places, the collectors united to change this reality, by giving visibility to the problems they faced, seeking recognition of their dignity and citizenship, and fighting for acknowledgment of the value of their work. In addition to redemption of social status, the collectors' organization contributed to higher income for the workers by the ability to accumulate materials in volumes high enough for the negotiation of better prices with the intermediaries,[26] in the Brazilian case, and with the industries, in the Colombian case.

Collectors' Organization: Characteristics and Strategies

Organizations of solid waste collectors take on specific and diverse characteristics according to the context within which they emerge, and according to their objectives. Such characteristics are found in the ventures' organizational formats and business models. By evaluating their respective influences on the effectiveness of the organizations, one can delineate the main characteristics conducive to good performance.

Organizational Configurations

As a group, collectors may participate in several types of organizations, ranging from social movements with little formalization to large associations and cooperatives structured around collective efforts. The three Latin American cases reveal that these organizational models are strongly focused on the improvement of the quality of life of collectors and their families, with economic inclusion and social value generation occurring as well.

The organization of solid waste collectors entails legal formalization to allow them to draw up commercial contracts and render services. That is a necessary step toward institutionalizing collective initiatives, which primarily begin in an informal manner. Work cooperatives have been the predominant organizational form adopted, because they provide the best configuration for a fair distribution of generated income and for member participation in the management of the institution. However, the commercial and administrative limitations of cooperatives sometimes lead to a call for adjustments, or even a search for new models, which can mean the creation of associations and private firms.

While they share common difficulties and managerial challenges, the organizations studied are distinct in size. Colombian Porvenir and Argentine El Ceibo are small organizations, with fewer than 50 members, but they have similar problems to those faced by Brazilian Asmare, which comprises 250 members. One hard task has been to single out adequate leaders and managers from the pool of collectors—a problem that hinders the exercise of self-management,[27] one of the main pillars of the cooperative organization model. This situation is worse in the Argentine and Brazilian cases as a result of the strong centralization of information and decision-making in the top management of each organization, although semi-hierarchic structures designed to ensure accountability and governance of the ventures are in place. By and large, the collectors' entrepreneurial spirit and competence in carrying out operational activities is not proof that they have developed the abilities required to manage the undertakings.

Porvenir has a team of 31 people to collect recyclable material, while 9 others carry out support activities such as driving garbage collection trucks and running the storage facility, besides performing administrative tasks. These workers participate in assemblies and their interests are represented in three committees (Education, Surveillance, and Communication). We observed that the difficulty in finding and developing leaders is attributed to low self-esteem and educational levels among the collectors, as well as their preference to remain involved in more familiar operational activities, those more directly related to their gains. Porvenir also presents high turnover rates, which heightens the difficulty of selecting cooperative members to take over managerial responsibilities. In 2004, a serious internal crisis caused by high administrative expenditures, tenuous financial control, production losses, and inefficient, expensive operations attested to the fragility of the organization. In order to improve this situation, the cooperative opted for outsourcing a professional administrator, whose management counts on the support and advice of the Bogota Recyclers Association (ARB).

Similar to Porvenir in size, El Ceibo has a type of structure that determines specializations in four positions: out of the 41 people working in the organization, 7 are in administrative support and 34 work in operations, out of which 15 are recyclers, 10 are environmental promoters, and nine are garbage sorters at the waste facility. El Ceibo counts on formal decision-making bodies, primarily the administration's council, which represents the members at structured meetings, as provided in the cooperative's bylaws. Other members of the organization meet when there are timely issues to be discussed. However, the cooperative is characterized by strong centralization of decisions and information in the figure of its manager and founder, which hinders the organization's development, the formalization of processes and policies, as well as the delegation of responsibilities and autonomy to other members. Nevertheless, El Ceibo intends to professionalize its administration, now oriented to entrepreneurial models, and has envisioned the idea of turning itself into a commercial firm, with a view to its economic and financial sustainability.

Though Asmare is an association rather than a cooperative, it adopted a horizontal organizational structure, aimed at sharing decisions and information within a self-management model. However, the growth the organization experienced along the last years gave rise to managerial inefficiencies, which in turn forced Asmare to reanalyze its model and resort to a semi-hierarchic structure, to facilitate and accelerate decision-making. Its 250 affiliates carry out four functions: collectors of recyclables, triage sorters (in charge of selecting the material donated), pressers (responsible for pressing and packing the material) and daily workers (who carry out support tasks). The administration team comprises some 40 people. To ensure the representation of the interests of the affiliates in the management of the organization, coordination is split among seven commissions: Press and Dissemination, Finance, Infrastructure, Environment, Religiosity, Health and Education, and Culture and Leisure. One representative of each commission participates in the Board of Directors, which is in charge of the decisions required for the organization's daily operations; assemblies with all affiliates take place quarterly. There is also a collegial entity to support the administration—The Council of Strategic Orientation—a consulting body that includes the Street Pastoral Mission and the Belo Horizonte city government through its Municipal Secretariat of Social Assistance and the Municipal Secretariat of Urban Cleaning.

Alliances and Collaborations

Alliances and collaborations with other organizations and actors have been important in the paths of the ventures studied and have enabled them to benefit from new opportunities and accelerate value generation and delivery in these initiatives. Different types of relationships with partners are identified in the cases studies.

Asmare's openness to embrace partnerships in its management approach resulted in collaboration among its partners in strategic decisions and shared responsibilities in the development of the organization. Building and keeping inter-sector alliances is another distinctive strategy of Asmare, which counted over 400 partner institutions in 2006, among them public and private organizations (companies and CSOs) and legal persons. At the state level, it interacts essentially with the city government of Belo Horizonte, which provides Asmare with financial resources and recyclables collected in transfer stations. In the third sector, a key partnership is with the Street Pastoral Mission, which has guided Asmare's affiliates in its process of organization and capacity-building, strengthening its autonomy and independence. Currently, the Pastoral participates in the coordination of support to the administration and refers street dwellers to the association. Asmare also counts on financial support from other outside organizations to develop special projects.

Integrating a network of cooperatives is also the strategy devised by Colombian Porvenir, which maintains a strong alliance with the Association of Recyclers (ARB) from Bogotá and the National Recyclers Association (ANR). Both play important roles in the connection between actors and institutions and in the efforts to eliminate the barriers and prejudices that create a distance between society and the collectors. Nevertheless, the consolidation of the cooperative network, which includes the government, has proved extremely difficult, thereby reducing the impact and the scope of what the network can accomplish. Collectors are therefore unable to participate in some supply chains, like that of plastics recycling, which reduces their opportunities for gains. But despite the difficulties with governmental support and the competition with private companies in the area of urban cleaning and recycling, the Colombian initiative has been obtaining results that ensure its sustainability and strengthen the lobby to improve its possibilities of operation.

Argentina-based El Ceibo, by contrast, does not seek to establish long-term alliances with other private or public organizations and institutions. More pragmatic in its approach, it establishes working alliances for specific projects, devoted to the improvement of its strategic positioning and access to resources. But the cooperative is experiencing the great challenge that the Argentine context imposes: the social articulation of collectors' groups and cooperatives at the local and national levels. The 2001 economic crisis led to the fast growth of the number of people surviving as waste collectors, in a process which, because it is recent, has not had time to go through the maturation observed in the Brazilian and Colombian cases. This is probably the reason for its lagging ability to form networks. Initiatives have been marked with some conflicts, causing the organization to have little capacity to voice its claims and to be a weak link in the supply chain.

Business Models

The three initiatives studied emerged in the 1990s, with the purpose of rescuing the dignity and civic rights of a population excluded from the formal labor market. Despite similarities in constitution, mission, and objectives, the ways in which these initiatives operate present distinct advantages and limitations. The business models of the three initiatives differ in two critical processes: obtaining raw material and selling collected and sorted materials.

The three cooperatives strive to obtain gains of logistics and scale, and to obtain raw material through partnerships with large generators (house complexes, public and private companies, hospitals), which provide large volumes of recyclable material to be collected, separated, baled, and sold. Colombia-based Porvenir focuses exclusively on this type of strategy, keeping 20 fixed contracts with 3 hospitals, 5 private firms, and 12 house complexes. Within a context of public policies which do not privilege waste collectors' organizations, this method of building partnerships appears to be the most adequate sustainability strategy for the organization. Such a strategy requires an effort of constant identification of opportunities in socially responsible entrepreneurship, and a continued commitment to Porvenir's objectives.

Brazilian Asmare also invests in partnerships with companies that generate large quantities of recyclable waste, and is presently working with 22 of them. It also maintains alliances with the local government, which results in gains of scale and logistical advantage. The local government of Belo Horizonte, where Asmare operates, delivers the recyclable material collected by the public collection trucks directly to the cooperative's warehouse. This material represents 15 percent of the organization's total raw material. In this model, sustainability results from the government's recognition and strengthening of the role played by the cooperatives and associations as agents in the waste supply chains, as evident in public policies that integrate those agents in the processes of environmental preservation and socio-economic development.

Unlike Asmare, the Argentine cooperative El Ceibo has not forged partnerships or agreements with the local government. Even so, its performance in the supply chain is strengthened by local legislation. Though garbage collection in Buenos Aires is conducted by private companies, legislation establishes that they must build landfills called "green centers," to be operated by the cooperatives. Thus the law provides implicit subsidies to El Ceibo and other cooperatives, adding value to the price of the material collected by the waste collectors and contributing thereby to the improvement of their quality of life. El Ceibo benefits by using its warehouse as a temporary green center for one of the companies employed in garbage collection. If the warehouse becomes a permanent green center, El Ceibo will gain scale and will be able to employ more people in the process of sorting the collected material.

The cooperative has reached agreement with some of the companies chartered by the local government to collect trash, dividing up areas and activities. This allows direct contact with the local population, which helps the cooperative to persuade and raise awareness on issues related to environmental preservation, through meetings between citizens and the cooperative's environmental promoters. Preceding the collection of the material, this step is carried out in homes at prearranged times. The cooperative deals with donors in 900 homes, in a largely unexploited market of 56,000 homes in El Ceibo's performance area. Given that the area lacks large scale trash generators, the strategy was effective to deal with the dispersion and low-density of the waste donors.

The second relevant process in the business models studied is that of selling the collected material. Participation and understanding of the waste management chain seem to maximize the generation of economic value by the cooperatives and associations of waste collectors. The economic value of a social enterprise is defined as "benefits earned or remunerated by the receivers, provided that the price exceeds the cost" and, in the case of cooperatives and non-profit organizations, it is measured in terms of financial sustainability, i.e., their capability of operating indefinitely (see Chapter 9).

Porvenir's strategy for reducing costs and obtaining gains of scale was to make arrangements with fixed suppliers that generate large amounts of waste. Also, it sells its products directly to various industries which use recyclable residues like cardboard, paper, plastic, and glass. Moreover, clients are responsible for the transportation of the material purchased from Porvenir, which brings down costs.

Reaching an appropriate scale of production, efficiency in the separation, processing, baling, and transportation of the material, and compliance with quality standards and legal requirements for the commercialization of the products generated, are the key challenges for organizations willing to participate in all stages of the supply chain and sell directly to industries. However, most waste collectors' organizations do not have the necessary resources to develop all those work steps. Their main clients, therefore, are companies acting as intermediate agents—facility owners, paper dealers,[28] scrap merchants,[29] and brokers. A resulting disadvantage is lower added value and less income for Porvenir's workers, as well as risks to the sustainability of the initiative.

It is estimated, for instance, that the end value of plastic is 200 percent above the price paid to the associations by scrap merchants. For this reason, in alliance with other similar organizations, Asmare expects to build a plastic recycling plant as a secondary income source to help eliminate the intermediaries and control the entire supply chain from collection to sale, including the transformation of recycled bottles and packages into new plastic products. El Ceibo, in turn, envisions the opportunity to work in the area of crafts and decorative art as an additional income source for the collectors.

Regardless of the specific conditions associated with each case, in terms of business models it is possible to say that Porvenir has, since its inception, been driven by the adoption of a sustainable business model, which caused it to build a warehouse to enhance storage capacity and facilitate transportation. Porvenir has also conducted a market study to identify potential clients and pricing in order to define its logistical needs and obtain gains of scale. To incorporate the model, it had to overcome the barrier of informality which characterized the collectors' work and eliminate the prejudices that separated the low-income population and client entrepreneurs. It is the only initiative that hired an outside professional to be in charge of administration, signaling its concerns about promoting changes in policies and practices so as to obtain higher economic gains for its affiliates. Because the largest margin of revenues comes from recycled paper, but paper accounts for only 30 percent of the total of the material collected, the cooperative has offered other types of services, such as the use of their space to serve as a landfill[30] site for hazardous waste. Its sustainability strategy is aimed at enhancing the number of partnerships with larger waste generators, which allows for gains of scale and production and reduction of logistics costs.

Asmare seeks to establish more partnerships and increase collection to obtain better prices through gains of scale. Asmare is not limited, however, to commercial activities between the low-income population and industries;

it also works to improve the collectors' work conditions by raising societal awareness of the importance of the cooperative's work, and facilitating workers' access to education, health, and housing. It obtains gains of scale and in logistics because its operation goes beyond collectors in the streets; additionally, it receives material collected by trucks from the municipal town hall and rented trucks that pick up donations by large generators. This material is separated, pressed, and commercialized in the association's two warehouses in the center of Belo Horizonte, which decreases logistics costs and adds value to the product.

El Ceibo has been seeking to develop consistent work and business strategies. Nevertheless, traces of informality, the expectation of immediate returns, and low professional levels persist. Its financial sustainability is assured through the use of its warehouse as a green center, as well as from donations specifically to the collectors' activities, allowing El Ceibo to keep its infrastructure and funds for specific projects. The initiative does demonstrate a healthy dose of pragmatism in handling these partnerships, and it intends to consolidate sustainability through increased waste collection and gains from production efficiency, all crucial factors in transforming the cooperative into a capitalist firm.

It is possible to imagine that technological innovations in collection and separation, in conjunction with the rationalization of tactical, operational, and administrative planning, could bring considerable efficiency to the management of this type of initiative. The fact remains, however, that the three cases studied can be viewed as rather simple organizational structures and unsophisticated management models. Two variables in their operation have a strong impact on efficiency, costs, and productivity: *scale*, referring to the volume of material collected and the capacity to store it; and *logistics*, encompassing transportation costs, scope of action, collection sources, and distribution. Maintaining a tactical view and a sense of opportunity while addressing these challenges is a key factor for financial sustainability, understood as the capacity to generate enough revenue to ensure the venture's life expectancy.

Financial and Economic Sustainability

Accounting records are unreliable in collaborative initiatives like cooperatives and associations. Mutual trust, a focus on the core activity, and the low degree of managerial professionalism of these organizations result in substandard records and projections. None of the three initiatives studied escapes this rule, though all show some indicators that explain how they have generated and maximized economic value.

Local government has a significant impact on the activities of solid-residue collectors through regulations of their performance and the operation of their cooperatives. Both can benefit from their association:while the collection and transportation of urban garbage are the responsibility of local governments, they constitute the main activity of the initiatives created by collectors. Hence increasing client portfolio, adjusting to current legislation, and improving infrastructure and logistics are key goals for collectors' organizations. Only by meeting them will collectors advance in the value chain, reach better financial results, and maintain good relations with their respective municipalities.

As discussed in the section entitled Business Models, enhancing operational processes for increasing the scale of production and reducing logistics costs are essential to the sustainability of those undertakings. At the same time, the collectors need to invest in organizational development, triggering internal changes that offer technical support to operations. Following this strategy, Colombia's Porvenir has been improving its financial performance by reducing administrative expenditures; excluding affiliated collectors that did not adapt to the organization's work routine; decreasing losses of material; intervening in several lines of operation to make them more efficient and productive; significantly decreasing expenses associated with the maintenance of vehicles and fuel; and improving the accounting system, making it more accurate and reliable. Those measures resulted in a 20 percent reduction in annual fixed costs and 15 percent in variable costs. At US$42 per ton on average for the margin of aggregate contribution from collected residues, Porvenir had a surplus of US$9,682 in 2006.

Strong sustainability indicators contribute to Porvenir's generation of economic value. Its organizational evolution and operational improvements enabled the establishment of strictly commercial relationships between the cooperative and the most powerful and influential organizations of the supply chain-end buyers. Moreover, Porvenir privileges the maintenance and development of fixed partnerships with large residue generators. That is an important strategy, because the local environmental regulation for organic waste (Solid Residue Master Plan) represents a threat to the collectors working in the streets without fixed trash sources. Porvenir thus gains financially as it ensures greater stability in production.

Avoiding dependence on governmental subsidies is important for the sustainability of the solid-residue social entrepreneurships. Brazil-based Asmare seeks to increase the growth trend of its overall revenue by increasing the sales of recyclable material to industries. The organization's revenue grew by 17 percent between 2001 and 2005, a period in which the sale of solid waste to companies—Asmare's main business line—increased by 28 percent. From the total resources allocated to it by the city government, which correspond to 50 percent of the organization's annual revenue, only 10 percent comes from the City Cleaning Authority and is allocated to its core activity. The rest comes from the Social Assistance Secretariat and is allocated to Asmare's social activities (in this respect Asmare differs from the other two initiatives studied, whose activities are exclusively economic). In terms of sustainability, debt reduction associated with a more rigorous accounting control, and investment in machinery and equipment that increase productive capacity, indicate Asmare's development toward a better performance in the near future.

Our analysis of economic sustainability of these three initiatives identifies the determinant factors in driving productivity, improving economic and financial performance, and enhancing the creation of economic value:

- Strengthening of the capacity to organize and structure collectors' activities and the operation of the cooperatives and associations that they constitute.

- Improving control and formalization of operational and managerial accounting records.

- Reducing the dependence on external resources coming from charity funds and subsidies—a factor associated with increased generation of income—through the commercialization of solid waste and derivates.

- Focusing on gains for scale in the acquisition of raw material and on the sale of solid waste and derivates.

- Improving the quality of the material collected, which is determined by its degree of cleanliness and separation (paper, aluminum, etc). Optimizing the routes of collection and delivery of materials, and improving the cost-benefit ratio through the rationalization of the operation logistics.

- Creating a strategic plan to consolidate the undertaking and strengthen its effective insertion in the supply chain.

- Forging relationships based on trust and direct negotiations with industries, thereby limiting the participation of brokers.

It is evident that the cooperative's relationship with the municipal authority must be handled within its respective socio-political context. If this context is favorable, as in the Brazilian and Argentine cases, it is important for the cooperative to build alliances and seek to establish influence in the formulation of public policies focused on the management of solid waste. More hostile contexts, like the Colombian case, indicate the importance of strengthening the generation of economic value through strictly economic pathways. In all contexts, however, it is essential that the organization maintain flexibility with regard to regulatory landmarks and arrangements within the supply chain that influence the activity of collectors' cooperatives and associations, in order to anticipate and respond adroitly to changes.

Economic Inclusion of the Collectors

The professional competence and increased efficiency of the collectors' enterprises provide important benefits to their constituents, such as lower economic and social vulnerability; better safety and hygiene work conditions; gains and economies of scale which increase the affiliates' bargaining power in commercial relationships; a decrease in the power of the brokers, allowing collectors to secure a higher income; an increase in the collectors' purchasing power; and improvements in their quality of life.

Nevertheless, the analysis of the generation of economic value along the waste management chain shows that this chain is characterized by unequal profit sharing. The case of the cardboard recycling chain to which Colombian-based Porvenir belongs illustrates this point.[31]

Cardboard collectors, who constitute the first link of the chain (E1), collect a zero value product for society, since it is a material discarded as garbage. If it does not follow to recycling, this material is taken to a landfill site by one of the urban cleaning consortia, at a cost of US$0.05[32] per kilo. In other words, when dumped in the garbage, cardboard has a negative value for society. This value starts to become positive when collectors modify its value by adding their labor to it, recovering it, and selling the kilo at US$0.13, on average, if they belong to an organization like Porvenir.

The broker is the second link of the chain (E2). Porvenir accrues value at this level because it packs the material and makes it ready for sale at US$0.20 to the third link of the chain. Cartón de Colombia is the agent in this link (E3), responsible for transporting large quantities of the material to the Smurfit Cartón de Colombia factory, which buys the material per kilo, still raw, at an average value of US$0.36. This factory is the fourth link of the chain (E4); it transforms the material and sells the product at US$0.57 per kilo on average.

Though profit margins are unknown at each link of the chain, it is possible to calculate the aggregate economic value per each link and calculate an "appropriation percentage," as demonstrated in Table 7.1.[33]

Table 7.1
Value Appropriation in the Recycling Chain

Link	Aggregated value	Accumulated	Appropriation %
E1	0.18	0.13	32.7%
E2	0.07	0.20	53.3%
E3	0.15	0.36	73.9%
E4	0.21	0.57	60%

These values indicate that the collectors' share of the total added value of the product generated in the recycling chain is 30 percent. Yet they gain only 32.70 percent of the value they contribute, in contrast to the large warehouses of recyclable material, which contribute 24 percent of the total aggregate value and appropriate 73.9 percent of the generated value. Brokers, who constitute the link between collectors and large warehouses, answer for 11 percent of the overall added value of the chain, and appropriate 53.3 percent of the value they generate. The recycling industry, responsible for 35 percent of the total aggregate value of the chain, appropriates 60 percent of the value it generates.

Analysis of these data allows us to conclude that collectors constitute the link that appropriates the lowest percentage of value generated, despite assuming the highest degree of uncertainty and risk. However, when collectors in an association form an intermediate cooperative, they start to operate also in the second link of the chain. Conjointly, they appropriate 86 percent of the value they generate, which strengthens their economic position in the chain. Still, they do not supplant the third and fourth links—the warehouses of recyclable material and the recycling industries—which take up, respectively, 74 percent and 60 percent of the value generated. Moreover, cooperatives do not limit themselves only to the cardboard industry, often accepting less profitable materials in an effort to generate a minimum income for the affiliated collectors; this adds another nuance of its unfavorable economic position vis-à-vis other links of the value chain.

A solid-residue management chain can also be understood as part of a circle originating in the industries that generate residues (paper, glass, and plastic), but not terminating at the end consumer; rather, the circle extends toward the collector. In this sense, the collector is a member of the link who effectively generates more economic value and offers the largest contribution to environmental preservation, even though collectors constitute the link with the lowest return. The brokers and large warehouses, conversely, make the least contribution to the generation of economic value in the chain, but appropriate the largest percentage of value generated. Thus, a state of imbalance ensues and permeates the supply chain.

In Argentina-based El Ceibo, collectors' average monthly income is US$240, 13 percent below the minimum wage defined by law in that country (US$275). In Colombian Porvenir, this difference is 21 percent, the average income of the collector being US$133, and the minimum wage US$191.82.[34] Finally, in Brazilian Asmare, even though collectors' monthly income of US$360 is 116 percent above the minimum wage of US$166.67,[35] it is 52 percent lower than the cost of living in Brazil (US$745.01).[36] In El Ceibo, this relation is 20 percent lower, with a cost of living of US$300, and in the case of Porvenir, it is 31 percent lower, with a cost of living of US$168.38. Though the family income may equal or rise above the minimum levels of cost of living through remunerated activities carried out other family members, in none of the three cases analyzed is the income obtained by the collector enough to sustain a family, according to the cost-of-living indicators of each country.

Another illustration of the economic disparity between collectors' income and that of the general population is evident in the comparison of the affiliated collectors' monthly income and per capita monthly income in each country, namely US$493.52 in Brazil,[37] US$478.77[38] in Argentina, and US$242.08 in Colombia.[39] Again, collectors' income is always below per capita income: 27 percent lower in Brazil, 50 percent lower in Argentina, and 45 percent lower in Colombia, comparisons that reveal the socio-economic inequality that characterizes these countries and the living conditions of the workers engaged in solid-waste collection.

Despite these statistics, it is important to bear in mind that the collectors associated to the enterprises studied still obtain gains above those of non-associated collectors. At Porvenir, the income of an associated collector is 118 percent higher than that of a non-associated one; at Asmare, it is 100 percent higher and at El Ceibo, 25 percent higher.[40] In this last case, the enterprise adds less value to the collectors' work, probably because of their comparatively small presence in the solid-residue management chain and the managerial immaturity of the enterprise.

Thus it is clear that this category of workers faces many difficulties in reaching equitable economic inclusion. The gain obtained is insufficient to ensure minimum quality-of-life standards, which places organized collectors at some type of intermediate stage, not in destitution but still apart from the mainstream of society.

Social Value Generation for the Collectors

Though the prospect of better living conditions has been the driving force behind the organization and formalization of the activities of the solid-residue collectors, the years these people have lived apart from society have brought consequences that hinder efforts toward sharing responsibility and effective collaboration in social and work relationships. That weakness, in turn, hampers the maintenance of the affiliates of their organizations. Thus changes in behavior and attitude are required, as they will have a direct impact on work productivity and quality. Above all, such changes will promote the generation of social value,[41] One of the first steps Asmare and Porvenir took to enact these changes was to establish criteria for the entry and permanence of the collectors in the organization.

Brazilian Asmare only accepts as members people who collect solid waste as a livelihood. Formal entry into the organization requires acceptance of the terms of the bylaws and, consequently, obedience to the rights and duties defined. To become members, collectors must also participate in capacity-building programs offered by the organization. Once accepted at Asmare, collectors can perform at several stages of the process (collection, selection, pressing), and they are prepared to become entrepreneurs and managers of their own businesses. This strategy has been carried out since January 2003, when collectors started to manage the association, supported by two administrative technicians hired by their former coordinator originally from the Street Pastoral Mission.[42]

Criteria are even more severe at Colombian Porvenir: good references must be presented or collectors (with no legal problems) must undergo a probation period before their employment status becomes permanent. They also participate in training programs and must obey rules defined by the organization. When collectors cannot abide by the cooperative's rules and maintain high productivity levels, they are fired. People sometimes find it hard to commit fully to the organization and its mission, because they are used to individualistic behavior, short-term results, and unilateral benefits. Once they are organized, however, Colombian collectors feel differentiated from informal collectors and develop characteristics of entrepreneurs or "small-business entrepreneurs."

El Ceibo's Argentine collectors act only at the beginning of the chain, collecting and storing the recyclable material, a fact that differentiates this undertaking from the other two. Still, all three cases studied are similar in terms of the social value arising from the initiatives, particularly the accomplishment of income-generating activities, reduction of social exclusion and drug use, the development of a sense of belonging to a group and sharing a collective sense of work. In contrast to El Ceibo, however, the collectors of Asmare and Porvenir also qualify for other roles, such as those required in negotiation and leadership, and in the strengthening of participative spaces. Asmare contributes to the formal education not only of collectors but also of their children, who, besides benefiting from changes arising from their families' improved economic situation, find more opportunities to enter the formal labor market than their parents. Such prospects of social mobility for future generations are also seen in Colombia, where solid-waste collection is an activity involving all family members. Collectors become organized to move from a subsistence economy to a sustainable productive project, but they do not want their children to work in that job. Their aim is to provide their children with education, to give them a chance to seek other professions.

Solid-waste collectors' organizations and regional movements aim to enhance their participation in the production of recyclables and strengthen their social and political structure by forging partnerships with companies and government agencies. A case in point is the CSO Fundación Social de Colombia, which has since 1986 supported the creation of collectors' cooperatives with financial resources and assistance in legal, administrative, and commercial matters.

Above all, regional and national movements and associations seek to dignify the work of informal collectors and educate society on the social and environmental benefits of their work. These are the aims of the Bogotá Recyclers Association (ARB), the National Movement of Cardboard Collectors (MNCR), Recyclers and Social Organizations (MNTCRyOS) from Argentina, and the National Movement of Recyclable Materials Collectors (MNCR) from Brazil.

To attain the recognition and valorization of this category of workers, MNCR seeks to exert influence on public policies, so that the collection of solid waste could provide a better remuneration at current values, and so that collectors might participate increasingly in all steps of the supply chain. In the social sphere, MNCR aims to obtain better living conditions—housing, health, and education—for collectors and their families. In the more encompassing sphere, MNCR advocates the end of "garbage dumpsites"[43] in favor of sanitary landfills, so that collectors' work might take place in warehouses, with fewer risks to their health and survival.

As these initiatives show, great advances have been made in value generation and consequent social inclusion of the collectors. But many challenges still lie ahead in improving the processes and relationships within the solid-residue management supply chain, before all of this potential to generate social, economic, and environmental benefits can be fulfilled.

Lessons of Solid-Waste Management Initiatives for Low-Income Citizens

The main positive impact of the initiatives developed by solid-residue collectors lies in the reduction in the level of social exclusion they experienced prior to their organization. The possibility of economic inclusion and related improvements in living conditions, and the prospect of benefiting from "substantive freedoms"[44] are clear results in the cases studied. Being affiliated with a formal organization helps collectors and their families to recover self-esteem and dignity, besides contributing to the social capital of their community.

The changes triggered by these initiatives are more obvious when the conditions of destitution, social exclusion, lack of resources and low self-esteem that historically mark the lives of these persons are taken into consideration. It takes an enormous effort to recover dignity and the capacity to participate in groups structured around common objectives. The influence of support organizations such as CSOs and social entrepreneurs with practical knowledge of the reality experienced by the collectors, were central to the first groups that originated the initiatives studied. Public or private social programs should take this background into consideration to avoid becoming mere assistance programs with low capacity for social transformation.

Public agencies have an important role in the solid-residue management chain. They hold the means to create conditions that favor the creation and development of collectors' cooperatives. Some cases studied have shown that action of the local government may be decisive, either through policies and laws for the management of solid waste or through agreements and partnerships for the collection and transportation of urban garbage. In situations where attempts to form partnerships with local municipalities proved less fruitful, the unity of efforts among collectors with the support of CSOs has created fertile terrain for the institution of formal cooperatives.

Private companies also play an important role in the solid-residue management chain: as generators of large volumes of residues; as collectors of urban garbage hired by local public administration; and as buyers of residues for milling and recycling. Whatever the position of the company in this chain, the establishment of strategic alliances with collectors' cooperatives and associations can bring numerous advantages for both sides, by forcing the redesign of the value-generating chain and repositioning the brokers; reducing storage, transport, or raw material costs; raising awareness among workers, clients, and suppliers of the social and environmental impacts of collecting and recycling; and triggering affirmative acts of social inclusion.

Additionally, the solid-residue management chain is characterized by a constant interaction among government, brokers, companies, and collectors' cooperatives. Cooperatives work in several stages of the chain, but mainly in the initial residue collection. In this occupation, the requirements concerning the qualification of the workers and the use of equipment are minimal. As initiatives evolve, other stages, like separation, storage, pressing, and even final commercialization are absorbed by collectors, steps that allow better sustainability for their initiatives and generate more income for their members. However, the relations among the agents participating in the value-generating chain are often marked by conflicts with public bodies and difficulties in overcoming the influence of brokers, to the detriment of the performance and growth of the cooperatives and the distribution of the value generated in the process. Forming networks of partners and local and regional coalitions of collectors has been the way the initiatives overcome those difficulties. Strategic alliances help the initiatives to carry out timely projects or to get on with their own business, as long as the business model is based on the collaboration and fair distribution of power and value generated.

Collectors' organizations have experienced huge internal difficulties operating under the collective principles that guide their creation. Decision-making in horizontal structures tends to be slow and low-participative, caused by the lack of natural leaders within these groups. Consequently, the management of the initiatives tends to become a semi-hierarchic model with low organizational development and little participation. Developing internal competencies aimed at full self-management, aligned with the requirements of reactivity, agility, and transparency imposed by the market and by partners, is critical to the professional development of those initiatives.

The generation of economic value by collectors' initiatives derives from the construction of business models adapted to the opportunities identified in their environment. Gains in logistics for obtaining raw material can be achieved in two ways: receiving large volumes of urban garbage from massive waste generators such as companies and buildings, or selling the material collected and separated directly to the industries that use it as raw material, thereby cutting out brokers and adding more economic value to output. Obtaining both efficiency and quality in the operation of solid waste collection, milling, and commercialization is the main objective that the value-generating chain imposes on the sustainability of collectors' cooperatives.

Economic inclusion of the collectors, through increment of income earned, is the driver of many initiatives and it will never cease to be one of their objectives. The increase in the number of cooperatives and associations is visible in Latin America, and the simultaneous consolidation and enhancement of those initiatives was shown in the cases studied. Nevertheless, the financial valorization of the collectors' activities is still low, since their income remains below the cost of living and the per capita income in all three of the initiatives' respective countries. In addition, their work, hygiene, and safety conditions are precarious. For this reason, the development of collectors' cooperatives has not been exclusively oriented toward the creation of efficient businesses. The political performance of these organizations through the union of collectors' efforts and the creation of organized movements have been crucial for the recognition and valorization of the role played by these workers in solid-residue management.

Notes

1. Heloisa V. de Medina, "Reciclagem de materiais: Tendências tecnológicas de um novo setor," CETEM—Centro de Tecnologia Mineral, Ministério da Ciência e Tecnologia, http://www.cetem.gov.br/tendencias/agenda/parte_III/Reciclagem %20de%20materiais.pdf.
2. The values and principles of cooperativism have historical routes in utopian socialism, the pioneer of which was Englishman Robert Owen (1771–1858), with his proposal, in 1817, of creating Cooperative Villages.
3. "What Is a Cooperative?" International Cooperative Alliance, http://www .ica.coop/coop/index.html.
4. Paul Singer, *Introdução à Economia Solidária* (São Paulo: Perseu Abramo, 2002).
5. Robert D. Putnam, *Making Democracy Work: Civic Traditions in Modern Italy* (Princeton, N.J.: Princeton University Press, 1993).
6. World Bank calculations suggested that the number of people working as collectors in 2004 could surpass the figure of 60 million in the world. Martin Medina, "Oito mitos sobre a reciclagem informal da América Latina," BIDAmérica, http://www.iadb.org/idbamerica/index.cfm?thisid=3075.
7. "Gestão Integrada de Resíduos Sólidos," Asociación Interamericana de Ingeniería Sanitaria y Ambiental, http://www.aidis.org.br/eng/ftp/polis_aidis.pdf.
8. Ibid.
9. "Oito mitos sobre a reciclagem informal da América Latina," BIDAmérica, http://www.iadb.org/idbamerica/index.cfm?thisid=3075.
10. "Gestão Integrada de Resíduos Sólidos," Asociación Interamericana de Ingeniería Sanitaria y Ambiental, http://www.aidis.org.br/eng/ftp/polis_aidis.pdf.

11. "Oito mitos sobre a reciclagem informal da América Latina," BIDAmérica, http://www.iadb.org/idbamerica/index.cfm?thisid=3075.

12. Pablo Schamber, "No se presta atención a los cartoneros como engranaje de un sistema económico," Página 12, http://www.pagina12.com.ar/imprimir/diario/sociedad/3-87058-2007-06-24.html.

13. Maricel Drazer, "O poder dos coletores informais," Tierramérica, http://www.tierramerica.info/nota.php?lang=port&idnews=170.

14. Asociación Nacional de Recicladores (ANR).

15. Pólita Gonçalves. "A Reciclagem Integradora dos Aspectos Ambientais, Sociais e Econômicos." DP&A / PHASE. Rio de Janeiro, 2003.

16. Intersectorial Relations Studies Group, "Movimento Nacional dos Catadores de Materiais Recicláveis (MNCR). Database of the record for sampling of the survey on the Workstation" (Salvador: GERI-Pangea/UFBa [Federal University of Bahia], 2005).

17. Ministério do Trabalho e Emprego, "Atlas da Economia Solidária no Brasil," http://www.mte.gov.br/Empregador/EconomiaSolidaria/conteudo/atlas.asp.

18. Interview with Roberto Laureano–National Movement of Collectors of Recyclable Materials. Aug 29, 2006.

19. Organized within the Archdioceses, the "pastorais" are structures that transcend the parochial limits, seeking to promote solidarity and citizenship, as well as redeeming human dignity when it is threatened.

20. César Rodríguez, "À procura de alternativas económicas em tempos de globalização: o caso das cooperativas de recicladores de lixo na Colômbia," Centro de Estudos Sociais, Faculdade de Economia da Universidade de Coimbra, http://www.ces.uc.pt/emancipa/research/pt/ft/rescatar.html.

21. Maricel Drazer, "O poder dos coletores informais," Tierramérica, http://www.tierramerica.info/nota.php?lang=port&idnews=170.

22. Thiago Guimarães, "Coleta seletiva de lixo cresce 38% no país," FolhaOnline, http://www1.folha.uol.com.br/folha/cotidiano/ult95u124738.shtml.

23. The Archdiocese of Belo Horizonte in Brazil, for example, provides capacity-building programs for Asmare's collectors. Operating at national level, their Nenuca Institute for Sustainable Development (INSEA) is a not-for-profit organization providing technical consultation for the creation and development of environmental management models identified with the premise of social inclusion. Also worth noting, though not bearing any direct relation with the sample studied, is the work of Peruvian Ciudad Saludable, which develops capacity-building activities thus bringing together the work of civil society organizations and public and private companies in the Andes region.

24. Rimisp Manuel Chiriboga, "Mecanismos de articulación de pequeños productores rurales con empresas privadas, síntesis regional," Mesa de Trabajo en Desarrollo Económico de RURALTER, 80. Quito, Ecuador, 2007.

25. "Termos de Referência para Monitoramento em Direitos Humanos," Instituto Nenuca de Desenvolvimento Sustentável (INSEA), December 2005.

26. Intermediaries are those who purchase solid waste (paper, metal, and plastic) from small and medium-sized generators (stores, banks, supermarkets, homes, schools, government offices, etc.), as well as from collectors. These materials are stored in their sheds, where they are sorted, packed in bales, and sold to the recycling industries.

27. Self-management is a democratic type of administration in which decisions are made in assemblies with all members of the organization or their authorized representatives. These assemblies define the guidelines to be followed by the organizations' managers. It is, therefore, the opposite of hetero-management, a traditional model of hierarchic administration, formed by successive authority levels. See Paul Singer, *Introdução à Economia Solidária* (São Paulo: Ed. Perseu Abramo, 2002).

28. These are called *aparistas* in Portuguese. They buy used paper scraps and cutting waste from companies and households, and send them to their depositary, where paper is selected and baled and then sold to paper industries.

29. These are locally called *sucateiros,* people who collect, receive, and store several types of solid residues to commercialize them.

30. Sanitary landfills are areas prepared for receiving the waste, with treatment for the gases and liquids that result from decomposition of materials, so as to protect the soil, the water, and the air from pollution.

31. Franklin Luis Combariza and Roberto Gutiérrez, "Apropiación de valor en la cadena de reciclaje del cartón," *Responsabilidad & Sostenibilidad,* 2008.

32. The Unidad Ejecutiva de Servicios Públicos (Public Services Executive Unit). An average household is calculated to generate 120 kg of garbage per month. Activities paid for are collection, transportation, and final disposal.

33. The "appropriation percentage" is determined by subtracting the purchase value from the sale value, and comparing this resulting proportion to the purchase value per each link.

34. "Salario Mínimo Legal Diario (Col $)," Banco de la República de Colombia, http://www.banrep.gov.co/estad/dsbb/srea_020.xls.

35. "Salário mínimo nominal e necessário," Departamento Intersindical de Estatística e Estudos Socioeconômicos, http://www.dieese.org.br/rel/rac /salmindez07.xml.

36. Ibid.

37. "Time Series Management System," Banco Central do Brasil, https://www3 .bcb.gov.br/sgspub/consultarvalores/telaCvsSelecionarSeries.paint.

38. "World Economic Outlook Database," International Monetary Fund, http://www.imf.org/external/pubs/ft/weo/2006/02/data/weoreptc.aspx?sy=2003 &ey=2007&scsm=1&ssd=1&sort=country&ds=.&br=1&c=213&s=NGDP_R %2CNGDP_RPCH%2CNGDP%2CNGDPD%2CNGDP_D%2CNGDPRPC% 2CNGDPPC%2CNGDPDPC%2CPPPWGT%2CPPPPC%2CPPPSH%2CPPP EX%2CPCPI%2CPCPIPCH%2CLP%2CBCA%2CBCA_NGDPD&grp=0&a= &pr.x=75&pr.y=9.

39. "World Economic Outlook Database," International Monetary Fund, http://www
    .imf.org/external/pubs/ft/weo/2008/01/weodata/index.aspx
40. The average income of collectors who are not members of cooperatives or asso-
    ciations is, on average, US$180 in Brazil, US$192 in Argentina, and US$61 in
    Colombia.
41. Social value is defined as "the pursuit of societal betterment through the
    removal of barriers that hinder social inclusion, the assistance to those tem-
    porarily weakened or lacking a voice, and the mitigation of undesirable side
    effects of economic activity." SEKN, ed., *Effective Management of Social Enter-
    prises Lessons from Businesses and Civil Society Organizations in Iberoamerica*
    (Cambridge, MA: Harvard University, David Rockefeller Center for Latin Amer-
    ican Studies, distributed by Harvard University Press, 2006), 266.
42. The Belo Horizonte Pastoral de Rua had an important role in the involvement
    of the collectors of that municipality and in the consequent creation of Asmare,
    as detailed in section 3 of this chapter.
43. Garbage dumpsites are places where the garbage collected by public services is
    disposed of without any treatment.
44. According to Sen, substantive freedoms are associated with an increase in the
    capacity for deliberate choice in five instrumental spheres: (1) political free-
    doms, (2) economic facilities, (3) social opportunities, (4) transparency guar-
    antees, and (5) protective security. Access to them contributes to promoting an
    individual's general capacity. Amartya Kumar Sen, *Development as Freedom*
    (New York, NY: Oxford University Press, 1999).

8

Agribusiness and Low-Income Sectors

John C. Ickis, Francisco Leguizamón, Juliano Flores, and Michael Metzger

Case studies on innovative agribusiness ventures that include low-income sectors (LIS) may offer new knowledge to fight poverty in Latin America. Over more than forty years, John Mellor and others have pointed out, with convincing data, that "agricultural growth and only agricultural growth effectively mitigates poverty in low income countries with a substantial agribusiness sector."[1] This conclusion was recently reaffirmed by the statement that "any rural income increase has a disproportionate impact on global poverty, which is mostly rural."[2] James Austin has argued that agribusiness projects create a demand for agricultural sectors to produce greater quantities of more diverse crops, and when this happens, farming employment generally grows.[3] Thus, agribusiness holds a promise to drive agricultural growth and rural poverty reduction.

This chapter examines nine research cases[4] of agribusiness ventures that have incorporated LIS into value creation activities. The key driver for agribusiness owners is economic, but that does not imply that wealth creation among LIS is not equally relevant. Regardless of underlying motivations, the key questions we explore in this chapter are, how do agribusiness ventures incorporate LIS into their value chains differently than in the past? How do these market-based initiatives enhance the potential to create economic and social value? What barriers hinder LIS incorporation, and how can they be overcome?

To answer these questions, we will use the agribusiness chain analytical framework described in the following section, which enables us to identify the roles played by LIS in the ventures studied. Next, we will examine how LIS incorporation has influenced business models and evaluate whether it has contributed to their competitiveness. There are many barriers, ranging from logistical to social and cultural, that prevent successful LIS incorporation. The next section will discuss these barriers and some practices used to overcome them. Finally, we will present some conclusions in reference to our initial questions.

Context and Challenges in the Value Chain of Agribusiness

An agribusiness chain includes the raw materials, the processing stage, and any upstream and downstream activities. Thus, agribusiness chains include operations spanning from agricultural input production activities to end-product delivery to consumers. These operations involve agricultural products grown on the soil and livestock-derived goods. The transformation of agribusiness products varies extensively, ranging from cleaning and packing to chemical alterations, but they are all characterized by three features of their raw materials. First, raw materials are perishable and cannot be stored for long periods of time, especially fruits and vegetables. Second, most harvests are seasonal, while food demand is usually stable. Third, farm product quality is much more variable than that of manufactured products. These traits impose logistical and operative challenges on agribusiness management and create opportunities for LIS incorporation as business partners.

Agribusiness logistical and operating challenges were first studied by Ray Goldberg,[5] who developed a system framework for their analysis known as "the agribusiness chain," later applied by generations of Harvard Business School students to analyze case studies. In developing nations, James Austin proved the analytical prowess of this tool and elaborated his own framework to explore agroindustry projects.[6] We will use this latter model to examine LIS incorporation strategies in agribusiness ventures.

There are three major links in the chain identified by Austin: acquisition (field), transformation (factory), and trade (market).[7] The first one refers to planting, growing, and harvesting processes. At the factory link, raw materials are transformed, and decisions are made regarding end-product packaging, storage, and transportation to distributors. The market link handles matters relating to consumer preferences, market segmentation, demand forecasts, pricing, distribution channels, as well as competitive force analysis and management. The tasks involved in each link are performed by primary actors—farmers, processors, distributors, and other parties directly managing products. In addition, other support actors provide assistance, loans, and other services, as well as coordination elements that enable efficient product flow. A close coordination among field, factory, and market links becomes crucial, given agribusiness products' seasonality and perishable nature.

The strength of this analytical framework lies in its ability not only to identify value activities carried out by each chain link, but also to determine who holds the greatest negotiating leverage and why. Indeed, this framework complements the strategic analysis model introduced by Michael

Porter—competitive pressures among rivals, buyers, newcomers, and substitute goods producers,[8] as well as the value chain with its primary and supporting activities.[9] Combined, these models prove useful to gain a better understanding of how LIS integration to agribusiness can create economic and social value.

Innovative Models That Allowed For the Inclusion of LIS

The nine cases studied reveal a range of roles performed by LIS in agribusiness—mostly at the field link, sometimes at the processing link, and less frequently in the market. There is only one case, Palí Supermarkets (Costa Rica and Nicaragua), which illustrates the incorporation of LIS as end consumers in agribusiness chains. It was precisely this LIS role—as profitable customers—that inspired C. K. Prahalad to research business at the base of the pyramid and to elaborate his work on the wealth held by this population segment. In contrast, all cases in our sample, except one, served mid and high-income segment customers.

The Tierra Fértil (Central America) and Cativen (Venezuela) ventures include LIS as fresh and perishable product suppliers for supermarket chains. In two other cases, LIS also provide perishable produce for downstream processing—organic grains received by Irupana from Bolivian farmers are naturally processed, while pupae in cocoons, shipped to CRES by Costa Rica's breeders, are classified, packaged, and exported to butterfly exhibitors. In the two cases dealing with palm oil and byproduct production, elaboration is greater, but there is a key difference among them: at Agropalma (Brazil), LIS participants still serve as field producers, whereas at Palmas del Espino (Peru), the producers' association promotes downstream integration and shares in factory profits. In fact, many farmers become factory employees, and, although their union demands better salary conditions, they double the wage paid to farm workers.

At APAEB (Brazil) and the Wild Fruit Pickers (Chile), LIS are fully involved in more complex transformation activities for natural hemp tapestry and carpets manufacture, in the former case, and for dried wild fruit elaboration and marketing, in the latter. In fact, Swedish buyers contact this pickers' association directly to purchase mushrooms, which proves LIS engagement in trade operations as well.

At first glance, these LIS roles are not that different from those traditionally performed by small farmers—selling their crops to market intermediaries or processing plants, or working as employees at agribusiness factories. However, when we examine business models and their changes as a result of LIS incorporation, we realize how different these roles truly are.

Let us begin by analyzing Palí, as this case clearly illustrates the notion of "business model," and it is the only case in which LIS perform the role envisioned by Prahalad—that of profitable customers. This business model reveals how activities are designed to produce value—i.e., how revenues drawn from customers' free choices exceed activity costs. Neighborhood stores' business model involves providing convenience and credit services in exchange for high unit prices, so that LIS customers traditionally pay more, as Prahalad has broadly highlighted in his research.[10] In contrast, Palí offers prices below those of other supermarkets, although it sells much fewer products than a typical supermarket. According to company estimations, 90 percent of its Nicaraguan customers and 70 percent of its customers in Costa Rica belong to D and E socio-economic segments,[11] i.e., LIS.

How does Palí do it? Palí chain supermarkets provide a pleasant, dignified albeit austere atmosphere, with products—mostly B-brands—displayed in their original shipping crates. These supermarkets do not sell fruit or vegetables requiring refrigeration, which LIS buy at public markets. Originally, they did not even carry milk or meat to save energy. Customers bring their own bags or purchase them at the stores, as Palí does not give bags away. Supermarket employees are trained for multitasking, flexibility, and productivity. Pursuant to this cost leadership strategy, Palí has built its core competency on overall operating efficiency.

This business model is highly innovative in Costa Rica and Nicaragua, where traditional supermarkets compete for higher-income segments. It was inspired on Aldi supermarkets' model, a small-store format with limited product assortment that originated in Germany in the postwar era.[12] The first Palí supermarket was inaugurated in 1979 in Costa Rica's low-income Desemparados district. Amidst an economic crisis, the model was largely welcome since inception. Until mid 2007, Palí's points of sale grew rapidly, consistently focusing on its target LIS customers. Currently, Palí stores account for over 60 percent of the overall sales of this corporation's supermarket formats. The company estimates that monthly store visits total 1.5 million customers in Costa Rica (roughly 30 percent of the country's population) and 1.2 million customers in Nicaragua.

Palí supermarkets not only contribute the most sales to CSU-CCA's corporate holding, but also post the highest return on investment. Investment recovery periods at Palí supermarkets average three years, while other store formats take over five years to recover investments. Referring to Palí supermarkets' profitability, the corporate affairs manager from the multinational that later acquired a controlling stake at CSU-CCA group stated: "[Our corporation] does not accept projects or new openings with unproven profitability."[13]

The business model for Tierra Fértil and Cativen is completely different. It is not based on low prices, low costs, and high volumes but on creating superior value that customers deem worthy of higher prices. These super-markets cater to middle- and higher middle-income customers who prefer one-stop shopping, and whose diet includes fruits, salads, and other healthy foods. These agribusinesses realize that one of the few ways available to stand out among their competitors, who sell the same food product brands, hinges on fruit and vegetable variety and freshness. Additional costs incurred to ensure this differentiation include training for producers, refrig-eration, transportation, and handling. Higher costs are offset not only by higher prices but also by customers' choice to do all their shopping at these supermarkets rather than at competing stores.

Cativen also illustrates how LIS incorporation in value-adding activities reshapes business model schemes. By developing small agricultural and fish vendors, Cativen managed to do away with intermediaries and save their 20 percent margin. In addition, treating directly with small producers enabled this supermarket chain to eliminate corruption in its purchasing department. With its former scheme, intermediaries, who marketed large volumes, often bribed Cativen's buyers in order to secure product purchases. Thus, by getting rid of intermediaries, the company also managed to improve its business practices.

Irupana's business model is also based on high prices that customers are willing to pay for organic products supplied by indigenous farmers. How-ever, this model shows two differences with those in the preceding cases. First, Irupana is not involved in retailing, and, second, it does not serve all segments in some socio-economic strata but only segments in domestic and export markets that value their products' differentiated traits.

In Costa Rica, around a hundred farmers and even some indigents have become butterfly breeders to provide pupae to CRES, an organization that exports these live pupae to butterfly exhibitors in Europe and the United States. This business model is also based on some transformation activities (classification, packing, and exports) that are valued by customers. It is quite innovative but still replicable, and, as such, threatened by the emergence of competitors. While the model's success has relied on increasing demand from abroad, supply growth jeopardizes this business and raises the need for a strategy to compete.

Both Agropalma and Palmas del Espino agro-ventures pursue business models with greater and more complex manufacturing operations. Palm fruits are transformed into industrialized products—palm oil and byprod-ucts. This affords LIS an opportunity to take part in agroindustrial chains, not only as farmers but as processors, for the business builds new employment sources. So, what is new about these cases? Changes lie in management practices that recognize the value of human capital. These practices are evident at the level of oil producers, with increased productivity as a result of human capital investments creating economic value. This finding was documented in SEKN's earlier book,[14] and later described by an Inter-American Development Bank (IADB) publication.[15]

APAEB, a nonprofit founded in 1980 by a group of hemp producers, is another agribusiness that, like Cativen, has modified its business model by eliminating intermediaries. This organization was created to command fairer prices for regional farmers by selling hemp fibers directly to textile companies. To this end, APAEB implemented joint storage and collective sales schemes. Once this first stage was consolidated, APAEB principals focused their efforts on downstream vertical integration by building a factory to manufacture tapestry and carpets with hemp fibers. By 2006, 60 percent of this plant's output was exported to the United States and Europe, securing profits for all participants.

The business model underlying the Wild Fruit Pickers' Cooperative, like APAEB's, encompasses activities along the entire agribusiness chain, from raw material production (i.e., in this case, collection) through trade operations. In these models, LIS are fully involved not only in field and factory operations but also in market-based activities, a feature that renders this model innovative. Small farmers have traditionally been excluded in agribusiness as indirect suppliers—linked in the chain by intermediaries—and, therefore, uninvolved in supply, manufacturing, and marketing operations. The deep engagement of small producers in APAEB's and Wild Pickers' business models has enabled their access to greater profits than ever before. The small farmers and pickers presented in both cases have not only improved their income and living conditions but have also developed new capabilities and skills. Improvements in their technical capabilities as a result of training and support have been noteworthy, as compared to other agribusinesses that engage small producers only peripherally as indirect suppliers or temporary substitutes.

One of the farmers benefited by APAEB recalled the difficulties he faced in the 1980s to exploit his 17-hectare (42-acre) property. "Back then, I couldn't make enough money to provide for my family . . . Before APAEB, there was no technical information available to endure droughts. There were no fruits; there was no fodder to feed the animals. We didn't even have a tank to store drinking water." With APAEB's help, this farmer managed to grow his estate; by breeding goats and growing hemp, as well as other products, he increased his income and introduced significant improvements in his farm.

He was able to build cement tanks to store water for irrigation and drinking water for family consumption. APAEB also helped him to access funding and trained him to enhance his planting and animal breeding techniques.

Another significant variable to be noted in APAEB's and Wild Fruit Pickers' business models is their organizational scheme. Using a cooperative scheme with committees to organize small farmers and pickers worked quite well in both cases, paving the way for the delivery of other key services, such as training, financial support, and technical capability development. The organizational scheme adopted by Wild Fruit Pickers is discussed later, in the section on barriers.

LIS and Competitive Advantage

In the previous section, we saw how LIS have been incorporated throughout agribusiness chains with innovating business models. We also discussed how business models differ, with some of them focusing on activities that reduce costs and others geared to increase customer value. These choices on how to compete are associated with generic cost leadership and differentiation strategies introduced by Michael Porter.[16] Competitive dynamics was not the research focus of the cases reported in this book; yet several of the nine cases studied provide information on competitive forces, proving that LIS incorporation has effectively contributed to the competitive advantage of these agribusiness firms.

Palí's competitive advantage has been built on its operating setup. It operates with few, high-turnover products; a small, multitasking workforce; simpler shelves, and relatively low energy and water consumption rates. LIS contribution to this competitive advantage is the most straightforward one, as this business model was originally designed to cater to this segment. This model does not work without LIS involvement. In Costa Rica and Nicaragua, Palí does not have any close competitors. Its swift growth, with profitable returns, tends to confirm Prahalad's thesis—LIS can be profitable customers.

Tierra Fértil's program was built in Costa Rica as a result of competitive pressures endured by Hortifruti, a supermarket chain also owned by the CSU-CCA's corporate holding, which sought to outdo its competitors by providing fresh produce of superior quality, freshness, assortment, hygiene, and safety. LIS incorporation was one key, as variety was only attainable through the acquisition of produce from regions with diverse weather conditions and scattered small farmers. However, variety in itself is not a source of competitive advantage—it may be obtained by purchases in the wholesale market. A true competitive advantage comes from the combination of attributes sought by customers. This combination is hard to imitate because it requires investments in training and forging long-term relationships with LIS.

CRES, like Tierra Fértil, introduced a new business model that favored the incorporation of a LIS producers' network. Butterfly exhibitors' demand for a larger diversity of species drove this agribusiness to recruit independent breeders from diverse micro-climates. Yet, as opposed to the settings where large retail chains like Palí, Cativen, and CSU operated, entry barriers in this business were lower, and new competitors imitated CRES's model. Now, CRES competes by providing customers with detailed information on the geographies and micro-climates where its cocoons originate. This requires a close, trust-based collaboration with suppliers who report these data.

Irupana, a pioneer in organic product manufacture and marketing that has been broadly recognized by organizations such as the World Economic Forum,[17] has pursued a high segmentation strategy to concentrate on a market niche. It offers organic food products to European and American customers. These products are elaborated with crops such as quinoa, amaranth, *cañawa*, soy, wheat, and a variety of fruits grown by indigenous farmers in the Andes, Amazonia, and Bolivia's Chaco regions. In a market dominated by large single-crop plantations for consumer markets, Irupana targets a niche of consumers who are willing to pay premium prices for organic products with positive social and environmental impact. The company elaborates over 80 products in five lines: grains, poultry products, whole-grain bakery, fruits, and coffee.

Irupana's large assortment of organic crops is made possible by means of an extensive LIS supplier network in eastern Bolivia's micro-climate areas, which are quite unsuitable for mechanized farming. Several governments tried to promote farming in these mountainous regions to no avail. This case presents a paradox: the lack or deficiency of natural or basic resources that prevents farming and acts as a deterrent for competition created an opportunity for Irupana and its organic food business. As in the cases of Tierra Fértil and Cativen, this uneven terrain turned into an advantage for the production of a variety of crops as a result of diverse weather conditions. Indigenous farmers' dispersion, added to their ancient, clean farming techniques, has become a source of competitive advantage for Irupana's market segment of choice—European and American consumers who are concerned about their health, environmental sustainability, and native culture preservation.

Irupana's social work has enabled the company to convey a positive international image that has appealed to cooperating agencies and superior partners, paving the way to new business opportunities. With support and funding from international cooperation agencies and a Bolivian CSO called PRORURAL, Irupana has built an initiative entitled "Suppliers' Program," a key instrument to enhance vendors' productive capability and therefore to increase the company's exports.

By connecting Bolivia's indigenous communities to markets demanding organic products, Irupana has effectively improved farmers' living conditions while preserving their cultural heritage and crops and, at the same time, avoiding negative environmental impacts. Thus it has transformed many Bolivian farmers, formerly dependent on government and development agencies' charity, into micro-entrepreneurs.

The above descriptions of competitive forces at play in some sample cases lead us to conclude that there is no one special way to compete in agribusinesses that incorporate LIS. Tierra Fértil and CRES sought to compete with products highly valued by their customers, whether in terms of quality, variety, or fulfillment reliability. Irupana focused its marketing efforts on a segment that was willing to pay premium prices for organic products. Palí chose to compete on low costs. All three ways to compete benefited LIS.

Barriers Faced By These Initiatives

LIS incorporation in agribusiness chains is not self-evident. All nine cases illustrate that it is often plagued by logistical, organizational, skills, and cultural barriers that hinder a successful execution of business models. Overcoming each barrier type calls for specific resources and capabilities.

Logistical barriers. These are mostly found in the field link and, to a lesser extent, in markets. Small farmers' geographical dispersion, which may prove beneficial to secure a vast variety of fruits and vegetables from diverse micro-climates, as in the case of Irupana's suppliers in Bolivia's plateau area, hinders their market integration because of difficulties to ship raw materials to their destinations. In several sample cases, geographic dispersion obstructed communications and access to information, likely raising transaction costs. Precarious road conditions and a lack of knowledge as to how intermediaries operated turned collection into an isolated, lonely task. In this setting, fruit marketers needed intermediaries to guarantee product stocking and delivery to processing plants.

Geographic dispersion is compounded by the absence of transportation, energy, water, and health infrastructure in the field link. The lack of access roads accounts for a significant barrier to the acquisition of raw materials. For Irupana, in a country with an overall area of 1.1 million square kilometers (425,000 square miles), the vendor nearest to company facilities was seven hours away by car due to poor local roads. Tierra Fértil's program faced a similar barrier in Nicaragua and Honduras. This barrier became more significant as products were perishable.

In addition to poor roads, Tierra Fértil's buyers also came upon another communication barrier with small Nicaraguan and Honduran farmers: lack of telephone service. Since small producers had no access to telephones, buyers could only call on farmers at their farms—a hard option due to poor rural road conditions. For an ongoing supply scheme as the one required by this program, fluent communications serve to arrange shipments, to negotiate prices, or to deal with quality or other issues.

Organizational barriers. The lack of organization and coordination among small producers hinders harvest sales, for it forces companies to negotiate with each farmer individually. Cativen faced this problem among both small farmers and traditional fishermen. Although Venezuela had already attempted to gather these small producers, these organizations were not very effective, and the company was forced to build producers' associations to facilitate technical assistance and price negotiation. In contrast, CRES, the butterfly marketer, maintained relationships with each supplier. The company founder had tried to bring vendors together but found little interest on their part. Individual relationships with suppliers were easy to manage for CRES, as Costa Rica is small and cocoon breeders were located near highways or roads with year-round access.

Skills barriers. Low educational and technical levels constitute a recurrent barrier in all sample cases, mainly in the field and factory links. LIS farmers have practically no education as a result of public education deficiencies in many Latin American rural areas. The need to start working at an early age and the lack of nearby schools and adequate learning materials curtails LIS education and opportunities to seek better paid jobs.

Cultural barriers. Unawareness of the differences between the corporate culture and that of low-income rural populations stands in the way of business relations between companies and LIS. This shows in the business sector's frequent indifference for LIS, coupled with both parties' inability to build mutually satisfying relationships. Overcoming this barrier may become even harder as a result of differing beliefs, values, ideas, or behavior patterns.[18]

The cultural distance between agribusiness managers and LIS is present throughout the value chain, but it becomes more evident when LIS act as suppliers. An agribusiness owner depicted this relationship as "two worlds coming together." The cases studied provide valuable information on how these dissimilar groups approach and get to know each other in the field. According to Verónica Salas, leader of the Cultural Action Network, "the dialog between pickers and local business leaders brought two mutually unknown worlds together. Businessmen started to regard pickers as individuals with a face and a story, and vice versa." Similarly, dwellers at the José Carlos Mariátegui community could relate to Ruperto Raygada, as he knew and shared both cultures. Thus, he acted as a link between these two worlds (Palmas del Espino Company and small farmers in the community).

Although the cultural distance between agribusiness managers and LIS is more obvious in the field, it applies to the entire agribusiness chain. At factories, LIS have trouble adjusting to company culture, conversion pace, and new tasks requiring special skills. Formal markets are unfamiliar with LIS segments' traditional purchasing practices.

Overcoming Barriers

Targeted investments. The Tierra Fértil case shows that despite unchangeable physical barriers or infrastructure deficiencies, logistics can be enhanced, and transaction costs may be reduced with modest investments in storage and technology centers.[19] Even though communication and transportation problems cannot be solved by organizing LIS producers, sample cases illustrate how organization facilitates transactions among geographically dispersed producers. This is an example of horizontal coordination mechanisms at work in agribusiness. For instance, Nestlé, the world's largest dairy product manufacturer, has developed a targeted investment strategy to overcome logistical barriers. This company builds "dairy districts" for milk collection and refrigeration centers for small dairy farmers' production, which is later shipped to processing plants.[20]

Organizational capabilities. The small farmers' organization facilitated contacts with retired Palmas del Espino workers, who provided technical advice. Irupana cooperated with a CSO to gather numerous, geographically dispersed families from Bolivia's plateau region to provide them with technical and financial support in order to strengthen their ability to supply organic products to the company.

In the case of Bío Bío Wild Fruit Pickers, monthly meetings were held to promote networking among collectors and, at the same time, provide technical training. As a result of these meetings, eight committees were built at small communities; these committees came together to establish a coordinating commission that negotiated directly with companies purchasing wild fruits from intermediaries. By organizing themselves, these pickers were able to sell their products to large buyers at fairs, farming trade shows, and fair-trade networks.

The development of new organizational capabilities for LIS seems to yield competitive advantage in several sample cases. The experiences of Tierra Fértil, Palmas del Espino, and Wild Fruit Pickers illustrate the development of genuine and profound ties with LIS, as well as the creation of unique networks that are hard to replicate.

Technical training. To overcome capability and qualification barriers, several agribusinesses that have incorporated LIS producers as suppliers have built support programs intended to improve farmers' technical readiness and education. Cativen's initiative with LIS farmers—for the most part poorly educated and technically unprepared—has included technical assistance, production process supervision, and harvest planning. Thus, Cativen has gone from "buyer to developer," as described by its corporate affairs manager. By turning into a developer, the company came to understand the reality of LIS and agriculture itself. To this end, Cativen forged several partnerships—one of them with Universidad Central de Venezuela's School of Agronomics, which helped design a technical support plan.

Outreach and dialog. Overcoming cultural distance starts with a dialog between producers and companies, sometimes aided by a CSO—as the Cultural Action Workshop (TAC) organization did in the case of wild fruit pickers. A study conducted by this organization revealed valuable information on female pickers. At Palmas del Espino, this facilitation role was performed by Mr. Raygada, who served as a liaison for both parties. For the Tierra Fértil program, cultural differences with potential vendors were overcome with the help of buyers, who needed both market and agricultural knowledge to advise and support LIS producers throughout their farming process. In a similar approach, Cativen hired new kinds of buyer who resembled farming advisors. These buyers had greater technical knowledge, a disposition to leave their desks to go out into the field, an ability to relate to small farmers and traditional fishermen, and a willingness to live in the hinterlands, near storage centers.

In some cases, cultural barriers were overcome by complying with traditional LIS purchase practices or by using surveys. At Palí, traditional markets and farming fairs have been a valuable source of information to gain a better understanding of customer tastes and preferences. At these fairs, approximately 90 percent of stalls sell fresh vegetables and fruits, and although Pali doesn't sell produce, the information it collects there is very valuable, as it helps the company to create new offerings, to adjust product packaging, and to learn more about its target segment in general. In addition, Palí complements this information with customer surveys, intended to provide a greater insight into LIS preferences as well as customer satisfaction with company offerings.

Greater contact and dialog among individuals helped to mitigate cultural differences. It is harder to tackle distrust issues, often compounded by different values associated with notions about time, manual work, interpersonal relationships, laws, and loyalty.[21] These cultural barriers may separate not only businessmen from LIS but also farmers from each other. At Bío Bío, wild fruit collection was viewed as a predominantly female task, and some men refused to do it, as it amounted to a public recognition of unemployment and lack of any other job opportunities. Male disdain for collection tasks was also attributed to the low income made by women in this activity, as intermediaries purchasing their fruits for sale to large distributors and exporters captured most of the profits. In this case, TAC managed to restore the dignity of collection work by associating it with age-old traditions of local native peoples. In order to legitimize fruit collection as a stable and sustainable labor source, TAC worked with pickers to expand their wild fruit portfolio, eliminating idle months. This enabled pickers to increase their income and enhance collective appreciation for their task.

Fair prices. The way to build trust and closeness with LIS farmers has required the establishment of fair pricing policies. CRES, for example, promoted a fair pricing policy among its suppliers and overseas customers, but, as a result of excess market supply, it was unable to stop international prices from falling. To offset this trend, the company changed its sales policy, offering customers 30 percent more pupae "at the same price," increasing purchase volumes and maintaining overall revenues for butterfly breeders. Additionally, CRES tried to differentiate its supply with an optimum mix in an effort to safeguard higher market prices. Irupana's business model also featured a fair pricing practice. The company paid vendors a 20 percent premium to reward product quality.

Integration of LIS and Social Change
The practices used to overcome barriers for LIS incorporation have often produced changes in the ecosystems where these agribusiness chains operate. These ecosystems tend to be complex, as shown in Figure 8.1. Many actors can advance or hinder full LIS incorporation to agribusiness chains. As mentioned in our description of agribusiness chains, LIS are often

geographically isolated, plagued by disadvantages in accessing services and markets. Thus, they are vulnerable to exclusion or exploitation.

Social change management skills are required to overcome these barriers. Let us consider the Tierra Fértil program. At the time of its inception, Costa Rica's fruit and vegetable industry ecosystem featured intermediaries, known as "coyotes," who bought and resold products in traditional markets or fairs. The company initially joined this agribusiness chain, purchasing products for supermarket distribution through these traditional channels. This ecosystem changed with the arrival of new actors—civil society organizations (CSOs)—that provided support, training, pricing information, and technical assistance to small LIS farmers. At the same time, Tierra Fértil reached out to producers, buying directly from them and eliminating two chain links—coyotes and wholesalers. In addition, farmers rely on CSOs for training, information and technical support services. Tierra Fértil approaches LIS directly to discuss quality expectations and prices.

A similar structural change came about at Irupana. The original ecosystem included only dispersed, isolated LIS farmers at risk of intermediaries' exploitation. The company depended on thousands of farming families with limited productive capabilities and low product quality. As in the case of Tierra Fértil, this organizational ecosystem changed with the arrival of the CSO called Prorural, which, in addition to training and technical support, offered financial and organizational assistance. The outcome was Irupana's direct involvement in organizing the producers and greater efficiency in overall process logistics.

The transformation of Costa Rica's butterfly ecosystem was even more dramatic. Before CRES initiated its business development, the breeding of butterfly pupae was non-existent. Current breeders used to work as farmers. When the new business started exporting pupae to American and European butterfly exhibitors, it brought a new opportunity for low-income rural populations. Currently, these segments enjoy a close relationship as suppliers, and benefits flow in both directions in this agribusiness chain. Furthermore, this ecosystem has become enriched with eco-tourism activities involving LIS.

In all these cases, changes occurred in the structure or relationships among actors in the ecosystems where LIS resided as a result of their engagement in agribusiness operations. The most outstanding were efforts to move LIS from geographical, economic, social, and cultural isolation to a position of inclusion and organization, as well as an effort to educate them and to turn them into active participants in agribusiness chains.

These cases also illustrate the key role played by supporting agents and coordination mechanisms—crucial elements in Goldberg and Austin's analytical framework presented earlier.[22] These support agents include CSOs that offer technical assistance, training, and funding in order to promote and facilitate LIS incorporation to ecosystems. These CSOs may act as coordinators to forge agreements and conventions and serve as honest brokers. Other coordination mechanisms in agribusiness chains are associations that promote horizontal coordination among producers and regulating organizations, which can legitimize contracts and futures markets. Environmental regulation has been a key factor in several projects involving LIS, such as Irupana. Costa Rica's government, through its Environmental Ministry, has tried to play a regulatory role to ensure that butterfly breeders' practices are compatible with environmental sustainability standards.

In ecosystems, support agents may also serve as *social inclusion* agents. InBio, a renowned research center in Costa Rica, is a service organization that promoted LIS incorporation as CRES suppliers by training former farmers in the breeding of butterfly pupae. CSOs often act as social inclusion drivers. Those that provide technical assistance or training constitute a special category of service organizations because of their motivations, which stretch beyond business relationships, and their close relationships with LIS. Quite a number of CSOs around Hortifruti and Irupana play a significant role in the new proximity between agribusinesses and LIS.

With significant barriers overcome among the many organizations studied, as in the case of the small producers associated with APAEB, not only has income increased, but the LIS has developed new skills and competencies. The APAEB model is substantially different from that of traditional agribusiness, which incorporates small family farmers into the business activity as peripheral suppliers only. In nearly every case mentioned in this chapter, the benefits obtained reach not only the small producers of the LIS, but their surrounding communities as well.

The examples we have seen of economic, social, and environmental sustainability are impressive in terms of their impact on the LIS. The varied forms of sustainability that were accomplished suggest that these agribusiness models do offer some innovative ideas in the fight against poverty and social exclusion in Latin America. These models have simultaneously driven business growth while reducing poverty and social exclusion, and in several instances, such as Irupana, made significant contributions to maintaining the environment and biodiversity of the regions in which they operate.

Lessons on Agribusiness Initiatives for Low-Income Citizens

Let us return to the questions posed at the beginning of the chapter. First, how can LIS be incorporated into agribusiness chains differently than in the past? The answer lies in the innovations we have found in business models. Some, like Palí's, are copied from successful models in other regions (Aldi, Germany); others, like Cativen's, introduce changes to traditional relationships among actors, and in some cases, like CRES, Tierra Fértil, APAEB, and Wild Fruit Pickers, new business models have been built.

Turning LIS from "indirect suppliers" into "direct vendors" (with no intermediaries) in agribusiness chains also surfaces as a new element in traditional agribusiness operations. This transformation is visible in several sample cases (e.g., Cativen, Pickers, Tierra Fértil), and, though subtle, it becomes very significant given the changes and innovations stemming from direct integration.

Second, how do these market-based initiatives enhance the potential to create economic and social value? As we have noted, several agribusiness experiences have succeeded on both dimensions. For one thing, they have developed business models that are consistent with the roles played by LIS in the value chains. Successful agribusinesses have developed their internal resources and leveraged external resources to build competitive advantage. External resources have commonly included natural resource endowments and capabilities drawn from partner organizations, like CSOs and government agencies.

Third, what barriers hinder LIS incorporation, and how can they be overcome? In this regard, our sample cases are educational. We conclude that multiple logistical, social, and cultural barriers obstruct LIS integration. Logistical barriers, despite being hard or impossible to change, may be mitigated with modest technological investments and by organizing producers to facilitate transportation and communications. Existing social service deficiencies, like public education, may be overcome with technical education programs. The cultural divide between business managers and LIS may be bridged by changing distorted perceptions. Distrust may dissipate with fair pricing policies. In some cases, several actions took place simultaneously: in the case of Chile's Wild Fruit Pickers, a legitimate mediator (TAC) was engaged; a fair pricing policy was set in place; pickers were organized in committees and trained, and logistical support was provided to connect them to agribusiness fruit buyers.

Five sets of conclusions may be drawn from the analysis of cases that incorporate LIS into agribusiness chains.

1. High Potential for Economic and Social Benefits
The incorporation of LIS into agribusinesses is important because these businesses operate in rural areas, where socio-economic statistics identify the largest pockets of poverty. In some of these geographically isolated areas, LIS incorporation in one way or another is inevitable. The characteristics of agribusiness raw materials—perishability, seasonality, and product variability—make close coordination among agribusiness chain links crucial. Thus, there is an opportunity to integrate LIS to agribusiness chains that can potentially benefit this sector and enhance business income.

2. Multiple Engagement Points
LIS may be brought in at any agribusiness chain link. Our sample cases illustrate innovations in LIS incorporation into business models. The greatest innovations were found in experiences engaging LIS as raw material suppliers. These innovations include some that contribute to the products' perceived value, and others that increase business productivity and efficiency.

3. Obstacles as Opportunities
Geographical dispersion and conditions often unsuitable for farming may be obstacles to efficient chain coordination, but at the same time may offer opportunities to incorporate small LIS producers. Mountainous landscapes that seem unfavorable for farming and small farmers' dispersion enable businesses to procure a great variety of products from diverse micro-climates, as illustrated by Irupana, Tierra Fértil, CRES, and Cativen.

4. Changes in Key Ecosystems
LIS integration comes, in all cases, with changes in organizational ecosystems or in relationships among actors. If these changes—ranging from the involvement of a CSO to the elimination of supply chain links—do not take place, expected outcomes will be unlikely. A significant outcome derived from LIS incorporation to agribusinesses is precisely an ecosystem shift towards greater balance and closeness, as well as a new opportunity to capture shared value. In addition, relationships built on this basis are hard to replicate by competitors.

5. LIS as a Source of Competitive and Social Advantage
LIS incorporation to agribusiness chains may contribute to building competitive advantages. This is both the most meaningful and boldest conclusion drawn from our study—and it does not apply to all cases. The evidence

is strongest in Palí's case, with its cost leadership strategy based on LIS as customers, and Tierra Fértil, whose small producers' supply program has provided a competitive advantage based on product range expansion, ongoing supply, and substantial quality and safety improvements. Tierra Fértil's contribution to business value creation has driven the company to replicate this program throughout Central America. There is also convincing evidence that LIS incorporation as vendors has been critical to Irupana's successful segmentation strategy.

Figure 8.1
Participants in an Agribusiness Ecosystem

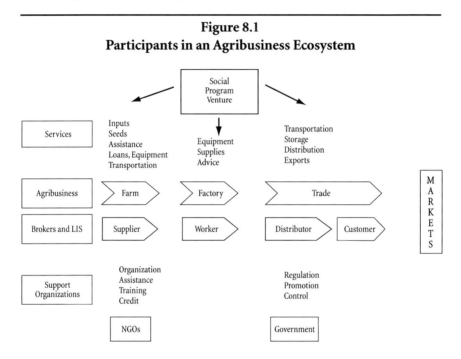

Notes

1. This literature is summarized in John W. Mellor, "Faster, More Equitable Growth—The Relation Between Growth in Agriculture and Poverty Reduction Agricultural Policy." Development Project Research Report 4, Abt Associates Inc. Cambridge, MA: October 1999.
2. "The End of Cheap Food," *The Economist*, December 8, 2007.
3. James E. Austin, *Agroindustrial Project Analysis: Critical Design Factors*, 2nd ed. (Baltimore, MD: Johns Hopkins University Press, 1992).
4. The cases that have served as a basis for this chapter are: Tierra Fértil (Central America), CRES (Costa Rica), Cativen (Venezuela), Palmas del Espino (Peru), Agropalma (Brazil), APAEB (Brazil), Recolectores de Frutos Silvestres (Chile), Irupana (Bolivia), Palí (Costa Rica and Nicaragua). We have also included the case of Pantaleón (Guatemala), studied by the SEKN network in a previous cycle, to illustrate the role of LIS as employees.
5. Ray Allan Goldberg, *Agribusiness Coordination; A Systems Approach to the Wheat, Soybean, and Florida Orange Economies* (Boston, MA: Division of Research, Graduate School of Business Administration, Harvard University, 1968).
6. James E. Austin, *Agroindustrial Project Analysis: Critical Design Factors*, 2nd ed. (Baltimore, MD: Johns Hopkins University Press, 1992), 19.
7. These operational links appear in ibid, in its earlier edition (1981), pages 14–20.
8. Michael E. Porter, *Competitive Strategy: Techniques for Analyzing Industries and Competitors* (New York, NY: Free Press, 1980), chapter 1.
9. Michael Porter, *Competitive Advantage: Creating and Sustaining Superior Performance* (New York, NY: Free Press, 1985), chapter 2.
10. C. K. Prahalad and Allen Hammond, "Serving the World's Poor, Profitably," *Harvard Business Review* (2002): 5.
11. Interviews conducted at Palí by Professor Francisco Leguizamón and Researcher Juliano Flores, March 2007.
12. For a description of this model, see Dieter Brandes, *Bare Essentials: The Aldi Way to Retail Success* (Frankfurt: Cyan-Campus, 2004).
13. Aquileo Sánchez, Wal-Mart Central America's Corporate Affairs Manager, interview conducted on March 27, 2007 by Francisco Leguizamón y Juliano Flores, both of INCAE.
14. SEKN, ed. *Effective Management of Social Enterprises: Lessons from Businesses and Civil Society Organizations in Iberoamerica* (Cambridge, MA: Harvard University Press with David Rockefeller Center for Latin American Studies, 2006).
15. Francisco Leguizamón and Julio Guzmán. "Caso Ingenios Pantaleón. El argumento empresarial de la responsabilidad social," INCAE / IADB. 2007. Pantaleón, Central America's leading sugar producer, has benefited from an aggressive human development policy and invests heavily in labor benefits. For

every payroll dollar, Pantaleón pays an additional US$0.72 that includes legal counsel, food, medical services, education, and other services.

16. Michael E. Porter, *Competitive Strategy: Techniques for Analyzing Industries and Competitors* (New York: Free Press, 1980), chapter 2.

17. The company CEO was chosen the 2002 Social Entrepreneur, invited to join the Schwab Foundation and the World Economic Forum for two consecutive years.

18. For a discussion on cultural analysis, see Vijay Sathe, "¿Qué es cultura?" 13292 INCAE. 1981.

19. Tierra Fértil provided cellphones to low-income producers.

20. Ray A. Goldberg and Kerry Herman, "Nestle's Milk District Model: Economic Development for a Value-Added Food Chain and Improved Nutrition," in *Business Solutions for the Global Poor: Creating Social and Economic Value*, ed. Kasturi Rangan, et al. (San Francisco, CA: Jossey-Bass, 2007).

21. Vijay Sathe. "¿Qué es cultura?" 13292 INCAE. 1981.

22. James E. Austin, *Agroindustrial Project Analysis: Critical Design Factors*, 2nd ed. (Baltimore, MD: Johns Hopkins University Press, 1992), 15.

9

Market-Based Initiatives for Low-Income Sectors and Economic Value Creation

*Josefina Bruni Celli and Rosa Amelia González**

C. K. Prahalad[1] urges companies to serve poor consumers' markets, arguing that they hold an untapped purchasing power with great wealth potential. However, for other observers, the notion that there is fortune at the base of the pyramid is at best a "harmless illusion," and at worst, a "dangerous delusion."[2] The fact is that empirical research on the profitability of market-based initiatives involving low-income sectors (LIS) remains scarce, except in the field of microfinance.[3]

This chapter intends to contribute to the debate, offering the empirical evidence drawn from 33 cases to answer the following questions: to what extent do market-based initiatives with LIS create economic value for sample organizations? Which experiences feature greater accomplishments or difficulties? What can we learn from these experiences about the scope and boundaries of market-based initiatives targeted to the poor to create economic value?

Our sample includes organizations of several types—companies, civil society organizations (CSOs), and cooperatives. They belong to various economic sectors and incorporate LIS as customers, suppliers or entrepreneurs. Indeed, the answers to our questions vary as a result of changes in these variables.

Since we are discussing several organization types, some focusing on profit creation and others driving social change, how can we analyze economic value? Clearly, private companies rely on a very specific definition—to them, economic value means profitability. For these organizations, a market-based initiative must provide enough revenues to pay for all production and opportunity costs (the value of the best option available for investors). In turn, social enterprises (cooperatives and CSOs) create economic value when revenue streams from market-based initiatives contribute to ensure their sustainability. Whether we are talking about private companies, cooperatives, or

CSOs, *it is safe to say that economic value creation occurs when revenue streams from market-based initiatives contribute to accomplishing financial sustainability.* This materializes in the manner described in Table 9.l.

<hr/>

Table 9.1
Definition of Economic Value Creation According to Organizational Form

Business companies	Profitability: returns on investments made by shareholders exceed opportunity costs.
CSOs	Initiatives' net income is positive and reduces organizations' dependence on donations.
Cooperatives	Operation surpluses minus compensations to associates are enough to prevent the impairment of revolving funds and productive assets.*

*In cooperative, "operation surpluses" are equivalent to net income in business companies, while "revolving funds" are equivalent to business companies' working capital.

<hr/>

In the case of companies, if organizations were not profitable, shareholders would withdraw their capital to invest it elsewhere (based on opportunity costs). Profitability is not, however, relevant to cooperatives' and CSOs' financial sustainability because, in these cases, there are no investors seeking returns.

In this chapter we begin by discussing economic value notions, as well as some challenges faced in measurement processes. The next sections show the results for each organization type, including economic value creation assessments and consideration of key factors involved in the economic performance of market-based initiatives in our study. Finally, major study findings are summarized.

Measuring Economic Value

Even after clearly establishing the meaning of economic value creation concepts and their components for the three types of organizations under study, it was truly challenging to measure the creation of economic value with empirical accuracy. Next, we discuss some of the obstacles found in the operationalization process, and how researchers dealt with them.

Two types of business companies were studied for their relationships with LIS. One is companies that started working with LIS since inception, and thus their customers or suppliers are exclusively LIS. The other type is companies whose customers or suppliers have traditionally been other sectors;

these companies have started to incorporate LIS in their exchanges in recent years.[4] In each group, the analysis units—i.e., market-based initiatives studied—are different. In the first group, companies themselves are market-based initiatives, and therefore economic value is determined by calculating companies' profitability as a whole. In the second group, market-based initiatives are specific investment projects executed to incorporate LIS as customers or suppliers; thus, their economic value is determined by calculating these projects' profitability. From now on, we will use the term "company=initiative" to refer to market-based initiatives in the first group, and the term "project=initiative" to refer to those in the second group.

For companies=initiatives we chose returns on assets (ROA)[5] and equity (ROE)[6] as profitability measurements. Calculations for economic value measurements (ROA and ROE) were possible in only half of these cases, as the other companies did not show their balance sheets.

For projects=initiatives, selected profitability measurements included internal rate of return (IRR) and net present value (NPV). These calculations require information on invested sums and cash flows throughout projects' lifecycles. In addition, to calculate NPV, it is necessary to know the opportunity cost of capital for investors, and none of these companies revealed any data on opportunity costs. Indeed, we found that most companies do not systematically record their investments when building relationships with LIS. At best, we just managed to determine whether project revenues exceeded costs. In other cases, we simply collected data such as project contribution to company profitability, investment payback period, cost reductions or savings for companies, and revenue increases. This rather unsystematic accounting approach to investments may be attributed to the lack of project accounting systems, initiatives' relatively small size, or the fact that these ventures are closer to the field of corporate social responsibility.

To analyze cooperatives' economic value creation, we used organizations themselves as analysis units, as, in these cases, organizations and market-based initiatives are one and the same. We have stated that in order to measure economic value creation in these organizations, we would evaluate whether an operation's economic results prevent revolving fund and productive asset impairment. This evaluation factored in organizations' ability to operate without subsidies. An organization's capacity to maintain or improve productive assets is reflected in its net income added to the depreciation reported on its income statements. An organization's capacity to maintain its revolving fund is seen in its cash and cash equivalents added to its accounts receivable, minus its accounts payable, plus its inventory reported on its Balance Sheet. In practice, no cooperative provided any financial statements that complied with generally accepted accounting principles; thus, at best, this study could only approximate gross earning figures. Gross profit is calculated by subtracting sales from the cost of goods sold. Most sample cooperatives reported sales, labor, and raw material costs, but only a few had any information on other components of their cost of goods sold, such as depreciation, inventory turnover, utility costs, and infrastructure use directly associated with productive operations. Even more erratic was their information on administrative expenses—so much so that net income calculations for these organizations are quite unreliable. This gap points to limited management capabilities at some of these organizations.

For CSOs, "organizations" were used as analysis units when they were equivalent to initiatives, and "projects" were used when initiatives had been taken up later by CSOs. The measurements recorded were initiatives' net income and net income minus subsidies, to zero in on the initiatives' actual contribution to organizational sustainability. The four organizations=initiatives studied provided enough financial information to calculate and analyze these measurements. For reasons similar to those found in companies, in projects=initiatives, financial information turned out to be insufficient.

A functional rather than legal criterion was used to classify sample organizations in company, cooperative, or CSO categories. Thus, for example, Comunanza was characterized as a company; though it had been legally incorporated as a foundation, its founders intend to turn it into a business company as soon as its operations reach the scale required to cover regulatory compliance costs. Similarly, all productive organizations engaging LIS as both workers and partners were classified as cooperatives, even if they had another legal status—such as APAEB (Brazil), CIAP (Peru) and Wild Fruit Pickers (Chile).

Economic Value Creation in Business Initiatives with LIS Consumers

This section analyzes the economic value created by all 13 sample business initiatives with LIS consumers, taking into account whether they are companies=initiatives or projects=initiatives and what are their business drivers. Figure 9.1 classifies initiatives according to these dimensions and groups them on the basis of detected patterns.

All companies=initiatives (group 1) focus on economic value creation through volume markets, and they are or plan to be profitable soon, even though most of them are very new (founded in 2005). Cruzsalud and Comunanza have been posting earnings from their first operating year—

Figure 9.1
Economic Value Creation in Business Initiatives with LIS Consumers

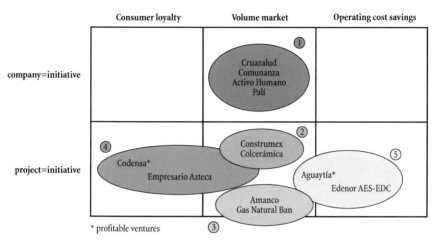

quite an accomplishment for any business. Additionally, there is sound evidence to indicate that Comunanza has been profitable (higher ROE than opportunity cost) from its first year of operation. Activo Humano does not yield earnings yet, but the interest shown by multinational Working Links to invest in this business points to its great potential to create shareholder value.[7] Finally, Palí,[8] the oldest company in our sample, shows signs of prosperity since its first operating year, as well as strong consolidation in Costa Rica, where it boasts a 45 percent of the market share. Each new Palí store's IRR is estimated at 15 percent, while payback takes a year in Costa Rica and one to two years in Nicaragua.

It is not as clear that the nine projects=initiatives in this sample are creating economic value. Only two of them are clearly profitable at present. The others are unprofitable, or their margin contribution to overall company profitability has not been clearly quantified.

The only two projects=initiatives that are clearly profitable (Codensa and Aguaytía, both marked with asterisks in Figure 9.1) share a common feature: they both maximize the use of an existing resource, thus exploiting prior investments—this surely helps them when it comes to calculating their profitability. On the one hand, Codensa, Colombia's electricity distribution company, built a credit system to sell home appliances to LIS at very low cost, using its electricity service invoice and collection platform. On the other, the LPG sold by Aguaytía to LIS is a byproduct of the company's core business (dry gas) that cannot be marketed in urban areas at competitive prices because of high transportation costs from jungle-based oilfields.

Other initiatives in our sample, such as Colcerámica and Construmex (group 2), expect to be profitable in the coming years. However, it should be noted that sample projects-initiatives are rather new (all launched between 2001 and 2004), and need time to mature. A business model develops slowly, with learning based on trial and error, especially when there is no previous experience with LIS markets. For instance, Colcerámica had a lot to learn. When its project was initiated, management thought that it would post profits after a year. Later, it became clear that an effective distribution model for LIS was not simple, and the company had to take some time to redesign its scheme. It may be safe to say that nearly all sample companies underwent a similar process.

Amanco and Gas Natural Ban (group 3) have had a slow start because they do not create economic value for their respective companies unless initial investments are funded by third parties. These include LIS customers themselves, who contribute labor, plus governments and multilateral agencies that provide non-refundable contributions, or soft loans offered by state agencies to LIS. Mostly, this need for funding happens when the service supply requires the installation of a costly physical distribution infrastructure, like irrigation and natural gas networks. For example, from 2001 to 2006, Amanco had not managed to launch its first irrigation project because of the large number of actors (third parties and customers) that needed to be mobilized and engaged to participate in infrastructure financing. In such circumstances, companies need time and negotiation skills to successfully engage all actors. In turn, Gas Natural Ban has found that multiple actor engagement models are not entirely replicable and must be reformulated every time a new project is launched, demanding plenty of time to mobilize and negotiate with actors involved. In its first natural gas network expansion project (at Cuartel V, in Buenos Aires), multiple actors (multilateral banks, neighbors, state banks, the company and its social partner) set up a fiduciary trust called Solidarity Networks. The idea was to replicate this engagement scheme in subsequent projects, but location specificities led to completely different developments in each case. For instance, for Gas Natural Ban's second project (at La Juanita), no fiduciary fund was built, and the parties engaged were the company, a grass-roots organization (Comunidad Organizada), and a construction company. For the third project (at Los Tábanos), the local administration made a significant financial contribution, and the project was carried out by the company and the local government.

Some projects=initiatives may seem unprofitable, or, if very small, their monetary contribution to company profitability may be low. However, if their benefits—in terms of loyalty or savings—were adequately incorporated to companies' overall profitability, they would be viewed differently (see groups 4 and 5). For example, Codensa's[9] initial driver for its initiative (loans for home appliance purchases) was to prevent customers from switching electricity suppliers when the market was deregulated. If this initiative indeed managed to accomplish its goal, ensuring customer loyalty, then its economic value calculation should include the project's earnings (registered) and the value of retained customers (not registered). A similar calculation applies to projects=initiatives whose primary goal is to provide cost savings for companies. Such is the case of electricity distribution companies (Edenor and AES-EDC): their projects' profitability is probably higher than reported. For instance, Edenor's financial statements include its initiative's operating profits, as well as the company's technical loss savings (disconnection and reconnection costs), but some additional benefits have not been included, such as non-technical loss savings (energy theft) and the cost of potential accidents resulting from illegal connections.

To sum up, a profitability difference exists between companies=initiatives and projects=initiatives. Companies=initiatives display quick profitability, while most projects=initiatives are still in their experimental phase, with a very small scale. A significant reason underlies this difference. For companies=initiatives, survival hinges on profitability—if they were not profitable, they would not exist. In projects-initiatives, by contrast, income does not substantially affect the overall financial performance of their promoting companies. This difference may also be attributed to the fact that startups originate in innovations that intend to exploit market opportunities, whereas large companies that launch projects with LIS are more resistant to innovation and change.

Economic Value Creation in Business Initiatives with LIS Suppliers

Here, as in the preceding section, economic value creation patterns for business initiatives with LIS suppliers were classified according to business drivers and account for the difference between companies=initiatives and projects=initiatives (see Figure 9.2 below).

The search for price premiums is the business driver for both companies=initiatives studied—Irupana and Mariposas de Costa Rica or CRES (group 1). These companies are exporters, and both try to secure price premiums in international markets for their exotic products: quinoa and other organic foods from the Andes' plateau (Irupana), and tropical butterflies (Mariposas de Costa Rica). These companies are not far from financial distress, however. Irupana was not profitable as of this writing (with negative

Figure 9.2
Economic Value Creation in Business Initiatives with LIS Suppliers

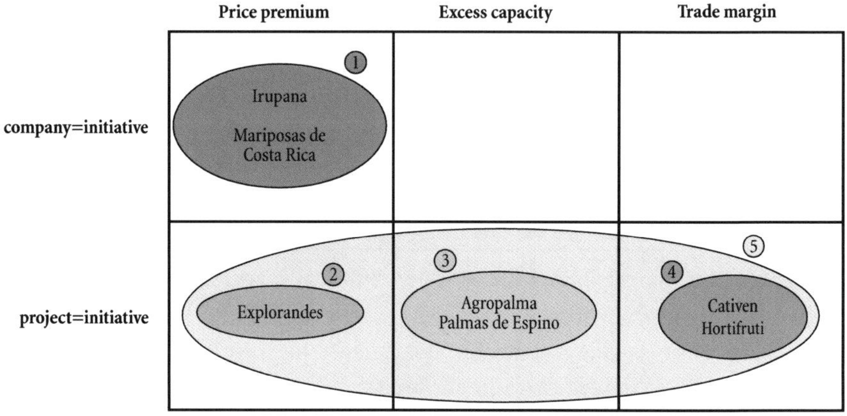

	Price premium	Excess capacity	Trade margin
company=initiative	① Irupana / Mariposas de Costa Rica		
project=initiative	② Explorandes	③ Agropalma Palmas de Espino	④ Cativen Hortifruti ⑤

ROA and ROE), although it planned to reach profitability in the short term. Company management reported that it ceased to be locally competitive as a result of its formal status, as Bolivia's traditional food market (including quinoa) is informal and, as such, pays no taxes. Its only opportunity to thrive is with exports, but securing them required volume and penetrating international markets has taken time and required significant new investments. For example, the company borrowed US$550,000 from private banks in 2006 to build the necessary warehousing to serve international markets. Mariposas de Costa Rica (CRES) does post profits, but its profitability dropped steadily in 2001 to 2005. This company faces, on the one hand, a small buyers' market with inelastic prices, and, on the other, LIS suppliers who tend to overproduce because this is a business with low entry barriers, replicated by many other small farmers who produce a lesser quality product but are willing to accept lower prices. Despite the company's efforts to control Costa Rica's butterfly overproduction, its ability to command premium prices for its exotic product has been undermined.

Among the projects=initiatives, one also featured price premiums as its key business driver—Explorandes' Titikayak project (number 2 in Figure 9.2). This initiative too offers an exotic product: adventure tourism involving indigenous communities. In contrast to the two cases mentioned above, this project is soundly profitable. On account of its small size, it could be assumed that this project is not very relevant for Explorandes' overall profitability; yet it is likely to create more value than its size could indicate, as it has enabled the company to position itself as an environmentally sustainable tourism provider—and because its kayak rides managed by natives count as a differentiating offering.

Agropalma's and Palmas del Espino's projects=initiatives are driven by their desire to exploit their excess capacity (group 3) when international markets are paying high prices for their products. These organizations' palm-oil producing plants boast a processing capacity that exceeds their ability to produce raw materials at their own lands, so both companies need to buy raw materials from independent producers. They have decided to engage LIS partly because of their proximity to these vendors, which results in significant transportation cost savings. However, this decision also intends to take advantage of national and local administrations' interest to consolidate a rural presence in those remote areas, which translates into financial and institutional support to companies' efforts to populate and develop these areas. As a result of these aggregated factors, both initiatives are viewed as sound business ventures by their promoters. Another neglected benefit is good relations between these companies and local neighbors—hardly a trivial benefit that goes well beyond public relations efforts. Palmas del Espino used to face a rather hostile environment, with squatting incursions in some of its properties. By engaging members from neighboring communities, the company has effectively turned aloof—even antagonistic—observers into partners who share its interest in venture success.

Cativen and CSU-CCA, Hortifruti's parent holding company (group 4), both own supermarket chains selling fresh fruits and vegetables. By streamlining their agricultural development operations and purchasing directly from small LIS farmers, these business groups benefit in several ways. First, they capture a 20 percent margin that used to go to intermediaries. With this additional margin, they can earn more, pay better prices to LIS suppliers, and even sell at lower prices to their own LIS customers—as illustrated by the relationship between Hortifruti and Palí. Second, with intermediaries, fresh produce waste at supermarkets is 25 to 30 percent higher than waste rates registered when these chains engage suppliers in planned harvest schedules. Finally, as a side effect, when direct relationships are forged with LIS vendors, business group managers believe they secure products of superior quality and appearance that leverage profitability at points of sale (supermarkets). Although both Cativen's and CSU-CCA's managements assured us that these ventures are profitable, they have also reported that it takes time and effort to make them work—among other reasons, because farmers need to be organized in order to reduce transaction costs in product purchases, so it takes time to train them and incorporate them into a harvest planning scheme (from which they stray rather easily).

In experiences with LIS suppliers, companies=initiatives are not or do not plan to be as soundly profitable as projects=initiatives. The latter are carried out by large companies, with significant control over products' value chains (transformation and marketing). Conversely, companies=initiatives are small ventures lacking such control—and, therefore, more vulnerable to markets. This study found another difference that separates companies=initiatives from projects=initiatives in this group. The former create economic value through a single mechanism: in sample cases, price premiums. In all projects=initiatives, however, companies create economic value not only through mechanisms such as price premiums, excess capacity, and profit margin, but also by securing a stronger position before their stakeholders (group 5). For instance, with its project, Explorandes comes across as a socially responsible company that respects both nature and indigenous cultures. Palmas del Espino and Agropalma are viewed as community development agents by local administrations and populations. Finally, Hortifruti and Cativen have not only become socially responsible corporate citizens but have also managed to market fresher, superior quality produce.

Key Factors to Assure Economic Value in LIS Business Initiatives

Economic value creation is challenging in any business—even more so in the inclusive type of venture, because learning to work with LIS takes time. In fact, impatience is a major threat to success, for it can lead promoters to abandon initiatives before potential economic benefits have had time to materialize. Construmex's example shows that getting to know LIS customers takes time. At first, the company wanted to serve the entire U.S. market of Mexican émigrés who send money to their home country by offering them a chance to buy construction materials and having them delivered at any location in Mexico. However, the company soon realized that not only its target market was smaller but it was actually restricted to a much smaller population—Mexico-born men with relatives in the United States, a formal place of residence, and some saving capacity—what it came to call the "*paisano* dream" segment. The company also understood that its initial market strategy, based on money transfers, alienated its customers' relatives in Mexico, who viewed Construmex as competing for incoming funds. Cemex, the parent company, was forced to change its strategy, clarifying that construction material purchases would be paid with "*paisanos*'" savings rather than money transfers to Mexico. If the company had not been patient and had not persevered to adjust its business models based on this realization, it would not have been able to draw any benefits from this initiative.

Colcerámica did not know LIS customers either. Aware of its ignorance, it sought the support of a social intermediary, hoping to find a quick solution—as illustrated by its initial profitability forecasts. However, when it started working with LIS communities, the company realized that market penetration would not come easy. It had to overcome prospects' distrust of strangers coming into their homes to sell them ceramic tiles that had to be paid for in advance. It took some time for the company to understand that pre-paid sales were not feasible and to develop a mechanism for credit sales. Once materials were sold, deliveries were difficult to accomplish, as orders were small and it was hard to access customers' homes. Finally, these problems were solved by making consolidated deliveries to community organizations' sites. The company did not anticipate these issues beforehand, and the entire venture execution process took much longer than expected.

Identifying how to organize internally to serve LIS markets also takes time and is subject to experimentation. At Colcerámica and Construmex, projects for LIS market development changed their location inside the companies several times before the right spot was found. Colcerámica started with a marketing pilot project that later became a formal marketing and sales program and was finally adopted as a new distribution channel by the Sales Department. In turn, Construmex was first assigned to the Self-Regulating Market Development Department, which reported to the Marketing Vice President, but, in 2006, as it was not receiving the required attention, it was moved to the Service and Social Projects' Department, reporting to the Institutional Relations and Communications Area created in 2005.

By analyzing these experiences, several key economic value creation drivers were identified in market-based initiatives with LIS. If these factors are adequately managed during both design and execution stages, the learning processes will be shortened, and returns on investment will increase.

Table 9.2
Key Factors to Assure Economic Value in LIS Business Initiatives

LIS as Consumers

LIS as consumers	LIS as suppliers
• Transaction costs	• Transaction costs
• Information asymmetries	• Technical and market know-how
• LIS expense structure instability	• Risk of impaired relationship with LIS
• Infrastructure investments (for utility service supply)	• Investments to develop new suppliers

Transaction Costs

Most companies selling goods or services to LIS use fragmented payment systems that reflect these buyers' low purchasing capacity. The large number of small exchanges multiplies costs associated with each customer. Companies must find ways to reduce these costs, as they cannot be transferred to consumers via price increases or taken from profit margins that are tight to begin with.

Technological innovations, such as meters and vending machines for pre-paid cards used to purchase electricity, provide a means to reduce transaction costs. Edenor deploys these vending machines at easy-access locations for LIS. A single machine can process a large number of purchases and automatically and electronically communicate service activation commands when customers introduce their purchase code. Although these technologies reduce the costs associated with each transaction, initial investments are significant. For instance, the special meter used—and paid for—by Edenor is six times as expensive as regular meters (approximately US$94 in Argentina, as compared to conventional meters that cost around US$15 to US$17). In addition, customer acquisition costs are substantially higher (approximately US$140 per customer) on account of their customization. Finally, pre-paid customers' consumption is lower, which also increases administration costs. While regular customers' administration costs account for 1 percent of their average consumption, pre-paid customers' administration costs range from 5 to 7 percent. This higher cost is offset only with a large customer base. For instance, if vending machines are located in areas with low population density, this arrangement does not add economic value to the company.

Institutional innovations provide another path to reduce transaction costs. A live medical consultation involves a certain fixed cost. In order to reduce costs and on the assumption that many simple consultations may be carried out over the telephone, Cruzsalud's managers incorporated a call-center feature, widely used in other businesses, to its service portfolio. This innovation, known as "24-hour overall telephone assistance center 0-800-Cruzsalud," reduced fixed costs associated with each transaction, guaranteeing a reasonable profit margin without compromising primary patient care quality.

Finally, AES-EDC's experience shows that community engagement and good relations with influential community leaders help reduce transaction costs. In hard-to-access, low-income areas, LIS service regularization can become profitable by using collective meters. This innovation reduces costs associated with meter amortization as well as readers' salaries, transportation, and security expenses. However, this case also proves that successful collective meter application also depends on the active involvement of a community leader with broad recognition and legitimacy who can engage meter subscribers and help them come to agreements on individual consumption and payment responsibilities.

Information Asymmetries
To sell goods and services to LIS, it is often necessary to extend loans, which leads to information asymmetry issues, as it is not easy for companies to accurately establish these customers' credit risk profile. The poor can only pay in small amounts, and this often calls for fragmented payment schemes. To this end, pre-paid or post-paid mechanisms can be used. Advanced payment systems, successfully employed by utility companies such as telephone and electricity service suppliers, involve no bankruptcy risks for companies, as goods or service delivery only takes place once payments have been made. Yet pre-paid systems are not always feasible: sample experiences prove that all attempts made to implant pre-paid mechanisms for durable goods failed. Thus companies have had to resort to credit schemes.

A lesson learned by sample company management teams is that LIS customers can only be attracted if credit approval requirements are reduced, as low-income individuals tend to belong to informal, no-banking sectors that render them unable to comply with traditional requisites. Yet companies do not know these customers' willingness and ability to pay, circumstances which increase insolvency risks and compromise profitability. So, how can this dilemma be solved?

Colcerámica used unconventional mechanisms to get to its customers. This company discovered that the best way to approach solvent customers was to employ female community members as sales promoters. As neighbors, promoters knew what to expect of many prospective customers— or, at least, knew how to come by useful information in that regard. Banco Azteca uses another unconventional—yet more formalized—mechanism to get to know its customers. It retains the services of a company called Círculo de Crédito (Credit Circle) that specializes in scoring LIS in Mexico. Both Banco Azteca and Círculo de Crédito belong to Grupo Salinas, a credit bureau. All group companies share the information collected by this outfit, building economies of scale that render this service economically feasible.

When Codensa joined the credit sale market, it initially outsourced credit risk evaluations to a company that used regular industry practices. Results were disappointing, and sales remained stagnant. Then the company decided to build an ad-hoc system employing statistical techniques (discriminant analysis) and company-based LIS market knowledge. With this system in place, Codensa's customer portfolio has grown at an average 170 percent annual rate. The company approves, in 48 hours, 85 percent of the applications submitted, and delinquency remains below 2 percent.

Activo Humano, a Chilean employment agency specializing in LIS job opportunities, faces an additional problem that closely resembles credit risk. The point is that not enough information exists on job applicants' credentials and background for employers to risk hiring them. This company has minimized this risk—and thus secured an excellent market position as headhunter—by engaging community leaders who vouch for candidates' good reputation.

LIS Expense Structure Instability
As LIS' available income is so limited, it is hard for them to make budget allocations for some recurring expenses, except for food. An occasional expense, like school supplies or a cooking pan, can deplete a substantial share of available income and curtail resources. For instance, every time Cruzsalud customers have to pay their membership fee, they have to choose between a contingent, abstract good—treatment for an occasional ailment—and more urgent expenses. Thus the company faces constant customer attrition. To deal with this problem, Cruzsalud has employed home collectors, who perform a twofold role: reminding customers and facilitating payments. Likewise, payback for loans granted to micro-entrepreneurs is also threatened by LIS expense structure instability. To offset this risk, Comunanza has enriched its credit products with funeral insurance policies—highly valued by LIS customers, as they prevent contingencies that might crush family and micro-venture budgets.

Infrastructure Investments
It is understood that utility service supply (e.g., natural gas or irrigation) to LIS often requires large infrastructure investments that companies cannot recover, given LIS customers' low payment capacity or "disposition to pay," as they view utilities as rights. Hence, in order to guarantee economic value creation, it becomes imperative to engage other actors, such as multilateral or government agencies and communities themselves, to contribute resources to infrastructure construction works. Sample evidence indicates that in these situations, LIS community-organized engagement plays a key legitimating role in fundraising processes.

LIS as Suppliers

Transaction Costs

LIS acting as direct business suppliers in value chains are small producers. For purchasing companies, this means multiple exchanges with numerous small vendors in order to secure an adequate quantity of supplies.

For agribusiness companies like Cativen, Hortifruti, Agropalma, and Palmas del Espino, engaging producers in cooperatives or associations has served as a key mechanism to reduce transaction costs associated with direct purchases to LIS. However, the job of organizing producers is a true challenge for companies, as this task is not usually included in usual management repertoires. Thus, in startup stages, sample companies often had to rely on experienced individuals who enjoy dealing with farmers, such as agronomists with a track record on farming advisory services.

Companies may also exploit prior community links to reduce transaction costs. For instance, Explorandes, a tourism company, identified existing social ties and forged a direct relationship with a local leader who was widely respected in the area where the company wished to operate. To motivate this leader, Explorandes had to earn his trust and persuade him of the project's benefits for his community. The company's horizontal relationship with this leader, as well as its sincere respect for the local culture and social fabric, also played a significant role in this initiative's feasibility.

Technical and Market Know-How

Incorporating LIS as direct suppliers only makes business sense if they add value to products and make them more attractive for consumers. Therefore a critical success factor for companies lies in their knowledge of their consumers and their ability to convey customers' technical requirements to LIS, as they monitor suppliers' compliance. For instance, Mariposas de Costa Rica (CRES) knows the preferences of a very specialized consumer niche—people who want to watch exotic butterflies emerge from their pupae. The company's owner and manager relies on his technical knowledge of butterfly breeding to train small producers to meet target market demands—pupae about to turn into butterflies.

Cativen's and Hortifruti's cases show that technical and market knowhow not only enhances company positioning but also ensures optimal benefits across value chains. In addition to capturing margins previously obtained by intermediaries, by working directly with LIS these companies have managed to secure a more diverse vegetable assortment of superior quality. They can now plan farming operations with producers, offering technical assistance and incorporating product washing and packing services. This translates into additional savings in waste reduction and lower costs associated with product preparation for shelf display.

In contrast, Irupana has found it hard to export traditional Andes plateau products to developed nations' health food markets. This difficulty has been attributed, in part, to the fact that this initiative was created by an individual who wanted to improve farmers' living conditions but knew nothing about the business and the infrastructure required to develop it. This is a key difference that separates this venture from more successful initiatives that incorporate LIS into operations that companies already know and execute well.

Risk of Impaired Relationship with LIS

Cativen and Hortifruti, which purchase vegetables from LIS, face an unsolved problem of LIS supplier desertion. Both companies employ a system of price ranges and harvest planning, guaranteeing to producers price and volume stability in exchange for loyalty. However, short-sighted LIS farmers forgo (desert) their agreements when market prices drift above company-set ranges. Companies are then forced to recruit new suppliers—a costly practice. As a result, companies deepen their relationship with the more reliable farmers. This ensures economic value creation, but it tends to favor less poor suppliers, who usually have a longer-term business vision.

Mariposas de Costa Rica is challenged by overproduction, which jeopardizes price stability and long-term product quality. LIS suppliers, both those selling to this company and independent breeders that have copied its technology, are motivated to produce more in order to earn more, but this is driving overproduction and pulling prices down, which, in turn, induces suppliers to lower product quality in order to reduce waste. This quality reduction threatens the business' long-term feasibility. The company tries to convince suppliers not to overproduce, but it is not always successful.

Irupana also faces a long-term business sustainability risk as a result of an environmental issue. Increased quinoa demand has driven small LIS farmers to single-cropping, which raises disease incidence in the Andes plateau. In turn, this fuels an incentive to use more pesticides—a practice that goes against quinoa's worldwide reputation as an environmentally sustainable, organic product.

In all the cases described so far, producer training has become paramount to ensure economic value creation. It seems that all sample companies expect suppliers to learn from the business relationship itself, but this may not be enough, and the absence of systematic training may drive LIS out of such a relationship. When several sample companies started working with highly vulnerable groups, they have tended to desert or companies have gradually cast these groups aside in—a "skimming" process that consolidates relationships only with less poor producers. Indeed, the most vulnerable suppliers are less willing to remain within a set price range (so if market prices go over the range established with companies, they have no qualms about selling their products to other buyers, defaulting in their commitments). Vulnerable farmers are also less reliable with regards to product availability and quality as a result of gaps between market demands and their own production standards, as well as their lack of resources to afford minimal investments required to guarantee steady quality.

Another problem may arise in places where companies and LIS share a geographical area (Palmas del Espino and Agropalma). In these circumstances, relationships between companies and LIS producers are asymmetrical as a result of the former's monopsony. Any abuse of monopsony-based powers may lead to violent outbursts by local communities, jeopardizing companies' operations. Thus, business feasibility depends on harmonious coexistence conditions, which demand significant company investments to build relationships based on mutual trust and respect.

Investments to Develop New Suppliers

Two situations were found to require investments to turn LIS into suppliers that could not be made by companies if their initiatives were to be profitable. Such were the cases of Agropalma and Palmas del Espino. These companies cannot recover the investments required to develop crops unless they pay prices below market average to their LIS suppliers. This would be unacceptable to all parties involved. As LIS have no means to make these investments by themselves, it is necessary to summon other actors, such as government agencies, to help finance these investments through donations or soft loans. Otherwise, the economic value created is not enough to ensure corporate interest in these initiatives.

In these circumstances, LIS community organization is also key—not only because of its legitimating role in obtaining funding, but also because it facilitates negotiations and reduces transaction costs associated with loan management.

Companies' regulatory frameworks may also threaten market-based initiatives with LIS by compromising their profitability. Among electricity distribution companies in this sample, the LIS business model that has been profitable for Edenor has not worked for AES-EDC, as a result of the latter's obligation to charge social fees that do not cover service supply costs. In 2007, Venezuela's government acquired AES-EDC and reinforced its social fee policy, rendering pre-paid electricity sales to LIS unfeasible. Economic uncertainty may jeopardize investments required to build these markets. Edenor's advanced payment initiative was launched as a pilot project; to scale it, the company would have to invest US$10 million. Argentina's electrical energy regulatory agency (ENRE) authorized the pilot test, but to date it had not approved its large-scale deployment.

Economic Value Creation in LIS Market Initiatives by Social Enterprises

The goals of all market-based initiatives launched by CSOs and cooperatives, encompassed under the term "social enterprises" in chapter 4, include the creation of economic resources to ensure their sustainability. Yet most sample initiatives do not create sufficient economic value to accomplish this goal, possibly because they focus on an additional social purpose: incorporating vulnerable groups to economic activities—a difficult task in itself. Table 9.3 classifies sample initiatives according to their key goals, offering also an overview of their economic results.

Table 9.3
Economic Value Creation in LIS Market Initiatives by Social Enterprises

	Creating surplus to support social mission	Incorporating LIS to demanding markets	Incorporating LIS to labor market
Cooperatives (LIS engaged as workers and partners)	*Cases:* *market-based projects= initiatives by Ciap and APAEB* Results: sound value creation	*Cases:* *Coopa-Roca, Bio-Bio Pickers* Results: they vary according to LIS vulnerability	*Cases:* *El Ceibo, Asmare, El Porvenir* Results: they vary according to exposure to market discipline
Civil Society Organizations (LIS engaged as beneficiaries)	*Cases:* *Salvation Army* Results: sound complementary value creation	*Cases:* *Oro Verde Corporation, Inacap* Results: they vary according to LIS vulnerability	*Cases:* *Futur Foundation, Andrómines, La Fageda* Results: sound complementary value creation

Some market-based initiatives carried out by business units within cooperatives (like CIAP and APAEB) and CSOs operate as profitability centers in commercial terms (column 1). These units are managed with strictly business criteria and operate independently within larger organizations. Their surplus—usually large—is used to support their organizations' mission-related social assistance and security services. For instance, Intercraft, an international marketer for Peruvian handicrafts and a subsidiary of Peru's Cross-Regional Artisan Center (CIAP), has skillfully gained a sound market position at the fair-trade circuit. Its surplus is used to fund services provided by CIAP, such as a cultural center, training programs for artisans, and other technical assistance and organizational programs for grass-roots groups. In addition, Intercraft's surplus supports the development of new businesses, such as Pachamama (an alternative tourism agency) and Bazar Perú (an online handicraft store).

Argentina's Salvation Army chapter, a CSO, also features a profitable business unit called Escudo Rojo that provides funds to help support its mainstream assistance services. However, Escudo Rojo is as not as important to the Salvation Army's sustainability as cooperatives' business units are for their parent organizations. Donations continue to be a significant source of funding for CSOs like the Salvation Army. For cooperatives like APAEB and CIAP, however, market-based initiatives account for clusters of interrelated businesses that, combined, become primary financial sources for them and their social services.

Another group of initiatives intends to provide LIS with access to demanding markets (column 2). For example, Chile's National Training Institute (Inacap) trains youths who are usually excluded from higher education programs to compete in the labor market for professionals and technicians. Coopa-Roca connects artisans who live in *favelas* (slums) with top Brazilian and international designers. Similarly, Oro Verde tries to link very poor miners to ecological gold buyers in markets around the world. The economic results of these initiatives have varied. The best performers are Inacap and Coopa-Roca. In 2006, Inacap posted net earnings of US$7.8 million and is using these funds for expansion. Coopa-Roca posted profits for several years, and its sales have grown steadily, although it has registered accounting losses since 2005 as a result of unrecorded past labor liabilities.

The ventures that have created the least economic value are the Wild Fruit Pickers (henceforth Bio-Bio) and Oro Verde Corporation. Bio-Bio is a small operation with interesting growth, but it is still far from self-sustainability. Its members have very little education and are therefore highly dependent on a CSO that provides free administration and international marketing services. Oro Verde, a Colombian organization founded in 2000 to provide access to international, environmentally responsible mining markets to subsistence miners, shows no surplus yet; management forecasts expect this to happen by 2009. This organization finances its operating losses (all administrative expenses) with funds from international technical cooperation. One difference between Coopa-Roca/Inacap and Bio-Bio/Oro Verde that might explain their contrasting economic outcomes is that the former organizations work with urban LIS who are less poor and vulnerable as well as more educated than rural LIS involved in Bio-Bio and Oro Verde.

Among organizations devoted to LIS incorporation to labor markets (column 3), most depend on government support for economic results (the cooperatives Asmare and El Ceibo, both with waste recycling operations, and Spanish CSOs Andrómines, Futur and La Fageda), and one proves to be independent in this regard (recycling cooperative El Porvenir).

Revenues for the three Spanish CSOs have grown steadily year after year, while their net earnings, though low, have been always positive. It should be noted, however, that a significant share of these organizations' revenues (12% to 28%) comes from subsidies regularly granted by the Spanish government to so-called social inclusion companies. By comparison, Latin American cooperatives Asmare and El Ceibo have not always boasted positive or steady net earnings. Asmare registers highly volatile results (both negative and positive) as result of changes in local administration's support policies. El Ceibo experienced slight losses in 2006, despite receiving a subsidy from the city administration. In all likelihood, the more formal institutional framework that rules the relationship between CSOs and Spain's government explains why these organizations enjoy better economic performance.

Unlike these organizations, El Porvenir draws all of its revenues from private-sector sales. While it posted losses in 2003 through 2005, this organization started to report profits—albeit with lower sales—after it hired a professional management team in 2005.

To gain a better understanding of these outcomes, we will point out the critical factors that seem to influence cooperatives' and CSOs' ability to create the resources required to ensure their financial sustainability through market-based initiatives.

Key Economic Performance Factors for Social Enterprises' Market-Based Initiatives

We have mentioned that a major requirement for companies developing market-based initiatives with LIS is patience to get to know them and to learn how to work with them lest initiatives be abandoned before maturing and reaping fruits. For cooperatives and CSOs, a common challenge is to formulate an efficiency rationale to allocate and use resources without compromising social goals, such as serving a specific vulnerable population.

CSO managers and cooperative members do not usually appreciate—and may even frown upon—economic efficiency.[10] Yet if financial resources are not efficiently secured, their social endeavors will be limited by budgetary constraints. Their reluctance to adopt an economic efficiency criterion might be attributed to their fear that it could become an end in itself rather than a means to create resources for social mission support. This risk is ubiquitous. For example, Futur, a Spanish labor inclusion CSO that works in the food service industry, seeking to boost its business efficiency, gradually hired qualified waiters instead of the former convicts and other socially excluded individuals that it was supposed to train for employment.

How can organizations become more efficient without straying from their social mission? Sample cases prove that organizations need to set the boundaries for their economic value creation endeavors. These boundaries result from a clear definition of non-negotiable premises for social value creation. For instance, CIAP is determined to support and strengthen the most vulnerable artisans, who are categorized as "level C" by a performance measurement system, and, as such, are not ready to successfully compete in international markets. Although Intercraft, CIAP's trading subsidiary, primarily sells products manufactured by more qualified artisans (belonging to levels A and B), it does not exclude level-C artisans. Profits from sales of products manufactured by more qualified artisans are used by the organization to provide the necessary training and technical assistance to help the most vulnerable artisans to qualify for exports. Thus CIAP manages to pursue an efficient approach in its international business without compromising its social mission.

At times, there is no clear definition of non-negotiable or core premises for social value creation, and this may threaten economic value creation as well. For example, Escudo Rojo has been historically viewed as a business unit intended to create financial resources to support the social services provided by Argentina's Salvation Army as part of its mission. In its early years, Escudo Rojo additionally set out to hire people with very poor employment prospects. As a result, venture productivity was very low, and the business was posting losses. When a new manager took over in 1994, Escudo Rojo returned to its original purpose. Productive and commercial processes were professionalized, and the initiative began to yield the financial resources required to support the Salvation Army's social services in Argentina.

In short, it is crucial not to confuse economic and social aspects. Keeping sound accounting records is essential to accomplish this goal, as organizations can then assess their economic performance and determine how much it costs to produce its social services. They can then determine whether they have additional financing needs. This practice also provides the transparency and legitimacy required to request donations and grants.

Abiding By Market Discipline

Becoming "market-oriented" is a means to ensure organizational efficiency and effectiveness. Recycling cooperative El Porvenir, unlike other recycling initiatives explored, receives no subsidies and maintains business agreements with private-sector customers. In late 2004, this cooperative posted losses as a result of disloyal member behavior, capital reduction, high costs associated with night waste collection, and shady accounting. In order to assure its feasibility and following a customer's advice, cooperative leaders hired a professional manager to review its processes and find a way to reduce operating costs. In 2005, night routes were discontinued; production lines were revised; a new accounting system was implemented; a result-based compensation scheme replaced former time-based payments and ended disloyal member behavior (members used to add disposable materials to waste or soak cardboard). The cooperative's economic performance improved soon after.

Argentine El Ceibo's leader knows that this recycling cooperative's vulnerability lies partly in the instability of subsidies received from state agencies. She is also aware that in order to sell directly to companies without intermediaries—a move that would significantly improve member income—this cooperative needs to streamline its waste separation process, increase its volume, adopt a legal invoicing system as well as administrative and accounting systems, and secure adequate transportation. However, unlike El Porvenir, El Ceibo views this migration to a "market-oriented" approach as very costly, and this is keeping its members tied to subsistence income. It should be noted that this organization was created as a political movement pursuing social vindication rather than as an economic organization.

An organization may be market-oriented even if it does not aspire to use only its revenues to cover all the costs incurred by a market-based initiative. For example, Spanish social-inclusion CSOs receive subsidies intended to compensate for the fact that their workers' productivity—as a result of their vulnerability—may be lower than that of business companies' regular employees. However, except for their recruiting practices, their other business procedures are similar to those found in competitive companies. For instance, La Fageda is a CSO that provides job opportunities for mentally challenged individuals in dairy product manufacture. All the same, the organization pursues a sophisticated marketing strategy and has developed competitive products. For example, its "La Fageda farm natural yogurt" ranks third in market share in Catalonia, following multinationals Danone and Nestlé.

Market orientation is closely related to the existence of professional management. A common factor among sample CSOs that might explain their sound financial performance is that their founders and leaders are professional managers. Additionally, there seems to be a connection between professional management and cooperatives' financial performance as well. El Porvenir, APAEB, and CIAP—the most solid organizations, with members drawing the highest income—are all managed by professionals.

Having Resources for Formalization

A willingness to abide by market discipline does not seem to suffice when it comes to guaranteeing sustainability, however. Organizations need to have the necessary resources (capital) to do so. For instance, El Porvenir lost an important hospital contract because it did not have the money to apply for ISO 9000 certification, although this cooperative did comply with ISO 9000 process quality standards. Likewise, some leaders of El Ceibo attribute their accounting flaws to high costs of implementing an auditing system.

Internal Leadership

All cooperatives with good independence potential have an organizational leader who is able to initiate inner change and improvement processes. Bio-Bio and Asmare have no such leader, which renders them highly dependent on CSOs or government agencies that support them. In comparison, organizations with dynamic leaders, like APAEB and CIAP, display a greater ability to shape their own destiny. These leaders' capability derives not only from their charisma, but from their competencies (these individuals are typically well educated) and their commitment to members' well-being.

LIS Vulnerability

Not all LIS are equal. Contrasting results from Oro Verde and Inacap raise the need to analyze economic value creation difficulties found when LIS are extremely poor or vulnerable. Oro Verde, the recycling cooperatives, Spanish "labor inclusion" CSOs, and Bio-Bio continuously depend on subsidies and donations, because the integration of indigents, subsistence farmers, and handicapped individuals is complex and costly. Organizations like Inacap that work with "the less poor among the poor"—i.e., LIS with social mobility aspirations—have a less costly task at hand, as their LIS customers are already willing and able to pay for their services. El Porvenir shows that it is not always possible to continue working with the most vulnerable LIS and create economic value. This cooperative's members ranged from lower-income individuals to those who lived below the poverty line and indigents.

When organization leaders decided to hire a professional management team and become market-oriented, nearly half its associates refused to adjust to the new rules and chose to leave the organization—they preferred to work on their own for mere subsistence income.

Fixed Costs for Social Services

To fulfill its solidarity mission, the cooperative conglomerate APAEB provides several social services (cultural center, agricultural family school, learning center, IT school, Internet access service, social club, radio station, TV show). These services imply fixed costs that can hardly be adjusted at economic downturn periods caused by external factors, such as exchange rate appreciation. If these costs were to exceed profits, APAEB's sustainability would be jeopardized. For example, the conglomerate would risk depleting its revolving funds or postponing investments for profit-creation centers in order to continue its social services.

Finally, it should be noted that institutional environments bear a significant influence on CSOs' and cooperatives' ability to become sustainable. Many sample initiatives—particularly, recyclers Asmare and El Ceibo, as well as Spanish social-inclusion CSOs (Andrómines, Futur and La Fageda)—provide services that would otherwise be provided by governments: serving mentally-challenged individuals (La Fageda); offering environmental education (El Ceibo); or supplying job training and legal counsel to waste collectors (Asmare). Thus, when governments financially support these organizations, they are actually outsourcing a service, albeit with more benevolent conditions than in regular market transactions.

Generally, governments and social service outsourcers are bound by contracts that parties must honor. Yet Latin American cooperatives like El Ceibo and Asmare find that despite the existence of formal agreements, subsidies are often delayed and even suspended unilaterally. In Spain, by contrast, the rules governing subsidies for social inclusion are clearly established by law, with institutions set up to oversee compliance. For the most part, this explains Spanish social-inclusion CSOs' financial stability as opposed to their Latin American counterparts' high financial volatility.

Summing up, the challenges associated with cooperative and CSO sustainability varied depending on organizations' focus (social inclusion, access to demanding markets, or profit generation). For organizations devoted to social inclusion, sustainability seems to hinge on credible contracts between organizations and the state. To accomplish sustainability, organizations that focus on incorporating LIS to demanding markets need to embark on "market intelligence" efforts, seeking to identify buyers, to determine their demands and preferences, and to convey their technical specifications to LIS producers. If organizations fail to institutionalize an internal competency by retaining a professional management team that embraces a business rationale, they will largely depend on external agents or individuals, becoming increasingly vulnerable in these agents' absence. For organizations intending to create resources to support social initiatives, the key to successful sustainability lies in a clear separation between business and social tasks.

Discussion and Conclusions

Business Initiatives with LIS as Consumers

Prahalad[11] and Weiser et al.[12] use data on LIS purchasing power and consumption capacity to argue that there is a fortune at the base of the pyramid. However, they fail to assess the profitability of the initiatives they study—they just assume that those initiatives are profitable. Our findings indicate that profitability is uncertain in business initiatives engaging LIS as consumers.

Economic value creation analyses of our sample companies revealed mixed results. Only modest market-based ventures by companies=initiatives proved to be profitable early on. Only two of the projects=initiatives, usually carried out by large companies, were profitable, although all are expected to become profitable eventually. Another outstanding finding is that all projects=initiatives—profitable or not—account for a very small share of promoter companies' overall revenues. In fact, most of these initiatives have been nothing but pilot experiences.

This fact may be attributed to the observation that large companies' traditional market knowledge and expertise are not all that useful when it comes to forging relationships with LIS consumers. Sample evidence indicates that profitable sales to LIS depend largely on companies' having a micro- or fragmented payment system for indivisible goods (e.g., home appliances or ceramic tiles). Building a credit or advanced payment scheme to enable LIS customers to buy those goods counts as an innovation—not an extension of previous practices. From another perspective, it may be argued—as a hypothesis in need of future validation with new research—that when companies are able to fragment products instead of payments, their prior experience can be more useful to approach LIS markets. Such would be consumer goods available in smaller packages or financial products that can be reformulated into smaller loans (micro-loans) and combined with specific sales force efforts. Theoretically, at least, this seems to match previous research findings on micro-finance[13] and consumer goods.[14]

As fragmented payments become more significant, initiatives' economic success depends to a larger extent on companies' ability to gather information on LIS customer reliability and to build a cost-effective collection system, which, according to our findings, requires the development and introduction of several institutional and technological innovations. This also calls for effective relationships with community counterparts and the exploitation of existing community structures and organizations. None of these abilities is included in the usual or traditional repertoire of companies venturing into LIS markets. Thus learning takes time and delays profitability. As Gunnar Eliasson points out, companies may lose heart or enthusiasm in the process, abandoning initiatives before they reach maturity or investing fewer resources and efforts in their ventures, which soon become mere pilot projects with no growth prospects.[15] This is why it is so important for companies to approach LIS markets with a medium-term perspective.

In addition, for a group of initiatives associated with utility services (electricity, natural gas or water), the variable that hinders economic value creation is the size of investments required to build distribution and collection systems. To become profitable, these initiatives need to engage governments, multilateral agencies, or users (with their labor) to support investments that, in practical terms, are non-recoverable with LIS consumption and fee levels. Carlos Rufín and Luis Arboleda point out how important it is for these companies to mobilize other actors who are willing to invest in these initiatives.[16]

Companies=initiatives—while modest in scale—achieved quick profitability, whereas large companies' projects=initiatives failed to do so. This finding may be attributed to an "attrition" bias: company=initiative survival depends on profitability; if companies=initiatives are not profitable, they do not exist. According to Aneel Karnani,[17] small and medium-sized companies seem to be better equipped to deal with LIS than large companies, as competitive advantages in these markets do not depend on economies of scale but on companies' ability to address LIS culture and priorities in each region or location. A common trait in sample cases, in support of Karnani's views, is that companies=initiatives (all modest in scale) test and adjust their approaches more rapidly, responding to LIS specificities, as compared to large companies, which need to fight their own inertia to launch their projects. However, some successful experiences by large companies, such as Mexico's Farmacias Simis and Elektra, suggest that the key performance driver in these ventures is LIS market centrality rather than size. In practical terms, this means that in companies that have not had LIS markets as part of their core business, initiative leaders need to make an extraordinary effort to ensure management commitment and willingness to invest time and creativity in venture development.

Business Initiatives with LIS as Suppliers

Karnani [18] argues that writings about the fortune at the base of the pyramid focus on LIS as consumers, whereas it is necessary to view LIS as suppliers, as the best way to mitigate poverty is to raise their income. Nonetheless, turning LIS into well-paid producers and, at the same, ensuring economic value creation for companies is not that easy. Our research findings show that the more vulnerable LIS are, the more uncertain profitability becomes.

Karnani's argument, inspired on ITC's e-Choupal case (documented by Prahalad[19] and by Anupindi and Sivakumar[20]), is based on the proposition that companies offer more efficient markets to LIS suppliers, and that in those scenarios, the latter capture more value and more revenues. Several sample cases have corroborated this statement; indeed, by approaching LIS in this manner companies also manage to build more efficient market mechanisms to capture greater value themselves (e.g., Cativen and Hortifruti). In short, win-win relationships are possible. However, our sample also showed that when companies start working with very vulnerable LIS groups, a "skimming" process ensues, leading companies to finally consolidate their relationships only with the less poor of the poor.

Based on these findings, we posit a hypothesis—to be verified with future research—that when companies' source of economic value in their relationship with LIS lies in greater value chain efficiency, a skimming process tends to ensue. This is not the case when companies' economic benefit source is a reputation improvement. Weiser et al. state that nowadays, "intangible assets, like reputation, have become a major source of shareholder value";[21] as a result, the use of fair-trade mechanisms, purchases to underprivileged groups, and the adoption of some international standards for supplier interactions have become increasingly important practices for companies. Both Explorandes and Irupana, which actively pursued customer satisfaction abroad, deployed explicit efforts to incorporate visibly excluded segments.

Two other cases showed no signs of skimming practices. In these cases (Agropalma and Palmas del Espino), companies tried to engage LIS as suppliers to enhance their reputation in the communities where they operate. This finding also confirms the observations of Weiser et al.[22]

Contrary to research findings associated with market-based initiatives featuring LIS as consumers, when LIS are engaged as suppliers, modestly scaled companies=initiatives tend to face greater difficulties to secure or maintain profitability than projects=initiatives involving larger companies. Additionally, the latter seem to be better equipped to guarantee LIS product business value and therefore income improvements. Except for palm oil producing companies, the advantage enjoyed by projects=initiatives may be attributed to the value chain integration achieved by large companies, from purchases from producers to retail sales. On the one hand, when chains are integrated all the way through retail operations, companies know more about their markets and, as a result, are able to provide adequate technical assistance to their LIS suppliers. On the other hand, overall value chain integration renders companies less vulnerable to market cycles, enabling them to plan suppliers' production and to ensure purchase volumes and prices. Conversely, suppliers for smaller companies whose value chains are not integrated all the way through retail operations are not engaged in harvest planning processes and are thus more inclined to overproduce, lowering prices and shaking markets to LIS detriment.

Social Enterprises' Market-based Initiatives with LIS

Like companies, CSOs and cooperatives also faced greater challenges to create economic and social value with their market-based initiatives when approaching more vulnerable LIS. Organizations of extremely poor people (Bio-Bio Pickers and Oro Verde Corporation) have run into many difficulties to create value and to provide LIS with a reasonable income. Moreover, when organizations like El Porvenir and Futur Foundation set out to create more economic value, they experienced skimming processes resembling those of companies that incorporate LIS as suppliers.

Marwaha et al. noted that the productive capacity of the poor is latent and requires external catalysts to activate. Social inclusion cases showed that the more vulnerable LIS segments are, the greater their dependence on external agents to create economic value for themselves.[23] In most cases, rather than a catalyst, these organizations need ongoing support and technical assistance to even survive.

Foster and Bradach argue that nonprofits lack "business perspective," mentioning, among other examples, their inability to keep cost accounting records.[24] This problem was found in organizations with the poorest economic value creation performance. In addition, among organizations that have indeed adopted a business approach, those with greater knowledge of consumer markets (market intelligence) have been able to exploit the opportunities presented by fair-trade institutions favoring LIS products (CIAP-Intercraft vis-à-vis Oro Verde Corporation). There seems to be a clear connection between organization size and age and its market intelligence, as well as among the adoption of a business approach, direct sales to end buyers, and the commercial value of products sold (El Porvenir vis-à-vis El Ceibo and Asmare).

Another problem found—also mentioned by Foster and Bradach[25]—is how easily CSO or cooperative social missions clash with economic value creation. The cases of sample Spanish CSOs highlight the significance of institutional environments to minimize dilemmas stemming from this tradeoff. In Spain, unlike normally in Latin America, the state is willing to grant stable subsidies for organizations to strike a balance between their economic and social goals.

In closing, our case studies prove that exchanges with LIS—either as consumers or suppliers—are more costly than in other markets as a result of information asymmetries and transaction costs. In addition, they also indicate that only initiatives that introduced technological and institutional innovations to overcome those obstacles have managed to operate profitably or expect to do so soon. This is consistent with Prahalad's findings about the significance of innovation in the design of products and services, distribution channels, transportation, and consumer education to approach base-of-the-pyramid markets.[26]

Notes

* The authors wish to express their gratitude for the invaluable contributions from Patricia Márquez and Ezequiel Reficco to this chapter. They are also grateful to Marguin Paradas, Norqui Peña and Juan Pablo Molina for their support as research assistants in this project.

1. C. K. Prahalad, *The Fortune at the Bottom of the Pyramid: Eradicating Poverty through Profits* (Upper Saddle River, NJ: Wharton School Publishing, 2005).
2. Aneel G. Karnani, "Fortune at the Bottom of the Pyramid: A Mirage" (Working Paper No. 1035, University of Michigan, Stephen M. Ross School of Business, 2006), 16.
3. Michael Chu, "Microfinance: Business, Profitability and the Creation of Social Value," in *Business Solutions for the Global Poor: Creating Social and Economic Value*, ed. Kasturi Rangan, et al. (San Francisco, CA: Jossey-Bass, 2007).
4. Empresario Azteca is the only exception in this group. This project was launched by Mexico's Salinas Group, whose business units focus primarily on LIS markets.
5. Calculated as net earnings divided by total assets, including investments (this index is often referred to as ROI).
6. ROA (return on assets) measures asset utilization efficiency, while ROE (return on equity) measures shareholder returns.

7. Activo Humano is a personnel recruiting agency that specializes in poorly qualified human resources. In 2006, Working Links, a renowned public-private nonprofit consortium devoted to job recruitment for labor-excluded individuals, partnered with Activo Humano.
8. Pali is a supermarket chain for LIS with stores in Costa Rica and Nicaragua. It is part of CSU-CCA, a group that owns other food retailing businesses.
9. Codensa's project for home appliance sales to LIS is profitable, but it accounts for a very small portion of the company's overall profits (2.2% in 2005 and 1.7% in 2006).
10. Gregory Dees, "Enterprising Nonprofits," *Harvard Business Review*, January 1998.
11. C. K. Prahalad, *The Fortune at the Bottom of the Pyramid: Eradicating Poverty through Profits* (Upper Saddle River, NJ: Wharton School Publishing, 2005).
12. John Weiser et al., *Untapped: Creating Value in Underserved Markets* (San Francisco, CA: Berrett-Koehler Publishers, 2006).
13. Michael Chu, "Commercial Returns at the Base of the Pyramid," *Innovations* (Winter–Spring 2007); "Microfinance: Business, Profitability and the Creation of Social Value," in *Business Solutions for the Global Poor: Creating Social and Economic Value*, ed. Kasturi Rangan, et al. (San Francisco, CA: Jossey-Bass, 2007).
14. Kasturi Rangan, "The Complex Business of Serving the Poor," in *Business Solutions for the Global Poor: Creating Social and Economic Value*, ed. Kasturi Rangan, et al. (San Francisco, CA: Jossey-Bass, 2007).
15. Gunnar Eliasson, "The Role of Knowledge in Economic Growth." Royal Institute of Technology, Stockholm, TRITA-IEO-R (Stockholm, 2000).
16. Carlos Rufín and Luis Fernando Arboleda, "Utilities and the Poor: A Story from Colombia," in *Business Solutions for the Global Poor: Creating Social and Economic Value*, ed. Kasturi Rangan, et al. (San Francisco, CA: Jossey-Bass, 2007).
17. Aneel G. Karnani, "Fortune at the Bottom of the Pyramid: A Mirage" (Working Paper No. 1035, University of Michigan, Stephen M. Ross School of Business, 2006).
18. Ibid.
19. C. K. Prahalad, *The Fortune at the Bottom of the Pyramid: Eradicating Poverty through Profits* (Upper Saddle River, NJ: Wharton School Publishing, 2005).
20. Ravi Anupindi and S Sivakumar, "A Platform Strategy for Rural Transformation," in *Business Solutions for the Global Poor: Creating Social and Economic Value*, ed. Kasturi Rangan, et al. (San Francisco, CA: Jossey-Bass, 2007).
21. John Weiser et al., *Untapped: Creating Value in Underserved Markets* (San Francisco, CA: Berrett-Koehler Publishers, Inc., 2006), 94.
22. Ibid.

23. Kapil Marwaha et al., "Creating Strong Businesses by Developing and Leveraging the Productive Capacity of the Poor," in *Business Solutions for the Global Poor: Creating Social and Economic Value*, ed. Kasturi Rangan, et al. (San Francisco, CA: Jossey-Bass, 2007).

24. William Foster and Jeffrey Bradach, "Should Nonprofits Seek Profits?," *Harvard Business Review* (February 2005).

25. Ibid.

26. C. K. Prahalad, *The Fortune at the Bottom of the Pyramid: Eradicating Poverty through Profits* (Upper Saddle River, NJ: Wharton School Publishing, 2005).

10

Inclusive Business and Social Value Creation

Felipe Portocarrero and Álvaro J. Delgado*

Although there is incipient regional consensus about the need for greater alignment between economic and social value creation in market-based initiatives, the notion that business profitability and social inclusion are different organizational goals and that it is impossible to combine them in a unique value-creation proposition is still quite widely accepted. This opinion may be largely attributed to the fact that current socially inclusive market-based initiatives have only recently begun to be systematically studied.[1] However, an increasing number of organizations take into account—more responsibly and professionally, though still slowly and inconsistently—the social consequences of their own economic activities.[2] The focus of this chapter is to identify the common traits or factors that can help to determine the success of these kinds of socially inclusive, market-based initiatives, turning them into sustainable projects that can eventually be replicated on a larger scale.

Which market-based initiatives create social value, and what kinds of social value are created? Are there significant differences between organizations that have incorporated low-income sectors (LIS) as suppliers or producers and those that have incorporated them as customers? How different (or similar) are patterns of creation of social value in non-profits, cooperatives, and civil society organizations (CSO)?

These questions have no easy answers. As this is a new field of study, except for the area of micro-finance, there is little evidence available to gauge the impact of these experiences on the lives of the poor and on social value creation. Also, the evasive nature of the concept of social value requires a definition of its content and scope, to evaluate how significant are the transformations that create socially inclusive market-based initiatives. This is especially important if we take into consideration, above all, the persistent structural asymmetries of power, information, and influence normally found in LIS settings. The key goal of this chapter is to seek the answers to these questions in the 33-case sample included in this collective study (see Tables 10.1 to 10.4, at the end of chapter).

This chapter is divided into seven sections. The first one briefly examines the notion of social value based on four analytical dimensions in order to classify and analyze sample cases in an orderly fashion. The second section offers an overview of the scope and limitations of social value creation in some cases. The third, fourth, fifth, and sixth sections analyze major findings organized by each analytical dimension used. Finally, we present brief conclusions drawn from previous sections.

Social Value: Conceptual Approach and Classification

Although the value created by an organization is basically indivisible when economic, social, and environmental values are intertwined in a single dynamic,[3] its analysis becomes more relevant when these factors are separated. Several authors have contributed to the debate about the social impacts of market-based initiatives involving LIS, originally inspired by the publication of an article written by C. K. Prahalad and A. Hart[4] and a book by Prahalad[5] about the wealth at the "base of the pyramid."[6] In both works, the main goal is to find new ways to integrate LIS (base of the pyramid) into the market, providing them with products that, directly or indirectly, increase LIS consumption alternatives. The cornerstone of this view is that the aggregated economic resources of LIS can both yield profits for companies offering them several products and create a social impact or value by turning LIS into consumers who are able to diversify their purchase opportunities, improve their living conditions, and escape poverty. As opposed to the more traditional, assistance-based approach, the concept of using market mechanisms to help LIS escape poverty recognizes that despite their low income, LIS are engaged in various commercial activities—at least those who overcome subsistence levels. Moreover, LIS must not only be considered as consumers but also as producers, because they can provide alternatives for creating more efficient, competitive, and inclusive markets, thus producing benefits.[7]

In light of the findings from previous studies, our approach attempts to go a step farther, as we understand that the term "social value" refers to "the pursuit of societal betterment through the removal of barriers that hinder social inclusion, the assistance to those temporarily weakened or lacking a voice, and the mitigation of undesirable side effects of economic activity."[8] From this point of view, LIS market inclusion is not limited to the role they may carry out as consumers or producers.[9] Rather, this inclusion may be understood as a mechanism that integrates LIS as citizens in full exercise of their rights, as agents in formal economies, or as managers of their own businesses and social projects.

In fact, this is the ideal aspiration for those who seek to overcome the social fragmentation that characterizes Latin American countries and, to a lesser extent, Spain. However, apart from this ethical concern, the active participation of low-income people in economic and social life, as well as their recognition by other actors, is the path that leads to reinforcing their sense of belonging, strengthening their collective identity, and enhancing the legitimacy of the initiatives they undertake.

In order to document social value creation as rigorously as possible, we pose four analytical dimensions that will allow us to classify and analyze the 33 sample cases in an orderly fashion. The first two dimensions—increased income and access to goods or services—refer to the tangible results that favor the groups of the socially inclusive market-based initiatives studied. Citizenship construction and social capital development correspond to intangible dimensions necessary to improve LIS living conditions.

Increased income. One of the most important components and, in fact, one of the first stages of social inclusion hinges on access to a labor market that provides stable jobs (or self-employment at small ventures, or the exercise of a trade), which, in turn, provide higher disposable income in decent conditions. Increased income goes beyond simple monetary increase (i.e., more economic value) to become a source of social value, as this is how LIS can broaden their life options—or, as Dahrendorf put it, "life chances."[10] However, social value creation is not limited to the improvement of LIS choices and purchasing power as a result of stable jobs. Another way to increase income and create social value is to incorporate the poor into productive chains, as suppliers of goods or services, not only as consumers. That is the reason why increased income does not exclusively entail a new consumer status for LIS. In some cases, social inclusion also involves the necessary resources to promote an entrepreneurial spirit that will turn LIS into wealth drivers. This spirit or the reflective attitude and commitment required for responsible decision-making are especially visible in cases where low-income individuals participate in initiative coordination, organization, or management, as pointed out in chapter 5.

Access to goods or services. Barrier reduction or elimination is viewed as an opening to provide access to goods or services for the satisfaction of unmet needs. Normally, these barriers are associated with relatively high prices (as compared to LIS income), distribution problems in rural and city outskirts, LIS inability to pay cash for some products, as well as their difficulty to access loans to afford utility network installations. These barriers may be overcome by means of information to improve decision-making processes; training to acquire professional or organizational competencies that enhance business offerings, individual job eligibility, and productivity; new and more cost-effective business models; and access to financial credit mechanisms in order to develop micro-ventures.

Citizenship construction. There are other legal, symbolic, and cultural obstacles in the path towards social inclusion and poverty eradication that prevent need satisfaction or the recognition and exercise of rights. In addition to power, influence, and information asymmetries, a major hindrance lies in the difficulty of low-income sectors to build an identity as members of the wider society, a sense of belonging that goes beyond the narrow boundaries of their own communities.[11] Similarly, it should be noted that in developing countries, especially among rural populations in Latin America, direct market engagement may be a mirage or a hard-to-reach goal. Frequently, products offered by LIS fail to reach the market or do so through dishonest middlemen who abuse these producers, holding them captive and poor. Likewise, certain situations of social exclusion make it hard for LIS groups to join the labor market and exercise their right to work. Among other things, self-esteem improvements as well as the respect for and recognition of cultural differences are also important. Poverty and educational gaps hinder the exercise of citizenship as they weaken the capacities for autonomous and active information, organization, and participation required for social life. Socially inclusive market-based initiatives that recognize people's dignity and rights effectively promote personal and collective success. These initiatives can also help to overcome the social stigmas associated with LIS poverty.

Social capital development. LIS resources (emotional, economic, political, symbolic, organizational, etc.) can be significantly increased by building efficient networks based on trust, reciprocity, and mutual cooperation. Thus, ongoing contact and interaction lead to more resources. Thus social capital creation facilitates joint projects, builds synergies among latent capabilities, and brings together individual interests that would otherwise be fragmented or dispersed.[12] Leadership and empowerment of LIS are also important, as they enable people to channel and express their demands, exercise the right to disagree, and avoid being subjugated and excluded.[13] As expected, socially inclusive market-based initiatives create different kinds of social capital by strengthening social relationships among people engaged in these efforts (bonding social capital) or through the bonds these groups establish with other social groups, local governments, ventures, new markets or customers (bridging social capital).[14]

In the effort to establish the conceptual boundaries of our analysis, we find that some of these analytical dimensions have overlapping and intertwined qualities and components. Is this an insurmountable obstacle in the theoretical construction of a concept? First, our sample lacks the necessary critical mass to accurately delineate our analytical dimensions. Second, some of its components are only dimly present in more than one of our analytical fields. Does this render our attempt to build a social-value rationale invalid or futile? The answer is no, if we bear in mind that this is a preliminary approach that may shed some light on major sources of social value in socially inclusive market-based initiatives. Future researchers will surely fine-tune our proposition and build the foundations for a more complete theoretical framework.

Market-Based Initiatives and Social Value

According to our collective research, which are the main factors that make a special impact on social value creation?

First, we should note the **heterogeneity of both LIS and the economic sectors involved**. Market-based initiatives are developed in a broad range of geographical locations in Latin America and Spain, spanning from the most remote regions of the Andean Plateau to the thick Amazonian rainforest to densely populated neighborhoods located around urban areas or in city historical centers. As a result of this diversity, low-income populations carry out several economic activities to overcome barriers and to mitigate their poverty. Our sample includes, for instance, electricity service users that regularized their access to this public service, seizing benefits such as enhanced home safety, better treatment, and payment alternatives suitable for their income flow (pre-paid system); this occurred under the electricity services provided by AES in Caracas and Edenor in Buenos Aires. Also included in our sample are butterfly breeders who export their products to Europe and the United States through Mariposas de Costa Rica; artisans from Peru's CIAP, who try to preserve their cultural identity and improve their living conditions by selling their products through fair-trade mechanisms; and farmers who forgo illegal and unstable coca plantations to become oil palm suppliers for the Peruvian company Palmas del Espino.

Second, we find LIS presence **in different value chain stages**, acting as consumers and customers as well as suppliers of larger ventures, even as owners of their own businesses—personal, family-centered, or in cooperatives—and producers of goods or services not only for domestic markets but also for export to various countries and customers. It is clear that the structures and processes of some of the organizations studied underwent several adjustments in order to reach out to LIS by means of cooperation and co-management mechanisms that have given way to new interactions. This was the case of Venezuela's Cativen supermarket chain and LIS farmers in Timontes. Another means, unilateral value chains, was used in the case of the Mexican transnational Cemex, interested in promoting home improvements with a savings and micro-credit program carried out by Construmex, an initiative that channels the resources from Mexican immigrants in the U.S. toward construction material purchases.

Finally, **several types and extents of social value are created by these initiatives**. Not all of the sampled market-based initiatives are intended to create the same types of value, and not all accomplish their goals. Indeed, some manage to build a vast network that promotes social value creation in their ecosystems but fail to drive any significant changes in LIS access to new goods or services; others boost LIS citizenship and dignity but fail to introduce substantial improvements in the more tangible dimensions of their physical well-being. We will return to this issue later, when we examine the intangible dimensions of social value creation.

Most socially inclusive market-based initiatives in this sample are still in their early development stages. However, we should analyze their progress in all four dimensions involved in social value creation. The following sections will address these issues.

Income Increase: Expanding Life Options

In the long run, social value creation always brings about economic consequences that favor LIS to a greater or lesser extent.[15] However, this section will only analyze how socially inclusive market-based initiatives in our sample directly influence the increase of income for LIS—or do so as an immediate result of their activities. More than half of these initiatives explicitly set out to increase their beneficiaries' income, yet their results have differed greatly. First, we will discuss the cases in which lower-income people have managed to escape poverty, followed by cases in which there are realistic prospects for doing so in the medium or long term. Next, we will analyze those initiatives that show no signs or probabilities of eradicating poverty, but in which an increase in income does contribute to mitigating poverty in the near future. Finally, we will look at companies that sell goods to LIS which the poor already use—or substitute products LIS consume—at better prices, thus providing savings that translate into increased disposable income.

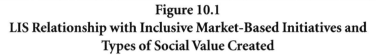

Figure 10.1
LIS Relationship with Inclusive Market-Based Initiatives and Types of Social Value Created

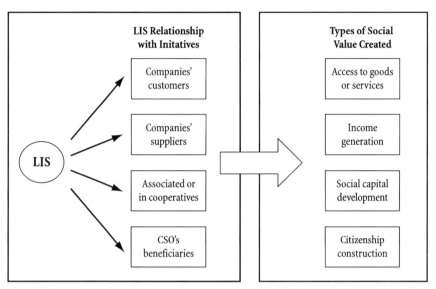

Our sample includes three leading cases in which the groups involved have managed to produce enough income to definitely overcome poverty. At Agropalma, a Brazilian agribusiness company that manufactures oil palm products, 80 percent of the 150 families that abandoned traditional and subsistence crops to join in as growers and suppliers of raw materials for Agropalma raised their monthly income from approximately US$27 in 2001 to US$345 in 2005. This substantial improvement is clearly conveyed by the optimistic comment from one project beneficiary who was used to the typical deprivations of rural people in developing nations: "*my family is no longer needy. We have a future.*"

Similarly, Mariposas de Costa Rica engages LIS as butterfly suppliers for its export operations, enabling nearly 150 low income people who ventured into pupae breeding to double and even triple their income over a 15-year period. As a breeder points out, their living conditions have improved as a result of their income increase.

I joined the butterfly business through my father-in-law . . . I went from riding a bike to having a motorcycle and a cell phone; I was able to pay off my debts, and, then, I could build my home. I've recently sold the motorcycle, and I bought a car.

The mechanism used in both cases to enable LIS to escape poverty has hinged on consolidating a business relationship with LIS serving as suppliers—with no intermediaries—for a company that provides a guaranteed market for their products and protects them from informal schemes' typical price speculation.

A similar scenario was found at APAEB, a Brazilian regional association created in 1980 by hemp producers to do away with intermediaries involved in their product sales. This case is particularly interesting because APAEB, with its 700-member base, is an organization built by LIS themselves, with no third-party intervention. Members' income has increased between 400 and 600 percent over the past 20 years, especially in the 1990s, as a result of their industrialization and exports of their products. APAEB posted revenues of US$8.7 million in 2005, primarily from exports of hemp carpets and tapestry manufactured at their own factory. As successful hemp producers and carpet manufacturers, these LIS have managed to escape poverty and promote their community development, benefiting over 4,500 families in a region besieged by poverty, neglect, droughts, and lack of opportunities.

Though still startups, a few organizations seeking economic improvements show some potential to produce enough income to enable LIS to escape poverty in the medium or long term. The most advanced is Palmas del Espino, an agribusiness company with a project in Peru's rainforest resembling that of Agropalma in Brazil. Palmas del Espino's project expects to increase LIS income in the future, as LIS oil palm harvests only started in late 2007. Increased income for over 50 families in the town of José Carlos Mariátegui, who shifted from raising coca plants to planting oil palm trees in 2003 in order to sell their production to Palmas del Espino, has materialized only recently—with the first harvest after four years—but will become more significant once the loan used to fund this project is paid off in 2013.

There is another group of sample cases in which income creation mitigates LIS poverty, although these initiatives do not aim at poverty eradication. In other words, these operations provide an additional, limited income or enable LIS to stabilize their income flow or ensure its continuity, but they do not help LIS to escape poverty—not even in the far future.

In this group, most cases displaying the best relative results are also business initiatives—like Cativen in Venezuela, Hortifruti in Costa Rica, and Irupana in Bolivia—that engage LIS as farming suppliers and account for their major, if not sole, income source. Indeed, Cativen and Hortifruti are supermarket chains that sell perishable and fresh products bought directly from LIS farmers, promoting programs to improve LIS producers' processes, to offer superior quality products, and thus to increase their income. Intermediary elimination, guaranteed payment, new packaging techniques to reduce waste, and direct product pickup by companies have driven income improvements for fishermen and vegetable and fruit growers. As noted by Hortifruti's Agricultural Development Director:

> Farmers were used to packing their produce in wooden crates that didn't last long, were unhygienic and hazardous for both fruits and people . . . Three years later, 80% of Hortifruti's farming suppliers were working with plastic crates, and today 100% of them do . . . Back then, the waste from harvest, classification, packing, transportation, plant arrival, and shelf display operations was nearly 25%. Today, that waste is below 5%. In those days, fruits were touched by 10 or 15 hands; only two or three hands touch each fruit. This enabled us to pay more to producers and to receive more of their produce, because that 25% was thrown out.

Another venture, Irupana, exports organic farming products purchased from rural Bolivian dwellers, paying 20 percent more than regular market prices with the twofold intention to build supplier loyalty and to promote product improvement and standardization. Using "fair-trade" and "organic product" labels that enable it to command higher prices than its competitors can get, lacking those attributes, Irupana targets market niches that value the social and environmental qualities of its productive processes as well as the well-being of the populations involved. Irupana's purchases account for half the income of its vendor families, which means that their overall incomes have increased by approximately 10 percent.

An interesting case of artisan mining is that of Oro Verde Corporation, which intends to connect artisan gold extraction, the usual activity of Colombia's Chocó region, with domestic and international markets, venturing into fair-trade and/or environmentally responsible niches through a non-profit organization. With the creation and standardization of economic, social, and environmental criteria, gold and platinum are certified, and miners are paid a bonus of 2 percent over the international price of each metal. Even though Oro Verde was supposed to be a growing, productive model, it still requires resources from international cooperation and depends on subsidies, although for the next years a progressive reduction of the latter is expected.

Most of the other initiatives that partially alleviate LIS poverty through income creation are cooperatives or associations built by LIS themselves, even though none has been as successful as APAEB. The remaining six cases in this group include three recycling organizations, whose members manage, at best, to scrape a minimum wage or an income 20 percent higher than free-lance waste collectors'. Two other organizations gather artisans and produce other forms of social value with greater impact than the meager income increase they manage to secure for their members. Especially noteworthy are the three Spanish non-profits (Andrómines, Futur Foundation, and La Fageda) working to provide labor inclusion opportunities for relatively poor, socially excluded, and vulnerable people. Although these organizations enable excluded individuals to secure or increase their income, their initiatives pursue other types of social value.

Finally, our sample includes 12 cases with LIS engaged by companies as customers or consumers. While these initiatives do not produce a nominal increase in income, they can increase available income if they manage to lower the prices of goods or services usually purchased by LIS. The most relevant case is that of Pali supermarkets in Costa Rica and Nicaragua. Their commercial system provides customers with an average 15 percent savings on groceries as compared to conventional supermarkets. Considering that the largest share of LIS family budget is spent on food,[16] savings afforded by Pali could be meaningful. Similarly, Aguaytía Energy has enabled LIS to enjoy significant savings in transportation and household fuel as a result of its efforts to change local energy schemes in its Peruvian jungle operating area. The company promotes the use of liquefied petroleum gas (LPG), a fuel that costs half as much as gasoline. Some estimates indicate that LIS spend over 80 percent of their income in food, clothing, and fuels.[17]

On the basis of the 33 cases selected to illustrate market-based initiatives with LIS in Latin America and Spain, it seems safe to say that the model that secures the best outcomes in terms of increased LIS income calls for their incorporation as suppliers to business, particularly in farming activities in rural areas. These findings support the thesis that the most effective strategies to alleviate poverty involve direct improvements in LIS actual income, which can be raised by offering opportunities for them to engage in new activities, not only as consumers but primarily as producers.[18] In nearly all other initiatives, income increases are so minimal that, if no changes were introduced in the other dimensions, these ventures' impact on LIS living conditions would be rather insignificant.

Companies that purchase LIS products as raw materials are mostly responsible for promoting these initiatives, fostering supplier engagement, and providing training, technical support or other services required to build functional relationships with them. When LIS suppliers are organized in efficient and effective productive chains, it forces them to accomplish and maintain high quality and compliance standards to continue selling their products. Income increases become significant because farmers switch from traditional or subsistence farming practices to much more profitable crops or operations, learning and applying new techniques that substantially enhance their productivity. Furthermore, direct relationships with purchasers enable these LIS suppliers to increase and stabilize their income by eliminating intermediaries and accessing practically guaranteed—albeit demanding—markets. It is also interesting to consider geographical factors. Whether producers are located near purchasing companies or not does not seem to be a success factor for initiatives, as proven by Mariposas de Costa Rica, Irupana, Cativen, and Hortifruti, which operate with suppliers in several regions within their countries of operation. Geographic dispersion and isolation may be overcome when companies implement efficient commercialization chains. However, Agropalma and APAEB—two of the three most successful cases—as well as Palmas del Espino deal with suppliers located in their operating areas. In any case, more research is required to determine how important the location of the initiative and beneficiary is for project success.

   In all other sample cases, market mechanisms by themselves do not provide a clear path to eradicate poverty through income increases or to create enough additional income to improve LIS living conditions significantly. This does not mean, however, that these initiatives do not create other types of social value, which are essential to overcome the profound inequities and social exclusion threats faced by these populations.

Access to Goods and Services: Improving Living Conditions

This category is complementary to the preceding one, if we consider only the 15 sample cases that explicitly seek to favor LIS access to some goods or services. All of them improve LIS living conditions as a direct or immediate result of the inclusive business or social ventures analyzed, but with substantial differences among business models employed and in the type or significance of goods or services offered. Thirteen cases involve companies that engage LIS as customers, offering goods such as medical, electricity, and natural gas services, construction materials, food products, and consumer items such as home appliances, as well as micro-loans. Only three of these companies focus primarily on LIS: Venezuela's Cruzsalud and Comunanza Foundation, which provide medical care with pre-paid and microcredit schemes, respectively, and Pali supermarkets, with operations in Costa Rica and Nicaragua.

Unlike organizations that also offer goods or services to LIS, Cruzsalud has focused exclusively on low-income markets to provide needed medical services, rendering health care and medicines more affordable and offering payment fragmentation to allow LIS to plan and anticipate their expenses. This organization's ambulances drive to excluded urban areas, and its personnel makes medical house calls in locations where such services did no exist. This initiative has had a clear impact on living conditions for Cruzsalud customers, who now register lower disease and job absenteeism rates as a result of the timely and effective medical assistance they receive. Comunanza Foundation provides micro-loans for subsistence entrepreneurs; although it charges the highest rate in Venezuela's formal market—28 percent annual interest plus commissions—some of its customers used to pay up to 170 percent to informal lenders. While Pali supermarkets' customers do not necessarily belong to low-income sectors, this chain serves rural social groups who used to shop elsewhere, and its reduced prices are lower than or similar to those found at fairs and traditional markets, even while Pali offers superior service and greater product security, safety, and hygiene.

The other ten cases in the group of for-profit companies that have incorporated LIS in the last link of their productive-commercial chains—i.e., as end customers—are mostly large, long-established companies that primarily target market segments with greater spending capacity. However, they also serve LIS as a means to expand their markets, create new consumption niches, or remedy inefficient commercial practices, without losing sight of their profitability and efficiency goals. It should come as no surprise, then, that their key investments are intended to remove barriers preventing LIS access to their products or services.

Four sample cases are energy providers. Venezuela's AES Electricidad de Caracas (AES-EDC) and Argentina's Edenor have expanded or formalized their electricity distribution services by means of pre-paid systems and other steps that ultimately implied free meter installation. A group of their new LIS customers received electricity services for the first time ever, while another group regularized its connections, eliminating the risk of accidents from hazardous, illegal connections as well as frequent appliance malfunctions, in addition to rationalizing electricity utilization. Likewise, Argentina's Gas Natural Ban collaborated in natural gas network installation in order to serve people who could not afford overall installation costs on their own, even when this distribution system gives them access to a lower-cost fuel. While these companies are driven by their business interests, this does not undermine the social impact resulting from initiatives that provide

LIS with market access. As Gas Natural Ban's Marketing and Commercial Coordination Manager points out, "we could have stayed in business with the customers we had, but we made a strategic decision to grow and target lower-income sectors."

Similarly, Peru's Aguaytía Energy has invested in changing energy consumption patterns in the jungle area where it operates to lead LIS to use LP gas instead of gasoline in transportation (cabs, motorcycles and small boats) or wood in cooking.[19] To this end, the company has covered engine LPG conversion costs and has distributed stoves for free or at subsidized prices. Additionally, in order to ensure demand continuity and service payment regularity, companies invest to boost customer loyalty, which may bring about greater additional benefits for LIS.

The remaining five companies engage LIS as customers by offering assorted products with credit options. Although only two sample cases specialize in micro-finance (Empresario Azteca in Mexico and Comunanza Foundation in Venezuela), several experiences have indirectly turned LIS into credit-eligible individuals in order to provide access to other assets. One of these, Amanco (Mexico), built modern irrigation systems that enhance poor farmers' productivity, enabling them to become supermarket chain suppliers; similarly, Construmex (Mexico) offers construction materials for home improvement that are guaranteed by cash transfers sent from abroad by beneficiaries' relatives. In two Colombian cases, credit facilities are used to purchase consumer products: low-cost ceramic tiles, formerly out of LIS reach, at Colcerámica; and home appliances at Codensa, available through consumer loans that were previously out of reach. The impact of these initiatives is described quite eloquently by one beneficiary:

> I got a loan at Codensa because it was very easy. I had looked elsewhere for a loan, but I was unable to get one—they asked for many guarantors and an initial installment, and I didn't have the money to pay for it at that moment. We needed a new fridge at home, because we didn't have a place to keep refrigerated stuff. With three documents, I got the fridge. When the fridge was delivered at home, my wife jumped with joy.

Similarly, an Empresario Azteca's micro-loan program beneficiary recalled, "I asked for a loan to buy two sewing machines, so that my daughters could start helping out. The machines paid for themselves, and, later, I was able to buy another one with cash. The truth is, if you don't have credit, you can't do anything."

The notion of selling goods or services to the poor, especially to those who cannot afford their basic needs, has been criticized on ethical grounds,[20] and has also been put into question from a strictly economic standpoint.[21] However, as noted by Hammond et al., it is a fact that practically all families—poor or otherwise—exchange money or labor to satisfy their needs.[22] It is also easy to corroborate that significant, basic LIS needs go unmet, and that they often suffer so-called LIS penalties—higher prices, lower quality, or inability to access various goods and services.[23] The arrival of new companies in new markets may encourage competition and lower prices, but, although this would improve LIS living conditions, it is unlikely to mitigate their poverty, except for some successful micro-loan ventures. Additionally, price reductions might be directly associated with lower-quality goods, unless profits and/or costs are lowered or a significant technological improvement takes place. Some authors argue that quality/cost tradeoffs might be acceptable for LIS, as long as they are duly informed.[24]

Some civil society organizations are also committed to providing LIS with access to goods or services. Chile's National Professional Training Institute (Instituto Nacional de Capacitación Profesional, henceforth Inacap) offers quality higher education programs, with no admission tests, for individuals who would be otherwise unable to join such programs. Indeed, most public school students are excluded from other higher, professional, or technical education options, as they are highly unlikely to pass mandatory admission tests. To ensure that program admittance is not hindered by income limitations, Inacap offers student loans or scholarships. Another organization that enables LIS to access goods is Argentina's Salvation Army, with its Escudo Rojo venture that collects and sells second-hand clothing, furniture, appliances, and books at very low prices and, in some exceptional cases, with flexible payment schemes. The Spanish cooperative La Fageda, in addition to engaging in productive operations with its mentally challenged partners and employees, also provides assistance services, such as monitored housing management.

Another venture that made a visible transformation of LIS living conditions through access to products is APAEB, a cooperative that has become the leading economic agent at Valente (Bahia State, Brazil), diversifying its operations into several farming, handicraft, educational, cultural, recreational, and communication activities in its area. While the goods and services now accessed by this population were not part of the organization's explicit goals and extend far beyond supplies required for hemp growing, industrialization, exports, or byproducts, this organization is included in this group, as its original initiative benefits both its members and its community. Other cases could have been included in this category as well, but were left out because the goods or services accessed by LIS are not directly derived from those initiatives but result from income increases or from the sheer presence of a company in a region—although it may not have interacted with LIS— or are services associated with production, like training or technical advice.

Strategies hinging on low-cost products, fragmented or advanced service payments, and loans to acquire products or services enable LIS to stay in control of their consumption. It may be safe to say that the most important social value contribution created by initiatives in this group has been expanded access to products and services—many of them inaccessible to or unattainable by LIS, or, like energy, formerly accessed in an irregular fashion. In any case, low-income people can now access these goods or services because they have been made more inexpensive, payable in installments, or easy to access. Market incorporation and increased consumer choices may be viewed as a benefit[25] that improves the living conditions of the poor, as it prevents them from turning to informal, inefficient, costly, poor, even illegal conditions—like illegal electrical connections—or those that are hazardous for both the environment and their health, like the use of contaminating fuels or the daily exposure to wood combustion.

Note that the initiatives in this sample, with a few exceptions, have not yet reached the poorest of the poor, but rather a less deprived lower-income segment,[26] as at a minimum they must be able to pay for the products and/or services they acquire, albeit at lower prices and with fragmented or flexible payment schemes. In fact, LIS may be classified in several strata, leading some authors to assert that market-based initiatives to mitigate poverty for the lowest LIS segments are not available or are insufficient.[27]

Some arguments questioning the engagement of LIS for commercial purposes point out that, as their income is not increased, in order to buy new products, they necessarily have to relinquish others. This could eventually discourage the acquisition of goods that satisfy basic nutritional, educational, and health-related needs,[28] or, instead of satisfying unmet demands, it could create new ones.[29] In any case, it is clear that LIS are entitled to make their own consumption decisions, without any kind of patronizing influence.[30] However, bearing in mind that the acquisition of goods or services compromises their resources, it would be reasonable to expect that their basic unmet needs, especially those associated with nutrition, health, and education, be prioritized. Clearly, with more options available, educated consumers' well-being improves, but a larger number of options do not necessarily or significantly mitigate LIS poverty.[31] Although any group's preferences can be influenced, the poor are usually more vulnerable as a result of their educational, economic, and other shortcomings and their limited access to information. Indeed, bad consumption choices will have worse consequences for LIS.[32]

Building Citizenship and Restoring Rights

Simply put, citizenship may be defined as the full exercise of people's rights and duties in equal conditions. However, different aspects of citizenship—political, economic, and environmental, among others—may experience unequal development. Political citizenship involves a sense of belonging to a community of peers and drawing recognition from it.[33] Economic citizenship refers to every individual's right to enjoy adequate living conditions that satisfy basic food, clothing, and housing needs.[34] Finally, the incorporation of concerns about the environment and non-renewable resources into the set of people's rights and obligations constitutes what some have called environmental citizenship.[35] A third of our sample cases feature explicit objectives to build some of these citizenship rights directly, but many other cases accomplish similar results in an indirect fashion.

The more obvious attempts to build political citizenship are those found in recyclers' cooperatives or associations in Colombia, Brazil, and, to a lesser extent, Argentina. These groups' organization was necessary even for their survival, as during the 1980s their lives were threatened by "social cleansing" actions against recyclers and street dwellers. Asmare is a Brazilian recyclers' association that works with poor populations, defending its beneficiaries from these attempts to eradicate homeless individuals from the streets by violent means. As one of Asmare's members recalls in a dramatic testimony,

> The police used to attack us at dawn. They would come to take whatever we had—waste, paper, etc. . . . This Association was created to stop that discrimination, that suffering, that violence against us . . . Asmare works for people who have lost everything, who are on the streets, who have no home, and who don't even know what it is like to be citizen—not because they don't want to, but because society has always deprived them of those rights.

A similar situation unfolded in Colombia before the Porvenir Recyclers' Cooperative was created. These extreme cases, with lives at risk, clearly illustrate the importance of social recognition for underprivileged individuals, whose poverty and vulnerability may prevent the exercise of even their most basic citizen rights. Currently, Bogotá's Recyclers Association (including Porvenir) has organized and trained more than 3,000 recyclers. In addition, it engages in political advocacy, representing recyclers and lobbying for their legitimacy. In some cases, recyclers' organizations afford members upward social mobility through access to activities or new jobs that are viewed as more dignifying than recycling.

As economic proceeds from waste recycling are not substantial even after LIS free themselves from abusive intermediaries, the most relevant social value created by recycling initiatives resides in intangible improvements— i.e., citizenship and the restoration of dignity for individuals involved. The case of Wild Fruit Pickers is similar to that of recyclers, albeit with better income. The pickers work with fruits, vegetables, and medicinal herbs they collect from forests in southern Chile, adding value to these products by dehydrating, packing, and selling them with no intermediaries. Visibility and dignity components are quite significant in this type of work as well. In most relevant cases in this category, LIS dignity and self-esteem restoration is explicitly highlighted, especially among CSOs or LIS cooperatives and associations. In contrast, key intangible improvements seem to be missing in business ventures that have incorporated LIS as customers.

Social recognition and visibility are also relevant in other cases. For instance, Cristóbal Colón, La Fageda's founder and president, emphasizes one of this organization's most important accomplishments: "We have boosted mentally challenged people's visibility and normalcy. We have proven that town 'fools' can also provide a service to our community." Thus, La Fageda contributes to restoring human dignity for individuals who are usually excluded from society. In a similar setting, we should also mention the political advocacy initiative launched by Peru's Cross-Regional Artisan Center (CIAP) to petition for the approval of the Traditional Artisan Act, intended to promote more favorable conditions for artisans involved in informal micro-ventures and small businesses. The "voice" afforded by this organization at national forums enables local artisans to reach markets that would be impossible for them to access on an individual basis.

Economic citizenship, as defined, may be promoted from several angles. Several sample cases do so by fostering employment and labor rights for excluded populations; others provide unregistered LIS with utility invoices that validate their identity, enabling them to access financial services. Economic citizenship may be built not only through access to goods and services but also by physically connecting people and their products to markets.

Ventures that offer social and labor inclusion opportunities to vulnerable, discriminated, and excluded individuals notably include the three Spanish cases in our sample—Andrómines (second-hand clothing collection and sales), Futur Foundation (food services), and La Fageda (dairy product manufacture). Although beneficiaries in these cases are not necessarily poor, the people assisted by the first two ventures face relative poverty and social exclusion (former convicts, drug or alcohol addicts, homeless individuals, battered women or single mothers, gypsies, immigrants, people who have been unemployed for long or are elderly), while La Fageda helps mentally challenged individuals who have virtually no other possibility to earn a living. In order to accomplish their goals, these organizations need to overcome prospective consumers' prejudices and habits; as a result, in most cases, they service NGOs or institutions that value their social components.

The only sample initiative specifically dedicated to labor inclusion in Latin America does target typical LIS. In Chile, Activo Humano, a company known as "the headhunter for the poor," compensates for the deficiencies of the Municipal Labor Intermediation Agencies. Two other sample cases, Brazil's Coopa-Roca and Explorandes in Peru, indirectly offer job opportunities for excluded individuals without qualifications. The Brazilian cooperative streamlines the work of poorly or non-qualified older women or mothers who cannot work outside their homes; for many of them, Coopa-Roca is their only job option, despite the limited income procured for beneficiaries. As one artisan pointed out, "I have been separated for two years now, and, before that, this money used to be an additional income. Right now, I'm trying to survive on this money." In contrast, Explorandes is a large adventure tourism broker with an ecological tourism venture in a community that used to be excluded from traditional tourist destinations. The company trains community members, offering them a chance to diversify their income sources.

The three sample cases that focus on LIS incorporation into energy (electricity and natural gas) distribution networks have indirectly provided these segments with property ownership or with the means for validation of their identity, which enables some of them to access financial services through their service invoices, which constitute a legal proof of residence. This positive external effect favors the exercise of economic citizenship also for Codensa's customers, who have purchased appliances with installment payments and, as a result, have started to build a credit record that enables them to access other financial services more easily. Venezuela's Comunanza Foundation has gone a step farther; for example, some of its loan recipients are unregistered aliens, who would face significant entry barriers to exercise their economic citizenship rights. As most members of LIS, these individuals are excluded from global markets and economies, as well as from their benefits.[36] Thus, connecting LIS to markets is a way to promote their economic citizenship. Several sample cases try to bolster LIS economic citizenship

(Cativen supermarkets, Hortifruti, Irupana and CRES exporters, Amanco, CIAP, and others) by linking supply and demand in remote or excluded places, permitting more LIS individuals to join market and formal economy operations.

Finally, another significant improvement associated with sample ventures refers to greater environmental awareness and care. This has been an explicit accomplishment in at least eight cases, which have also promoted biodiversity and organic products. For instance, the use of natural gas for home cooking, instead of more contaminating fuels, brings a substantial health improvement for users, who cease to be exposed to direct smoke pollution from wood combustion. In addition, electricity consumption has become more rational after legal connections were built, improving resource utilization efficiency. The Futur Foundation, Oro Verde Corporation, and Palmas del Espino have adopted environmental certifications, while Agropalma has consistently shown leadership in observing the stringent environmental regulations in the Amazon rainforest—something that most companies present in the area cannot say. While some of these benefits stem from the existence of mandatory, formal standards, and others simply respond to market demands, they all contribute to building and strengthening environmental citizenship. In a more direct manner, personal hygiene practices explicitly fostered by Porvenir Recyclers' Cooperative drive a qualitative change in these people's living conditions, in addition to promoting city cleanliness and health, as do all other waste collection and management ventures.

Social Capital Development: Building Networks and Alliances

The notion of social capital, which has received much attention,[37] may be viewed as even more elusive and harder to materialize than social value. In synthesis, however, it is safe to say that its development is associated with the following areas: personal empowerment, construed as expanded freedom to choose and act, in addition to increased authority and power of individuals over the resources and decisions affecting their lives;[38] community social cohesion, interpreted as the "consensus among social group members about their sense of ownership in common projects or situations";[39] and networking to enhance the use of proximate and outer relationships (family, neighborly, friendly, and organizational) and resources (economic, social, symbolic, and emotional).[40]

Cases in this sample with the greatest impact combine LIS empowerment and social cohesion, as well as broader social networks (bridging social capital), as illustrated by recyclers' experiences at Asmare (Brazil), El Ceibo (Argentina), and Porvenir Cooperative (Colombia). In all of these cases, a path towards social inclusion is cleared by boosting local capabilities, improving organizational efficiency, creating a sense of belonging to a community, strengthening ties to neighbors and local administrations, while expanding LIS leverage to negotiate with glass, plastics, and recycled cardboard buyers. This amounts to a considerable social impact: because recyclers come from extreme exclusion, any improvement has a significant impact on their well-being. In any case, it is nearly impossible for them to change their predicament if they do not work together, which explains the emergence and development of a special teamwork mystique. Finally, in view of their activity, it is neither complicated nor costly to introduce primary improvements to their organizations' management as well as to their living and working conditions.

Other illustrative cases of social capital development are employment reentry initiatives in Spain and Chile. These organizations serve as bridges for excluded or poorly qualified groups to cross over from unemployment to labor inclusion, after, in some cases, a training and follow-up process. The decisive role played by this kind of intervention is proven by the testimony of an employer, an Activo Humano's customer, who elaborates, "I feel reassured that I'm not hiring a complete stranger, but someone who comes with a reliable recommendation." Thus, the eligibility of LIS workers associated with Activo Humano is enhanced as their close interaction with the company infuses them with the credibility it has earned in the market.

Similarly, as Futur Foundation is part of an ecosystem encompassing several networks of organizations with similar social purposes, its workers-users can exploit its connections to broaden their employment and development opportunities, or, at least, rely on a customer portfolio that guarantees the organization's continuity. Indeed, at La Fageda, mentally challenged employees have built such strong ties with the organization that, despite having other job offerings, they often prefer to stay at this venture. As widely reported, environments featuring significant social cohesion enhance productivity and economic development in a trust-based atmosphere.[41]

People from LIS may have some difficulty organizing themselves efficiently and effectively with a conventional business rationale. In addition, their knowledge and skills to access monetary and human resources are often limited, and they lack key connections to public and private sectors to manage their ventures efficiently, to create value, and to accomplish successful market continuity. Thus, it should come as no surprise that major social capital creation achievements in the other cases are mostly associated with LIS empowerment—enhanced by regained self-esteem—and organization, particularly among business suppliers who have received training and advice either to improve their techniques and procedures or to switch

to more profitable operations. In fact, just as important as specific technical knowledge, is the ability to identify the available assets at hand and the
willingness to put them to work to our advantage,[42] as explained in the
chapter on market ecosystems and social inclusion. Interactions between
companies and LIS develop the management abilities of the poor populations and, in some circumstances, strengthen their cultural identity, sal-
vaging traditional practices at risk of extinction. In the cases that also
consolidate cohesive communities (bonding social capital), like the palm-
growing families selling their crops to Agropalma and Palmas del Espino,
this impact is even more meaningful. In contrast, the majority of cases that
show no social capital development correspond to those companies
approaching LIS as customers or end consumers.

Final Thoughts

On the basis of the evidence presented throughout this chapter, we conclude that the notion of social value is not only elusive but also multi-
dimensional and complex (see Figure 10.2). To outline its key
characteristics, we have focused on tangible and intangible outcomes benefiting LIS as a result of the socially inclusive, market-based initiatives
launched by several organizations. While most of the ventures studied have
been recently developed and are limited in scope, the sample itself is diverse
and heterogeneous in terms of (a) organization size, age, structure, and type
(companies, LIS cooperatives or associations, and CSOs); (b) the role played
by LIS (customers, suppliers, beneficiaries, and partners-owners); and (c)
the sectors where they operate.

Far from hindering our analysis, this diversity has enabled us to identify
a large range of types and degrees of social value. The socially inclusive,
market-based ventures explored in this chapter prove that LIS experience
improvements in well-being of varying breadth and intensity when they are
engaged as consumers, raw material suppliers, or producers. However, the
effects of their engagement clearly go beyond those roles; as their purchasing power increases and their purchase options become more diverse, low-
income people strengthen their rights as economic agents and, therefore,
as full-fledged citizens. This is also a key driver for improvements in living
conditions and, ideally, for poverty eradication.

To pinpoint all major social value creation elements in our sample of
socially inclusive, market-based initiatives (see Figure 10.2), we have
grouped social value expressions found in four categories of both tangible
(income growth and access to goods or services) and intangible dimensions
(citizenship promotion and social capital development). Their analysis has
enabled us to draw the conclusions that follow.

Figure 10.2
Major Social Value Creation Elements in Sample
Market-Based Initiatives

Increased income	Access to goods and services
• Raw materials produced—mostly in rural areasfor companies, especially farming and farming-related products. • Producers' organization and association or incorporation to productive chains. • Increased productivity as a result of training and technical advice. • Elimination of intermediaries. • Certification for differentiated products. • Better marketing channels. • Savings in frequent purchases.	• Reduced prices. • Fragmented payment for goods and services, and pre-paid systems. • Physical presence in rural and poor urban areas. • Private investments in equipment, infrastructure, and distribution networks. • Flexible access to loan mechanisms. • Elimination of barriers for education.
Citizenship promotion	Social capital development
• Recognition and exercise of basic rights (life, work, etc.). • Political advocacy. • Increased visibility and dignity for LIS and excluded groups. • Labor intermediation for handicapped people, excluded groups, poorly or non-qualified individuals. • Identity validation for unregistered individuals. • Physical access to markets to sell LIS production. • Environmental awareness. • Promotion of good hygiene habits, order, and rational consumption.	• Networking, local relationship, and capability strengthening. • Building a sense of belonging to a community. • Social networking; trust, reciprocity, and cooperation development. • Greater availability of own and third-party resources through contacts and interactions. • LIS empowerment to streamline and express demands. • Self-esteem enhancement. • Association of individual interests. • Connecting dispersed social groups with local administrations, companies, new markets, or customers.

Several ventures have been able to encourage LIS to create additional income or to better exploit their resources by means of steady, dignified jobs, incorporation into productive chains, the sale of their products, or the purchase of goods and services with reduced prices or payment facilities. These initiatives are most successful when they directly help LIS to come out of poverty, although this outcome is not very frequent among sample cases. However, if these exemplary cases are coupled with others that mitigate poverty substantially, then this group of initiatives accounts for a fifth of the sample sharing similar characteristics. The most significant income increases for LIS results from their engagement as suppliers or farming producers or producers in associated agribusiness sectors. They are able to improve their productivity as they replace subsistence activities with more profitable operations, joining other LIS producers, eliminating trade intermediaries, and receiving advice or training—from companies that are interested in their products—to apply new techniques, reduce waste or improve product quality. As a result, they command better prices and forge long-lasting business relationships. Other cases of partial poverty relief primarily include LIS cooperatives or associations, whose economic outcomes make it difficult to assume that the individuals involved will overcome poverty completely any time soon. However, these initiatives do create other forms of social value that eventually lead to significant improvements for members' living conditions.

Most initiatives favoring LIS access to goods or services have been launched by companies that have incorporated them as customers. Their strategy hinges on physically reaching rural or excluded urban areas with innovating services, superior quality products, and reduced prices or flexible payment terms. These initiatives successfully eliminate barriers that deprive LIS from adequate market attention. Along with goods and services, the initiatives provide consumption control. Additionally, they prevent LIS from seeking informal, inefficient, more costly, poor in quality, and even unhealthy alternatives.

While improvements are introduced to LIS living conditions (as consumers, customers, or beneficiaries), these ventures are only marginal to eradicating poverty, except for some successful micro-loan and job-training initiatives. In addition, so long as LIS gain no extra income, what they spend on new products or services necessarily means they give up something else, and in this tradeoff, they don't always make the best decisions. Furthermore, these ventures' efforts do not reach the lowest LIS levels, for goods or services offered must be paid for, however little. Thus, market-based initiatives by themselves are insufficient to mitigate poverty for lower LIS strata—i.e., those suffering the most extreme form of poverty.

In experiences featuring LIS cooperatives or associations with no significant income increase, the most outstanding social value created is citizenship promotion. Perhaps the most illustrative cases in this regard are those of recyclers who came together to survive and to gain visibility and social recognition, dramatically raising their self-esteem and changing their living conditions. Citizenship refers to the full exercise of people's duties and rights, such as the right to work, promoted by labor inclusion initiatives especially for excluded, disabled, or at-risk individuals, although other sample ventures indirectly foster employment for people with limited skills as well. Similarly, unregistered individuals can access financial services when they become customers at some organizations and use their invoices to prove their identity and place of residence.

In other cases, LIS organizations provide individuals with a voice to express their demands or a means to bring their products to the market (as a counterpart to their access to goods and services) through supply chains built by supermarkets, efficient stocking companies, or exporters, thereby reducing the number of intermediaries involved. Additionally, LIS gain environmental awareness as a result of the policies implemented by some companies and organizations on matters ranging from personal hygiene all the way to resource management and biodiversity preservation.

Finally, social capital development is clear in initiatives launched by organized low-income people themselves, as well as in labor organizations and, to a lesser extent, companies engaging low-income suppliers. Conversely, the most significant shortcomings in this regard are found in companies that have incorporated LIS as customers or end consumers. For instance, recycling initiatives produce recyclers' empowerment, enhance their leverage, develop comradeship that contributes to social cohesion, and help form social networks that improve their access to relationships and resources of all kinds. In fact, intangible benefits (citizenship promotion and social capital development) are more frequent in initiatives deployed by CSOs or LIS organizations than in ventures launched by companies. Nonetheless, it should be noted that any social initiative ruled by market principles—whether promoted by a company, a non-profit, or a LIS cooperative or association—must maintain a balance between profitability or economic value creation and tangible as well as intangible social value creation, in order to accomplish the greatest and most sustainable impact possible on LIS well-being and human dignity.

Table 10.1
Companies with LIS Customers

CASE	Income increase	Access to goods and services	Citizenship promotion	Social capital building
Activo Humano (employment agency, Chile)	It provides greater income stability for poorly qualified unemployed individuals.		Exercising the right to work.	This organization serves as a liaison among several social groups. Raises expectations and social mobility.
AES-EDC (electricity, Venezuela)	Cost savings through appliance repairs and connections; hazard reduction.	Better and more extended electrical service (pre-paid and other projects) in poor urban areas.	Identity validation for undocumented individuals (through service invoice). Increased security with public area lighting.	Community leadership promotion.
Aguaytía Energy (natural gas, Peru)	Very significant savings (505) through fuel switch (LPG instead of gasoline).	Cheaper and less contaminating fuel.	Environmental awareness.	
Amanco (irrigation systems, Mexico)		Access to modern irrigation systems through associations and loans.	Small farmers' access to markets.	Strengthening local ties and capabilities. LIS organization and empowerment.
Codensa (appliances, Colombia)	Income increase or saving costs.	"Easy" credit to purchase home appliances.	Proof of "citizenship" for individuals with no access to formal markets.	
Colcerámica (ceramic tiles, Colombia)	Savings for LIS customers and income for local promoters (part-time salary) based on sales.	Ceramic tiles for home improvement. Customers previously excluded from the market.	Identity validation for undocumented individuals and credit record.	

Table 10.1
Companies with LIS Customers (continued)

CASE	Income increase	Access to goods and services	Citizenship promotion	Social capital building
Construmex (construction materials, Mexico)		Construction materials, advice, blueprints, housing.		
CruzSalud (health services, Venezuela)	Ability to plan for medical expenses. Lower morbidity leads to job absenteeism reduction. Some local jobs.	More accessible medical care by means of pre-paid plans.	LIS visibility and dignity.	
EDENOR (electricity, Argentina)	Rational energy utilization leads to savings.	Pre-paid electricity, free meters. Access to loans.	Social inclusion. Identity validation (through service invoice).	
Empresario Azteca (micro-loans, Mexico)	Loans (and services) micro-entrepreneurs.	Financing, advice, legal counsel, training.	Information on people with no credit record or collateral.	
Fundación Comunanza (micro-loans, Venezuela)	Loans at better rates than informal credit. Some local jobs.	Loans for subsistence entrepreneurs. Higher rates than formal market, but lower than informal lenders.	Illegal aliens as customers. Risk management (sickness and life insurance).	Flexible, part-time jobs for mothers.
Gas Natural Ban (natural gas, Argentina)	Savings through changes in natural gas consumption.	Natural gas network access (installation costs too high for LIS).	Property deed regularization (through service invoices).	The company engages state agencies, local administrations, CSOs and communities.
Palí (supermarkets, Costa Rica y Nicaragua)	Average 15% savings in groceries as compared to other supermarkets.	Lower or traditional market/fair prices, with better service.		

Table 10.2
Companies with LIS Suppliers

CASE	Income increase	Access to goods and services	Citizenship promotion	Social capital building
Agropalma (oil palm, Brazil)	Family income increase from around US$27 to US$345 a month.	Infrastructure, home appliances, loans, health care, etc.	Steady jobs. Environmental awareness and other, indirect benefits.	Empowerment and strengthened ties with local administrations and neighbors.
Cativen (supermarkets, Venezuela)	Payment guarantee, income stability.	Technical advice, production schedules and quality control.	Formal producer engagement. Access to markets.	Producers' organization.
Explorandes (tourism, Peru)	Income to complement subsistence activities, insufficient to overcome poverty.	Improvements on basic services and infrastructure, training.	Access to markets. Better self-employment conditions.	Female empowerment. Reduced migration, appreciation for traditions.
Hortifruti (supermarkets, Costa Rica)	New techniques secure lower costs and increased income.	Training, access to stocking centers.	Market access through efficiency.	Social inclusion. Farming continuity.
Irupana (organic products, Bolivia)	20% overprice for organic products accounts for 50% of family income.	Strategic alliances for advisory services and financing for producers.	Market share: access to organic retail chain in Bolivia and international markets.	Community development; promotion for social entrepreneurs and SMEs.
Mariposas de Costa Rica (CRES)	LIS double their income and overcome poverty.	Access to goods as a result of higher income.	Access to international markets.	Trust-based relationships with suppliers and customers. Safety reduces transaction costs.
Palmas del Espino (oil palm, Peru)	Farming wage until palm trees yield fruits. Clear prospects for overcoming poverty.	Loan access, formal land ownership, technical advice.	Legal livelihood (foregoing illegal coca plantations).	Social inclusion, conflict resolution.

Table 10.3
CSOs with Market-based Initiatives Involving LIS

CASE	Income increase	Access to goods and services	Citizenship promotion	Social capital building
Andrómines (second-hand clothing, Spain)	Income creation or increase for groups at risk of exclusion (working poor).	Second-hand clothes and other products.	Exercise of right to work. Environmental awareness (waste reduction and management).	A bridge to cross the divide between unemployment and labor inclusion. Training and support.
Fundación FUTUR (food services, Spain)	Income creation or increase for relatively poor or socially and labor excluded individuals.		Right to work for worker-users. Organic, local and fair-trade product promotion. Environmental awareness.	Ties to networks and organizations with similar social goals exploited by worker-users.
Instituto Nacional de Capacitación Profesional—INACAP (job training, Chile)	Indirectly, through education or training (after program completion).	Quality higher education, with no admission tests (for segments that could not access education otherwise).	Social inclusion. Technical education upgrade.	Institutional agreements to grant scholarships or loans. Social mobility.
La Fageda (dairy products, Spain)	Income creation or increase for mentally challenged individuals and their families.	Assistance services for mentally challenged individuals (job therapy and monitored housing).	Access to labor market (very low turnover). Recognition and dignity.	Strong ties to organization, which employs over 20% of the local mentally challenged population.
Oro Verde Corporation (environment-ally-friendly mining, Colombia)	Miners receive a 2% "bonus" over international gold prices.	Greater consumption and trade as a result of income increase. Access to information technologies.	Social and environmental impact monitoring.	Empowerment, individual capability strengthening, and engagement in public affairs.
Salvation Army (second-hand clothing, Argentina)	Savings on used goods purchases. Only resellers could escape poverty.	Clothes, furniture, home appliances, second-hand books.	Charity and pastoral work; servicing basic needs.	Ties as a result of shared goals.

Table 10.4
LIS Cooperatives or Associations

CASE	Income increase	Access to goods and services	Citizenship promotion	Social capital building
APAEB (hemp fiber carpets, Brazil)	Very significant income increase. Poverty definitely overcome in 1990s.	Education and several other services.	Dignity. Full citizenship exercise.	Empowerment. Local capability development.
Asmare (recycling, Brazil)	Members obtain at least minimum wages.	Infrastructure, food, health.	Citizenship, self-esteem, trust, etc. Employment re-entry (other activities), education, housing.	Recyclers' engagement. Social inclusion.
CIAP (handicrafts, Peru)	Members satisfy their basic needs but do not escape poverty. Other entrepreneurial ventures built on this experience.	Fair prices, loans and market access (incomplete regularization).	Artisans' act approval. It contributes to eliminate distance, language, and other barriers.	Empowerment, female appreciation, entrepreneurship.
Coopa-Roca (handicrafts, Brazil)	Stable artisans (fewer than 20) get minimum wage.	Working at home, education, trips, etc.	Only job opportunity for older women and mothers.	Local capability and safety strengthening.
Cooperativa de Recicladores Porvenir (recycling, Colombia)	Not significant. Not all value added is recognized.	Basic goods, knowledge, etc.	Dignity, self-esteem, etc. Recognition for recyclers. 10% are senior citizens.	Capability and leverage strengthening. Engagement in public affairs.
El Ceibo (recycling, Argentina)	Variable, but below poverty line. Estimated at 20% over non-affiliated recyclers' income.	Employment for vulnerable population (at risk, extreme poverty). Training.	Work, dignity and recognition. Raised environmental and public cleanliness awareness.	Improved organizational capability. Sense of belonging to a community. Better relationships with neighbors and government.
Recolectores de Frutos Silvestres (wild fruits, Chile)	Steady monthly income. Elimination of intermediaries and product portfolio expansion boost profits.	Training in management and organization; access to technologies.	Visibility, dignity and innovations.	Recyclers' engagement.

Notes

1. The Private Sector Mapping (PSM) project shows a remarkable effort to document, in thirteen different countries of Latin America and the Caribbean (Argentina, Bolivia, Brazil, Chile, Colombia, Ecuador, Peru and Trinidad and Tobago), the different ongoing initiatives of inclusive ventures. "A Firm-Level Approach to Majority Market Business: Private Sector Mapping (PSM) Project Final Report" (Washington, D.C.: SNV Netherlands Development Organization and Inter-American Development Bank, 2008).

2. Nancy E. Landrum, "Advancing the 'Base of the Pyramid' Debate," *Strategic Management Review* 1, no. 1 (2007): 4.

3. Jed Emerson and Sheila Bonini, "The Blended Value Map: Tracking the Intersects and Opportunities of Economic, Social and Environmental Value Creation," www.blendedvalue.org, http://www.blendedvalue.org/Papers/97.aspx.

4. C. K. Prahalad and Stuart Hart, "The Fortune at the Bottom of the Pyramid," *Strategy + Business* 1, no. 26 (2002).

5. C. K. Prahalad, *The Fortune at the Bottom of the Pyramid: Eradicating Poverty through Profits* (Upper Saddle River, NJ: Wharton School Publishing, 2005).

6. According to Prahalad: "The poor cannot participate in the benefits of globalization without an active engagement of private enterprises with the base of the pyramid and also due to the fact that the poor lack such products and services that represent global quality standards. They need to be exposed to the range and variety of opportunities that inclusive globalization can provide. The poor represent a 'latent market' for goods and services. The active engagement of private enterprises at the base of the pyramid is a critical element in creating inclusive capitalism, as private-sector competition for this market will foster attention to the poor as consumers and it will create choices for them." Ibid., 8.

7. Allen L. Hammond et al., *The Next 4 Billion: Market Size and Business Strategy at the Base of the Pyramid* (Washington, DC: World Resources Institute and International Finance Corporation, 2007), 21.

8. SEKN, ed., *Effective Management of Social Enterprises Lessons from Businesses and Civil Society Organizations in Iberoamerica* (Cambridge, MA: Harvard University Press with David Rockefeller Center for Latin American Studies, 2006), 266.

9. Herman B Leonard, "When is Doing Business with the Poor Good—for the Poor? A Household and National Income Accounting Approach," in *Business Solutions for the Global Poor: Creating Social and Economic Value*, ed. Kasturi Rangan, et al. (San Francisco, CA: Jossey-Bass, 2007).

10. Ralf Dahrendorf, *Life Chances, Approaches to Social and Political Theory* (London, UK: Weidenfeld and Nicolson, 1979).

11. SEKN, ed. *Effective Management of Social Enterprises Lessons from Businesses and Civil Society Organizations in Iberoamerica* (Cambridge, MA: Harvard University Press with David Rockefeller Center for Latin American Studies, 2006), 291; Tzvetan Todorov, *La vida en común. Ensayo de antropología general* (Madrid: Taurus, 1995), 35.

12. Felipe Portocarrero et al., *Capital social y democracia. Explorando normas, valores y redes sociales en el Perú* (Lima, Perú: Universidad del Pacífico, Centro de Investigación, 2006), 89.

13. Albert Hirschman, *Enfoques alternativos sobre la sociedad de mercado y otros ensayos recientes* (México D.F.: Fondo de Cultura Económica, 1989), 80–87.

14. Ross Gittell and Avis Vidal, *Community Organization: Building Social Capital as a Development Strategy* (London: Sage, 1998), 10.

15. SEKN, ed. *Effective Management of Social Enterprises Lessons from Businesses and Civil Society Organizations in Iberoamerica* (Cambridge, MA: Harvard University Press with David Rockefeller Center for Latin American Studies, 2006), 309.

16. Allen L. Hammond et al., *The Next 4 Billion: Market Size and Business Strategy at the Base of the Pyramid* (Washington, DC: World Resources Institute and International Finance Corporation, 2007), 14.

17. Aneel G. Karnani, "Fortune at the Bottom of the Pyramid: A Mirage" (Working Paper No. 1035, University of Michigan, Stephen M. Ross School of Business, 2006).

18. Herman B. Leonard, "When Is Doing Business with the Poor Good—for the Poor? A Household and National Income Accounting Approach," in *Business Solutions for the Global Poor: Creating Social and Economic Value*, ed. Kasturi Rangan, et al. (San Francisco, CA: Jossey-Bass, 2007); Aneel G. Karnani, "Fortune at the Bottom of the Pyramid: A Mirage" (Working Paper No. 1035, University of Michigan, Stephen M. Ross School of Business, 2006), 28.

19. Allen L. Hammond et al., *The Next 4 Billion: Market Size and Business Strategy at the Base of the Pyramid* (Washington, DC: World Resources Institute and International Finance Corporation, 2007), 4.

20. Nancy E. Landrum, "Advancing the 'Base of the Pyramid' Debate," *Strategic Management Review* 1, no. 1 (2007): 3; Aneel G. Karnani, "Fortune at the Bottom of the Pyramid: A Mirage" (Working Paper No. 1035, University of Michigan, Stephen M. Ross School of Business, 2006), 17–19.

21. Herman B Leonard, "When Is Doing Business with the Poor Good—for the Poor? A Household and National Income Accounting Approach," in *Business Solutions for the Global Poor: Creating Social and Economic Value*, ed. Kasturi Rangan, et al. (San Francisco, CA: Jossey-Bass, 2007).

22. Allen L. Hammond et al., *The Next 4 Billion: Market Size and Business Strategy at the Base of the Pyramid* (Washington, DC: World Resources Institute and International Finance Corporation, 2007), 6.

23. Ibid., 6 and 30.

24. Aneel G. Karnani, "Fortune at the Bottom of the Pyramid: A Mirage" (Working Paper No. 1035, University of Michigan, Stephen M. Ross School of Business, 2006), 25.

25. Allen L. Hammond et al., *The Next 4 Billion: Market Size and Business Strategy at the Base of the Pyramid* (Washington, DC: World Resources Institute and International Finance Corporation, 2007), 25.

26. Nancy E. Landrum, "Advancing the 'Base of the Pyramid' Debate," *Strategic Management Review* 1, no. 1 (2007): 4.

27. Ibid.: 5.

28. Aneel G. Karnani, "Fortune at the Bottom of the Pyramid: A Mirage" (Working Paper No. 1035, University of Michigan, Stephen M. Ross School of Business, 2006), 17.

29. Nancy E. Landrum, "Advancing the 'Base of the Pyramid' Debate," *Strategic Management Review* 1, no. 1 (2007): 3.

30. "To be sure, the greatest benefit of a free economy is that it produces products that consumers value—and their voluntary purchase and use of these products is the best indication we can reasonably expect to have that the products are producing perceived consumer value." Herman B. Leonard, "When Is Doing Business with the Poor Good—for the Poor? A Household and National Income Accounting Approach," in *Business Solutions for the Global Poor: Creating Social and Economic Value*, ed. Kasturi Rangan, et al. (San Francisco, CA: Jossey-Bass, 2007).

31. Aneel G. Karnani, "Fortune at the Bottom of the Pyramid: A Mirage" (Working Paper No. 1035, University of Michigan, Stephen M. Ross School of Business, 2006), 17.

32. Ibid., 18–19.

33. Elizabeth. Jelin, "Igualdad y diferencia: dilemas de la ciudadanía de las mujeres en América Latina," *Ágora. Cuadernos de estudios políticos* 3, no. 7 (1997): 189.

34. IIDH and CEPAL, *La igualdad de los modernos. Reflexiones acerca de la realización de los derechos económicos, sociales y culturales en América Latina* (San José: IIDH, CEPAL, 1997), 20.

35. Grupo Técnico Nacional de Ciudadanía Ambiental, "Estrategia Nacional de Promoción de la Ciudadanía Ambiental," CONAM, http://www.conam.gob.pe /documentos/ciudadania/index.asp.

36. Allen L. Hammond et al., *The Next 4 Billion: Market Size and Business Strategy at the Base of the Pyramid* (Washington, DC: World Resources Institute and International Finance Corporation, 2007), 4.

37. For a 'theoretical genealogy' of this notion, see Felipe Portocarrero et al., *Capital social y democracia. Explorando normas, valores y redes sociales en el Perú* (Lima, Perú: Universidad del Pacífico, Centro de Investigación, 2006).

38. Christiaan Grootaert and Thierry van Bastelaer, "Understanding and Measuring Social Capital: A Synthesis of Findings and Recommendations from the Social Capital Initiative" (Washington DC: World Bank, 2001), 1–31.

39. CEPAL, *Cohesión social: inclusión y sentido de pertenencia en América Latina y el Caribe* (Santiago de Chile: Naciones Unidas, 2007), 14.

40. Felipe Portocarrero et al., *Capital social y democracia. Explorando normas, valores y redes sociales en el Perú* (Lima, Perú: Universidad del Pacífico, Centro de Investigación, 2006).

41. CEPAL, *Cohesión social: inclusión y sentido de pertenencia en América Latina y el Caribe* (Santiago de Chile: Naciones Unidas, 2007), 17.

42. Patricia Márquez and Ezequiel Reficco, "The Unsuspected Player: Small Firms in Business with Low Income Sectors," in *Small Firms, Global Markets: Competitive Challenges in the New Economy*, ed. Jerry Haar and Jörg Meyer-Stamer (London and New York: Palgrave Macmillan, 2007).

11
Conclusions: Developing Inclusive Business

Patricia Márquez, Ezequiel Reficco, and Gabriel Berger

This book started out by recounting the stories of Marcela, a subsistence gatherer of wild fruit and mushrooms in Chile's Bio Bio region, and Jose, a Mexican migrant worker in the United States. Successive chapters examined how, in less than five years, with the support of the non-profit organization TAC, Marcela's little-valued work became part of a collective, going concern that conducted market transactions with companies in Chile and abroad. In probing several LIS experiences as suppliers, in both rural and urban contexts, we searched out how they add value to goods and services, and how they came to earn a fair income once integrated in dynamic value chains. The outcomes of such ventures were assessed at the individual, communal, and corporate levels.

In those opening pages, we also explored how Cemex shaped its Construmex initiative to address the needs of LIS consumers like Jose, who earned a living in the United States but had his plans and family back in Mexico. Construmex enables one of the world's leading cement companies to serve low-income consumers in communities of migrants dispersed throughout the United States. In-depth study of these consumers' needs, patterned on a previous blueprint (Patrimonio Hoy), allowed Construmex to bring a fresh mindset to a company dedicated to selling cement and home improvement: that is, servicing low-income consumers with a range of services including remittance transfers and credit. All told, SEKN authors scrutinized 33 market initiatives, whereby different kinds of organizations shaped challenging business models to engage LIS as consumers, suppliers, or business partners.

Market initiatives involving LIS cast organizations and individuals in a variety of roles. In the above chapters we have distinguished ventures developed by the poor, seeking to strengthen and scale up their business models ("organized LIS as producers") in order to move away from poverty, from those created by formal organizations to generate profits or fulfill their social mission (organization to LIS). The former operate at the very base of the income pyramid—indigent urban groups and the rural poor.

In this final chapter, we revisit the main findings of each of the preceding chapters, paying particular attention to the issue areas that structured our research, namely, the identification of: (a) the organizational forms, business models, and capabilities that proved most effective in engaging the poor; (b) the barriers that hinder this connection, and the strategies that help to overcome them; (c) the collaborative relations that support these initiatives and make them viable. In structuring these findings, we reproduce the modules that comprise the book—actors, sectors, and value generation. We then present an integrative view of critical factors in developing sustainable, socially inclusive business models. Specific business models and management practices suggested for developing market initiatives with LIS should help bring about what has been deemed a more inclusive kind of capitalism that "spreads wealth as it creates wealth" and "empowers the poor as it generates returns for investors."[1]

Actors

We now look at the different actors that took part in the 33 experiences examined: multinational and large companies, small and medium-size firms, and social enterprises.

Large and Multinational Companies

Much of the BOP literature holds that multinational companies (MNCs) command the kind of financial, infrastructure, and organizational resources required to serve poor consumers profitably. Fourteen of our sample cases were large firms, including multinationals providing services and products to low-incomes sectors. The results these large organizations achieved by the market initiatives with LIS varied widely from case to case. Few firms serving LIS found the activity profitable and readily scalable. Others considered that uneconomical relationships with low-income groups could be converted into profitable exchanges, although reaching scale implied deep transformations and commitments not always within their control. Building viable inclusive businesses appears to require a significant gestation period, during which a series of interrelated managerial, financial, sociocultural, geographical, and even political barriers may have to be overcome. Before a business focused on enlisting LIS becomes a going concern, a strategic path must be mapped, followed by a learning process that can prove challenging. Moreover, as chapter 2 showed, even the best-laid strategy needed successive iterations of adjustments, which eventually did lead to viable models. The chances of success in this process were substantially conditioned by the presence of specific enablers, both external and internal.

External enablers refer to conditions in the business environment that could facilitate overcoming barriers. The presence of existing organized communities or local leaders can be a make-or-break factor when it comes to gaining access to clients or developing appropriate distribution channels. The innovative use of preexisting technologies—such as the devices that enabled the Argentine utility Edenor to offer pre-paid electricity to LIS customers—allowed for significant savings in transactions costs. The quality of governmental regulation has also proven determinant. As Carlos Rufin points out, in any LIS market initiative the government "will make its presence felt, whether we like it or not."[2] This was most evident in the case of utility companies such as Argentina's Edenor or Venezuela's AES-Electricidad de Caracas, where inflexible regulation has curtailed scaling up the ventures.

Other enablers were internal to the organization. Chief among them was the culture of the organization. When a commitment to develop market initiatives to serve the poor was truly embedded in the beliefs and everyday practices of the organization, change proved feasible. Amanco, part of Grupo Nueva, was founded by a leading philanthropist, an outspoken pioneer in the global movement for sustainability. Accordingly, Amanco's culture and leadership revolved around the idea of business for social betterment and delivering along a triple bottom line. Company management had a mandate to reach 10 percent of sales from business with LIS by 2008.

Such a culture enables innovation and new ways of management. In order to market tiles to LIS consumers, Colcerámica had to link with the informal economy of urban slums. The corporation had to learn to operate in a setting in which it had no experience; to deal with issues management had never before considered; to recruit and train a different kind of field level manager; to build relationships where control was not always in company hands; and to work closely with non-traditional actors such as social entrepreneurs, community organizations, and a sales force made up of local women who worked part-time.

Changing "old ways" can encounter stiff resistance in large corporations.[3] Consider utility companies, where the pervasive dominant logic was that bill collection was to take place either through a local bank or at company offices. Mechanisms such as prepaid systems and community partnerships to ease payments ran against the grain of their organizational DNA. Unless engaging LIS becomes truly internalized as a core component of what the company is meant to do, the chances that these projects can move beyond the pilot stage appear unlikely.

Finally, a critical internal enabler for developing LIS initiatives in large companies is the existence of mechanisms for knowledge management; that is, transforming tacit knowledge into organizational know-how and effective processes for serving LIS. Our case sample shows that in large companies, the process of drawing useful lessons from experience and turning them into significant know-how is threatened by discontinuities at various points. A group of professionals working in an initiative might identify its key aspects but fail to bring the pieces together, as these individuals operate in different departments; information gathered by field staff may be incorrectly interpreted by higher-level managers with different sensitivities to what is happening in low-income sectors, or who have other priorities. Valuable insights obtained from pilot trials may be lost in making the transition to systematic management guidelines when they move up the organizational pyramid. Such failings illustrate gaps in the organization's learning loop. Preventing them is critical: it might only take one such discontinuity to kill a project.

In sum, success attained in generating economic and social value among large and multinational companies undertaking LIS market initiatives varied significantly from case to case. Our sample confirms the great potential of large corporations in inclusive ventures. At the same time, as chapter 2 showed, to a large extent this potential is not yet fully actualized, particularly when bringing ad-hoc models up to scale. The mixed results in profitability (see chapter 10, on economic value creation) are certainly part of the reason why we have not made much progress in scaling up these ventures. Building inclusive businesses tests companies' internal capabilities—its culture, leadership, and management skills. Such strong demands can discourage large companies from upping the stakes in LIS initiatives, which are not necessarily perceived as central to business survival.

SME and Startups

Six experiences in our study of small and mid-sized enterprises (SME)—some of them startups—bring out what it takes to develop market initiatives that both generate profits and shape social value: mission centered on LIS, flexibility, proximity, and capability to generate profits as well as social value. SMEs centered on targeting LIS as consumers appear to employ processes that are simpler, leaner, with lower fixed costs, and expressly conceived to deliver goods and services to consumers with little purchasing power. By starting with a clean slate, there is no need to alter the "company way of doing things." SMEs and startups focused on inclusive business tend to be closer to the poor than large corporations, and thus better understand their needs and develop empathy. Small firms which place LIS at the core of their mission and business model, interacting closely with the targeted group, are likely to maximize their chance for success. Considering the experience of an admittedly small group of startups and SMEs, and taking account of each context, the development of "local" solutions may offer more promising returns than seeking "global" reach.

SME cases in our sample are led by entrepreneurs with a clear business imperative: building a profitable business in which societal needs are also fulfilled: economic and social value are viewed as complementary. Commitment to society's betterment by doing business with LIS became a driving force in defining the strategy deployed to run operations—even when, for some, this meant passing up other opportunities. Their innovative business models entailed building markets from the ground up. They created markets: they saw opportunity where others only saw frustration and scarcity. In some cases, they proved the viability of a business model that others later replicated. Invariably, designing innovative business models involved the shaping of new practices by trial and error, learning from experience, and sheer resoluteness to overcome obstacles.

Doing business in Latin America's sprawling urban slums is daunting. The masses of LIS consumers that live there must put on with endless unmet aspirations, about which little is known, in a setting where violent crime, illicit trade, and lack of basic public services is the norm. Some of the SMEs examined here rose to the challenge of building viable business models to operate in such difficult settings, and upon discovering that LIS encompass a variety of market segments, they catered to this population through ad-hoc models. Perhaps due to their size and characteristics, these organizations effectively maneuvered within the sometimes disparate and inexorably related worlds of the formal and informal economy. Their suppleness suggests that this organizational model may hold greater prospects for undertaking profitable market initiatives with LIS than either large companies or social enterprises. To be sure, the initiatives studied are young; their capacity to become going concerns has yet to be proven. When the moment comes to expand and scale up, these startups will certainly face significant managerial bottlenecks and difficulties in gaining access to capital. However, they still offer valuable lessons in the quest for social inclusion.

Social Enterprises

This study grouped civil society organizations (CSOs) and cooperatives under the term "social enterprise," defined as mission-driven private organizations that rely primarily on market-based strategies to raise the necessary funds to create social value for their members or communities. In order to fulfill their social missions they have to develop "a business perspective." Like-lihood of success in their market engagements increased as they developed expertise in properly reading the market, which in turn often implied adjust-ments in their managerial practices and programs. They may have had to reinvent or redefine the organization's business model, to diversify into new markets, or to adjust the value proposition of their product or service. A good example of acute market reading are those ventures that capitalized market opportunities of fair trade institutions that favored the LIS origin of their products.

Social enterprises feature a capacity often lacking in multinational and large companies when it comes to engaging the poor: patience, deep knowl-edge of LIS, and trust. In their market initiatives, these organizations lever-age those assets, strengthening their source of legitimacy and seeking financial sustainability and autonomy. Nonetheless, as they strived to become "market-oriented," significant tensions with their social missions emerged. This might not be much of a discovery, as it follows the conven-tional split of the for-profit versus non-profit organizations. Spain's La Fageda, which seeks to bring mentally challenged individuals into the labor force, provides a most telling example: its first step was to map business opportunities, but lack of experience in understanding demand led to busi-ness failure in the two fields it tried: religious artistry and nurseries. It then turned to dairy products, launching a yogurt business that eventually became competitive in a very crowded market. La Fageda experience shows that social enterprises that seek to leverage the market need more than a good idea and a business plan; ideas must be aligned with suitable organi-zational capabilities and resources.

Some of the "organized-LIS-as-producers" initiatives featured in our study were undertaken by very poor individuals, even indigents. Although they lacked access to most basic needs, their spirit of survival and entre-preneurial zeal materialized into market initiatives through support from CSOs and, in some cases, government. The growth of these ventures was favored by a combination of circumstances: LIS performed a labor-inten-sive activity that earned them a living, in most cases by individuals with no other employment options (e.g. wild fruit gatherers, garbage collectors and sorters, artisan miners, etc.); supportive organizations were at hand; and market demand was clearly in evidence. Organized social enterprises of LIS-as-producers showed a capacity to leverage labor as a community resource and keen willingness to work closely with CSOs and government agencies. However, they usually lacked the skills needed to add value to output through forward integration, or by catering to specific demand niches, or even to interact effectively with large corporations. In these cases, "bridging" organizations helped to realize the sourcing opportunity.

On the downside, only modest economic gains were generally achieved by "organized LIS-as-producers" initiatives, given the many barriers faced by these groups in raising output and deploying bargaining power. Despite some progress, internal practices remain informal, drawing largely on personal ties and a relatively weak knowledge base. Their stock of capital has proven insufficient to expand operations: except for APAEB in Brazil and CIAP in Peru, the "organized-LIS-as-producers" social enterprises included in our study have not achieved great success in scaling up and expanding operations.

On the upside, however, some of these social enterprises showed a creative spark, reversing negative stereotypes by capitalizing on themes that appealed to up-market consumers—such as "native grown," "*favela* creation," and "local, legendary crafts." Even if their economic results were meager, they did succeed in linking with vibrant business ecosystems, gaining autonomy, empowerment, and self-esteem in the process. Skeptics will legitimately argue that little has been accomplished, for the targeted beneficiaries remain poor. A more benign view, on the other hand, will reveal that through their efforts LIS shifted from passive waiting for assistance or charity to active self-reliance. Turning indigents into budding micro-entrepreneurs striving to improve their lives is certainly a noteworthy step in the tortuous landscape of poverty and inequality.

Ecosystems

Our study reaffirmed that we live in a relational society, where the limits of the efforts by single organizations are becoming increasingly evident. We took the analysis beyond the single organization to encompass the work of partners, and beyond that, to include the context in which the alliance operated. The concept of "ecosystem" was defined as economic community supported by a foundation of interacting organizations involved in the production of goods and services. It is broader than value chains or value systems, in that it encompasses non-linear interactions that fall outside economic production. All members share a stake in the well-being of the community, but contribute to it in different ways: they may provide intellectual capital, governance, or social capital, besides creating wealth. Participants are interdependent, and their fates are intertwined. Business ecosystems tend to rely on the leadership of a pivotal organization that performs a stewardship role, aligning the behavior of other actors through positive incentives.

This is realized through *platforms*: assets that the leader offers to other ecosystem participants, to make interaction fluid and effective. In our sample, these platforms consisted of shared standards and practices that helped organize and support participants' activities. Platforms were prevalent in initiatives that targeted LIS as producers—like the one led by Venezuelan retailer Cativen—but some were also featured in initiatives that engaged the poor as consumers—such as Colombia's Colcerámica.

These platforms were successful only to the extent that they served to deliver ongoing, solid win-win benefits to all participants involved. By doing that, many pivotal organizations were able to redefine relations with key stakeholders and reshape their environment as they improved their bottom line. Platforms served to anchor expectations, providing stability in turbulent environments where neither the market nor government had a strong presence. In many cases, platforms filled in institutional voids through the construction of structured system of conventions, giving participants a sense of predictability and allowing successive interactions that sparked economic activity.

Such a pivotal organization could benefit from being at the center of this web of interactions. By simplifying interactions, platforms lowered transaction costs for all players. This is critical in inclusive business, as they operate with low margins per transaction and need scale to reach profitability. In many of our cases, the ecosystem leader needed to "build an interlocutor" in order to have a fruitful dialog: often this entailed creating or strengthening cooperatives and producers' associations, which could take a seat at the table as an autonomous partner. Additionally, shared platforms allowed pivotal organizations to accelerate returns and capture economies of time.

Moreover, the feeble presence of market and state results in weak or nonexistent contract enforcement. Engaging all members of the economic community can be the first step towards building a normative web of consensus-based responsibilities and duties. This is no substitute for a well-run judiciary, but it can be a cost-effective second best, which can trigger a virtuous process of wealth creation and demolition of exclusion barriers. Our cases show that this is best done through the leveraging of existing social networks and leadership, particularly when they are given a strong stake in venture success.

Finally, our analysis showed that committing to the organizational ecosystem can be an effective way to actively shape an organization's environment, changing the "rules of the game" under which it operates—something unthinkable for most organizations acting on their own.

Some of the sample organizations engaged external players for specific goals—such as opening up new distribution or sale channels or diversifying into new markets—while keeping strategic control of the initiative. We termed these ventures "unilaterally managed value chains." Other managers considered that the socially inclusive initiative had to rely on capabilities that could only be constructed collectively. In these cases, the organization that led the effort granted different levels of decision-making authority to its partners. In some cases, that amounted to *coordination* of activities between the organization and its low-income partners, with the company retaining overall control of strategic decisions. In others, it went one step further to encompass *consensus-based* decision-making on a more equal basis; in a third group, it reached the point of equal *governance*, with company and external partners negotiating all strategic decisions democratically.

The co-creation of shared value requires putting in place ad-hoc structures and processes, but it also calls for something else: the shaping of a new type of relationship with the poor. Our cases suggest the benefits of going beyond a market-transaction framework and building long-term, embedded relationships. This approach, termed here "business-friendships," has a strong human, non-economic component. It focuses more on potential and possibility than on assets and resources. It is willing to accompany and empower; it is patient, and it refrains from exploiting weaknesses or systematically maximizing short-term gains. Instead, it seeks to build material rewards that "satisfice" ("satisfy" + "suffice") all parties involved.

This study also highlighted the limitations of partnerships and embeddedness. As chapter 2 made clear, embedded relationships are context-specific assets, which are difficult to replicate and scale up. They can be useful to tear down historic barriers and capture elusive tacit knowledge in opaque environments, but they do not necessarily facilitate standardization and mass production. We go back to this theme below, in the discussion of recurring tensions in inclusive business ventures.

Sectors

Several cases in our sample were found in agribusiness and recycling, where LIS have traditionally been predominant actors; and public utilities (electricity and gas) where they have been invisible or poorly served. In agribusiness and recycling, challenges centered on integrating LIS in value chains; whereas in public utilities, companies experienced managerial dilemmas as they sought to broaden services to LIS consumers.

These sectors differed substantially, not only in that they engaged LIS in different capacities—producers, suppliers, and consumers—but also in that

LIS participants varied in their socio-economic condition. For example, while agribusiness initiatives engaged the rural poor, recycling initiatives engaged urban indigents who barely survived in waste collection. As chapter 8 explains, the two groups feature marked differences and require tailored approaches. Public utilities cases encompass both urban and rural poor. Below we review the challenges faced by these initiatives, and extract some lessons of relevance to other industries.

Utilities
Undeniably, improving access by the poor to basic services such as potable water, electricity, and gas affects substantially their quality of life; equally important, but less cited, it may also spur economic activity and social change. In much of Latin America, these services in poor communities are deficient, and sometimes enmeshed in social and political conflicts. Business models devised to improve service delivery in the region would offer more than simply a potential opportunity for growth; for some public utility companies, serving the poor has become a strategic imperative, where failure may threaten the company's entire investment in the country concerned.[4]

In our study of electricity companies, the challenge for them was how to turn large numbers of LIS households, long used to tapping power from public lamp post wiring, into paying customers, and most important, how to persuade them to keep paying. Companies competed against other products and services as poor consumers struggled to make the best of their meager or erratic income to fulfill their needs. In the case of power supply, prior to the new initiative most LIS had some access to electricity, even if it was obtained illegally and the quality was poor; accordingly, the choice of becoming a paying customer depended on whether the new service added real value. Gas companies competed with other sources of fuel; even if gas was cheaper, consumers had to bear substantial installation costs so it was essential to make clear to poor consumers the advantages and savings they could obtain over time by remaining customers.

Market initiatives in the public utility sector not only entailed understanding the consumer. Three power and light companies underwent significant internal changes as they sought to better serve urban consumers: first, as they moved from a technical mindset to a consumer orientation; and second, as they crafted the proper value proposition, key to the development of the new consumers' "willingness to pay."

Regardless of whether utilities were state or privately owned, a technical or engineering mindset had historically governed management decision-making. They were led by professionally trained engineers and dealt with

LIS consumers much in the same way they handled service to paying customers: by reviewing applications for service submitted to company offices
together with supporting documents, installing meters, billing, and cutting
power if payment was not made on time. Few LIS customers in slum communities could provide supporting documents—usually a property title or
notarized rental contract—for most of their dwellings were built without
proper authorization. Such communities dealt directly with the power supplier only when a company crew removed illegal connections and cut off
electricity.

Change in the organizational ethos was a first step. Company management had to shift from a "people come to us" attitude to a "customer orientation." Understanding how LIS earn a living and why a new value
proposition was required to turn free riders into paying customers came
next. Management practices had to be adjusted to ease payments by offering flexible conditions and developing LIS-centered payment systems. It
was a change from distributing a commodity to selling a consumer-oriented
service. The three power and light companies in our study made big strides
in their efforts to service the poor. However, only Codensa in Colombia was
able to reach significant scale. It remains to be seen whether this company's
market experience with LIS consumers truly evolves into fully-fledged business ventures, or eventually falls under the CSR portfolio.

The two gas companies market their product in competition with alternative substitutes. A value proposition that appealed to LIS needs and wants
was central to their success. Both Gas Natural Ban and Aguaytía had to undertake investments in market development in order to augment their customer
base. Their success ultimately depended on their ability to generate trust and
adapt to the peculiarities of specific LIS communities. At times, this was
achieved by working closely with community leaders and local actors.

Agribusiness

In Latin America, poor *campesinos* generally till undersized plots of land, are
often at the mercy of unscrupulous intermediaries, or work as day laborers
in company-owned plantations. For the most part, the region's rural poor
are devoid of basic public services, with little hope for a good education or
improved living conditions. In the nine agribusiness initiatives examined
in our study, each involving rural LIS, their role as producers and workers
was redefined. The organizations leading those ventures sought to generate
economic and social value by leveraging the advantages of vertical integration from source of supply to end-consumer, changing relations between
participating actors, and developing new models.

Companies and cooperatives worked with LIS producers to eliminate intermediaries, provide higher earnings, and improve market potential. This implied investments in better infrastructure such as new roads or telecommunication hubs. Significant challenges also emerged in addressing management capabilities and technical know-how: better product quality and consistency, products shaped to meet consumer preferences, finely tuned supply and demand levels. To meet these challenges firms needed to be involved in new partnerships, and contribute to the development of LIS-led organizations that encompassed individual producers and enhanced their productive capacities. Our nine cases in agribusiness show that direct integration of LIS with dynamic value chains created opportunity for small farmers, as they linked more effectively with large-scale markets. Such integration may also help to minimize the risks taken by poor suppliers worldwide, who often suffer the most from changes in market conditions—from price drops of commodities to foul weather. APAEB, a Brazilian social enterprise, evolved into an integrated organization exporting 60 percent of its sisal output. By adding value to a primary product through industrial processing, APAEB was able to reach significant scale and endurance. Support from development agencies allowed the organization to garner sufficient capital as well as technical and managerial capabilities.

Large companies, given their greater capital and market intelligence resources, may fare better than smaller ones in promoting an effective value chain for the benefit of small producers. Vertical integration in these cases allowed them to better match consumer demands to local production. Smaller operations such as Irupana in Bolivia revealed the burdens of lacking capital and having insufficient know-how and capacity to connect with market demands in an international arena. Yet some smaller organizations found success in new market niches, which they worked out through LIS initiatives. Rural LIS proved to be reliable suppliers for non-traditional, export-oriented businesses, such as silk cocoons or organic Andean products.

Solid Waste Recycling

The chapter on recycling (chapter 7) confirmed the contribution that these initiatives make to overcome social exclusion. On the one hand, the economic results of these initiatives, usually run by their beneficiaries, have not been impressive. The benefits distributed among workers remain below the cost of living of those countries: the monthly income of the recyclers in our sample remains 20 percent of the cost of living in Argentina, 31 percent in Colombia, and 52 percent in Brazil. On the other hand, however, it is important to keep in mind that wealth creation is only one of their goals. The gains made in self-esteem and social reintegration into the mainstream of society are at least as important. Here economic value is only a means towards a different end.

Our study revealed a painful reality: recyclers fail to capture most of the value they generate as participants in the value chain of urban waste, as the case of the Colombian cooperative El Porvenir shows. If the value created[5] by each segment of the value chain is divided by the price paid for its supplies, recyclers capture only 32.7 percent of that value; the companies that hoard waste to gain scale capture 53.3 percent, those who transport it in large quantities capture 73.9 percent, the industries that process it keep 60 percent. According to the authors, the managerial weakness of these cooperatives diminish their bargaining position and prevent them from extracting better exchange terms, or capturing some of that value through vertical integration.

The profit margins of urban waste recycling are determined by two critical factors: upstream, the capacity to gain scale in the intake of waste and implement efficient logistics and operations; downstream, in the output, the capacity to add value to those supplies so as to improve the exchange terms. Most of the cases analyzed have sought to gain scale through alliances with large waste producers, and are trying to rationalize their processes so as to decrease costs per unit. The main difficulty is to add value. Most of these organizations lack the necessary capabilities to integrate forward, although that this is where the largest opportunities lie. This study also confirms the critical importance of external enablers such as the regulatory framework. Effective regulation can create the incentives to stimulate the work of these cooperatives. But more than that, to improve the living conditions of waste recyclers it is crucial to increase the managerial capacity of those enterprises. The cooperatives from Brazil (Asmare) and Argentina (El Ceibo) benefited from favorable regulations, which granted them explicit or implicit subsidies or benefits. By contrast, the Colombian cooperative (El Porvenir) lacks any public support. For different reasons, both Asmare and El Porvenir have gone further in the process of adding value to supplies than El Ceibo, which limits itself to gathering waste and selling it to intermediaries. Comparatively, the first two can distribute more benefits to its associates: they double the income received by informal recyclers (118 percent higher for El Porvenir, 100 percent for Asmare), while the amount for El Ceibo is only 20 percent higher.

The organizational capacity of these cooperative to gain scale, efficiency, and value-adding capabilities remains insufficient. Here the sensible thing to do from an economic perspective is also the right thing to do from a social perspective. The challenge is to attract private investment to these ventures so as to increase productivity per worker, thus income. Support organizations have an important role to play here, providing seed capital training and brain power to redefine the business model and create new win-win relationships among the actors of this ecosystem.

Generating Economic and Social Value

To be successful, any market-based effort to engage LIS must bring about sustainable benefits to participating companies, organizations, and individuals. Such benefits are generally analyzed in terms of the emerging economic and social value, as defined in chapters 9 and 10. Findings from our sample of 33 market ventures with LIS show that companies and social enterprises generated mixed returns on both accounts. Largely, results appear determined by the centrality of LIS to the organization's mission; and by the organizational capabilities of the venture's leader, including the capacity to learn and innovate.

One of the tenets of mainstream BOP studies has been the importance of achieving scale in operations in order to maximize value creation, both economic and social. This focus on scale naturally became a normative preference towards large corporations. This study, albeit based in a limited sample, points to a different direction. For all their potential, large, well-established corporations felt short of expectations. They found it difficult to leave behind established practices and reinvent themselves in order to tackle the LIS segment successfully. In our sample, what drove impact and change was not so much scale as replicability. Small and mid-sized ventures based on innovative models have shown a capacity to generate economic and social inclusion that cannot be easily dismissed by arguments of scale. Promoting entrepreneurship and greater participation in regular markets can affect Iberoamerican societies in ways never imagined before.

Economic Value

It is not an easy task to gauge the economic value generated by a diverse sample of organizations—some focused on profit, others on social change. The yardsticks employed to measure economic success depend on the organization's mission. While companies measure success through profits (ROA or ROI), for social enterprises financial sustainability is only a means to pursue their social mission. The problem is further compounded by the variety of initiatives encompassed in the sample, which pursued very different goals and engaged LIS in different capacities. For some companies, serving LIS was a paramount objective; those initiatives were labeled "LIS-focused companies"; for other companies, LIS were only one segment in a wider market; those ventures were labeled "LIS-focused projects."

When LIS-focused companies target the poor as consumers, they must build volume and generate profits from their LIS initiative in order for it to survive. LIS-focused projects, by contrast, can survive longer if the sponsoring organization chooses to sustain support over time. In our sample, all but two LIS-focused companies generated profits or were close to doing so. LIS-focused projects in our sample turned out to be profitable—at least for the time being—in only two instances: Codensa and Aguaytía, both utilities. Most LIS-focused projects in our sample were in a pilot stage and represented a very small share of net overall sales.

When LIS were engaged as suppliers, our analysis showed that it was relatively easier for larger companies to generate profits than for smaller ones. Large companies were able to exert greater control over the distribution chain, thus assuring the commercial value of goods; for example, they were able to assist LIS producers in shaping product features to match consumer preferences, or adjust output to consumer demand. Such practices not only lead larger companies to earn greater profits, but also help generate higher income for the poor.

In all cases examined, a key factor for increasing return on investment is developing adequate mechanisms for reducing transaction costs. Invariably, technological innovations and some kind of credit mechanism proved necessary solutions in servicing LIS consumers. In addition, when companies procure from LIS, transactions costs were often reduced by developing LIS organizations such as cooperatives. Nevertheless, this can prove a daunting task because it requires skills that most companies lack.

Social enterprises, as noted earlier, seek to generate economic value to fulfill their social mission. However, very few generate sufficient revenue from their market engagements to achieve financial sustainability. This finding suggests that inserting the very poor and vulnerable in value chains is difficult and costly.

Despite noteworthy improvements achieved by LIS-centered organizations such as Wild Fruit Pickers in the Chilean Bio Bio region, and Corporación Oro Verde in Colombia, widespread poverty and isolation from mainstream markets made it very difficult for the respective ventures to generate enough revenue so that income among participants can rise above the poverty line. In these cases, organizations became dependent on external actors supporting them, such as CSOs or social entrepreneurs. Sometimes, actors drawn from the local community also played a critical role in bridging the "traditional" or "informal" economy of such participants with the modern economy in which larger companies operate. LIS in poor regions are easily intimidated, fearing to even step into a bank or credit agency. Other more successful cases in terms of economic value generation, such as El Porvenir and Fundacion Futur, relied on a "skimming" process of drawing on less poor LIS to generate higher returns.

Is there a "fortune" buried at the bottom of the income pyramid? Our study cannot issue a definitive verdict. Variance across cases is simply too wide to consider an encompassing answer to that question, and partial answers must be accompanied by caveats and specifications. This does not mean that the economic value generated was necessarily mediocre or negligible; it does mean that some good performers coexist with less impressive ones. This conclusion does not pretend to apply to all BOP initiatives, only to a very limited sample. Despite some undeniable achievements, as far as this study is concerned, the jury is still out.

Social Value

It is difficult to gain a clear understanding of the social value produced by market-based initiatives targeted to the poor, which explains the scarcity of previous research in this area. For starters, low-income sectors are not homogenous, as mentioned in the introduction. Their characteristics are influenced by the context in which they live—city or country, in stagnant or growing, developed or transitional economies—as well as by the resources available in their communities.

Our analysis of the social value created has focused on four dimensions, all of which are central to social inclusion: increase in personal and family income, enhanced access to goods and services, citizenship building, and development of social capital. Even though these four dimensions are differentiated for analytical purposes, the last three also have an indirect impact on the generation of income for the poor.

Increase in personal and family income broadens life options and opportunities. Several experiences in our case sample showed positive impact in this area through the generation of additional income, or the stabilization of irregular or uncertain cash flows. Among these cases were initiatives that engaged the poor as producers in niche markets, such as Oro Verde's sustainable gold production, or the recycling of urban waste. However, if the bar is raised to the point of lifting LIS out of poverty, only three cases showed success. Two of them are initiatives in which the poor become suppliers of corporations, thus part of well-established and profitable value chains. In the third case, thanks to the work of APAEB—an organization created and staffed by LIS members—income per capita in its region of influence increased 333% in two decades. This impressive improvement was secured through a process of forward integration during this time, which consistently added value to goods produced and secured better prices for its output. One single program (Programa de convivência com o semi-árido), between 2000–2002, generated substantial increases for participants: 40 percent of participating farmers saw their income doubled.

Fifteen of the 33 cases studied gave the LIS enhanced access to goods and services, from medical and health care to micro-credit, home appliances, or public services such as electricity or gas. In addition to the improvement of the quality of life that access to these goods and services entail per se, social value was created through additional benefits such as more disposable income, enhanced security in public places, or a safer supply of public utilities. Several of the initiatives provided different forms of micro-loans, which in most cases allowed the poor to get credit for the first time. All in all, access to good and services which were previously out of reach give poor people greater control over their consumption choices. However, it should also be recognized that when LIS were engaged as consumers, companies avoided the poorest of the poor. Moreover, whether this consumption improves the quality of life of the poor or just creates greater pressure on their limited income, with little impact in terms of poverty alleviation, is a question that must be assessed carefully.

A third of the cases studied explicitly pursued building political, economic, or environmental citizenship. The waste recycling organizations showed clear gains in terms of political citizenship and inclusion for their members, who by their own account recovered their dignity and self-esteem through work, despite its precarious nature. Greater visibility and social recognition are evident in several initiatives in our sample. A case in point is La Fageda. As expressed by its founder and leader, Cristobal Colón, "we have demonstrated that the dummies in town can provide a service to the community." As mentioned earlier, many of the cases turned the poor into subjects of credit. Beyond the immediate material advantages, such a step is significant as a contribution to economic citizenship that can facilitate subsequent commercial transactions. Another aspect expressed in at least eight cases is the promotion of greater environmental awareness and responsibility, which some authors have considered yet another expression of citizenship. If economic poverty leads to social exclusion, inclusive businesses can help the poor to exercise their rights and empower them as full-fledged citizens.

Several of the cases combine empowerment and greater social cohesion by bridging the poor into broader social networks. Development of social capital is then obtained by fostering the capacities of local people to get organized as a collective group with greater bargaining power and stronger organization. Cases in which LIS are partners, suppliers, or workers were those that showed greater gains in terms of social capital.

Overall, the most promising results for overcoming poverty through social value creation appear in those initiatives that engage LIS as suppliers in established value chains run by large organizations or networks. Our analysis showed that the benefits centered mainly on producers who are not extremely poor: the fragility of those living at the very bottom of the income pyramid appeared to be a handicap for success, and the gap between expectations and realities simply too wide to be bridged. Very poor farmers are usually unable to comply with standards on quality, quantity, and timing, soon dropping out of the project. Moreover, their lack of formal education and capital often renders them less reliable as suppliers of quality produce, creating a misalignment between their capacities and market demand.

Recurring Tensions

Eventually, socially inclusive market initiatives come to face a number of challenges that have no obvious solutions. One is the tension between the creation of economic and social value. Some ventures choose to accept sub-par economic returns and prioritize the positive impact on the community, either because they are managed by mission-driven organizations, follow a leadership mandate to pursue social benefit as part of their corporate strategy, or view it as a tactical option to insure buy-in by the community. Other ventures choose to maximize private profits, in order to demonstrate that the base of the pyramid can be an attractive commercial market.[6] Those who favor this route argue that only solid profits will attract private investment, increase scale, and maximize impact. At some point, all managers that venture into the terrain of inclusive business must confront this tension.

The dilemma is serious. On the one hand, one of the undeniable merits of the BOP approach has been to shake things up in the corporate world. By raising the prospect of an untapped "fortune" to be found among the forgotten poor, its proponents caught the attention of large multinational corporations. Only if there substantial profits to be captured will they mobilize the resources on the scale needed to tackle poverty. On the other hand, those expectations may turn out to be counterproductive. As mentioned earlier, those expecting to find a fortune may be disappointed by the results found in our study—acknowledging the bias imposed by a very limited sample.

Our analysis suggests the importance of balancing those expectations with the willingness to invest in the development of long-term markets.

Another recurring contradiction emerges between the imperatives of efficiency and openness. While some ventures prioritize vertical control and expediency in decision-making, others favor building trust, which implies putting more horizontal structures in place. Under what conditions does it make sense to relinquish control of the organization's value chain, to external partners? We have ventured a tentative answer to that question, but we have only begun to scratch the surface of the problem.

Finally, there is a recurrent tension between depth and breadth. It has been mentioned that socially inclusive ventures need to be patient, become socially embedded, and construct business friendships. The advantages of developing capillarity and strong local roots are clear, but at the same time, they may contradict the imperatives of geographical expansion and scale. Locale-specific assets cannot be transferred easily: once an organization has heavily invested in them, they become a sunk-cost that will generate incentives to exploit economies of breadth in the same area, as opposed to expanding the model to other venues. Yet capturing economies of scale is essential, both for economic and social reasons. Any business model that operates under thin margins, as most BOP initiatives do, will need critical mass to generate profits. Perhaps only through scale will business be able to make a dent on poverty. Our analysis has not produced any clear or definitive answers to these challenges. These points should inform the agenda for future research avenues.

Critical Factors

C. K. Prahalad likened the design of breakthroughs for building market initiatives with LIS to working in a "sandbox," alluding to the flow of shifting sand within the fixed constraints of a box as successive shapes are explored.[7] Lessons drawn from our study of 33 experiences in Iberoamerica bear out Prahalad's insight. Every large corporation, SME, and social enterprise encompassed in our sample interacted deeply with LIS consumers, suppliers, and partners, as they sought to forge viable business models and develop suitable management practices in all areas of business policy—from product design to pricing, distribution, promotion, and customer relations. A review of these lessons suggests the following as critical factors for any organizational form in shaping inclusive business in the region: undertaking institutional transformation; gauging the meaning of value; making the most of the learning loop; linking the parts of the ecosystem creatively; and developing a long-term perspective.

Undertaking Deep-Seated Institutional Transformation

For any organization, the institutional transformations required for building successful LIS market initiatives represent a major undertaking. For companies, the process may entail radical rethinking of business models, or significant departures from standard "business logic" in reckoning with the erratic or insufficient income-generating capacity of LIS. To make matters worse, this redesign rests on a poor knowledge base. For social enterprises, aligning the organization's mission and capabilities, as well as shaping the right mix of policies and practices required to operate effectively in the business world, may turn out to be extremely difficult. All cases in our sample show that building successful LIS market initiatives entails treading on unfamiliar terrain.

The analysis of our sample shows that sweeping organizational change enabled organizations to cope with LIS limited purchasing power, unreliable and irregular cash flows, information asymmetries, and infrastructure shortcomings. By way of illustration, consider the innovations in the Cruzsalud model, as managers realized that they could lower the fixed cost of in-house visits by establishing a "call center," much used by large corporations but rarely found in SMEs. In fact, this service increased patients' perception of the quality of service, for they could obtain medical attention 24 hours a day without stepping out of their homes—a highly valuable feature when you live on steep and crime-ridden hills.

Addressing the divergent requirements of product development, marketing, and customer service in mainstream *and* low-income markets simultaneously can stretch a company's resources and imagination. However, engaging LIS markets in a business-as-usual mode will most likely result in failure. The introduction of flexible payment schemes may be complex, but the alternative of extending credit to consumers with no traceable credit history, or enduring a rash of defaults by consumers with no collateral, looks no more promising. Our analysis suggests that the implementation of fresh structures and processes is usually the cost-effective way to go. Artificially extending models from mainstream markets to LIS initiatives will certainly generate additional costs, and transferring these costs to consumers would prove self-defeating. The same kind of rethinking and imagination are required when companies include LIS as suppliers in their value chains. Organizing LIS, training them, providing technical assistance, and adapting purchasing procedures and delivery practices must be done creatively, if we are to construct socially inclusive and economically viable businesses.

Gauging the Meaning of Value

Like beauty, the perception of value lies in the eye of the beholder. At times, managers wonder why LIS consumers reject a product or service offered at an exceptionally low price, or else show strong demand for high-end consumer products.[8] Others find it difficult to grasp why LIS customers perceive a start-out offer as valuable, but soon pass it up or fail to renew their purchase—the pre-paid healthcare plans offered by Cruzsalud, for instance. Not until organizations interacted deeply with their LIS target, and learned the reasons for their seemingly irrational buying habits, were they able to gauge how their product might be valued and why. For Cruzsalud, it meant learning that, for LIS customers with little cash in hand, making a monthly payment for pre-paid health care necessarily competes with paying for school supplies. Inclusive business ventures must gear the value parameters of a product or service offered in terms of LIS perceptions.

What holds value for the poor is not always simple to decipher. Organizations run by professional managers drawn from more affluent social strata are rarely aware of the full range and complexity of emotions that define value in impoverished contexts, where everyday decisions often center on how best to survive. A company that seeks to understand how members of a LIS target group value a particular good or service could simply follow a learning path of trial and error; but even this approach may fail, for the window of trust with such groups may close fast, and timing is crucial. To build the credibility upon which a market initiative with LIS can grow, scoring small but quick victories may be essential.

Most interesting, our research suggests that the meaning of value for any LIS group may blend individual wants with community needs. Among the impoverished, the two are inextricably linked in a logic that may replace, or at least complement, the traditional *"what's in it for me"* with *"how will we all be better off."* Gauging how value is perceived by any specific LIS group vis-à-vis a given offering may prove crucial to achieve success. In some organization-to-LIS initiatives, companies struggled to add value to their mainstream offerings so as to make them appealing to the poor; conversely, in organized-LIS-as-producers, some of them found it hard to figure out the "expected" value of the products and services they supplied. In our sample, this gap proved easier to bridge in ventures involving fair trade or organic products, where organizations were able to reach a greater alignment between their understanding of value added—matching what they could actually do—with their clients' expectations and demand. These organizations excelled at communicating with both ends of the chain, and were able to bridge gaps between expectations and realities whenever the poor encountered production bottlenecks.

Value Bundling

Ivar Pettersson, from AES Corporation, stated categorically: "in my opinion, the ability to serve the BOP in a few years will move from the nice-to-do to the must-do in the utilities business; and in order to do that, the bundling of value will be crucial." He should know. When AES-Electricidad de Caracas entered the low-income barrios, they strived to go beyond the provision of electricity: the good will of the community members—and most important, their willingness to pay—was won through efforts to improve not just their consumer experience (through a safer and more reliable energy stream) but also improved public spaces in parks and streets. A traditional, commoditized service was enriched with the addition of a public good, not as a philanthropic afterthought, but rather as part of an integrated value proposition.

The concept of value bundling is a neologism derived from the well-known marketing strategy of "product bundling," which is the offer of several products as one combined product, called by Mintzberg "differentiation by support."[9] When applied to inclusive business, value bundling consists in attaching additional layers to a well-established value proposition. When Cemex first approached low-income sectors through Patrimonio Hoy, the company realized that it could not just "sell cement": instead, it would need to enrich its value proposition, and throw in design, technical advice, and financing to the mix. Construmex went one step further, as it bridges geographically disperse (though emotionally tied) communities: the expatriates who have saving capacity and the family members at home, with scarce capital and huge unmet housing needs. Similarly, Amanco realized that it could not just sell "irrigation systems" to the poor: its traditional offer would need to be augmented with supplementary services at all stages of the LIS farming business, from planting to retailing. Only a holistic value proposition would address the needs of the poor, and most important, assure the poor farmers' commercial success. *The company would succeed commercially only if the targeted LIS succeeded commercially as well.* Because of the interdependence of the ecosystem, tasks traditionally associated with philanthropy become part of market development efforts.

As the chapter on public utilities argued, value bundling proved effective as a way to lure consumers into a value exchange with the company, and away from the free ride of irregular connections. The experience of Codensa shows that although penalties may have a role to play, incentives are much more effective in breaking with the culture of irresponsible free-riding that decades of populism have created in some low-income populations in Latin America. After a few years of hard efforts to reduce non-technical losses (i.e., illegal connections), Codensa launched an effort to win over its customers' loyalty through a new business unit that leveraged some of the corporations' core assets and delivered goods that poor consumers badly needed.

The idea of enriching the value proposition is critical for consumers for whom every dime spent has a huge opportunity cost. Every commercial proposition to the poor must seek to stand out among a myriad of alternative uses of those cents. This is particularly hard where the offering is intangible, as any marketing officer knows. Part of what Codensa sought to accomplish through the development of Codensa Hogar was to give a tangible dimension (consumer goods) to the value exchange with loyal and responsible customers.

The idea of value bundling, or adding layers to an existing value proposition, can also be useful for socially inclusive initiatives that target the poor as producers, as our industry-specific chapters showed. A trait that runs across virtually all such initiatives is that increased income is tied to value added. Earlier in this chapter, we mentioned that the capacity to add value was *the* most important factor in all the waste-recycling initiatives in our sample, when it came to improving income for the poor. That was also true for many of the agribusiness initiatives covered here. APAEB was able to lift its beneficiaries out of poverty through a relentless process of forward integration and value bundling that extended for over 20 years. At the beginning, its beneficiaries were selling unprocessed sisal fiber at US$150 per ton. In 1996, after APAEB opened a sisal processing facility, they were able to start selling sisal tapestry at US$350 per ton—and a decade later, at US$450 per ton. Unrelated diversification also helped: opening a tannery allowed its beneficiaries to increase their selling prices by a factor of 3.5 to 4, depending on the leather. Not surprisingly, per capita income in its area of influence went from US$15 to US$50 in the last 20 years. In other cases, the idea of adding value was not materialized through forward integration but through the addition of distinctive value that catered to the needs of a discerning niche of demand. CRES (Mariposas de Costa Rica) was able to increase the income of small farmers by a factor of 6, by linking them to an export-oriented agribusiness that puts a premium on high quality butterfly pupae. Irupana was able to increase the income of poor Bolivia farmers by 50 percent, linking them to an export-oriented agribusiness that produced high-quality organic produce from that country's high plains.

Pursuing the bundling of value may imply redefining the contours of the business. Cemex had also always considered itself a B2B company, but it learned that it would need to develop a customer orientation to tap the low-income segment successfully. Venezuela's Cativen had traditionally been a player in the retail industry, not in agriculture. All the company needed to know about farming was how much to buy, at given prices and quality standards. The integration of poor farmers into their extended value chain, however, led Cativen to become agricultural developers, which in turn implied developing new internal capabilities, processes, and structures. Gas Natural Ban learned that bringing natural gas to the poor would entail organizing demand—most often in partnerships—something hitherto outside its business model.

Linking customer loyalty or higher income with added value is not exactly a revolutionary concept in the mainstream commercial world. However, the idea that improved income is contingent on the capacity to deliver enhanced value has not been widely applied in traditional approaches to poverty alleviation. In fact, in some areas, it has been disputed. Javier Hurtado, founder and CEO of Irupana, recounts that, after many years of working with development CSOs, Bolivian farmers had grown accustomed to receiving *donations*, not investments. They had come to perceive external aid as a right, more than a reward for their efforts. Mr. Hurtado was convinced that such an outlook was detrimental for the peasants: he was determined to make a positive impact on their life, but considered that giving away something for nothing "would only prolong dependency."

When LIS were targeted as producers, adding value was instrumental to improving their income. When LIS were engaged as suppliers, value bundling was critical to ensure their commitment to the value chain in which they were integrated. When low-income sectors were targeted as consumers, value bundling brought the product closer to their realities and needs. The commercial drive that, in different ways, was present in all the initiatives studied, made the bundling of different layers of value a critical tool to secure both economic success and social betterment.

Developing The Learning Loop

Identification and comprehension of the economic, socio-cultural, political, and managerial barriers that stand in the way of inclusive business give rise to the search for effective means of dealing with them. It is vital to close the knowledge gap, which appears to be most effectively done through unconventional market research methods, sometimes very innovative and highly participatory in nature. It is not simply about finding out how people live or what decisions they make; learning is about empathy: identifying and experiencing feelings, thoughts, or attitudes of others, and drawing valid lessons from them. Sometimes mainstream managers view the attitudes of low-income individuals in a simplistic or patronizing manner.

When the organization is an "external actor," it must learn to fully understand the "economy of the barrio": who provided the services before the organization made its appearance, and under what conditions; what local actors exert influence on LIS groups targeted; how do these groups make decisions as economic actors. This knowledge must then be distilled by an organizational process: unstructured, tacit knowledge acquired by means of participatory interactions with LIS, translated into formalized, explicit knowledge, which can be systematized and communicated throughout the organization, in order to be used to support informed decision-making. Not only must the organization be equipped with a capacity to listen to what the poor are saying; information gathered must be sorted out and transmitted to other levels in the organization, and then converted into product features or support services which adequately respond to target group needs.

For LIS-centered initiatives, this learning process is critical for success and sustainability of operations. More than just gathering information aimed at operating more efficiency or fine-tuning product features, the learning process involves a soul-searching effort to examine, understand, and build on their own strengths, very often buried and hidden amid a complex reality. This process is best illustrated by the steps undertaken by several organizations included in our study: how Coopa Roca evolved a sense of haute couture aesthetics, to sell favela-made crochet to high fashion markets worldwide; how Recolectores in the Bio Bio region discerned the quality standards of up-market produce consumers. In sum, no game plan is at hand for building a venture with LIS; yet shaping a learning loop may be essential for the venture to reach scale and turn into an inclusive business.

Linking The Ecosystem Creatively

Earlier chapters show how and why ecosystems are built in socially inclusive businesses. To build partnerships and networks that draw on such ecosystems requires competence in mapping actors and groups that can influence economic activity in areas where an organization seeks to operate. Appropriate and useful linkages can be activated in direct or indirect ways; sometimes in ways that individuals and organizations do not anticipate. Once the organization actively engages its ecosystem, the strength of the relationships that will unfold among unequal actors will depend on reciprocal trust.

Inclusive business ventures often require setting up a long-term relationship with unusual market actors. Explorandes, a tour operator, engaged the inhabitants of a poor community on the shores of Lake Titicaca in Peru in order to contract hospitality services for foreign tourists—a creative linkage on its part. A first step was to identify business-minded community leaders with business sense who could understand the nature of the project, serve as intermediaries, and help recruit people willing and qualified to undertake the tourist support services. A next step was to ensure that the value obtained from undertaking the venture appealed to both participating families and the community at large, keeping in mind what the foreign tourists might expect regarding the service quality they would obtain and pay for. It was necessary to acquaint poor, isolated, and largely illiterate community members with minimal-quality levels of hospitality, lodging, and food services, while instilling the sense of a business proposition whereby the community and the tour operator stood to view each other as equal partners in the endeavor—where neither party could afford to fail.

The establishment of linkages among unconnected actors requires keen insight, careful planning, and patient effort. The payoff can be substantial. Co-creation of value brings new, multi-faceted identities to members of the ecosystem. End-consumers become distributors, valuable but passive stakeholders (like poor neighboring communities) become suppliers, or sales personnel, or even co-directors in a multi-stakeholder governance forum in charge of an ad-hoc cross-sector value chain. Such linkages allow for the flow of ideas, resources, and skills, as indifference and isolation give way to commitment and communication. As connectivity grows so does productivity, for connectivity usually stimulates specialization and economies of scale.

Entrepreneurship

A dimension that has been somewhat overlooked in the mainstream literature on BOP studies is the critical importance of entrepreneurship in the success of inclusive ventures. If we understand entrepreneurial management as "the pursuit of opportunity without regard to resources currently controlled,"[10] it is easy to see why nurturing this ability is crucial. The majority of our cases showed how difficult it is to command all resources needed to engage LIS commercially. Sooner or later, and with varying degrees of intensity, most organizations have needed to reach out beyond their boundaries to make their LIS ventures viable. This applies not only to traditional social entrepreneurs and start-ups, but also to large and well-endowed organizations, which brings to the fore the relevance of what has been called "corporate social entrepreneurship."[11]

In most sample cases, the innovating entrepreneurs were outsiders to the LIS communities served by the initiatives, in line with the "principle of external participation" posited by the BOP literature:[12] companies—both large and small—which not only brought new assets but also organized resources that existed within the community, putting them to innovate uses. Our evidence suggests that success in inclusive businesses might depend on entrepreneurs who can bring about innovations through bold leadership, engaging others to align resources outside their control to common ends. A crucial role for these entrepreneurs is to bridge disparate and previously disconnected groups or traditional and non-traditional market actors acting simultaneously at a local and global level, as a new value chain is created.

Traditionally, social entrepreneurship was distinguished from the traditional sort by two characteristics: the centrality of social value creation and heightened sensitivity to stakeholders.[13] Our analysis suggests an intriguing finding: the emergence of inclusive business appears to have blurred this hitherto clear conceptual frontier between social and commercial entrepreneurship. True enough, for the private companies that undertake inclusive business, social value creation is not central to their mission. However, our analysis suggests that to become a going concern in this new arena, creating social value *must* be central to their strategy. Inclusive businesses can only succeed to the extent that they deliver win-win benefits for all involved, particularly the poor. Even BOP scholars acknowledged this conclusion, when they spoke about the need to assure "mutual value creation"[14] or "mutually beneficial business opportunities."[15] This tentative hypothesis appears intriguing, and merits further investigation.

Similar observations apply to the need to engage stakeholders. In a traditional social enterprise, heightened sensitivity towards the interests and needs of stakeholders (such as funders, beneficiaries, partners, or others) serves as reassurance of the venture's capacity to create value. Additionally, the capacity to connect with the expectations and values of stakeholders infuses the initiative with commitment, talent, and resources.

Our analysis suggests that inclusive businesses share this trait, to different extents depending on the business model, and probably for different reasons. Consider the experience of Colcerámica. Its innovative business model was first tried out in Usme, a district of Bogotá, where the company implemented its first pilot. A year and a half later, the company sought to replicate and scale up the experience in other regions. At that point, many inside the company suggested doing away with the partnerships with grassroots communities in order to simplify processes, gain control, capture economies of time, and lower costs—in short, applying traditional business rationality to the enterprise. Alberto Sehuanes, Marketing Manager and responsible for the initiative "Your house as new, step-by-step," resisted that move, however. In his view, bypassing "social organizations" (as grass-roots organizations are called inside the company) would be problematic. "To make the initiative succeed," he explained,

> You really need the community on board. And you cannot do that just through financial incentives. You need to make sure that promoters [saleswomen from the community] honor their commitments and remain loyal to the initiative. Where are you going to turn to, if things go wrong . . . ? To the community organizations; you don't have any other choice. That is where their loyalty lies. Grass-roots organizations were on the ground before you arrive, and will be there after you leave. *We are outsiders, they are insiders. You really need that social tissue as a platform upon which to build your distribution network.* If you ignore that, your whole venture will be built on shaky foundations.

In the context of inclusive business, heightened sensitivity to stakeholders helps to make the business unfold through distribution channels, sales teams, working cooperatives. Webs of trust and reciprocity make up for the lack of market intermediaries and complementors, as well as for lax contract enforcement. Without this support, very little is left. Thus, much as it happens with social value creation, paying close attention to the needs and views of stakeholders is not just value-driven, but strategy-driven. It is not matter of choice, but a matter of necessity in the realm of inclusive business.

To sum up, our analysis suggests that inclusive businesses are driving a convergence[16] between traditional enterprise and social enterprise, with very different organizations behaving similarly—an idea that would merit investigation and testing.

Developing a Long-Term Perspective

The urgency of mobilizing private initiatives and business leadership for solving the world's intractable social ills has been acknowledged by many. A less heard message is that determination and boldness need to be linked to patience. A leading practitioner has recently claimed persuasively that "patient capital" is essential for business to truly contribute in addressing the problems at hand.[17] For business initiatives examined in our study, impatience was a threat to success. Obstacles were multi-dimensional and the solutions often involved deep-seated transformations that took considerable time to mature. As stated earlier, most organizations had to undergo a process or "unlearning-and-relearning," and then invest in market development, all of which takes time. Any company expecting returns in a LIS oriented initiative within a timeframe that could reasonable for mainstream markets is likely to abandon it too early, without ever getting to test its real potential. Had companies like Cemex lacked the patience and perseverance to invent an ad-hoc business model, benefits from its venture would not have materialized. Building trust, developing business ties, and finding organizational fit takes time. The same holds true for organizations setting out to forge new value chains with LIS producers. A considerable investment of time may be required to acquire know-how and new technologies, and develop the ecosystem.

Towards a New Business Imagination

This book started by reviewing the frustration generated by traditional approaches to poverty alleviation. Neither philanthropy nor the public sector can do it alone: any lasting solution to poverty will need to harness the markets. Our analysis of 33 initiatives in Iberoamerica confirms this view, but takes us full circle. Altruism alone will not do it, *but experience shows that markets alone will not do it either*. The emerging field of BOP studies cannot be left to the CSR departments, but CSR cannot be left out of it either.

This is not just about semantics: words can illuminate or obscure our understanding of reality, opening up or blocking new courses of action and transformation. Plus, the question of how much to emphasize the business case versus the social dimension in the development of inclusive businesses does not always have a clear-cut answer A leading Latin American research center devoted to social innovation recently organized a workshop on the private sector's role in sustainable development. The agenda included issues of enormous social impact, such as supply chain development, or the management of company's human capital. When the academic manager in charge of the organization was asked why the acronym CSR was nowhere to found in the agenda, his answer was categorical:

> We do not want to attract managers from Community Relations, or from corporate foundations. Experience suggests that when we frame the event using these words, the information is forwarded towards those departments—and away from the individuals who shape the business. If we want to influence decision-making we need to keep that dimension hidden.

This is really food for thought. It is paradoxical, to say the least, that concepts that are meant to promote the agenda of social transformation may end up weakening it; that the understanding of business's contribution to society in untainted altruistic terms may end up downgrading it. Latin America has had a tendency to shape normative models that were almost *too good*, so much so that most people opted to ignore them.[18] This is a reality that we have to deal with: those who promote the business case of so-called BOP initiatives do have a point. It is important that companies start thinking about these ventures in business terms, not just as a way to improve their PR or keep activists and public regulators off their backs.

At the same time, it is important to acknowledge that this is really new territory. Harnessing the power of business is essential, but the private sector's traditional "toolbox" has proven insufficient to connect with the poor. Throughout the book we have discussed the need to reinvent internal structures and processes and to recognize the role of innovation. Nonetheless, the analysis suggests the need to go one step further: it not just our organizations that need to change, but also *our minds*. We have discussed the need to invest "patient capital" and to develop "business friendships" with the poor. Discussing the relative weight of the business case versus the social case does not appear to be productive. What is really needed is a new outlook that integrates both in synergistic way.

As stated earlier, Latin Americans are perhaps used to hard-to-reconcile dualities. In the context of socially inclusive market initiatives, both theory and practice would benefit from a business imagination that bridged that gap. A novel approach is needed: one that blends commitment to flesh and blood human beings with accountability and commitment to results; one that blends resource-savvy altruism with enlightened self-interest. Only through the development of such a multi-faceted approach will we be able to blend compassion and efficiency, and make the call for business engagement in poverty reduction a reality.

Notes

1. Nicholas Sullivan, *You Can Hear Me Now: How Microloans and Cell Phones Are Connecting the World's Poor to the Global Economy* (San Francisco, CA: Jossey Bass, 2007).
2. Carlos Rufin, "The Role of Government: LIS Market Initiatives and the Public Sector," *ReVista Harvard Review of Latin America* (Fall 2006).
3. Niraj Dawar and Amitava Chattopadhyay, "Rethinking Marketing Programs for Emerging Markets," *Long Range Planning* 35, no. 5 (Oct 2002).
4. Carlos Rufin and Luis Fernando Arboleda, "Utilities and the Poor: A Story from Colombia" (paper presented at the Harvard Business School Conference on Global Poverty, Boston, MA, December 1–3 2005).

5. Sale price minus purchase price.
6. For example, in 1995 ACCION International, Calmeadow of Canada, FUNDES of Switzerland and SIDI of France created Profund, a Latin American investment pool that sought to demonstrate that investing in microfinance could be a financially attractive investment option.
7. C. K. Prahalad, "The Innovation Sandbox," *Strategy + Business* 2005.
8. In Argentina, low-income consumers spend on average 5% more on cellular phones than their top-of-the-pyramid counterparts. Sophisticated features, such as built-in MP3 players, photo cameras, or attractive designs are highly valued by LIS consumers. While only 6% of high-income consumers find important that the phone device is "fashionable," the percentage is 23% among low-income consumers. According to market research carried out by Latin-Panel, a consultancy, the reason is that the latter cannot afford dedicated equipment to take photos or listen to music, so they come to rely on their cellular phone to carry out various functions. Mercedes García Bartelt, "Los celulares más caros, preferidos por los pobres," *La Nación*, August 22 2008.
9. The strategy of differentiation by support occurs when a firm consciously promotes a cluster of products around its core products, in order to fulfill the complete needs of customers in a given segment. Henry Mintzberg, "Generic Strategies: Toward a Comprehensive Framework," *Advances in Strategic Management* 5 (1988).
10. Howard H. Stevenson, "A Perspective on Entrepreneurship" (Working Paper, Harvard Business School 1983).
11. James Austin et al., "Corporate Social Entrepreneurship: The New Frontier," in *The Accountable Corporation. Volume 3: Corporate Social Responsibility*, ed. Marc Epstein and Kirk Hanson (Westport, CT: Praeger, 2006); "Social Entrepreneurship: It's For Corporations, Too," in *Social Entrepreneurship: New Paradigms of Sustainable Social Change*, ed. Alex Nicholls (Oxford, GB: Oxford University Press, 2005); James Austin and Ezequiel Reficco, "Eine umfassende Transformation des Unternehmens," *Ökologisches Wirtschaften* special issue on social entrepreneurship (June 2009).
12. Ted London, "The Base-of-the-Pyramid Perspective: A New Approach to Poverty Alleviation" (Working Paper, William Davidson Institute/Stephen M. Ross School of Business, 2008).
13. J. Gregory Dees. "The Meaning of Social Entrepreneurship." Harvard Business School. Boston, MA, 1998.
14. Erik Simanis et al., "Strategic Initiatives at the Base of the Pyramid A Protocol for Mutual Value Creation." (Base of the Pyramid Protocol Workshop Group, Wingspread Conference Center. Racine, WI 2005).
15. Erik Simanis and Stuart Hart. "Beyond Selling to the Poor: Building Business Intimacy through Embedded Innovation." (Working Paper, Cornell University. Ithaca, NY, 2008).
16. James Austin et al., "Capitalizing on Convergence," *Stanford Social Innovation Review* (Winter 2007).

17. Jacqueline Novogratz, "Meeting Urgent Needs with Patient Capital," *Innovations: Technology | Governance | Globalization* 2, no. 1/2 (2007): 30.

18. In colonial times, the gap between normative standards and facts, as well as the low feasibility of enforcing the wishes of the Spanish crown, came to be reflected in the celebrated formula "I obey but I do not comply" (*obedezco, pero no cumplo*) used by Spanish Viceroys. Donald J. Mabry, "Government and Law in Spanish Colonial America (revised)," http://historicaltextarchive.com/sections.php?op=viewarticle&artid=296.

ANNEX: Case Sample

Argentina (UDESA)

Escudo Rojo:

Red Shield (or "Escudo Rojo," as known in Latin America) is a commercial venture launched by the Salvation Army—a British religious institution—over 75 years ago. In 2007, it boasted 40 employees and annual sales in excess of US$1 million. Serving 1,200 customers a day, mostly from low income neighborhoods in Buenos Aires and its suburbs, Escudo Rojo sells second-hand clothing, furniture, home appliances and books donated to the Salvation Army, with which it shares its proceeds.

Buenos Aires' underdeveloped second-hand market did not feature any private players, although it did encompass other social organizations (other CSOs, mostly religious, that also worked with donations). These performed poorly, primarily as a result of amateur management and the existence of resellers who served as intermediaries between institutions and end customers. Until the early 1990s, Escudo Rojo also experienced these constraints, but, with new leadership, it initiated several changes, lowering prices to reach end consumers, investing in infrastructure, optimizing internal process, announcing item prices more clearly, and separating its social goal from its commercial purpose by ceasing to hire Salvation Army beneficiaries.

Thus, Escudo Rojo became a benchmark for the city's used goods market, doubling its sales in 2004–2007. By offering low prices, it catered specifically to low-income consumers, providing them with access to clothes, furniture, and home appliances as well as fostering business ventures for intermediaries who resold merchandise purchased at Escudo Rojo.

El Ceibo:

El Ceibo is a cooperative created in the early 1990s in Palermo, a Buenos Aires neighborhood, by charismatic leader Cristina Lescano, to gather people for waste collection. Its 40 garbage collectors pursued an innovating supply strategy: first, they tracked prospective customers; then, they taught suppliers how to separate inorganic waste, so that they could collect it later. Finally, after processing inorganic waste, they sold it to intermediaries or to recycling companies. In 2006, El Ceibo posted revenues of approximately US$50,000.

This cooperative had been built by people who shared a particular trait: they were all squatters at abandoned homes. Its members, including a growing number of single mothers, collected garbage to secure an income.

Eventually, they realized that they could increase their income by working together. However, as garbage collecting in the streets was illegal and got them into trouble with both collection companies and neighbors, El Ceibo decided to change its approach, becoming an "urban recoverer" cooperative.

In the early 2000s, neighbors' interest in cooperative activities grew (El Ceibo's customers increased from 100 to nearly 1,000), and this initiative gained the support of Greenpeace, IAF, and several public, social and private national and international actors. El Ceibo developed a pragmatic policy to build partnerships with several actors and groups. As a result, it managed to secure sustainable income for excluded segments, while driving a positive environmental impact and promoting ecological values. Finally, El Ceibo also worked as an advocacy group, promoting changes in local regulations to favor garbage collection cooperatives with the operation of inorganic waste-recycling "Green Centers" in Buenos Aires garbage collection circuits.

EDENOR:
Edenor is a private company that originated in mid 1992, when electrical service supply was privatized in the northern Buenos Aires and Greater Buenos Aires area. By late 2006, the company had over 2.4 million customers, and, since 2005, it was owned by the national Dolphin Group, with a stake still held by its former controlling shareholder, France's EDF. Edenor developed a pilot program for advanced energy purchases, provided through pre-paid meters in Merlo (4,200 customers) and Escobar (100 customers). Pre-paid electricity cards were purchased at gas and railway stations as well as company branch offices.

High delinquency and free-riding among low-income customers during the 2001–2002 Argentine crisis drove Edenor to employ operating and commercial segmentation approaches. In order to retain troublesome customers and to lower transaction costs, the company built a dedicated structure to provide customer follow-up and support, and developed a mechanism to attract prospects, based on the installation of a computerized system to connect vending machines with the mainstream system to register purchases.

Project sales were around US$800,000, and the initial investment was recouped in 27 months. Most (60%) purchases were of less than a dollar. This system not only enabled Edenor to expand its electrical service and regular customer base; it also rationalized energy utilization by lowering regularized customers' consumption by 30%. Yet the project could not be scaled because the regulatory agency had not provided standards for such initiatives. However, other cities had shown interest in replicating this project, and

Edenor was exploring ways to incorporate it into larger-scale state housing projects (energy-efficient housing developments).

Gas Natural BAN

Gas Natural BAN is a Spanish-owned company that provides natural gas services in the northern Buenos Aires area since 1992, with a customer base of over 1.3 million by late 2006. Its initiative focused on expanding its natural gas network to low-income neighborhoods. High connection costs forced poor segments to use bottled gas, despite its higher unit price.

The company's first attempt to provide natural gas to low income sectors was a program called "Gas for Everyone," launched in the late 1990s. This initiative was marketed by certified gas installers, who recruited a large number of customers with unsustainable connections and delinquency problems. Then, the company sought a new model to approach low-income customers. The most successful experience unfolded at Cuartel V, a neighborhood where the company worked with a local social partner, Fundación ProVivienda Social (FPVS), to develop a fiduciary fund supported by local social capital and community engagement, identifying leading neighbors to streamline project subscriptions along with education to promote responsible gas utilization. The company incorporated 2,000 new customers. Later, with other funding schemes, Gas Natural BAN worked with several local partners (grass-roots organizations or local administrations) to expand its natural gas network to other low-income neighborhoods.

These projects not only enabled the company to penetrate an underserved market, incorporating over 3,000 new customers, but they also secured annual savings of US$100 at each home. These initiatives also increased gas supply safety, appreciated house value, and provided customers with access to credit services, using their gas bills as proof of residence. For local economies, these projects drove global savings that could be used to fund new ventures, to create more jobs and to promote microventures. The company is currently working to scale up this project in partnership with banks, national and state administrations, and multilateral agencies.

Brazil (USP)

COOPA-ROCA

Rocinha's Handicraft Work and Sewing Cooperative (*Cooperativa de Trabalho Artesanal e de Costura da Rocinha*, henceforth Coopa-Roca) is a cooperative that manages and coordinates the work of women who produce handicraft fabrics for clothing and design goods at the Rocinha *favela* (slum) in Rio de Janeiro. It started in the early 1980s to enable its members to work at home, boosting their families' income while taking care of their children and their house chores.

This cooperative began with a small production scheme focusing on decorative handicrafts made using traditional Brazilian techniques. In the 1990s, its scope grew along with the fashion industry in Sao Paulo and Rio de Janeiro. Fashion designers started to appreciate handicrafts, enabling Coopa-Roca to enter a new market segment and to work with garment manufacturers, participating in Brazilian fashion calendar events. By 2006, approximately 100 cooperative members worked on exclusive designs for renowned partners in the fashion, art, and interior design industries. Coopa-Roca's handicraft quality and uniqueness positioned its pieces in trade shows and runways in Brazil, the United Kingdom, Germany and France.

Coopa-Roca's work has improved living conditions for artisans and, indirectly, their families. This cooperative has boosted its members' qualifications, self-esteem, and collective learning.

APAEB

The Association for the Hemp Region's Sustainable and Solidarity-Based Development (*Associação de Desenvolvimento Sustentável e Solidário da Região Sisaleira,* henceforth APAEB) is a non-profit association created in 1980 by hemp fiber producers to guarantee trade opportunities for its associates. Its initial goal was to ensure fair prices for hemp fibers used in textile industries, minimizing the intervention of intermediaries. With APAEB, producers conducted collective sales and installed a community hemp processing facility to facilitate direct transactions with manufacturers. Later, by building its own plant, APAEB managed to add more value to farmers' products and to increase the number of jobs it created.

APAEB's carpet and tapestry factory is located at Valente, in Northeastern Brazil, 150 miles from Salvador, capital of Bahía state. In 2005, the factory accounted for 66% of APAEB's profits on consolidated revenues of US$5.5 million. It produced nearly 7 million square feet of carpet and created 630 direct jobs. Almost 60% of its production is exported to the United States and Europe, with APAEB ranking second among Brazilian exporters of similar products. The cooperative is Valente's second largest employer. Nearing US$8.4 million in annual gross profits, APAEB created 904 new jobs in 2005, benefiting over 4,500 families in surrounding communities. In addition to its business operations, APAEB seeks to promote its region's economic and social development.

ASMARE

The Association of Collectors of Paper, Cardboard and Recyclable Material (*Associação dos Catadores de Papel, Papelão e Material Reaproveitável*, henceforth Asmare) was created in 1990 by a small group of paper collectors who worked on the streets of Belo Horizonte, capital of Minas Gerais state. Asmare's core business encompasses the collection, classification, pressing, and commercialization of recyclable materials found on the streets and donated by companies and local administration agencies. It also offers training workshops in sewing, carpentry, and paper recycling and hosts community events to raise public awareness and appreciation for collectors' work and initiatives.

Asmare organized the work of member collectors, effectively enhancing their leverage to market recyclable materials. Formerly socially excluded, they became recognized as workers and providers of a socially and environmentally significant service. Members' monthly income can be as high as US$360, an amount that gives access to food, medicines, clothing, and home appliances. They currently enjoy better working and living conditions, with more hygienic and safe homes, while their children have joined the public education system. Their job situation also strengthens their self-esteem, citizenship and family ties.

This venture has become the largest collectors' association in Belo Horizonte, and its work is recognized also for its contributions to the city's social and environmental conditions. In 2005, Asmare processed 390 tons of recyclable materials, with a net profit of US$26,361.17. In 2006, with 250 members, Asmare processed 35% of all recyclable materials of the city's urban waste.

AGROPALMA

The Agropalma Group has operated in agribusiness since 1982. It comprises six companies that produce, refine, and market palm oil and fruit. (Palm oil is mostly used for cooking, but also serves as a substitute for diesel oil and in the manufacture of soap, candles, fat, lubricants and vulcanized products.) These companies have become Brazil's largest and most modern agribusiness conglomerate devoted to palm oil, accounting for 80% of the nation's overall production and providing 2,800 direct jobs. This group is considered as Latin America's leading palm oil producer, with 5.5 million palm trees and 120,000 tons of oil produced yearly. Its annual revenues total US$184 million, and its operations encompass the entire palm oil production cycle. Based in Northern Brazil, its plantation and extraction areas expand across 79,000 acres in the Tailândia, Acará and Moju region, 93 miles away from Pará state capital.

The company promotes social and economic development actions for small local producers, including the Dendê Family Farming Project. This project engages farming families in Moju and Tailândia to plant palm trees. Agropalma provides technical assistance and commits to buying their entire production at fair prices. Initiated in July 2001, this project is also supported by government agencies, including Banco de la Amazônia (Basa). Its farming development strategy relies on large corporate buyers to purchase small farmers' production.

By 2005, the Dendê Family Farming Project had successfully planted palm trees on 3,700 acres, accomplishing an average monthly production of 228 tons of palm bunch, with a yearly productivity of 15 tons per hectare. The project provided an income for 150 families, with a monthly income increase of over 1000% for 80% of the families.

Chile (PUC)

Instituto Nacional de Capacitación Profesional (INACAP)
Chiles's National Professional Training Institute (INACAP) was created in 1966 as a non-profit with state funding to provide quality job education. In the late 1980s, amidst a domestic economic crisis, the state stopped providing funds for INACAP, forcing it to find its own resources to ensure its long-term sustainability. Four decades after inception, INACAP is the nation's largest higher education institution, with over 54,000 students, 26 sites across the country, and an online site, delivering over 170 technical and professional programs. Since its inception, INACAP has catered to people who lacked any other way of obtaining quality professional training, particularly those who came from sub-par public schools. This institute offers daytime and evening programs, enabling students to study and work at the same time. Despite its reputation for academic excellence, INACAP does not require admission tests. Its mission states that it is an inclusive institution, open to all, with no academic screening. Thus, its teaching methodology is based on hands-on learning principles.

Currently, INACAP runs a Technical Training Center, a Professional Institute, and a University—all enabling it to deliver a modular curriculum scheme that addresses students' training needs. Students can organize their higher education plans to balance their training needs and job demands. They can join INACAP's Technical Training Center first and then move on to INACAP's Professional Institute to pursue a professional degree. Eventually, they may enroll at INACAP's University for a B.A. program.

Activo Humano

Activo Humano (AH) is a Chilean private company, created in 2005 to provide employment opportunities to poorly qualified individuals. This initiative is primarily addressed to Santiago's low-income unemployed. Until AH's inception, Chile's Municipal Labor Intermediation Offices (OMILs) acted as intermediaries between employers and poorly qualified job candidates. Though free, OMIL's services were viewed as unsatisfactory by users. In general, employers did not trust these state agencies, and those who did use them offered only temporary jobs.

Client companies of AH are willing to pay a modest fee for successful placements when workers retain their jobs for more than three months. AH recruits adequate candidates through community leaders—teachers, religious leaders, etc.—who live in the same neighborhoods as unemployed individuals.

By 2007, as a result of its high retention rates (90% of its hired candidates held their jobs for more than three months), AH's effectiveness was quite well-known. This fledgling initiative already boasted a significant client company portfolio that hired its candidates for truck driver and loader, furniture assembly, worker, mason, and carpenter jobs.

Coordinadora Regional de Recolectores y Recolectoras de Frutos Silvestres de la Región del Bío-Bío

Bío-Bío Regional Wild Fruit Pickers was created in 2004 to bring together collectors from eight communities in Southern Chile's Bío-Bío region—the country's second poorest area, with one of the highest unemployment rates in the nation. Bío-Bío pickers have joined their efforts to market their wild fruits more effectively and profitably.

This initiative emerged under the auspices of Taller de Acción Cultural (TAC), a CSO that helped the pickers to organize in order to negotiate directly with distribution companies. Until then, wild fruit pickers worked in isolation as a result of their geographical dispersion. Their work provided an inadequate income, as most profits went to intermediaries. In addition, large forest owners did not allow pickers on their lands for fear of fires and damage. Through their organization and supported by TAC, Bío-Bío pickers managed to overcome these barriers, securing an improved income and bolstering their occupation's dignity.

At present, as a result of a collaboration network of public institutions and universities, this organization has broadened its field, and pickers now process and market their wild fruits, including mushrooms, medicinal herbs and wild fruits. They dehydrate their produce and package them at the organization's plants to sell them in domestic and international markets.

Colombia (Uniandes)

Codensa

Codensa, an electrical service provider in Bogotá and Cundinamarca, has been controlled by Endesa, a Spanish multinational, since 1997. In four years, Codensa opened 13 customer service centers, offered new facilities for energy invoice payments, created a reward system for customers, and established a direct communication channel with users through community engagement programs. Technically, the company also introduced improvements into systems that prevented electricity theft and street lighting. Improved service quality, coupled with the development of a payment culture and technical interventions, enabled the company to cut energy losses by half and to reduce monthly bill delinquency to a fourth of former rates.

Starting in 2001, Codensa formulated new strategies to approach customers and to enrich its value proposition. Its "Codensa Home—Easy Credit for Everyone" program exploited the company's billing platform to build a value chain that engages large store chains and home appliance manufacturers to "improve home living conditions." Challenged to find a financial partner for its consumer loans for low-income sectors, Codensa decided to grant these loans using its own liquidity surplus. By late 2007, Codensa Home had issued loans for US$600 millions to finance 730,000 home appliance purchases—two thirds of these loans had gone to customers who had never taken out formal loans before. Codensa was viewed by both employees and customers as a company with two strong businesses: electricity distribution and consumer loans.

Colcerámica

Colcerámica was created in 1935 as a vertically integrated ceramic manufacturer. In the 1990s, the company faced decreasing sales as a result of Colombian government's economic opening policies. In 2004, Colcerámica decided to approach low-income consumers. By 2007, the company posted US$353 million in consolidated sales, with production plants in Colombia and the United States and exports to several countries in the Americas, Europe, Russia, and Israel. In 2007, its low-income segment business brought in nearly US$300,000 in sales and was projecting revenues in excess of US$24 million for this market in the medium term.

In its efforts to penetrate the local low-income markets, Colcerámica was assisted by a social leader who knew and worked with poor neighborhoods. Together, they launched a project called "Your Home, Built Anew, Step by Step" with active community involvement. Existing grass-roots organizations

at Usme—a town next to Bogotá—recruited and supervised local sales promoters. Two years into the Usme project, Colcerámica moved forward to
expand its initiative into other Bogotá districts and other Colombian cities.
To meet project objectives, Colcerámica relied on its vertically integrated
chain, but it found some difficulties in formulating the most adequate distribution scheme to serve low income consumers. In addition, as a large company approaching this market with a view to securing profitability and
growth, Colcerámica has been challenged by lack of information, risks associated with poor areas, poor community education and training, low consumer purchasing power and banking access, distrust for private companies,
and transaction informality.

Cooperativa de Recicladores Porvenir
Colombia's cardboard industry is partially sourced—40%—with recycled
cardboard. To reuse it, cardboard must be collected, stocked, and processed.
The Porvenir Recyclers' Cooperative, founded in 1990, groups 40 garbage
collectors, 9 stationed at its warehouse and 20 working at "sources." For
recyclers, working at a source means to have a workplace with a stable flow
of materials over several months, with a predictable income. Conversely,
not having a source obliges them to roam the streets in search of garbage
bags before collector trucks start their routes.

Intermediaries used their leverage to prevent the growth and strengthening of recycler cooperatives. In addition to their lack of organizational
experience and financial resources for warehousing materials, cooperatives
were forced to abide by trade standards in order to do business with companies. It was not easy for recyclers to meet formal business demands of
reliability, volume, and professionalism. However, since the 1990s, some
value chains have been set up, doing away with intermediaries and securing
better prices for recycler cooperatives.

Without the support of Colombia's public sector, recyclers have organized themselves to fight for improvements in their living conditions and to
participate in public policy making. Bogotá's Recyclers Association has
encouraged cooperatives to engage other organizations and to develop leadership and motivation among its nearly 2,000 affiliated families. Over
almost two decades, violence against recyclers has diminished, and 3,000
recyclers have been trained in forming associations, stocking, accounting,
and public policies, while significant improvements have been accomplished
in recyclers' identity and 65% of Porvenir's associates have improved their
living conditions.

Corporación Oro Verde

Colombia's Chocó department houses one of the world's poorest populations. Many combine subsistence farming with primitive extraction operations (gold and platinum mining). In the late 1990s, in order to create the Oro Verde Corporation (COV), Fundación Amigos del Chocó (Amichocó) built an alliance with Fundación Las Mojarras and community councils at Tadó and Condoto—these councils were instituted in 1993 to collectively manage African Colombian territories. COV's purpose has been to provide mining communities with a dignified livelihood through sustainable utilization of natural resources, certification and income generation, food production, and ethnic organizational strengthening.

COV launched its Oro Verde initiative to promote sustainable gold extraction—i.e., without contaminating agents and action to recover mined areas and selling it at fair-trade international and national markets. Clients at these markets are willing to pay extra for certified gold, and surplus proceeds are invested in a fund to guarantee model sustainability. Amichocó expects to transfer the initiative to community councils for replication at other communities.

International gold certification has been a great challenge to Oro Verde. The Pacific Ocean Environmental Research Institute, an agency reporting to Colombia's Environment Ministry, was in charge of formulating criteria and procedures to certify "environmentally responsible" miners, validating these standards with producing communities and prospective clients. In order to standardize the certification process, COV promoted the creation of the Association for Responsible Mining, a cross-sector partnership among 66 organizations from around the world.

Costa Rica and Bolivia (INCAE)

Irupana Andean Organic Food

By 2006, Irupana Andean Organic Food had been working for 19 years on food products based on produce naturally grown by indigenous farmers in Bolivia's Andes, Amazon and Chaco regions. This company was created to help poor farmers in rural Bolivian areas to gain access to markets, to receive technical and financial support, and, primarily, to command fair prices for their crops. In 1987, Irupana launched the first 100% organic roasted coffee into Bolivia's market. Since then, the company diversified its offerings until it reached a total of nearly 150 products. Additionally, in 2002, Irupana started exporting Andean grains, especially quinoa and amaranth.

Irupana works with small farmers who live on less than US$700 a year. The company's economic success made it possible to develop this environmentally and socially responsible business in a country with huge biodiversity potential but also plagued by severe poverty in its rural areas.

Palí

Pali is a discount supermarket chain. It is part of the CSU-CCA group, one of Costa Rica's leading business conglomerates. Palí supermarkets operate in both Costa Rica and Nicaragua, with relatively low margins and large sales volumes. Palí intends to sell products at low prices, making them accessible for low-income sectors.

Palí's business scheme has evolved as the company has learned more about its target market's needs. For instance, it increased its product assortment (number of SKUs) and expanded its points of sale from urban to rural areas. Palí supermarkets feature simple, efficient, and cost-saving operations, with a limited assortment that includes leading national and private brands to cater to families' basic needs, in a pleasant, yet austere, atmosphere that matches its low-cost philosophy.

Currently, Palí serves one-third of Costa Rica's market (nearly 1.5 million people) and accounts for 50% of CSU's consolidated supermarket sales. In Nicaragua, Palí serves approximately 1.25 million people, accounting for 69.4% of CSU Nicaragua's overall sales.

Mariposas de Costa Rica (CRES)

Costa Rica's butterflies are a source of wealth for approximately 100 low-income families. In 1983, Costa Rica Entomological Supplies (CRES) was created to breed, pack, and export pupae to butterfly exhibitors in the United States and Europe. However, the company's goals were not only business-oriented but also social. Its founder, Joris Brinckerhoff, sought a business opportunity that would contribute to Costa Rica's development without jeopardizing its rich environment.

Since 1986, the company's exports have included, in addition to CRES' output, butterfly pupae bred by independent producers. Initially, CRES recruited former company employees who had started to breed butterflies on their own, but eventually its supplier network expanded across the nation, including low-income rural dwellers and providing job opportunities for nearly 100 families. Pupae breeding grew rapidly, and, in the 1990s, production exceeded the demand from clients overseas. New exporters joined the market, offering to purchase breeders' overproduction at lower prices and selling pupae at international marketplaces for less. In 2006, CRES' founder wondered how to maintain the company's fair-price policy in order to both safeguard breeders' income and ensure its continuity.

Hortifruti's Tierra Fértil Program

Hortifruti, a produce company owned by CSU-CCA, developed its "Tierra Fértil" (Fertile Land) program in Costa Rica in the 1970s to support its low-income, small farming suppliers in order to ensure its produce supply, to expand its assortment for supermarkets, and to raise the quality, hygiene, and safety standards of the fresh products provided to CSU-CCA.

In 1973, with only five supermarkets, CSU-CCA had a hard time supplying its points of sale with quality fresh products to respond to its consumers' demands. As a result, Hortifruti started to organize Costa Rican farmers to establish some business criteria, including profit margins, quality standards, and production programs based on market demands. Thus, the Tierra Fértil program was born.

Hortifruti's work with small farmers also promoted more efficient and safer product delivery schemes. It introduced safer and more hygienic packaging methods and crates. In 1985, a nationwide, two-year campaign was launched to train farmers on rational and efficient chemical product utilization. Tierra Fértil's success fueled its replication in other Central American countries, including Nicaragua, where it was launched in 1998, and Honduras, where it was initiated in 2001.

Spain (ESADE)

Andrómines

Andrómines Social Association works to provide social and labor inclusion for excluded groups at environmentally friendly and sustainable projects, such as second-hand clothing and IT component collection and reutilization. Its low-income beneficiaries include gypsies (28%), single mothers (18%), long-term unemployed individuals (12%), and immigrants (12%).

Andrómines is affiliated with the Ropa Amiga (Friendly Clothes) Program, an employment reentry project based on second-hand clothing, including collection, recycling, and sales. This joint venture by 17 labor inclusion organizations was promoted jointly by the Un Sol Món Foundation, associated with Obra Social de Caja Cataluña; Aires (Asociació Intersectorial de Recuperadores y Empresas Sociales de Catalunya), a cross-sector organization consisting of 32 employment reentry companies, and Cáritas Catalunya, a Catholic Church charity.

The Ropa Amiga program was created to exploit significant synergies by encouraging a group of labor-inclusive organizations to collaborate, expanding their market and consolidating their operations. Through these organizations' voluntary engagement, Fundació Un Sol Món's financial and technical support, and the creation of collective intervention criteria, this program has addressed common problems, especially those associated with production processes and value chains that each organization could not tackle on its own.

Futur

Futur is a small non-profit founded in 1996 in Barcelona to provide labor and social inclusion opportunities for people who have completed their prison terms, single mothers with no income, homeless individuals, drug and alcohol addicts, as well as immigrants who have recently arrived in Barcelona from Latin America and Northern Africa.

Futur started working in the textile industry but later changed its focus to food services, concentrating on ecological and fair-trade products offered at three restaurants and a catering service. More recently, it has successfully expanded its operations to school cafeterias—four at first, then eight on the following school year, and projecting a total of 12 for the coming year. Its latest project—still under study—involves selling organic, fair-trade products on the streets with salespeople on bicycles. In 2007, Futur posted nearly 1.5 million euros in sales (roughly, three times its revenues in 2005), with 52 employees—18 of them from socially excluded groups.

La Fageda

La Fageda (Catalonian for beech forest) is a non-profit organization that had managed, since its inception in 1982, to employ over 100 mentally challenged local people. This organization runs a 37-acre farm located at the heart of the Volcano Region Natural Forest in Fageda d'en Jordà, a beech forest known for its flat, low-altitude location and breathtaking beauty.

La Fageda's founder, Cristóbal Colón, had been committed to proving that it was feasible to conduct economically viable business ventures with handicapped employees. This led him to look for projects that would be therapeutic for the mentally challenged and, at the same time, would address a specific market need in order to become sustainable. He first ventured into gardening and forest maintenance, later moving on to dairy farming and, eventually, to diary product manufacturing and successful yogurt production.

Twenty-five years later, La Fageda's team and its founder could take pride in the fact that the organization's yogurts, produced in a small town far away from Barcelona, were displayed at supermarkets alongside Danone's products, the industry's undisputed leader. La Fageda had secured this outstanding shelf positioning by manufacturing a quality yogurt consumers viewed as a wholesome, natural farm product.

How can La Fageda preserve its standing in the yogurt distribution circuits? On the one hand, large food multinationals have ever increasing leverage with distributors; on the other hand, some leading distributors prioritize their own brands. La Fageda needs to find adequate strategies to maintain its competitive positioning while upholding its foundational spirit.

Mexico (EGADE)

Amanco

Ashoka, a civil society organization that supports social entrepreneurs, developed its Hybrid Value Chain program to promote collaborations that combine value-chain capabilities to bring products and services to low-income communities at fair prices. A pilot project for this program was conducted in Mexico with Amanco, a leading irrigation system company, to provide advanced irrigation systems to small farmers by combining company capabilities with those of social entrepreneurs.

This initiative was based on a strategic network built by Amanco, Ashoka and owners of small lemon orchards in Mexico's Guerrero and Oaxaca states. The goal of this chain is to provide farming solutions to low income producers. Amanco's corporate objective was to draw 10% of its revenue from low-income sectors. Thus, the company accepted Ashoka's invitation to build a hybrid value chain.

Once Amanco decided to launch this project in Mexico, the company realized that small farmers lacked competitiveness as a result of their location and inability to access resources. Their plantations were old, and they were not exploiting their subsoil appropriately, partly because they had no access to loans and no knowledge of farming technologies. Thus, Amanco set out to provide solutions to farmers, including incentives for them to come together and technical support for irrigation system utilization.

Construmex (Cemex México)

Construmex is an initiative launched by Cemex, a leading cement manufacturer, to provide housing support in Mexico (house construction, refurbishing or purchase) to Mexican émigrés in the United States. Construmex relied on local distributors to provide the materials used to build or refurbish houses in émigrés' hometowns.

This initiative intended to position Cemex in a new market niche. The idea was to capitalize on a business opportunity and to provide a new value proposition for Mexico's certified distributors. Associated with Cemex's mission, Construmex sought to offer services that satisfied construction needs. Some of the challenges faced by this initiative included émigrés' distrust for this type of services as a result of earlier disappointments with other providers. In addition, Cemex had to adjust its business model and to learn more about this particular market.

Asociación del Empresario Azteca (Grupo Salinas)

Empresario Azteca is a support and financial service for low-income sectors interested in developing micro-ventures in Mexico. With this initiative, the Salinas Group services the need for credit (through its Banco Azteca business unit) and for supplies (through its Elektra store chain) to small businesses. Empresario Azteca pursues a loyalty-building strategy, offering customers, in addition to loans and products, a complementary service network, including discounts on medical services, legal counsel, business training and advertising. This scheme is set in motion when Banco Azteca grants a loan to a customer; Elektra offers its products by means of an electronic catalog, and Empresario Azteca Association (AZMAZ) provides a membership for the customer to access all program services. Thus, both Salinas Group's business units are incorporated into the program.

Perú (UP)

Palmas del Espino

For over 25 years, Palmas del Espino has been a vertically integrated company devoted to oil palm plantation, palm oil extraction and, more recently, to byproduct manufacture (oil, butter, soap, etc.), in the Alto Huallaga valley, in the Peruvian Amazon region. Its operating area has been at the center of the most significant conflicts in recent Peruvian history, associated with drug trafficking and terrorism. It is also one of the poorest regions in Peru. In this risky setting, Palmas del Espino has managed to become a profitable, efficient company that contributes to local development with market-based initiatives and land ownership schemes, providing surrounding communities with an alternative to coca leaf production.

Palmas de Espino employs over 1,500 people, including executives, employees, and workers. In 2005, it posted consolidated revenues of US$37.1 million, with net profits of US$4.9 million. Company operations, spanning from raw material production to end product manufacture, focus almost exclusively on its 22,200-acre plantation and factory in the jungle, but its products are marketed nationwide. It even exports butter to Chile.

The company engages low-income sectors in two primary ways: it employs migrant workers on a temporary basis at its plantation, and it purchases fresh palm fruits from independent farmers who become its regular suppliers.

Titikayak Consortium

The Titikayak Consortium is a community and adventure tourism initiative promoted by Explorandes, a tourism agency that has operated in Peru for the past 30 years. The Titikayak Consortium is the result of a strategic alliance with Llachón Turs, a company owned by local community leader Valentín Quispe, to develop kayaking tours on Lake Titicaca. This operation engages Llachón community members as suppliers of lake transportation, lodging, and food services.

Llachón is located on the Capachica peninsula, on the coast of Lake Titicaca, nearly 10,000 feet above sea level. This is primarily a rural area, with subsistence farming and cattle raising. Over 80 peasant families live in this area and participate in tourism activities, organized in associations based on their individual services—food, lodging, and lake transportation. These families are direct suppliers for Llachón Turs, thereby significantly complementing their household income without neglecting other activities.

Explorandes offers both Titikayak and Llachón Turs services to major wholesale tourism agencies in the United States, the United Kingdom, and other European countries. Currently, Titikayak offerings are included in international wholesalers' packages for trips to Peru.

CIAP

Peru's Cross-Regional Artisans Center (Central Interregional de Artesanos del Perú, henceforth CIAP) is a non-profit created in 1992 by Peruvian artisans from several regions, who have focused their handicraft production to sell in international markets, where customers share fair-trade values.

CIAP members view this initiative as an experience that strengthens and develops their individual and collective work, based on self-management. The artistic venture serves to preserve their local cultural wealth and builds social capital. Although handicraft operations have yet to help some CIAP members to escape poverty, they have contributed to satisfying the basic, unmet needs of a low-income segment in Peru.

CIAP members have founded four companies to streamline their joint business ventures. These companies include Intercrafts Perú, the association's leading company created in 2003 to export handicrafts; an alternative tourism agency created in 2001 to promote responsible tourism packages with local community engagement; a savings and loans cooperative created in 2002 to provide favorable financial services to CIAP members, and PRO-Ecosol, a complex built in 2006 that houses a fair-trade cafeteria and a handicraft store offering CIAP products.

Aguaytía Energy

Aguaytía Energy produces and distributes natural gas and its byproducts in Peru's central jungle, the Ucayali Region. It is part of the first overall development project to exploit natural gas in Peru. It started operating in 1998, and, since 2002, it has developed a program to expand the use of LPG (liquefied petroleum gas) in its area of operation. This initiative has a twofold social and business purpose: to promote the use of LPG for both household applications (cooking) and public transportation in order to create a local market for its production, to improve local living conditions, and to reduce the environmental impact of other, more contaminating fuels.

Through fuel sales, Aguaytía Energy covers the conversion costs for small gasoline engines, recovering its investment in two to three years, depending on the type of vehicle and its LPG consumption. The company's margin is higher in local sales, as a result of high transportation costs. Public transportation vehicles' owners or licensees are low-income individuals who cannot afford engine conversions. Similarly, local families, who used to cook mostly with wood or kerosene, have received free gas stoves, as well as discounts to purchase their first LPG bottles, as part of the company's strategy to expand its local market. While Aguaytía's goal is to convert 50% of all local vehicles, it has managed to turn a little over 7% into natural gas, and it has distributed nearly 50,000 gas stoves to local community families.

Venezuela (IESA)

AES Electricidad de Caracas

Electricidad de Caracas (EDC) was founded in 1895 and became one of the largest private companies in Venezuela as well as one of the few listed at Caracas Stock Exchange. In 2000, the company was acquired by AES through a hostile takeover. AES-EDC was the exclusive electricity service provider in the Caracas metropolitan area, with a population in excess of 5 million. By 2006, it served 1,062,300 customers—888,035 were household consumers, and 591,933 lived in low-income neighborhoods.

AES-EDC approached low-income sectors in 2003 with a view to reducing energy losses and to building a profitable business with LIS. Its first attempt was a pilot project involving the installation of pre-paid meters at La Morán neighborhood. However, this initiative failed to appeal to consumers, and the state regulatory agency banned the use of pre-paid electricity systems. A second company project sought to secure payment for hundreds of overdue service bills from a social housing development. Another project focused on removing cable tangles caused by illegal connections, encouraging consumers to become regular company customers. Eventually, these initiatives were grouped under the heading "Electrical Neighborhood." In the first quarter of 2007, Venezuela's President, Hugo Chávez, nationalized AES-EDC.

Cativen

Cativen is a retailer subsidiary of France's Casino Group. In 2001, it acquired the CADA supermarket chain in Venezuela. In 2001–2004, Cativen invested approximately US$200 million in Venezuela to refurbish the CADA chain and develop its Q´PRECIOS (stores in low-income areas) and ÉXITO (hypermarkets) chains. For 2005–2009, the company has planned investments nearing US$400 million to turn Cativen into Venezuela's leading retailer.

Cativen's strategy to approach low-income sectors is to eliminate vegetable distributors and intermediaries and buy directly from small farmers. The company's initiative relies on the installation of "proximity platforms" in farming areas. These platforms include purchasing, stocking, and distribution centers, which also engage in social activities to support small farmers' development.

Through these "proximity platforms," Cativen's employees negotiate directly with small farmers, building long-term relationships based on the company's commitment to purchase their production and producers' agreement to abide by harvest schedules and quality standards. In order to render these relationships more cost-effective for producers, Cativen buyers promote their association into cooperatives, providing the necessary support for these cooperatives to open bank accounts and to register for tax payments. Cooperatives also receive technical assistance in farming and harvest-planning, to prevent over- or underproduction and to respond to Cativen customers' demands. Finally, the company pays more to cooperatives that add value to their produce (washing and packing it).

Comunanza

Comunanza is a private non-profit foundation, certified in January 2005 by the Micro-Financial Development Fund (FONDEMI) to serve as a Venezuelan micro-financial system agency. It provides financial services to subsistence entrepreneurs. In 2006, its US$165,000 revenues came from loans and interest on temporary cash surplus placements. By November 2006, Comunanza served 720 active customers, with nearly 200 customers about to reactivate their recent credit lines.

This organization has two sites—an administrative office at a shopping mall in Caracas' financial district, and an operating office at Petare, a section of the city where 30% of its population lives (two million people), including many subsistence entrepreneurs. By November 2006, Comunanza employed 16 people.

Comunanza works with low-income sectors (strata D and E). At the time of its inception in 2004, stratum D accounted for 22% of Venezuela's financially served population, including micro-entrepreneurs who manage inventories, hire employees, and, albeit in a limited fashion, could access banking institutions for financial services. Stratum E accounted for 58% of Venezuela's population, primarily consisting of "subsistence micro-entrepreneurs"—i.e., self-employed individuals making a living with mostly informal micro-ventures and limited access to financial services. Their personal and business economies overlapped and affected their payment capacity.

By incorporating LIS to formal financial circuits, Comunanza expects to create social value: first, by providing them with banking and financial services, and, later, with its second-generation products, by helping micro-entrepreneurs to separate their personal and business finances. Experience shows that low-income family crises affect micro-ventures and vice versa. Thus, by promoting long-term saving plans and health-care service affiliation, reserve funds are created to serve family needs and to preserve business ventures' financial soundness.

Cruzsalud

Cruzsalud is a medium-sized company founded in 2004 to provide health-care solutions to low-income sectors in Eastern Caracas. Its mission is to "become an organization with sustained growth promoted by its people, providing innovating health care solutions efficiently and profitably for everyone." By late 2006, Cruzsalud had some 70 employees; it also relied on 70 affiliated physicians in several specialties and 15 associated institutions (clinics, labs) to provide services for its 10,000 members. It expected its membership base to grow to 100,000 by 2010.

Its business model is based on pre-paid medical insurance, with subscribers receiving a number of healthcare services in exchange for a fixed monthly fee. Cruzsalud offers four health plans: Family, Kit, Look After Me, Overall, with monthly fees ranging from US$4 to US$18.6. All four plans offer a common service base, including a 24-7 hot line, house calls, and ambulance service for emergencies. The Kit, Look After Me and Overall plans also include additional services, such as a supply kit for medical care, dental emergencies, medical check-ups and specialty consultations.

Cruzsalud targets Venezuela's E population segment, usually served by public hospitals, outpatient clinics, and the Misión Barrio Adentro. The company believes that the E population segment comprises people who can barely survive and must be assisted by the government and another group, with some purchasing power and unmet health-care needs, who is willing to pay for some services. Cruzsalud's goal is to offer healthcare services to this E+ segment, providing products that address their payment capacity and needs.

Bibliography

Acs, Zoltan J., Pia Arenius, Michael Hay, and Maria Minniti. "Global Entrepreneurship Monitor. 2004 Executive Report." Babson Park, MA, and London, UK: Babson College and London Business School, 2005.

Anderson, Beth Battle, Gregory Dees, and Jed Emerson. "Developing Viable Earned Income Strategies." In *Strategic Tools for Social Entrepreneurs: Enhancing the Performance of Your Enterprising Nonprofit*, edited by J. Gregory Dees, Jed Emerson and Peter Economy, 191–234. New York, NY: Wiley, 2002.

Anupindi, Ravi, and S Sivakumar. "A Platform Strategy for Rural Transformation." In *Business Solutions for the Global Poor: Creating Economic and Social Value*, edited by Kasturi Rangan, John Quelch, Gustavo Herrero and Brooke Barton., 193–206. San Francisco, CA: Jossey-Bass, 2007.

Austin, James E. *Agroindustrial Project Analysis: Critical Design Factors*. 2nd ed. Baltimore, MD: Johns Hopkins University Press, 1992.

Austin, James E., and Michael Chu. "Business and Low-Income Sectors: Finding a New Weapon to Attack Poverty." *ReVista Harvard Review of Latin America* (2006).

Austin, James, Roberto Gutiérrez, Enrique Ogliastri, and Ezequiel Reficco. "Capitalizing on Convergence." *Stanford Social Innovation Review* (Winter 2007): 24–31.

Austin, James, Herman Leonard, Ezequiel Reficco, and Jane Wei-Skillern. "Corporate Social Entrepreneurship: The New Frontier." In *The Accountable Corporation. Volume 3: Corporate Social Responsibility*, edited by Marc Epstein and Kirk Hanson. Westport, CT: Praeger, 2006.

———. "Social Entrepreneurship: It's for Corporations, Too." In *Social Entrepreneurship: New Paradigms of Sustainable Social Change*, edited by Alex Nicholls. Oxford, UK: Oxford University Press, 2005.

Austin, James, Patricia Márquez, Ezequiel Reficco, Gabriel Berger, et al. "Building New Business Value Chains with Low Income Sectors in Latin America." In *Business Solutions for the Global Poor: Creating Economic and Social Value*, edited by Kasturi Rangan, John Quelch, Gustavo Herrero and Brooke Barton. San Francisco, CA: Jossey-Bass, 2007.

Austin, James, and Ezequiel Reficco. "Eine umfassende Transformation des Unternehmens." *Ökologisches Wirtschaften* special issue on social entrepreneurship, (June 2009).

Austin, James, Ezequiel Reficco, Gabriel Berger, Rosa Maria Fischer, et al. *Social Partnering in Latin America: Lessons Drawn from Collaborations of Businesses and Civil Society Organizations*. Cambridge, MA: Harvard University, David Rockefeller Center for Latin American Studies, distributed by Harvard University Press, 2004.

Ayyagari, Meghana, Asli Demirguc-Kunt, and Thorsten Beck. *Small and Medium Enterprises across the Globe: A New Database*: SSRN, 2003.

Bloom, Paul N., and Gregory Dees. "Cultivate Your Ecosystem." *Stanford Social Innovation Review* 6, no. 1 (Winter 2008): 47–53.

Brandes, Dieter. *Bare Essentials: The Aldi Way to Retail Success*. Frankfurt: Cyan-Campus, 2004.

Brown, L. David. "Bridging Organizations and Sustainable Development." *Human Relations* 44, no. 8 (1991): 807–31.

Burnside, Craig, and David Dollar. "Aid, Policies and Growth." *American Economic Review* 90, (2000): 847–68.

Carroll, Glenn R. "Organizational Ecology." *Annual Review of Sociology* 10, (1984): 71–93.

Castells, Manuel, and Alejandro Portes. "World Underneath: The Origins, Dynamics, and Effects of the Informal Economy" In *The Informal Economy: Studies in Advanced and Less Developed Countries,* edited by Alejandro Portes, Manuel Castells and Lauren A. Benton, 11–37. Baltimore, MD: Johns Hopkins University Press, 1989.

CEPAL. *Cohesión social: inclusión y sentido de pertenencia en América Latina y el Caribe*. Santiago de Chile: Naciones Unidas, 2007.

———. "Panorama social de América Latina 2007." Comisión Económica para América Latina y el Caribe, 2007.

Combariza, Franklin Luis, and Roberto Gutiérrez. "Apropiación de valor en la cadena de reciclaje del cartón." *Responsabilidad & Sostenibilidad*, 2008.

Comisión Económica para América Latina. "Anuario estadístico de América Latina y el Caribe." Santiago: Naciones Unidas, División de Estadísticas y Proyecciones Económicas, 2007.

"Consejo Nacional de la Vivienda. Programa II: Habilitación Física de Zonas de Barrios." CONAVI, http://www.conavi.gov.ve.

Chesbrough, Henry. "Business Model Innovation: It's Not Just about Technology Anymore." *Strategy & Leadership* 35, no. 6 (2007): 12–17.

Chiriboga, Rimisp Manuel. "Mecanismos de articulación de pequeños productores rurales con empresas privadas, síntesis regional." 80. Quito, Ecuador: Mesa de Trabajo en Desarrollo Económico de RURALTER, 2007.

Christensen, Clayton, Thomas Craig, and Stuart Hart. "The Great Disruption." *Foreign Affairs* 80, no. 2 (2001).

Chu, Michael. "Commercial Returns and Social Value: The Case of Microfinance." Paper presented at the research symposium at Harvard Business School "The Business of Reaching the Global Poor," Boston, MA, December 2005.

———. "Commercial Returns at the Base of the Pyramid." *Innovations* (Winter–Spring 2007): 115–46.

———. "Microfinance: Business, Profitability and the Creation of Social Value." In *Business Solutions for the Global Poor: Creating Economic and Social Value*, edited by Kasturi Rangan, John Quelch, Gustavo Herrero and Brooke Barton, 309–20. San Francisco, CA: Jossey-Bass, 2007.

D'Andrea, Guillermo, and Gustavo Herrero. "Understanding Consumers and Retailers at the Base of the Pyramid in Latin America." Paper presented at the Harvard Business School Conference on Global Poverty, Boston, MA, December 1–3 2005.

Dawar, Niraj, and Amitava Chattopadhyay. "Rethinking Marketing Programs for Emerging Markets." *Long Range Planning* 35, no. 5 (Oct 2002): 457–74.

de Medina, Heloisa V. "Reciclagem de materiais: Tendências tecnológicas de um novo setor." CETEM - Centro de Tecnologia Mineral, Ministério da Ciência e Tecnologia, http://www.cetem.gov.br/tendencias/agenda/parte_III/Reciclagem%20de%20materiais.pdf.

Dees, J. Gregory. "Enterprising Nonprofits." *Harvard Business Review*, January 1998.

———. "The Meaning of Social Entrepreneurship." Boston, MA: Harvard Business School, 1998.

Demirguc-Kunt, Asli, Thorsten Beck, and Ross Levine. *Small and Medium Enterprises, Growth, and Poverty: Cross-Country Evidence*. SSRN, 2003.

Drazer, Maricel. "O poder dos coletores informais." Tierramérica, http://www.tierramerica.info/nota.php?lang=port&idnews=170.

Drucker, Peter F. *Innovation and Entrepreneurship: Practice and Principles*. 1st ed. New York: Harper & Row, 1985.

Easterly, William Russell. *The Elusive Quest for Growth: Economists' Adventures and Misadventures in the Tropics*. Cambridge, MA: MIT Press, 2001.

Easton, Tom. "The Hidden Walth of the Poor." *The Economist*, November 5 2005a.

Eliasson, Gunnar. "The Role of Knowledge in Economic Growth." Stockholm: Royal Institute of Technology, Stockholm, TRITA-IEO-R, 2000.

Elsner, Wolfram. "The 'New' Economy: Complexity, Coordination and a Hybrid Governance Approach." *International Journal of Social Economics* 31, no. 11 (2004): 1029–49.

Emerson, Jed, and Sheila Bonini. "The Blended Value Map: Tracking the Intersects and Opportunities of Economic, Social and Environmental Value Creation.," http://www.blendedvalue.org/Papers/97.aspx.

Emery, F. E. , and E. L. Trist. "The Causal Texture of Organizational Environments." *Human Relations* 18, (1965): 21–32.

"The End of Cheap Food." *The Economist*, December 8 2007.

Epstein, Marc J., and Christopher A. Crane. "Alleviating Global Poverty through Microfinance: Factors and Measures of Financial, Economic, and Social Performance." Paper presented at the Harvard Business School Conference on Global Poverty, Boston, MA, December 1–3 2005.

Fagerberg, Jan, David C. Mowery, and Richard R. Nelson. *The Oxford Handbook on Innovation*. Oxford, UK: Oxford University Press, 2004.

"A Firm-Level Approach to Majority Market Business: Private Sector Mapping (PSM) Project Final Report." Washington, DC: SNV Netherlands Development Organization and Inter-American Development Bank, 2008.

Förster, Michael, and Marco Mira d'Ercole. "Income Distribution and Poverty in OECD Countries in the Second Half of the 1990s." Paris, France: OECD Social, Employment and Migration Working Papers, 2005.

Foster, William, and Jeffrey Bradach. "Should Nonprofits Seek Profits?" *Harvard Business Review* (February 2005).

Freeman, R. Edward. *Strategic Management: A Stakeholder Approach*. Boston, MA: Pitman, 1984.

García Bartelt, Mercedes. "Los celulares más caros, preferidos por los pobres." *La Nación*, August 22 2008.

Gasparini, Leonardo, and Leopoldo Tornarolli. "Labor Informality in Latin America and the Caribbean: Patterns and Trends from Household Survey Microdata." In *Documento de Trabajo Nro. 0*. La Plata, Prov. Buenos Aires: Centro de Estudios Distributivos, Laborales y Sociales, Universidad Nacional de La Plata, 2007.

Gawer, Annabelle, and Michael A. Cusumano. "How Companies Become Platform Leaders." *MIT/Sloan Management Review* 49, no. 2 (Winter 2008).

"Gestão Integrada de Resíduos Sólidos." Asociación Interamericana de Ingeniería Sanitaria y Ambiental, http://www.aidis.org.br/eng/ftp/polis_aidis.pdf.

Gittell, Ross, and Avis Vidal. *Community Organization: Building Social Capital as a Development Strategy*. London: Sage, 1998.

Goldberg, Ray A., and Kerry Herman. "Nestle's Milk District Model: Economic Development for a Value-Added Food Chain and Improved Nutrition." In *Business Solutions for the Global Poor: Creating Economic and Social Value*, edited by Kasturi Rangan, John Quelch, Gustavo Herrero and Brooke Barton. San Francisco, CA: Jossey-Bass, 2007.

Goldberg, Ray Allan. *Agribusiness Coordination; A Systems Approach to the Wheat, Soybean, and Florida Orange Economies*. Boston,: Division of Research, Graduate School of Business Administration, Harvard University, 1968.

Gómez, Henry, Patricia Márquez, and Michael Penfold. "Cómo AES-EDC generó relaciones rentables en los barrios pobres de Caracas. Harvard Business Review América Latina." *Harvard Business Review América Latina* (diciembre 2006): 68–75.

Gonçalves, Pólita. "A Reciclagem Integradora dos Aspectos Ambientais, Sociais e Econômicos." Rio de Janeiro: DP&A / PHASE, 2003.

Grootaert, Christiaan, and Thierry van Bastelaer. "Understanding and Measuring Social Capital: A Synthesis of Findings and Recommendations from the Social Capital Initiative." 1–31. Washington DC: World Bank, 2001.

Grupo Técnico Nacional de Ciudadanía Ambiental. "Estrategia Nacional de Promoción de la Ciudadanía Ambiental." CONAM, http://www.conam.gob.pe /documentos/ciudadania/index.asp.

Guimarães, Thiago. "Coleta seletiva de lixo cresce 38% no país." FolhaOnline, http://www1.folha.uol.com.br/folha/cotidiano/ult95u124738.shtml.

Gulati, Ranjay, Sarah Huffman, and Gary Neilson. "The Barista Principle: Starbucks and the Rise of Relational Capital." *Strategy & Competition* Third Quarter, (2002).

Hagel, John, John Seely Brown, and Lang Davison. "Shaping Strategy in a World of Constant Disruption." *Harvard Business Review* (October 2008).

Hammond, Allen L., William J. Kramer, Robert S. Katz, Julia T. Tran, and Courtland Walker. *The Next 4 Billion: Market Size and Business Strategy at the Base of the Pyramid.* Washington, DC: World Resources Institute and International Finance Corporation, 2007.

Hannan, Michael T., and John Freeman. *Organizational Ecology.* Cambridge, MA: Harvard University Press, 1989.

Hart, Stuart, and Clayton Christensen. "The Great Leap: Driving Innovation from the Base of the Pyramid." *MIT/Sloan Management Review* 44, no. 1 (2002).

Hart, Stuart, and Ted London. "Developing Native Capability: What Multinational Corporations Can Learn from the Base of the Pyramid." *Stanford Social Innovation Review* (2005): 28–33.

Hirschman, Albert. *Enfoques alternativos sobre la sociedad de mercado y otros ensayos recientes.* México D.F.: Fondo de Cultura Económica, 1989.

Holliday, Charles, Stephan Schmidheiney, and Philip Watts. *Walking the Talk: The Business Case for Sustainable Development.* Sheffield: Greenleaf Publishing, 2002.

Iansiti, Marco, and Roy Levien. *The Keystone Advantage.* Boston, MA: Harvard Business School Publishing, 2004.

———. "Strategy as Ecology." *Harvard Business Review* (March 2004).

IIDH, and CEPAL. *La igualdad de los modernos. Reflexiones acerca de la realización de los derechos económicos, sociales y culturales en América Latina.* San José: IIDH, CEPAL, 1997.

"Indicadores de concentración del ingreso, total nacional, 1990 - 2006 (cuadro 14)." Comisión Económica para América Latina y el Caribe, http://www.eclac.org /publicaciones/xml/5/30305/PSE2007_AnexoEstadistico.xls.

Intersectorial Relations Studies Group. "Movimento Nacional dos Catadores de Materiais Recicláveis (MNCR). Database of the record for sampling of the survey on the Workstation." Salvador: GERI-Pangea/UFBa (Federal University of Bahia), 2005.

Jarillo, Carlos. "On Strategic Networks." *Strategic Management Journal 9:31–41.* 9, no. 1 (1988): 31–41.

Jelin, Elizabeth. "Igualdad y diferencia: dilemas de la ciudadanía de las mujeres en América Latina." *Ágora. Cuadernos de estudios políticos* 3, no. 7 (1997): 189–214.

Karnani, Aneel. "The Mirage of Marketing at the Bottom of the Pyramid." *California Management Review* 49, no. 4 (Summer 2007).

———. "Fortune at the Bottom of the Pyramid: A Mirage." Working Paper No. 1035, University of Michigan, Stephen M. Ross School of Business, 2006.

Kerlin, Janelle A. "Social Enterprise in the United States and Europe: Understanding and Learning from the Differences." *Voluntas* 17, (2006): 247–63.

Klein, Michael. In *Creating Opportunities for Small Business*. Washington, DC: International Finance Corporation, World Bank Group, 2007.

"La pequeña y mediana empresa. Algunos aspectos." In *LC/R. 1330*: CEPAL, 1993.

"La pobresa a Catalunya. Informe 2003.." Fundació UN SOL MÓN de l'Obra Social de Caixa Catalunya, http://obrasocial.caixacatalunya.es/CDA/ObraSocial/OS_Plantilla3/0,3417,1x3y355,00.html.

Landrum, Nancy E. "Advancing the 'Base of the Pyramid' Debate." *Strategic Management Review* 1, no. 1 (2007).

Leguizamón, Francisco, and Julio Guzmán. "Caso Ingenios Pantaleón. El argumento empresarial de la responsabilidad social.": INCAE / IADB, 2007.

Lenoir, René. *Les exclus*. Paris: Seuil, 1974.

Leonard, Herman B. "When Is Doing Business with the Poor Good – for the Poor? A Household and National Income Accounting Approach." In *Business Solutions for the Global Poor: Creating Economic and Social Value*, edited by Kasturi Rangan, John Quelch, Gustavo Herrero and Brooke Barton. San Francisco, CA: Jossey-Bass, 2007.

Lodge, George C. "The Corporate Key: Using Big Business to Fight Global Poverty." *Foreign Affairs* 81 no. 4 (2002): 13–18.

London, Ted. "The Base-of-the-Pyramid Perspective: A New Approach to Poverty Alleviation." Working Paper, William Davidson Institute/Stephen M. Ross School of Business, 2008.

———. "Beyond 'Stepping Stone' Growth: Exploring New Market Entry at the Base of the Pyramid." Working Paper, William Davidson Institute/Stephen M. Ross School of Business, 2006.

London, Ted, and Stuart L Hart. "Reinventing Strategies for Emerging Markets: Beyond the Transnational Model." *Journal of International Business Studies* 35, (2004): 350–70.

López, Ramón, and Alberto Valdés. *Rural Poverty in Latin America*. New York: St. Martin's Press, 2000.

Mabry, Donald J. "Government and Law in Spanish Colonial America (revised)." http://historicaltextarchive.com/sections.php?op=viewarticle&artid=296.

Márquez, Gustavo, Alberto Chong, Suzanne Duryea, Jacqueline Mazza, and Hugo Ñopo. *Outsiders? The Changing Patterns of Exclusion in Latin America and the*

Caribbean. Washington, DC and Cambridge, MA: Inter-American Development Bank and David Rockefeller Center for Latin American Studies, Harvard University, 2007.

Márquez, Patricia, and Ezequiel Reficco. "The Unsuspected Player: Small Firms in Business with Low Income Sectors." In *Small Firms, Global Markets: Competitive Challenges in the New Economy*, edited by Jerry Haar and Jörg Meyer-Stamer. London and New York: Palgrave Macmillan, 2007.

Marquez, Patricia, and Henry Gomez. *Microempresas: alianzas para el éxito*. Caracas: Ediciones IESA, 2001.

———. *Alianzas con microempresas*. Caracas: Ediciones IESA, 2001.

Márquez, Patricia, and Ezequiel Reficco. "SMEs and Low-income Sectors." In *Small Firms, Global Markets: Competitive Challenges in the New Economy*, edited by Jerry Haar and Jörg Meyer-Stamer. London and New York: Palgrave Macmillan, 2008.

Marwaha, Kapil, A. Kulkarni, J. Mukophadyay, and S. Sivakumar. "IBENEX: Business Effectiveness—the Next Level: Being Served by the Poor, as Partners." Paper presented at the Harvard Business School Conference on Global Poverty, Boston, MA, December 1–3 2005.

Marwaha, Kapil, Anil Kulkarni, Jipan Mukhopadhyay, and S. Sivakumar. "Creating Strong Businesses by Developing and Leveraging the Productive Capacity of the Poor." In *Business Solutions for the Global Poor: Creating Economic and Social Value*, edited by Kasturi Rangan, John Quelch, Gustavo Herrero and Brooke Barton. San Francisco, CA: Jossey-Bass, 2007.

Medina, Martin. "Oito mitos sobre a reciclagem informal da América Latina." BIDAmérica, http://www.iadb.org/idbamerica/index.cfm?thisid=3075.

Mellor, John W. "Faster, More Equitable Growth—The Relation Between Growth in Agriculture and Poverty Reduction Agricultural Policy." In *Development Project Research Report*. Cambridge, MA: Abt Associates Inc., October 1999.

Milstein, M.B., Ted London, and Stuart Hart. "Revolutionary Routines: Capturing the Opportunity for Creating a More Inclusive Capitalism." In *Handbook of Cooperative Colaboration: New Designs and Dynamics*, edited by S.K Piderit, R.E. Fry and D.L. Cooperrider. Stanford, CA: Stanford University Press, 2007.

Ministério do Trabalho e Emprego. "Atlas da Economia Solidária no Brasil." http://www.mte.gov.br/Empregador/EconomiaSolidaria/conteudo/atlas.asp.

Mintzberg, Henry. "Generic strategies: Toward a Comprehensive Framework." *Advances in Strategic Management* 5 (1988): 1–67.

Mintzberg, Henry, and James Brian Quinn. *The Strategy Process: Concepts, Contexts, Cases*. 2nd ed. Englewood Cliffs, NJ: Prentice Hall, 1991.

Moore, James F. *The Death of Competition: Leadership & Strategy in the Age of Business Ecosystems*. New York, NY: HarperBusiness, 1996.

———. "Predators and Prey: A New Ecology of Competition." *Harvard Business Review* (May 1993).

Novogratz, Jacqueline. "Meeting Urgent Needs with Patient Capital." *Innovations: Technology | Governance | Globalization* 2, no. 1/2 (2007).

ONU-Hábitat. *El estado de las ciudades en el mundo 2006/2007*. Nueva York: NY: Programa de las Naciones Unidas sobre Asentamientos Urbanos, 2007.

Osterwalder, Alexander, Yves Pigneur, and Christopher Tucci. "Clarifying Business Models: Origins, Present, and Future of the Concept." *Communications of the Association of Information Systems* 16 (2005).

"Panorama social 2007 de América Latina." Comisión Económica para América Latina y el Caribe, http://www.eclac.org/publicaciones/xml/5/30305/PSE2007_Sintesis_Lanzamiento.pdf

Porter, Michael E. *The Competitive Advantage of Nations*. New York, NY: The Free Press, 1990.

———. *Competitive Advantage: Creating and Sustaining Superior Performance*. New York, NY: Free Press, 1985.

———. *Competitive Strategy: Techniques for Analyzing Industries and Competitors*. New York, NY: Free Press, 1980.

Portocarrero, Felipe, Armando Millán, James Loveday, Bruno Tarazona, and Andrea Portugal. *Capital social y democracia. Explorando normas, valores y redes sociales en el Perú*. Lima, Perú: Universidad del Pacífico, Centro de Investigación, 2006.

Prahalad, C. K. *The Fortune at the Bottom of the Pyramid: Eradicating Poverty through Profits*. Upper Saddle River, NJ: Wharton School Publishing, 2005.

———. "The Innovation Sandbox." *Strategy +Business*, 2005, 1–10.

———. "Why Selling to the Poor Makes for Good Business." *Fortune*, Nov 15 2004, 70–72.

Prahalad, C. K., and Allen Hammond. "Serving the World's Poor, Profitably." *Harvard Business Review* (2002).

Prahalad, C. K., and Stuart Hart. "The Fortune at the Bottom of the Pyramid." *Strategy + Business* 1, no. 26 (2002).

Puente, Raquel. "Mercadeo para las mayorías." In *Compromiso Social: gerencia para el siglo XXI*, edited by Antonio Francés. Caracas: Ediciones IESA, 2008.

Putnam, Robert D. *Making Democracy Work: CivicTtraditions in Modern Italy*. Princeton, NJ: Princeton University Press, 1993.

Quinti, Gabrielle. "Exclusión social: el debate teórico y los modelos de medición y evaluación." In *De Igual a Igual. El desafío del Estado ante los nuevos problemas sociales*, edited by Jorge Carpio and Irene Novacovsky. Buenos Aires: Fondo de Cultura Económica de Argentina y Secretaría de Desarrollo Social de la Nación, 1999.

Rangan, Kasturi. "The Complex Business of Serving the Poor." In *Business Solutions for the Global Poor: Creating Economic and Social Value*, edited by Kasturi

Rangan, John Quelch, Gustavo Herrero and Brooke Barton., 309–20. San Francisco, CA: Jossey-Bass, 2007.

Reficco, Ezequiel, Roberto Gutiérrez, and Diana Trujillo. "Empresas sociales: ¿una especie en busca de reconocimiento?" *Revista de Administração da Universidade de São Paulo* 41, no. 4 (Oct–Dec 2006): 404–18.

Reficco, Ezequiel, and Patricia Marquez. "Socially Inclusive Networks for Building BOP Markets." Working Paper, School of Business Administration, University of San Diego, October 2007.

———. "Inclusive Networks for Building BOP Markets." *Business & Society* (forthcoming).

Richardson, George B. "The Organization of Industry." *Economic Journal* 82, (1972): 883–96.

Rodríguez, César. "À procura de alternativas económicas em tempos de globalização: o caso das cooperativas de recicladores de lixo na Colômbia." Centro de Estudos Sociais, Faculdade de Economia da Universidade de Coimbra, http://www.ces.uc.pt/emancipa/research/pt/ft/rescatar.html.

Rufin, Carlos. "The Role of Government: LIS Market Initiatives and the Public Sector." *ReVista Harvard Review of Latin America* (Fall 2006): 45–46.

Rufín, Carlos, and Luis Fernando Arboleda. "Utilities and the Poor: A Story from Colombia." In *Business Solutions for the Global Poor: Creating Economic and social Value*, edited by Kasturi Rangan, John Quelch, Gustavo Herrero and Brooke Barton. San Francisco, CA: Jossey-Bass, 2007.

Rufín, Carlos, and Miguel Rivera-Santos. "Global Village vs. Small Town: Understanding Networks at the Base of the Pyramid." Unpublished paper, 2008.

Salamon, Lester M. "The Rise of the Nonprofit Sector." *Foreign Affairs* 73, no. 4 (1994): 109–22.

Salamon, Lester M., and Helmut K. Anheier. *The Emerging Nonprofit Sector: An Overview*. Manchester, UK: Manchester University Press, 1996.

Salamon, Lester M., and Dennis Young. "Commercialization, social ventures, and for-profit competition." In *The State of Nonprofit America*, edited by Lester M. Salamon, xi, 563 p. Washington, DC: Brookings Institution Press, 2003.

"Salario Mínimo Legal Diario (Col $)." Banco de la República de Colombia, http://www.banrep.gov.co/estad/dsbb/srea_020.xls.

"Salário mínimo nominal e necessário." Departamento Intersindical de Estatística e Estudos Socioeconômicos, http://www.dieese.org.br/rel/rac/salmindez07.xml.

Sathe, Vijay. "¿Qué es cultura." INCAE, 1981.

Schamber, Pablo. "No se presta atención a los cartoneros como engranaje de un sistema económico." Página 12, http://www.pagina12.com.ar/imprimir/diario/sociedad/3–87058–2007–06–24.html.

Scherer, A.G., and G. Palazzo. "Toward a Political Conception of Corporate Responsibility: Business and Society Seen from a Habermasian Perspective." *Academy of Management Review* 32, no. 4 (2007): 1096–120.

Seelos, Christian, and Johanna Mair. "Profitable Business Models and Market Creation in the Context of Deep Poverty: A Strategic View." *The Academy of Management Perspectives* 21, no. 4 (2007).

———. "Social Entrepreneurship: Creating New Business Models to Serve the Poor." *Business Horizons* 48, no. 3 (2005): 241–46.

SEKN, ed. *Effective Management of Social Enterprises: Lessons from Businesses and Civil Society Organizations in Iberoamerica.* Cambridge, MA: Harvard University Press with David Rockefeller Center for Latin American Studies, 2006.

Sen, Amartya Kumar. *Development as Freedom.* New York, NY: Oxford University Press, 1999.

Sharma, Sanjay, and Frances Westley. "Strategic Bridging: A Role for the Multinational Corporation in Third World Development." *Journal of Applied Behavioral Sciences* 30, no. 4 (1994): 458–76.

Simanis, Erik, and Stuart Hart. "The Base of the Pyramid Protocol: toward next generation BoP strategy." (2008), http://www.wdi.umich.edu/files/BoPProtocol 2ndEdition2008.pdf.

———. "Beyond Selling to the Poor: Building Business Intimacy through Embedded Innovation." Ithaca, NY: Working Paper, Cornell University, 2008.

Simanis, Erik, Stuart Hart, Gordon Enk, Duncan Duke, et al. "Strategic Initiatives at the Base of the Pyramid A Protocol for Mutual Value Creation." In Base of the Pyramid Protocol Workshop Group Wingspread Conference Center. Racine, WI 2005.

Singer, Paul. *Introdução à Economia Solidária.* São Paulo: Perseu Abramo, 2002.

SNV & World Business Council for Sustainable Development. "Inclusive Business: Profitable Business for Successful Development." (2008), http://wbcsd.typepad .com/wbcsdsnv/wbcsd_snv_alliance_brochure_march_08_web.pdf.

Stevenson, Howard H. "A Perspective on Entrepreneurship." Working Paper, Harvard Business School, 1983.

Stronza, Amanda. "Because It Is Ours: Community-Based Ecotourism in the Peruvian Amazon." Ph.D. Dissertation, University of Florida, 2000.

Sullivan, Nicholas. *You Can Hear Me Now: How Microloans and Cell Phones Are Connecting the World's Poor to the Global Economy.* San Francisco, CA: Jossey Bass, 2007.

Tencati, Antonio, and Laszlo Zsolnai. "The Collaborative Enterprise." *Journal of Business Ethics* (2009): 367–76.

"Termos de Referência para Monitoramento em Direitos Humanos." Instituto Nenuca de Desenvolvimento Sustentável (INSEA), December 2005.

"Time Series Management System." Banco Central do Brasil, https://www3.bcb.gov .br/sgspub/consultarvalores/telaCvsSelecionarSeries.paint.

Todorov, Tzvetan. *La vida en común. Ensayo de antropología general.* Madrid: Taurus, 1995.

Trujillo Cárdenas, Diana, and Roberto Gutiérrez. "The Base of the Pyramid, Citizenship above Consumerism: Colombia's Colcerámica." *ReVista Harvard Review of Latin America* (Fall 2006).

USAID. "Innovative Approaches to Slum Electrification." Washington, DC: Bureau for Economic Growth, Agriculture and Trade, December 2004.

Weiser, John, Michele Kahane, Steve Rochlin, and Jessica Landis. *Untapped: Creating Value in Underserved Markets.* San Francisco, CA: Berrett-Koehler Publishers, 2006.

Westley, Frances, and Harrie Vredenburg. "Strategic Bridging: The Collaboration between Environmentalists and Business in the Marketing of Green Products." *Journal of Applied Behavioral Sciences* 27, no. 1 (1991): 65–90.

"What Is a Cooperative?." International Cooperative Alliance, http://www.ica .coop/coop/index.html.

Wheeler, David, Kevin McKague, Jane Thompson, Rachel Davies, et al. "Creating Sustainable Local Enterprise Networks." *MIT Sloan Review* 47, no. 1 (2005): 33–40.

World Economic Forum. "Latin America@Risk. A Global Risk Network Briefing." www.weforum.org/pdf/grn/LatinAmericaRisk.pdf

"World Economic Outlook Database." International Monetary Fund, http://www .imf.org/external/pubs/ft/weo/2006/02/data/weoreptc.aspx?sy=2003&ey=2007 &scsm=1&ssd=1&sort=country&ds=.&br=1&c=213&s=NGDP_R%2CNGDP _RPCH%2CNGDP%2CNGDPD%2CNGDP_D%2CNGDPRPC%2CNGDPP C%2CNGDPDPC%2CPPPWGT%2CPPPPC%2CPPPSH%2CPPPEX%2CPC PI%2CPCPIPCH%2CLP%2CBCA%2CBCA_NGDPD&grp=0&a=&pr.x=75& pr.y=9.

"World Economic Outlook Database." International Monetary Fund, http://www .imf.org/external/pubs/ft/weo/2008/01/weodata/index.aspx

Young, Dennis R. "Nonprofit Finance Theory." National Center for Nonprofit Enterprise, http://www.nationalcne.org/index.cfm?fuseaction=feature.display &feature_id=27.

———. "Social Enterprise in the United States: Alternate Identities and Forms." Paper presented at the conference L'Impresa Sociale In Prospettiva Comparata, Trento, Italia; Istituto Studi Sviluppo Aziende Nonprofit, Universidad de Trento, December 13–15, 2001.

Zevallos, Emilio. "Micro, pequeñas y medianas empresas en América Latina." *Revista de la CEPAL* 29 (2003): 53–70.

Contributors

Gabriel **Berger** is an associate professor at the Universidad de San Andrés (Buenos Aires, Argentina) Department of Management, where he directs the Center for Social Innovation. This institution coordinates training, research, and teaching activities for non-profit organizations, corporations engaged in CSR, and individual philanthropists, and the Graduate Program in Nonprofit Organizations. Professor Berger is serving as co-coordinator of Social Enterprise Knowledge Network (SEKN). Dr. Berger's teaching and research focus on strategic management and governance of social enterprises, corporate social engagement, and philanthropy. He has been an advisor to NGOs, businesses, and foundations in several Latin American countries and in the United States. He obtained a Ph.D. in Social Policy and a Master in Management of Human Services from the Heller School of Social Policy and Management at Brandeis University.

Leopoldo **Blugerman** holds a degree in Political Science (Universidad de Buenos Aires, Argentina) and an M.A. in International Relations (Università degli Studi di Bologna, Italy). Since 2009 he is a faculty member of the Administration Department, Universidad de San Andrés and has worked as a member of the research team of SEKN Argentina since 2005.

Monica **Bose.** A psychology graduate, she has a master's degree in Management and is currently finishing her Ph.D. at School of Economics, Management and Accounting of the University of São Paulo (FEA-USP). She is a project coordinator and researcher at CEATS, the Center for Social Entrepreneurship and Third Sector Management, which is part of FIA, the Management Institute Foundation, where she teaches graduate courses. Her main research areas are Social Entrepreneurship, Third Sector, Sustainable Development, and People Management. Her articles have been published in Brazil and abroad.

Josefina **Bruni Celli** holds a Ph.D. in Public Administration, New York University (2001); M.B.A. with concentration in Public Services and Public Enterprises, IESA (1988); and B.A. in Political Science, Yale University (1983). As a professor in the Centre for Public Policy in Venezuela's Instituto de Estudios Superiores de Administración (IESA), Dr. Bruni Celli teaches various classes in business and public policy including *Tools for Information*

Analysis, Evaluation and Design of Public Policy, Enterprise State and Society, and Corporate Social Responsibility in Latin America. She is an active member of Social Enterprise Knowledge Network (SEKN). The majority of her research on the social responsibility of business has been published outside Venezuela, including at the Harvard Business School.

Graziella **Comini** is an economist with an M.A. and a Ph.D. from the School of Economics, Management and Accounting of the University of São Paulo (FEA/USP); she teaches at the FEA/USP Management Department and at FIA, the Management Institute Foundation (Fundação Instituto de Administração) and is vice-coordinator of CEATS, the Center for Social Entrepreneurship and Third Sector Management (Centro de Empreendedorismo Social e Administração em Terceiro Setor), which is part of FIA, the Management Institute Foundation . Her research and consulting work centers on Social Entrepreneurship, Sustainability, Third Sector and Organizational Management, and People Management. She has had articles published in Brazil and abroad.

Álvaro J. **Delgado** studied Social Sciences, specializing in Sociology at the Pontificia Universidad Católica del Perú, and in Economics at the Universidad del Pacífico. He currently works with public relations and lobby of Peruvian industrial companies of the food industry at the Sociedad Nacional de Industrias. He used to work as a Research Assistant in the Research Center (CIUP) at the Universidad del Pacífico, where he also contributed to the development of teaching cases about CSOS and organizations that practice or encourage social responsibility and the inclusive business in the agriculture, mining, and energy sectors.

Verónica **Durana** is a research assistant in the School of Management at the Universidad de los Andes. She has an undergraduate degree in psychology (with a minor in philosophy) from the Universidad de los Andes. She is currently a student in the M.B.A. program at the Universidad de los Andes.

Rosa Maria **Fischer**. A sociologist with an M.A. and a Ph.D. from the School of Social Sciences of the University of São Paulo (USP), she is a senior professor appointed by examination (livre-docente) at USP's School of Economics, Management and Accounting (FEA-USP), where she teaches undergraduate and graduate courses. She is founder and coordinator of CEATS, the Center for Social Entrepreneurship and Third Sector Management, which is part of FIA, the Management Institute Foundation. She is USP's representative to SEKN, of which she is one of the founding members.

She coordinates research and interventions in Social Entrepreneurship, Sustainability, Corporate Governance, Third Sector and People Management, besides advising private-sector organizations and CSOs. She has had several books and articles published in Brazil and abroad.

Juliano **Flores**, M.B.A. by INCAE, is a Researcher at INCAE's Centro Latinoamericano para la Competitividad y el Desarrollo Sostenible (CLACDS), and coordinates SEKN-related activities at INCAE. He has been involved in various research projects on corporate social responsibility, and has co-authored various chapters on that subject. His main areas of professional interest are corporate social responsibility, social entrepreneurship, inclusive business, ethic investment, and responsible competitiveness.

Natalia **Franco** is a professor of Public Management and Social Entrepreneurship in the School of Management at the Universidad de los Andes. She has an undergraduate degree in Political Science from the Universidad de los Andes (1998) and a graduate degree as a Specialist in International Resource Management from the University Jorge Tadeo Lozano (2001). She is currently enrolled in the Ph.D. Program in Management (with emphasis in Organizational Behavior) at Tulane University. She has worked as a researcher and management consultant for the non-profit sector.

Henry **Gómez-Samper** is Professor Emeritus at the Institute for Advanced Studies in Administration (IESA) in Caracas, and Visiting Professor at the Universidad de los Andes School of Management in Bogotá. He obtained a Ph.D. (1965), M.B.A. (1954), and B.S. (1952) from New York University. He is a former president of IESA (1981–1991) and of the Council of Latin American Graduate Schools of Management (CLADEA); and founding president (1989–1998) of the Global Network for Management Development (INTERMAN).

Rosa Amelia **González** holds a Ph.D. in Political Science, Universidad Simón Bolívar (2002); M.B.A. with concentration in Public Service and Public Enterprises, IESA (1988); Urban Planner, Universidad Simón Bolívar (1981). As Associate Professor in the Public Policy Center of IESA, she teaches the course *Enterprise, State and Society* in the M.B.A. program. She also teaches the courses *Public Management I* and *II* in the Master in Public Administration program. Professor González is a member of SEKN Network and coordinates the project in Venezuela. Her research on Corporate Social Responsibility and Social Enterprise has been published outside Venezuela in articles, books, and teaching cases.

Roberto **Gutiérrez** holds a Ph.D. in Sociology from The Johns Hopkins University and is an Associate Professor in the School of Management at the Universidad de los Andes since 1995. He has published academic articles on social entrepreneurship, partnerships, education, and sustainable development in journals such as *American Sociological Review, Review of Educational Research, Journal of Management Education, Stanford Social Innovation Review* and *Harvard Business Review América Latina*. Dr. Gutiérrez co-edited *Effective Management of Social Enterprises* (2006).

John C. **Ickis** holds a D.B.A. from Harvard University and is a Full Professor in Business Administration at INCAE. His research work focuses on Strategic Processes in Social Organizations. Dr. Ickis co-authored "Beyond Bureaucracy" and has published several articles in the *Harvard Business Review* and *World Development*.

Mladen **Koljatic** is a professor at School of Management of the Pontificia Universidad Católica de Chile. He holds an M.B.A. from the University of Michigan and an Ed.D. from Indiana University. He has taught marketing and advertising management, and more recently corporate social responsibility and non-profit management. Articles of his have recently appeared in *Journal of Business Research, British Journal of Educational Technology,* and *Psychological Reports*, and several Latin American journals.

Francisco **Leguizamón** holds a D.B.A. from IESE, Universidad de Navarra, Spain, and is a Full Professor at INCAE, where he has also served as Dean and Academic Director. Professor Leguizamón lectures at graduate programs and executive seminars on Organizational Behavior, Business Strategy, Negotiation and Small Company Management. He has authored two books on support programs for small and medium-sized companies. He has also written several articles and numerous case studies dealing with contemporary challenges in business administration.

Iván Darío **Lobo** is a professor of Management and Entrepreneurship in the School of Management at the Universidad de los Andes. He holds an M.Sc. in Political Science (2008), and a B.A. in Industrial Engineering (2000), both from the Universidad de los Andes. His research and teaching activities focus on social enterprise, general management, strategy for non-profit organizations, and—more recently—inclusive businesses and social entrepreneurship. He has coauthored chapters and articles from previous SEKN research cycles.

Gerardo **Lozano** holds a Ph.D. in Business Administration with a major in Marketing and International Business. He is a professor at the Graduate School of Business Administration and Leadership (EGADE—Tec de Monterrey), where he leads the Mexican chapter of the Social Enterprise Knowledge Network (SEKN). Since 2001, he has taught at the Social Leaders' Program, an initiative undertaken by the Virtual University of Monterrey Tech, the Nature Conservancy, the World Bank, and the Mexican Center for Philanthropy (CEMEFI). This program provides distance capacity-building training to CSOs in Latin America.

Patricia **Márquez** is an Associate Professor at the University of San Diego and a Visiting Professor at IESA in Caracas, Venezuela. She was the Cisneros Visiting Scholar at the David Rockefeller Center for Latin American Studies (DRCLAS) and at the Harvard Business School for the academic year 2005–2006. Her research centers on corporate social responsibility, social enterprise, and business initiatives for poverty alleviation. Márquez received her B.A. in Mathematics from Bowdoin College and her Ph.D. in Socio-Cultural Anthropology from University of California, Berkeley.

Michael **Metzger** is a faculty member at INCAE Business School, where he teaches Marketing, Strategic Marketing and Marketing of Services. Prof. Metzger also taught graduate-level courses at the University of Michigan School of Business. His research interests focus on corporate social responsibility, social marketing, and marketing for non-profit organizations. He has consulted extensively on the implementation of socially responsible business plans and sustainable business practices.

Felipe **Portocarrero** has a Ph.D. in Sociology, St. Antony's College, University of Oxford; M.Phil. in Sociology with mention in Demography, and a B.A. in Social Sciences with mention in Sociology. He is President of the Universidad del Pacífico, Lima, Perú, as well as the former Head of the Department of Social Sciences and Political Sciences, Director of the Research Center (CIUP), and President of the Editorial Board at the Universidad del Pacífico (1991–2009). He participated as researcher in the Johns Hopkins Comparative Nonprofit Sector Study, was Fellow in the Kellogg Foundation's Leadership in Philanthropy Program, and was Director of the Program on Leadership and Social Development in the Andean Region. He is member of the Advisory Committee of AVINA, member of the Board of Directors of ISTR, and Director of the Peruvian team of the Social Enterprise Knowledge Network (SEKN).

Ezequiel **Reficco** is currently a Professor of Strategy at the School of Management of the Universidad de los Andes (Bogotá, Colombia). He was a Post-Doctoral Fellow (2002–2004) and a Senior Researcher (2004–2008) at the Harvard Business School. He co-authored *Social Partnering in Latin America* (2004), and co-edited *Effective Management of Social Enterprises* (2006). His work was published in popular and academic journals, such as the *Stanford Social Innovation Review, Business & Society* and the *Harvard Business Review América Latina*. He received a Ph.D. in Law & Diplomacy from The Fletcher School, Tufts University. Dr. Reficco currently sits on the Inditex Social Council; he is also a member of the Advisory Council to the IADB's Multilateral Investment Fund, and an external advisor to Johnson & Johnson's Latin American Contributions Committee.

Paulo **Rocha Borba** has undergraduate and master's degrees from the School of Economics, Management and Accounting of the University of São Paulo (FEA/USP) and is currently completing his Ph.D. at that school. He is a researcher at CEATS, the Center for Social Entrepreneurship and Third Sector Management, which is part of FIA, the Management Institute Foundation. He has research and consulting experience in Business Administration, in particular in Financial Management, Corporate Social Responsibility, Strategy and Third Sector.

Mónica **Silva** is a Research Associate at the School of Management of the Pontificia Universidad Católica de Chile. She received her undergraduate degree in Psychology from the Pontificia Universidad Católica de Chile and an M.S. and Ph.D. form Indiana University. Her research focuses on educational assessment and research methods, and her articles have appeared in *Evaluation and Program Planning, Journal of Business Research, Journal of Cross-Cultural Psychology, British Journal of Educational Technology* and *Psychological Reports*, as well as local Latin American journals.

Diana **Trujillo** is a professor at the School of Management of the Universidad de los Andes. She received her Master's degree in Education from that University in 2006 and is currently enrolled in the Ph.D. Program in Public Administration at New York University. Her research focuses on management and public policy and explores the interaction between private organizations and the public sector in Latin America. She has contributed chapters to *Effective Management of Social Enterprises: Lessons from Businesses and Civil Society Organizations in Iberoamerica* (2006) and *Social Partnering in Latin America: Lessons Drawn from Collaborations of Businesses and Civil Society Organizations* (2004).

Alfred **Vernis**, head of training of the Institute for Social Innovation-ESADE, holds a Ph.D. in Public and Non-Profit Management from the Robert F. Wagner School of Public Service (New York University). He is Associate Professor in the Department of Business Policy and the Institute of Public Management at ESADE (Universidad Ramón Llull). He directs the program "The Managerial Role in Non-Governmental Organizations" (Fundació "la Caixa" – ESADE) and coordinates all SEKN activities at ESADE. He has published numerous articles and books on third-sector management and on cross-sector collaboration. He co-authored *Management of Nonprofit Organizations* (1998) and *Nonprofit Organizations: Challenges and Collaboration* (2006). He sits on the Inditex Social Council and is a member of the Editorial Board of the Spanish Journal of the Third Sector (Luis Vives Foundation, Madrid).